First World War
and Army of Occupation
War Diary
France, Belgium and Germany

29 DIVISION
Headquarters, Branches and Services
General Staff
9 October 1915 - 31 December 1917

WO95/2283

The Naval & Military Press Ltd
www.nmarchive.com
Published in association with The National Archives

Published by

The Naval & Military Press Ltd

Unit 10 Ridgewood Industrial Park,

Uckfield, East Sussex,

TN22 5QE England

Tel: +44 (0) 1825 749494

www.naval-military-press.com

www.nmarchive.com

This diary has been reprinted in facsimile from the original. Any imperfections are inevitably reproduced and the quality may fall short of modern type and cartographic standards.

© **Crown Copyright**
Images reproduced by permission of The National Archives, London, England, 2015.

Contents

Document type	Place/Title	Date From	Date To
Heading	29th Division General Staff Sep-Dec 1917		
Heading	War Diary October HQ G.S. 29D Vol 32		
Heading	War Diary General Staff 29th Division For The Month Of October 1917. Volume XXXII		
War Diary	J Camp Map Ref. & Sheet 28 N.W. 1/20,000 A.8.A.	01/10/1917	02/10/1917
War Diary	Elverdinghe	03/10/1917	10/10/1917
War Diary	Proven	11/10/1917	15/10/1917
War Diary	Basseux. 1/40,000 Sheet 51.C.	16/10/1917	31/10/1917
Miscellaneous	List Of Appendices.		
Heading	Operation Orders Instructions		
Operation(al) Order(s)	29th Division Order No. 157. App II	30/09/1917	30/09/1917
Miscellaneous	29th Div. No. C.G.S. 72/57.	01/10/1917	01/10/1917
Operation(al) Order(s)	Addendum To 29th Division Order No. 157.	01/10/1917	01/10/1917
Miscellaneous	Appendix "A". Creeping Barrage.		
Map	Barrage Map		
Miscellaneous	29th Division Operations. Instructions No. 18. Machine Gun Scheme.	30/09/1917	30/09/1917
Miscellaneous	29th Division H.G. Barrage.		
Miscellaneous	Addendum To Instruction No. 18. Machine Gun Scheme.	01/10/1917	01/10/1917
Miscellaneous	29th Division Operations. Instruction No. 19. Administrative Arrangements.	30/09/1917	30/09/1917
Miscellaneous	29th Division Operations. Amendment to Instruction No. 19. Administrative Arrangements.	01/10/1917	01/10/1917
Miscellaneous	29th Division Operations. Instruction No. 20. Communications.	30/09/1917	30/09/1917
Miscellaneous	29th Division Operations. Instruction No. 21. Counter Attack Machine.	03/10/1917	03/10/1917
Miscellaneous	29th Division Operations.	02/10/1917	02/10/1917
Miscellaneous	29th Division Operations.	03/10/1917	03/10/1917
Miscellaneous	29th Division No. I.G. 94/20.	03/10/1917	03/10/1917
Miscellaneous	Amendment to 29th Division Order No. 159.	06/10/1917	06/10/1917
Map	Secret Reference Broembeek Map 1 10,000		
Map	Langemarck		
Map	Broembeek		
Miscellaneous	3rd Battn Of Yorks 4 Oct 1917	04/10/1917	04/10/1917
Miscellaneous	Brigade Major 86th Infy Bgde.	07/10/1917	07/10/1917
Miscellaneous	Brigade Major 86th Infantry Bgde.		
Miscellaneous			
Miscellaneous	Attention From The Enemy Artillery	07/10/1917	07/10/1917
Miscellaneous	Report On Operations Carried Out By 1st Bn. Royal Dublin Fusiliers On The 4th October 1917 At Langemarch.	04/10/1917	04/10/1917
Operation(al) Order(s)	29th Division Order No. 158. Appx III	03/10/1917	03/10/1917
Miscellaneous	March Table Issued In Conjunction 29th Division Order No. 158		
Miscellaneous	Location Table Issued in conjunction with 29th Div. Order No. 158		
Miscellaneous	Amendment to 29th Division Order No. 158.	04/10/1917	04/10/1917
Miscellaneous	Administrative Order No. 18	03/09/1917	03/09/1917

Miscellaneous	29th Division No. C.G.S. 67/60.	04/10/1917	04/10/1917
Operation(al) Order(s)	29th Division Order No. 160. Appen V	07/10/1917	07/10/1917
Map	Reference Maps Bixschoote & Westroosebeke 140,000 Section 29th Div 7.10.17		
Miscellaneous	Reference 29th Division Order No. 160	07/10/1917	07/10/1917
Operation(al) Order(s)	Addendum No. 1 To 29th Division Order No. 160.	07/10/1917	07/10/1917
Map			
Miscellaneous	29th Division Operation. Instruction No. 22.	05/10/1917	05/10/1917
Miscellaneous	29th Division Operations. Instruction No. 23. Machine Gun Scheme.	06/10/1917	06/10/1917
Miscellaneous	Locations-29th Division Midnight 7th/8th October, 1917. including moves in progress.	07/10/1917	07/10/1917
Operation(al) Order(s)	29th Division Order No. 159 Appen IV	06/10/1917	06/10/1917
Miscellaneous	March Table issued in conjunction with 29th Division Order No. 159		
Miscellaneous	Location Table Night 7th/8th.		
Miscellaneous	Amendment to 29th Division Order No. 159.	06/10/1917	06/10/1917
Operation(al) Order(s)	29th Division Order No. 162. Appen VII	08/10/1917	08/10/1917
Miscellaneous	Location Table "B".		
Miscellaneous	March Table Issued In Conjunction 29th Div Order No. 162		
Miscellaneous	M.C. Barrage Table.		
Miscellaneous	Addendum No. 1 To Instruction No. 23.	07/10/1917	07/10/1917
Miscellaneous	29th Division Operations. Instruction No. 24. Administrative Arrangements.	07/10/1917	07/10/1917
Miscellaneous	29th Division Operations. Instruction No. 25. Communications.	07/10/1917	07/10/1917
Operation(al) Order(s)	29th Division Order No. 161 Appen VI	07/10/1917	07/10/1917
Miscellaneous	March Table Issued In Conjunction With O.O. No 161.		
Miscellaneous	29th Division No. C.G.S. 67/74.	08/10/1917	08/10/1917
Miscellaneous	29th Division Warning Order.	12/10/1917	12/10/1917
Map	Broembeek		
Map	Langemarck		
Miscellaneous			
Miscellaneous	C Form. Messages And Signals.		
Heading	File Of War Diary		
Miscellaneous	C Form. Messages And Signals.		
Miscellaneous	A Form Messages And Signals.		
Miscellaneous	C Form. Messages And Signals.		
Miscellaneous	A Form. Messages And Signals. Appendix VIII		
Miscellaneous	C Form. Messages And Signals.		
War Diary		09/10/1915	10/10/1915
Miscellaneous	29th Division Warning Order.	12/10/1917	12/10/1917
Miscellaneous	29th Division No. 2014/2.	13/10/1917	13/10/1917
Miscellaneous	Entrain Houpoutre Detrain		
Operation(al) Order(s)	29th Division Order No. 163. Appen X	14/10/1917	14/10/1917
Miscellaneous	Reports On Operations Miscellaneous		
Miscellaneous	29th Division No. C.G.S. 72/62.	07/10/1917	07/10/1917
Miscellaneous	Notes For Companys Commander.	29/10/1917	29/10/1917
Miscellaneous	29th Division No. I.G. 103/19.	15/10/1917	15/10/1917
Miscellaneous	Period 7th August, 1917 to 11th October, 1917.	07/08/1917	07/08/1917
Miscellaneous	29th Division No. C.G.S. 70/54.	25/10/1917	25/10/1917
Miscellaneous			
Miscellaneous	29th Divisional Conference-Basseux 18th October, 1917. (Brigadiers and Commanding Officers attending).	18/10/1917	18/10/1917
Miscellaneous	29th Division CGS. 78/25	20/10/1917	20/10/1917

Miscellaneous	Table "A".		
Miscellaneous	Table "B". Instructional Staff for Depot Battalion.		
Miscellaneous	Reference VI Corps Winter Sports Programme.	21/10/1917	21/10/1917
Miscellaneous	Some Lessons From Recent Operations At Ypres by Major-General Sir Beauvoir de Lisle, K.C.B., D.S.O.	23/10/1917	23/10/1917
Miscellaneous	Training Instructions Schemes		
Miscellaneous	Locations		
Miscellaneous	Changes In Locations-29th Division 6 p.m. 30th October, 1917.	30/10/1917	30/10/1917
Miscellaneous	Disposition And Movement Report No. 11a. 29th Division.	27/10/1917	27/10/1917
Miscellaneous	29th Division No. I.G. 93/147.	26/10/1917	26/10/1917
Miscellaneous	Changes In Locations-29th Division up to 6 p.m. 21st October, 1917.	21/10/1917	21/10/1917
Miscellaneous	Reference Disposition and Movement Report No. 2 (29th Division No. I.G. 93/138)	18/10/1917	18/10/1917
Miscellaneous	29th Division No. I.G. 93/138A.	18/10/1917	18/10/1917
Miscellaneous	Disposition And Movement Report No. 2. 29th Division.	18/10/1917	18/10/1917
Operation(al) Order(s)	Addendum to 29th Division Order No. 163.	14/10/1917	14/10/1917
Miscellaneous	Amendment To Locations-29th Division. Midnight 7th/8th October, 1917.	07/10/1917	07/10/1917
Miscellaneous	Changes In Locations-29th Division up to Midnight 3rd/4th October, 1917.	03/10/1917	03/10/1917
Miscellaneous	Changes In Locations-29th Division up to Midnight 2nd/3rd October, 1917.	02/10/1917	02/10/1917
Miscellaneous	Summaries		
Miscellaneous	29th Division Intelligence Summary 6 a.m. 30th Sept. to 6 a.m. 1st Oct. 1917.	30/09/1917	30/09/1917
Miscellaneous	29th Division Intelligence Summary 6 a.m. 1st October to 6 a.m. 2nd October, 1917.	01/10/1917	01/10/1917
Miscellaneous	29th Division Intelligence Summary 6 a.m. 2nd Oct. to 6 a.m. 3rd Oct. 1917.	02/10/1917	02/10/1917
Miscellaneous	Patrol Report.		
Miscellaneous	29th Division Intelligence Summary 6 a.m. 4th to 6 a.m. 5th October, 1917.	04/10/1917	04/10/1917
Miscellaneous	Patrol Report.		
Miscellaneous	29th Division Intelligence Summary 6 a.m. 5th to 6 a.m. 6th October, 1917	05/10/1917	05/10/1917
Miscellaneous	29th Division Intelligence Summary 6 a.m. 6th to 6 a.m. 7th October, 1917	06/10/1917	06/10/1917
Heading	HQ GS 29D War Diary November 1917 Vol 33		
Heading	War Diary General Staff 29th Division For The Month Of November 1917 Volume XXXIII.		
War Diary	Basseux	01/11/1917	16/11/1917
War Diary	Basseux Moislains	17/11/1917	19/11/1917
War Diary	Quentin Mill & Sorel.	20/11/1917	30/11/1917
Miscellaneous	Appendices.		
Heading	Appen A Mentioned In Diary Operation Orders.		
Operation(al) Order(s)	29th Division Operation Order No. G.S. 37/31. Appendix 1	14/11/1917	14/11/1917
Miscellaneous	Routine Order No. G.S. 37/30 by Major-General Sir Beauvoir de Lisle, K.C.B., D.S.O.	14/11/1917	14/11/1917
Operation(al) Order(s)	29th Division Order No. 164. Appen III	15/11/1917	15/11/1917
Miscellaneous	Restrictions as to Movement.	08/11/1917	08/11/1917
Miscellaneous	March Table for Transport 16/17th November.	16/11/1917	16/11/1917

Type	Description	Date 1	Date 2
Miscellaneous	March Table for Transport 17/18th November. Table "B"	17/11/1917	17/11/1917
Miscellaneous	29th Division Warning Order. Appen 4	15/11/1917	15/11/1917
Miscellaneous	Moves of Personnel 17/18th Table "C"		
Operation(al) Order(s)	29th Division Order No. 165 Appen IV	16/11/1917	16/11/1917
Miscellaneous	Moves of Personnel 17/18th Table "C"	17/11/1917	17/11/1917
Operation(al) Order(s)	29th Division Order No. 166. Appex 1	17/11/1917	17/11/1917
Miscellaneous	Moves of Infantry 18/19th November, 1917. Table "D".	18/11/1917	18/11/1917
Operation(al) Order(s)	29th Division Order No. 168. Appen VI	18/11/1917	18/11/1917
Miscellaneous	Assembly March Y/Z Night. Table "E".		
Map	Identification Trace for use with Artillery Maps.		
Operation(al) Order(s)	29th Division Order No. 167 Appen VII	18/11/1917	18/11/1917
Miscellaneous	29th Division No. C.G.S. 67/85.	20/11/1917	20/11/1917
Miscellaneous	29th Division No. C.G.S. 67/86.	19/11/1917	19/11/1917
Miscellaneous	Operation G.Y.	17/11/1917	17/11/1917
Miscellaneous	Secret No. C.G.S. 67/91	18/11/1917	18/11/1917
Operation(al) Order(s)	29th Division Order No. 169. Appen VIII	24/11/1917	24/11/1917
Operation(al) Order(s)	29th Division Order No. 170. Appen IX	27/11/1917	27/11/1917
Operation(al) Order(s)	29th Division Order No. 171.	29/11/1917	29/11/1917
Miscellaneous	Appen B Instructions		
Miscellaneous	29th Division Operations. Instruction No. 1.	11/11/1917	11/11/1917
Miscellaneous	Appendix 1 To 29th Division Instruction No. 1 Marking Of Tanks.		
Miscellaneous	Addenda and Corrigenda to 29th Division Operations Instruction No. 1.	13/11/1917	13/11/1917
Miscellaneous	Amendment No. 1 to 29th Division Instructions No. 1.	15/11/1917	15/11/1917
Miscellaneous	29th Division Operations. Correction To Instruction No. 1.	16/11/1917	16/11/1917
Miscellaneous	29th Division Operations. Instruction No. 3	13/11/1917	13/11/1917
Miscellaneous	29th Division Operations. Instruction No. 4. Communications.	13/11/1917	13/11/1917
Miscellaneous	Addendum No. 1 to 29th Division Operation Instruction No. 4.	19/11/1917	19/11/1917
Miscellaneous	29th Division Operations. Instruction No. 6 Medical Arrangements prior to Zero.	15/11/1917	15/11/1917
Miscellaneous	29th Division Operations. Instruction No. 7. Prisoner Of War, Refugees, Enemy Documents.	15/11/1917	15/11/1917
Miscellaneous	29th Division Operations. Addendum No. 1 to Instruction No. 7.	16/11/1917	16/11/1917
Miscellaneous	29th Division Operations. Instruction No. 9. Employment of Machine Guns.	16/11/1917	16/11/1917
Miscellaneous	29th Division No. C.G.S. 68/76	15/11/1917	15/11/1917
Miscellaneous	III Corps General Staff. G.O. 5963, November 9th, 1917	09/11/1917	09/11/1917
Miscellaneous	29th Division Operations. Instruction No. 10. Codes and Ciphers.	16/11/1917	16/11/1917
Miscellaneous	29th Division Operations. Instruction No. 11. Employment of R.E.	16/11/1917	16/11/1917
Miscellaneous	Amendment to 29th Division Operation Instruction No. 11.	18/11/1917	18/11/1917
Miscellaneous	29th Division Operations. Instruction No. 12. Dress, Equipment, etc.	16/11/1917	16/11/1917
Miscellaneous	29th Division Operations. Instruction No. 13. Administrative Arrangements.	18/11/1917	18/11/1917
Miscellaneous	Amendment No. 1 to 29th Division Order No. 167.	18/11/1917	18/11/1917
Miscellaneous	29th Division Operations. Instruction No. 14	19/11/1917	19/11/1917

Miscellaneous	Third Army No. G.14/289. III Corps G.O. 6739. 29th Div. No. C.G.S. 51/136	25/11/1917	25/11/1917
Miscellaneous		24/11/1917	24/11/1917
Miscellaneous	Appen C Intell Summaries and Location Lists.		
Miscellaneous	29th Division Intelligence Summary Period ending 6 a.m. 23.11.17	23/11/1917	23/11/1917
Miscellaneous	29th Division Intelligence Summary 6 a.m. 23rd-6 a.m. 24th Nov.	23/11/1917	23/11/1917
Miscellaneous	29th Division Intelligence Summary 6 a.m. 24th to 6 a.m. 25th Nov. 1917.	24/11/1917	24/11/1917
Miscellaneous	29th Division Intelligence Summary 6 a.m. 25th to 6 a.m. 26th Nov. 1917.	25/11/1917	25/11/1917
Miscellaneous	29th Division Intelligence Summary 6 a.m. 26th to 6 a.m. 27th Nov. 1917.	26/11/1917	26/11/1917
Miscellaneous	29th Division Intelligence Summary 6 a.m. 27th to 6 a.m. 28th Nov. 1917.	27/11/1917	27/11/1917
Miscellaneous	29th Division Intelligence Summary 6 a.m. 28th to 6 a.m. 29th Nov. 1917.	28/11/1917	28/11/1917
Miscellaneous	Change In Locations-29th Division 13th November, 1917.	13/11/1917	13/11/1917
Miscellaneous	Changes In Locations-29th Division 11th November 1917	11/11/1917	11/11/1917
Miscellaneous	Locations-29th Division.	16/11/1917	16/11/1917
Miscellaneous	Changes In Locations-29th Division 6 p.m. 5th November, 1917.	05/11/1917	05/11/1917
Map	Gouzeaucourt.		
Miscellaneous	Report on Operations by 29th Division on 20th November, 1917. Appendix D	20/11/1917	20/11/1917
Miscellaneous	Appendix "A".		
Heading	29th Division Reports On Cambrai Operations		
Map	Niergnies.		
Miscellaneous	Report on Operations by 29th Division on 30th November and following days.	10/12/1917	10/12/1917
Miscellaneous		30/11/1917	30/11/1917
Miscellaneous Diagram etc	29th Div. No. C.G.S. 70/79.	30/12/1917	30/12/1917
Miscellaneous	29th Divisional Artillery. Report on Operations of 30th November 1917. and following days.	30/11/1917	30/11/1917
Miscellaneous	Appendix "A". Action of Medium Trench Mortar Batteries of 29th Division November 30th and December 1st 1917.	01/12/1917	01/12/1917
Miscellaneous	Appendix "B".	30/11/1917	30/11/1917
Miscellaneous	29th Division No. C.G.S. 70/73.	30/11/1917	30/11/1917
Miscellaneous	Report on Operations near Masnieres on Nov. 30th and Dec. 1st by 86th Brigade.	30/11/1917	30/11/1917
Miscellaneous	Precis of Operations of 87th Infantry Brigade November 30th to December 3rd, 1917.	03/12/1917	03/12/1917
Miscellaneous	Report on Operations near Marcoing on Nov. 30th and Dec. 1st by 88th Brigade.	30/11/1917	30/11/1917
Miscellaneous	Summary Statement of Casualties Incurred By 29th Division In Active Operations S.W. Of Cambrai 20-11-17 To 3-12-17 Inclusive.	20/11/1917	20/11/1917
Miscellaneous	Report on Operations by 29th Division on 20th November, 1917.	20/11/1917	20/11/1917
Miscellaneous	29th Division-Captured Material.		
Miscellaneous	29th Division No. 311/66	30/11/1917	30/11/1917

Miscellaneous	Civilians Evacuated During Recent Operations.		
Miscellaneous	29th Division-Captured Material.		
Miscellaneous	Action S.W. Of Cambrai. 29th. Division. Statement Of Casualties.	20/11/1917	20/11/1917
Miscellaneous	Gouzeaucourt. 510th. (London) Field Coy. R.E.	08/12/1917	08/12/1917
Miscellaneous	Gouzeaucourt.	08/12/1917	08/12/1917
Miscellaneous	Narrative of the Events at Marcoing on December 3rd. 1917.	03/12/1917	03/12/1917
Miscellaneous	29th. Division. Report On Evacuation Of Wounded During Operations 20th November to 4th December, 1917	20/11/1917	20/11/1917
Miscellaneous	Report On The Use Of Hot Air Apparatus At An Advanced Dressing Station During Recent Operations Of The 29th Division.	04/12/1917	04/12/1917
Miscellaneous	Report on Operations by 29th Division on 20th November 1917.	20/11/1917	20/11/1917
Miscellaneous	Headquarters, 29th Division.	29/12/1917	29/12/1917
Heading	G.S. 29th Div December 1917		
War Diary	Trescault Sorel.	01/12/1917	04/12/1917
War Diary	Sorel Le Cauroy.	05/12/1917	05/12/1917
War Diary	Le Cauroy	06/12/1917	17/12/1917
War Diary	Hucqueliers	18/12/1917	31/12/1917
Miscellaneous	29th Division Warning Order.	29/11/1917	29/11/1917
Miscellaneous	Special Order Of The Day by Major-General Sir Beauvoir de Lisle, K.C.B., D.S.O. Commanding 29th Division.	11/12/1917	11/12/1917
Operation(al) Order(s)	29th Division Order No. 172.	14/12/1917	14/12/1917
Operation(al) Order(s)	29th Division Operation Order No. 175.	27/12/1917	27/12/1917
Operation(al) Order(s)	Addendum No. 1 to 29th Division Order No. 175.	02/01/1917	02/01/1917
Miscellaneous	C Form. Messages And Signals.		
Operation(al) Order(s)	29th Division Operation Order No. 176.	27/12/1917	27/12/1917
Miscellaneous	March Table Issued With 29th Division Order No. 176.		
Operation(al) Order(s)	Addendum No. 1 to 29th Division Order No. 176.	28/12/1917	28/12/1917
Miscellaneous	29th Division Warning Order	12/12/1917	12/12/1917
Miscellaneous	29th Division Warning Order.	29/12/1917	29/12/1917
Miscellaneous	Appendices.		
Heading	Appendix A Operation Orders Of Moves Summary Of Manages For Operations 30th Nov-4th Dec		
Operation(al) Order(s)	29th Division Administrative Order No. 22. Appen I	04/12/1917	04/12/1917
Miscellaneous	Entraining Table. Table A.		
Miscellaneous	Transport To Proceed By Rail. Table B.		
Miscellaneous	29th Divisional Conference held at Le Cauroy on December 8th, Brigadiers and Commanding Officers attending. Appen 2	08/12/1917	08/12/1917
Miscellaneous	29th Division Warning Order Appen 3	12/12/1917	12/12/1917
Operation(al) Order(s)	29th Division Order No. 172. Appen 3	14/12/1917	14/12/1917
Miscellaneous	29th Div. No. C.G.S. 5C/31 Appen 4		
Miscellaneous	Anti-Gas Measures. Syllabus Of Training For One Hour Twice Each Week.		
Operation(al) Order(s)	29th Division Order No. 174. Appen 5	20/12/1917	20/12/1917
Operation(al) Order(s)	29th Division Operation Order No. 175. Appen 6	27/12/1917	27/12/1917
Operation(al) Order(s)	29th Division Operation Order No. 176. Appen 7	27/12/1917	27/12/1917
Miscellaneous	March Table Issued With 29th Division Order No. 176.		
Operation(al) Order(s)	Addendum No. 1 to 29th Division Order No. 176.	28/12/1917	28/12/1917
Miscellaneous	S. end of Gouzeaucourt	00/11/1917	00/11/1917
War Diary	6th Division H.Q. Villers Plouich	00/11/1917	00/11/1917

Miscellaneous		01/12/1917	04/12/1917
War Diary	S. end of Gouzeaucourt	00/11/1917	00/11/1917
War Diary	6th Division H.Q. Villers Plouich	00/11/1917	00/11/1917
Miscellaneous		01/12/1917	04/12/1917
Heading	Appendix B. Locations		
Miscellaneous	Locations-29th Division for 8th December, 1917. Appen. I.	08/12/1917	08/12/1917
Miscellaneous	Amendment to Locations 29th Division No. I.G. 93/186. Appen. 2.	27/12/1917	27/12/1917
Miscellaneous	29th. Division. Report On Evacuation Of Wounded During Operations 20th November to 4th December, 1917 by A.D.M.S., 29th Division.	04/12/1917	04/12/1917
Miscellaneous	Report On The Use Of Hot Air Apparatus At An Advanced Dressing Station During Recent Operations Of The 29th Division.	04/12/1917	04/12/1917
Miscellaneous	A Form. Messages And Signals.		

29TH DIVISION

GENERAL STAFF

SEP - DEC 1917

(6202) W 11186/M1151 350,000 12/16 McA. & W., Ltd. (Est. 781) Forms/W 3091/3. Army Form W. 3091.

Cover for Documents.

Nature of Enclosures.

War Diary

October

Notes, or Letters written.

CONFIDENTIAL.

WAR DIARY

GENERAL STAFF

29TH DIVISION

FOR THE

MONTH OF

OCTOBER 1917.

-o-o-o-o-o-o-o-o-o-o-o-o-o-o-

VOLUME XXXII

-o-o-o-o-o-o-o-o-o-o-o-o-o-o-

Army Form C. 2118.

WAR DIARY
INTELLIGENCE SUMMARY

(Erase heading not required.)

Instructions regarding War Diaries and Intelligence Summaries are contained in F. S. Regs., Part II. and the Staff Manual respectively. Title pages will be prepared in manuscript.

OCTOBER, 1917.

Place	Date	Hour	Summary of Events and Information	Remarks and references to Appendices
"J" Camp Map Ref. & Sheet 23 N.W. 1/20,000 A.S.A.	Oct. 1st.		G.S.O.1 to forward area. Hostile Artillery active during night 30th Sept/1st Oct. Inactive during the day. G.O.C. and C.R.E. to forward area for reconnaissance. Capt. McConnel 20th Hussars, G.S.O.3, 4th Division appointed Brigade Major 88th Bde.	
	Oct. 2nd.		G.S.O.2 to forward area. Quiet day. Lieut. H.B.Thompson, Reconnaissance Officer, 29th Divl. Artillery, killed by sniper near JAPAN HOUSE (front line N. of railway). Colonel Drum of American Army Corps1 staff arrived for few days attachment to the Division.	
ELVERDINGHE	Oct. 3rd.		G.O.C. and Col. Drum to forward area. Quiet day. Divl. H.Q. moved to ELVERDINGHE CHATEAU. 1st Royal Dublin Fus. moved up into assembly positions for attack. (O.O.157 & Instructions)	Appendix I.
	Oct. 4th.		Attack by 1st Royal Dublin Fus. (See special account).	Appendix II
	Oct. 5th.		G.O.C. and G.S.O.2 to H.Q. 1st Royal Dublin Fus. LANGEMARCK. 2nd S.W.B's - 87th Bde took over the Divisional front. (O.O.158).	Appendix III
	Oct. 6th.		G.S.O.1 to forward area. Conference XIV Corps H.Q. 5-30pm. New Divisional boundaries in front area adjusted ready for next operation. (O.O.159 & /60)	Appendix IV Appendix V
	Oct. 7th.		Rain. Conference of Brigadiers. Moves to assembly positions commenced in accordance with 29th. Div. Order No.161.	Appendix VI

Army Form C. 2118.

WAR DIARY
or
INTELLIGENCE SUMMARY.
(Erase heading not required.)

Instructions regarding War Diaries and Intelligence Summaries are contained in F.S. Regs., Part II. and the Staff Manual respectively. Title pages will be prepared in manuscript.

Place	Date	Hour	Summary of Events and Information	Remarks and references to Appendices
	Oct. 8th.		Relief complete 3.am. Fine in early morning. G.S.O.2 to forward area. Enemy's Artillery more active. Rain commenced about 3.30pm and continued until midnight. (O.O.162).	Appendix VII
	Oct. 9th.		Attack (see special report). Army Commander visited Divl. H.Q. Relief of 1st Lancs Fus and 4th Worcesters by 2 Bns 51st Bde. 17th Div.	Appendix VIII
	Oct. 10th.		G.S.O.2 to forward area to arrange details of relief. Commander-in-Chief visited 29th Div. H.Q. Relief in front area by 17th Div. Relief complete by 5.am 11th inst. Units of 29th Div. by train from ELVERDINGHE to various areas P1, P5 and S1. Lieut-Col.C.G.Fuller D.S.O. G.S.O.1, 29th Div. appointed B.G.G.S. 3rd Corps.	
PROVEN	Oct. 11th.		Command of line passed to G.O.C. 17th Div at 10.am. Divl. H.Q. to PROVEN. G.O.C. visited 86th Bde after lunch.	
	Oct. 12th.		Rain. Attack by 2nd and 5th Armies continued. G.O.C. visited 88th Bde. Lt-Col.J.Moore D.S.O. Royal Berkshire Regt. arrived from G.S.O.2, 5th Corps, to take over duties of G.S.O.1 of this Division, vice Lt-Col.C.G.Fuller appointed B.G.G.S. 3rd Corps.	
	Oct. 13th.		Rain. G.O.C. attended Gala performance at Divisional Theatre.	
	Oct. 14th.		Quiet day, nothing to report. Advanced parties to 3rd Army Area despatched.(Warning Order).	Appendix IX

Army Form C. 2118.

WAR DIARY
INTELLIGENCE SUMMARY

(Erase heading not required.)

Instructions regarding War Diaries and Intelligence Summaries are contained in F.S. Regs., Part II. and the Staff Manual respectively. Title pages will be prepared in manuscript.

Place	Date	Hour	Summary of Events and Information	Remarks and references to Appendices
BASSEUX. 1/40,000 Sheet 51.G.	Oct. 15th.		Entrainment commenced. D.A.A.G. and G.S.O.2 to new area. (O.O.163).	Appendix X
	Oct. 16th.		Entrainment continued. G.O.C. to new area. H.Q. opened at BASSEUX 10.am.	
	Oct. 17th.		Weather fine. Detrainment complete. G.O.C. visited 87th Bde in billets in the morning and 86th and 88th Bdes in afternoon.	
	Oct. 18th.		Commanding Officers Conference 11.am. G.O.C gave lines on which training is to be carried out. G.O.C. inspected 1st Royal Dublin Fus. on parade prior to their transfer to 16th Div.	
	Oct. 19th.		1st Royal Dublin Fus. by march route to 16th Div. Army Commander visited G.O.C. 87th Bde of Drums played at Divl. H.Q. 4-30pm.	
	Oct. 20th.		G.O.C. visited 88th Bde training. 88th Bde of Drums played at Divl. H.Q. 4-30pm. Weather fine and cold.	
	Oct. 21st.		G.O.C. attended Church Parade. G.O.C. temporarily in command of VI.Corps in absence of G.O.C. VI.Corps. Visited H.Q. of Division in line.	

Army Form C. 2118.

WAR DIARY
INTELLIGENCE SUMMARY.
(Erase heading not required.)

Instructions regarding War Diaries and Intelligence Summaries are contained in F. S. Regs., Part II. and the Staff Manual respectively. Title pages will be prepared in manuscript.

Place	Date	Hour	Summary of Events and Information	Remarks and references to Appendices
	Oct. 22nd.		G.O.C. visited 86th Bde training. Saw rehearsal of Brigade of Drums.	
	Oct. 23rd.		Wet day. G.O.C. lecture at VI.Corps School.	
	Oct. 24th.		Cold and wet. G.O.C. visited 87th Bde training in the morning. G.O.C. attended Divisional Theatre with VI.Corps Commander. Orders received for Divl. R.E. to move to VII.Corps Area.	
	Oct. 25th.		G.O.C. visited 86th Bde training. Wet day. R.E. move completed. 29th Div. Artillery commence to arrive from XIV.Corps Area, detraining at DOULLENS.	
	Oct. 26th.		G.O.C. visited 87th Bde training. Wet day. Orders received for 2 M.G.Coys to be placed at disposal of 16th Div.	
	Oct. 27th.		G.O.C. to 3rd Army H.Q. 29th Div. Artillery completed detrainment and billetted in DOULLENS Area.	
	Oct. 28th.		Gen. Fuller and Gel. Hardress-Lloyd visited G.O.C.	
	Oct. 29th.		G.O.C. visited 16th Div. and presented medals to 1st Royal Dublin Fus. G.O.C. 16th Div. and Royal Dublin Fus. Bde (48th) under Gen. Ramsey on parade.	

Army Form C. 2118.

WAR DIARY
INTELLIGENCE SUMMARY.
(Erase heading not required.)

Instructions regarding War Diaries and Intelligence Summaries are contained in F. S. Regs., Part II. and the Staff Manual respectively. Title pages will be prepared in manuscript.

Place	Date	Hour	Summary of Events and Information	Remarks and references to Appendices
	Oct. 30th.		Rain. Nothing to report.	
	Oct. 31st.		G.O.C. and G.S.O.1 attended Conference at 111.Corps H.Q.	

A.T. Miller Capt. for H.T. Gen Staff
29th Div

10.11.17.

LIST OF APPENDICES.

-o-o-o-o-o-o-o-o-o-o-o-o-o-o-

Appendix "A" comprises:-

- (I). Orders and Instructions for attacks on 4th and 9th October.
- (II). Report on Operations by 1st R.Dublin Fus. on 4th October.
- (III). Reorganisation of XIV.Corps front on night 5th/6th October.
- (IV). Reorganisation of XIV.Corps front on night 5th/6th October.
- (V). Orders for attack on 9th October.
- (VI). Ordres and march table for march to assembly positions.
- (VII). Orders for relief of 29th Div. by 17th Div. in Centre Sector of XIV.Corps front on 9th October.
- (VIII). Telephone messages and wires received during attack on 9th October.
- (IX). Warning Order for transfer of 29th Div. from XIV.Corps to Third Army.
- (X). Order for transfer of 29th Div. from Fifth Army to Third Army.

Appendix "B" comprises:-   Date.

- (I). 29th Div.No.I.G.103/19. Report of casualties to Division in fighting during the months April - October 1917.   15.10.17.
- (II). 29th Div.No.C.G.S.70/54. Suggestions for preparation of attack from experiences gained on 4th October.   25.10.17.
- (III). 29th Div.No.C.G.S.72/57. Restriction in use of Telephones in Forward Areas.   1.10.17.
- (IV). 29th Div.No.I.G.94/20. Information regarding German Regiments opposite the Division.   3.10.17.
- (V). 29th Div.No.C.G.S.72/62. Flares for Contact Aeroplanes.   7.10.17.
- (VI). 29th Div.No.56/20. Notes for Coy. Commanders.   7.10.17.
- (VII). 29th Div.No.C.G.S.56/22. Notes of 29th Div. Conference at BASSEUX.   18.10.17.
- (VIII). 29th Div.No.C.G.S.78/25. Formation of Divl. Depot Battalion.   20.10.17.
- (IX). 29th Div.No.G.S.29/11. Winter Sports Competition.   21.10.17.
- (X). Agenda of Lecture by Major-General Sir Beauvoir de Lisle, K.C.B.,D.S.O., at VI.Corps School.   23.10.17.

Appendix "C" comprises:-

Locations of 29th Division.

Appendix "D" comprises:-

Summaries of 29th Division.

-o-o-o-o-o-o-o-o-o-o-o-o-o-o-o-

A

Operation Orders.

Instructions.

SECRET.   Copy No. ____4____

29TH DIVISION ORDER NO. 157.
-o-o-o-o-o-o-o-o-o-o-o-o-o-o-o-o-o-o-

BROEMBEEK 1/10,000, and
Ref. attached tracing.   30th Sept. 1917.

1.   The attack on the enemy's position is to be renewed by the XIV Corps, in conjunction with other operations to the South on a date and at an hour Zero to be notified later.

2. (a) The attack is to be carried out by the 4th Division on the right and the 29th Division on the left.
        The objectives and boundaries between Divisions are shewn on the attached tracing.
   (b) The attack is to be made in two bounds on the 4th Division front only. The 29th Division will complete the operations in one bound.
   (c) The 10th Inf. Bde. (4th Division) with Headquarters at ADELPHI (C.3.b.2.1.) will be on our right.

3.   The attack will be carried out by one battalion of the 86th Inf. Bde., under the orders of the G.O.C., 87th Inf. Bde., South of the railway, and by two platoons of the 87th Inf. Bde. North of the Railway.
        Two battalions of the 87th Inf. Bde. will be in Divisional Reserve, West of the CANAL, and will remain in their Camps ready to move at 15 minutes notice.

4. (a) In order to meet immediate enemy counter-attacks, fresh troops will be kept in hand behind the assaulting waves, ready to advance at once against any such counter-attack.
   (b) The most probable line of approach of a hostile counter-attack would appear to be on our right flank.
        A liaison detachment of   half a Company (detailed from another Bn. of the 86th Inf. Bde.) and two machine guns will consequently advance in echelon behind the right flank ready to fill any gap that may occur on the right flank, and to counter-attack the enemy if necessary.
   (c) Adequate mopping-up parties will be organised in rear of each assaulting wave, and all enemy dugouts or strong points, situated between the objective and protective barrage will be dealt with as soon as the lift of the barrage permits.

5.   The attack will be made under cover of :-

        (a) A creeping barrage.
        (b) A standing barrage.
        (c) A back barrage of 6" Howitzers and 60pdrs.
        (d) A distant barrage of Heavy Howitzers and 60pdrs.
        (e) A machine gun barrage.

        Three Brigades and two Batteries of Field Artillery will form the creeping and standing barrages.

        The creeping barrage will open 150 yards in front of the RED line; no troops will be in front of this line at Zero.
        The first lift will take place at Zero plus 3 minutes.
        Lifts will be 50 yards at a time.
        From the first lift, for 200 yards, the barrage will advance at the rate of 50 yards in two minutes. Thence to the first objective at 50 yards in three minutes.

                                                        / From

From the first objective to the second objective (on the 4th Division front) at 50 yards in four minutes.

The protective barrage covering the GREEN DOTTED line will become intensive at Zero plus 2 hours and 2 minutes, and commence to creep at Zero plus 2 hours and 10 minutes.

The Artillery barrage maps will be issued shortly.

The creeping barrage will be thickened by 8 Stokes Mortars, from the 86th Trench Mortar Battery, each firing 100 yards.

6. The left flank of the advance will be protected by a smoke screen, and by Artillery fire directed so as to keep down hostile fire from the north bank of the BROEMBEEK.

7. The dispositions of the 20 machine guns for the machine gun barrage have been issued in Instruction No. 18.

The 86th M.G. Coy. (less 1 section) is at the disposal of the G.O.C. 87th Inf. Bde. for/consolidation, and for the defence of the original front line. covering

Two sections of the 87th M.G. Coy. will assist the attack with covering fire from the line.

8. To ensure liaison with the Division on the right, special parties will be told off to get in touch with the 4th Division at

    (a) Road junction at U.18.c.95.55.
    (b) " " " U.18.d.3.8.

9. The following lines will be consolidated :-

    (a) The GREEN line.
    (b) KANGAROO TRENCH - T'GOED DER VESTEN FARM.

In addition to (b), a central support line will be consolidated from about U.18.c.4.0. to U.17.d.9.0.

Garrisons for these lines will be detailed in advance.

10. As soon as the objective has been captured, it will be consolidated.

An outpost line will be established in front of all lines during consolidation. When the consolidation is nearing completion the troops will be reformed, and organised in depth, and a reserve collected for counter-attacks.

The machine guns placed at the disposal of the Brigade, vide para. 7, will be used to strengthen the lines that are being consolidated, and will be disposed in depth.

11. Arrangements will be made to relieve the assaulting battalion by another battalion of the 86th Inf. Bde. on the night of the attack (Z/Z plus 1,night).

12. The S.O.S. Signal will be a succession of S.O.S. Rifle Rockets, each bursting simultaneously into four Red Lights.

No other light signal will be employed except RED flares, which will be used to shew the position of the infantry to contact aeroplane patrols.

13. A contact patrol will fly over the Corps front at :-

    Zero plus 1 hour and 30 mins.
    Zero plus 3 hours.
    Zero plus 5 hours.

and subsequently as ordered by Corps Headquarters.

/ RED

- 3 -

~~RED flares will be lit by the leading troops only when demanded by contact aeroplanes either~~ :-

    (a) By Klaxon Horn.
    (b) By a series of White lights.

The necessity for lighting flares will be impressed on all concerned, and an adequate supply of flares issued to the troops taking part in the attack, and to any reserves likely to be used in the operations. The flares will as far as possible be lighted in rows of three. Each Brigade and Battalion Headquarters will be marked by ground sheets of authorised shape, with the code letters of the unit laid out with white strips alongside. These letters should be 9 feet in depth. Signalling to aeroplanes will be carried out with Panels.

14.   Watches will be synchronised from Divisional Headquarters as soon after 12 Noon and 6 p.m. on "Y" day as possible, by a Divisional Staff Officer. Watches are on no account to be synchronised by telephone.

15.   Divisional Headquarters will close at "J" Camp at 6 p.m. on the 3rd October, and reopen at the same day and hour at ELVERDINGHE CHATEAU.

16.   <u>ACKNOWLEDGE.</u>

(signed)

Lieut-Colonel, G.S.,
29th Division.

Issued at   6 p.m.

Copies		
1 - 4	General Staff.	15 1/2nd Monmouths.
5	"Q".	16 A.D.M.S.
6	C.R.A.	17 A.P.M.
7	C.R.E.	18 D.M.G.O.
8 - 9	86th Inf. Bde.	19 14th Corps.
10 - 11	87th Inf. Bde.	20 4th Division.
12 - 13	88th Inf. Bde.	21 Guards Division.
14	Off. i/c Sigs.	22 29th French Division.
		23 9th Squadron R.F.C.

M.

War Diary

S E C R E T.   29th Div. No. C.G.S.72/57.

To all Units.

    Attention is again directed to the use of Telephones in the Forward Area.

    Telephones will not be used in front of Battalion Headquarters.   Fullerphones only may be used.

    The only exception is in the case of F.O.Os. who will be careful not to say anything that would be of the slightest value to the enemy.

    The telephones at Battalion Headquarters will only be used by responsible officers, and then only to speak to the flanks or rear, when all restrictions as to the use of the telephone in the danger zone will be adhered to.

A.T. Miller. Capt
Lieut-Colonel, G.S.,
29th Division.

1st October, 1917.

M.

S E C R E T.   29th Division No. C.G.S.67/63B.

ADDENDUM TO 29TH DIVISION ORDER NO. 157.
-o-o-o-o-o-o-o-o-o-o-o-o-o-o-o-o-o-o-o-o-o-o-o-o-o-

With reference to para. 5 of 29th Division Order No. 157, I forward herewith _____ copies of the Artillery Barrage Map.

The creeping barrage will remain on the "final protector" line until Zero plus 4 hrs. 38 mins.

After this hour the S.O.S. barrage, if called for, will fall on the following line (marked in RED on the attached map) :-

    Along the final protector from V.13.d.50.15. to U.18.a.0.1. - U.17.a.7.0. - NEY CROSS ROADS - thence along the line of the BROEMBEEK.

ACKNOWLEDGE.

C.J. Fuller.
Lieut-Colonel, G.S.,
29th Division.

1st October, 1917.

Copies to all recipients of 29th Division Order No. 157.

M.

CGS 68/67

APPENDIX "A".

CREEPING BARRAGE.

1st Objective.

1. The creeping barrage will fall at ZERO on the line A.A., 150 yards east of the "line of departure", and will remain there stationary for 3 minutes. No troops will be in front of the "line of departure" at ZERO.

At ZERO, the infantry will advance, and get <u>as close to the barrage as possible.</u> Should the infantry get up to the barrage too soon, they will kneel down, but they must not lie down.

The barrage will commence lifting back from the line A.A. at ZERO plus 3 minutes in lifts of 50 yards in two minutes, until it reaches the line F.F.

The barrage will pause 3 minutes on the line F.F., and lift back from F.F. at ZERO plus 14 minutes in lifts of 50 yards in three minutes, and will continue at this pace, until it reaches the line W.W., where it will remain stationary till ZERO plus 2 hours 10 minutes.

The leading infantry will halt on the "line of posts" and the GREEN line, and will be covered by the "final protector", shewn in BROWN, on the attached map.

2nd Objective (Right Division only).

2. At ZERO plus 2 hours 2 minutes the protective barrage covering the GREEN DOTTED line will become intensive, and will commence to creep at ZERO plus 2 hours 10 minutes, reaching the "final protector" on the right flank about ZERO plus 2 hours 38 minutes. During this period, the barrage opposite our front will remain on the "final protector" line.

3. The barrage will die down at ZERO plus 4 hours 38 minutes

4. Should the S.O.S. call (succession of S.O.S. Rifle Rockets, each bursting simultaneously into four RED Lights) be made after this hour, a protective barrage will be placed by the Artillery on the line :-

Along the final protector from
V.13.d.50.15. to U.18.a.0.1. - U.17.a.7.0.
- IVY CROSS ROADS - thence along the line
of the BROEN BEEK.

-o-o-o-o-o-o-o-

Copies sent to :- 86th Bde. 87th Bde. C.R.A.
D.M.G.O. 86th M.G. Coy.
87th M.G. Coy. 88th M.G. Coy.
227th M.G. Coy.

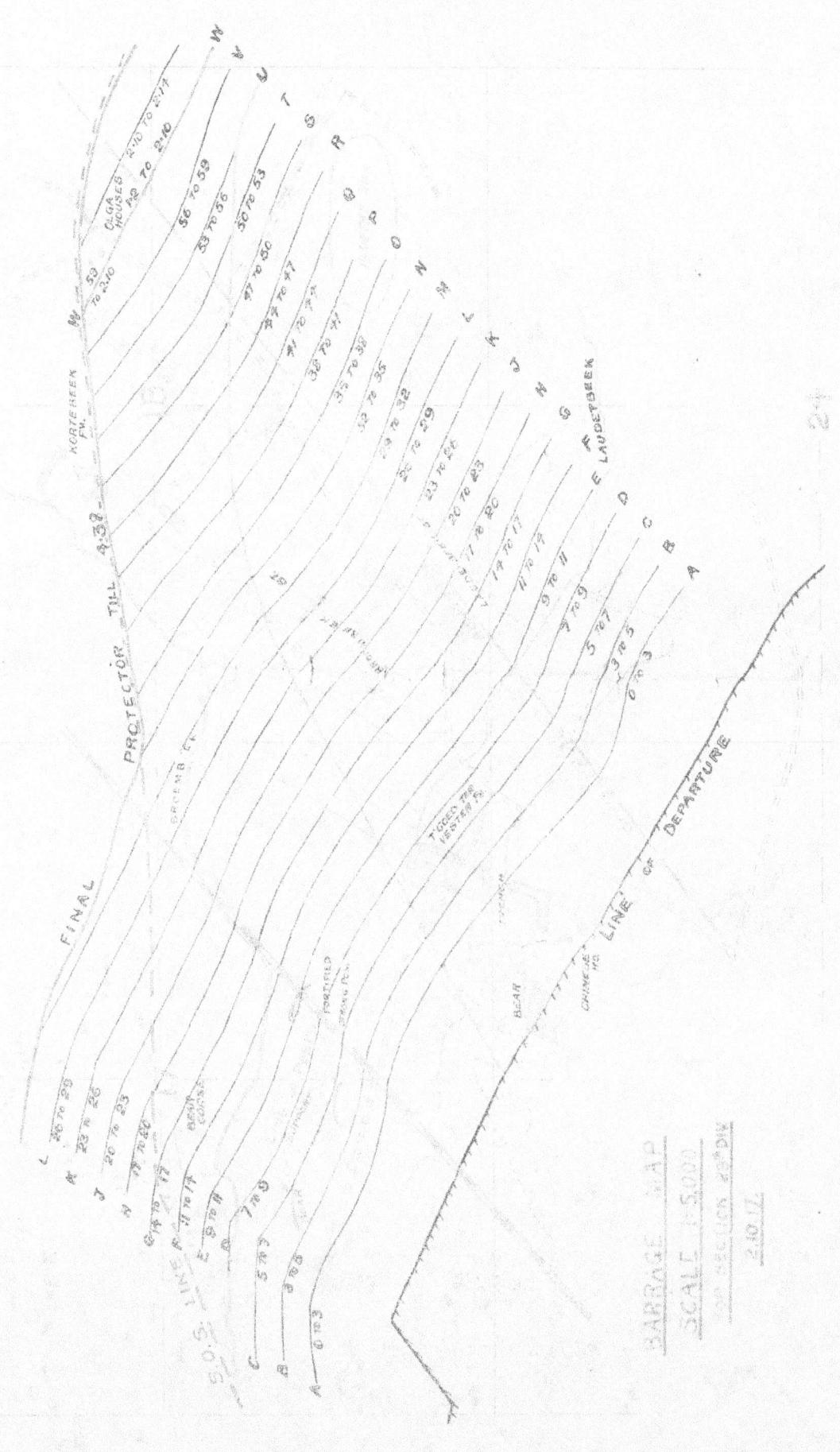

S E C R E T.   29th Division No. C.G.S.61/3.

29TH DIVISION OPERATIONS.

Instructions No.18.

MACHINE GUN SCHEME.

1. **Guns Available.**
   The following will be the dispositions of the Machine Guns of the Division.

   (a) For Barrage Purposes.
3 Sections	227th M.G.Coy.	12 guns.
1 Section	87th M.G.Coy.	4 guns.
1 Section	86th M.G.Coy.	4 guns.
	Total	20 guns.

   (b) At the disposal of G.O.C., 87th Bde.
       86th M.G.Coy (less 1 Section) 12 guns.

   (c) For covering fire from the line
       2 Sections, 87th M.G.Coy ..... 8 guns.

2. **Distribution of Barrage Guns.**
   Barrage guns will be divided into 5 Groups of 4 guns each. These will be situated at :-

   MONTMIRAIL FARM.
   U.15.d.5.0.
   U.21.c.9.9.
   U.21.d.3.7.
   U.21.d.7.4.

   The Groups will form a standing barrage along the general line, U.11.b. - U.11.d. - U.17.b. - U.18.a. Details of lines of fire and targets are given in the attached table.

3. **Ammunition.** Each gun will commence the barrage with 20 belts filled, and 10,000 rounds S.A.A. for bolt filling and reserve.

4. **Rate of fire.**   One belt in 4 mins during the advance.
                          One belt in 10 mins during consolidation, dropping to
                          One belt in 15 mins after Zero + 1 hour.

5. **Water.** One petrol tin for each gun must be at the gun positions before Zero.

6. **Barrels.** Each gun will commence barrage with a new barrel. These will be changed on completion of barrage.

7. **Danger Space.** Each Group Commander will arrange to mark out the danger space in front of his group and to warn troops in the neighbourhood.

8. **Covering Fire.** In addition to the barrage guns, the 8 guns of 87th M.G. Coy in the line, will assist the advance by firing on any target that appears on their front, engaging hostile M.G's and searching the line of the Railway.

9. Orders for the eventual disposal of the 20 Barrage Guns detailed in para 1, (a) will be issued from these Headquarters.

                                                                            Fuller
                                                                  Lieut-Colonel, G.S.,
                                                                         29th Division.

30th September, 1917.

29TH DIVISION M.G. BARRAGE.

Group.	Position.	Target.
A. 87th M.G.Coy.	MONTMIRAIL FARM.	2 Guns PASCAL Fm. - NAMUR CROSSING. 2 Guns U.17.b.0.6 - U.17.b.5.0.
B. 227th M.G.Coy.	U.15.d.5.0.	U.11.b. S.E. from Zero to Zero + 1 hour. S.O.S. Line KORTEBEEK Fm. U.18.a.
C. 227th M.G.Coy.	U.21.c.9.9.	KOEKUIT and U.11.d.
D. 227th M.G.Coy.	U.21.d.5.7.	2 Guns U.17.b. S.W. 2 Guns NAMUR CROSSING.
E. 86th M.G.Coy.	U.21.d.7.4.	Both sides of Railway from BROEMBEEK to NAMUR CROSSING.
Rate of Fire.	Z - Z + 20 mins. Z + 20 - Z + 1 hr. Z + 1 hr - Z + 5hrs. Intermittent fire all day S.O.S.	1 belt in 4 mins. 1 belt in 10 mins. 1 belt in 15 mins. 1 belt in 1 minute for 4 minutes, then 1 belt in 10 minutes.

S E C R E T.   29th Division No. O.G.S.61/Ca.

ADDENDUM TO INSTRUCTION No. 18.

MACHINE GUN SCHEME.

With reference to para 1 (b) of the above scheme.

1. The 12 guns of 86th M.G.Coy mentioned therein will be employed as follows :-

2 guns with Liaison Detachment (vide para 4 (b) of 29th Division Order No 157) on Right Flank.

2 guns now at U.23.a.4.7 will move up the Railway to a position in rear of the post to be established at U.17.d.3.6 during the attack. These guns will fire N.E. along BROEMBEEK VALLEY.

2 guns at U.23.a.6.5 will remain in their present positions, and will form a barrage across the road in U.18.b.6.5 to connect with the Machine Gun Barrage of the 4th Division.

The remaining 6 guns will be in reserve and will remain in their present Camp.

2. With reference to the Machine Gun Barrage Table, Groups A, B, D, and E, owing to posts being established along BEAR SUPPORT and on the Railway at U.17.d.3.6, the barrage on to U.17.b. must not fall South of the line U.17.b.0.3 - U.17.b.9.3.

Lieut-Colonel, G.S.,
29th Division.

1st October, 1917.

SECRET.   29th Division No. C.G.S.68/66.

29TH DIVISION OPERATIONS.

Instruction No. 19.

Administrative Arrangements.

The following are the Administrative arrangements for the forthcoming operations :-

1. AMMUNITION.

The dump at AU BON GITE (U.28.Central) belonging to the 4th Division will be drawn on as required.
Two Brigade dumps will be established at U.22.d.1.3., near REITRES FARM, and at U.22.d.95.10., LANGEMARCK.

2. PRISONERS OF WAR.

Collecting post will be at "THE ADELPHI" C.3.Central alongside the 4th Division Collecting Post.
The Divisional Prisoners Cage will be at CACTUS PONTOON.
The 86th Inf. Bde. will supply 2 N.C.Os. and 12 men to be under the control of the A.P.M., 29th Division, to take over prisoners at "THE ADELPHI", and conduct them down to CACTUS PONTOON, where the Military Police will take over and the Divisional Intelligence Officer interrogate.

3. STRAGGLERS POSTS.

Stragglers Posts will be established by the 4th Division at 5 Chemins Estaminet, PILCKEM MILL, BARD CAUSEWAY and CACTUS PONTOON. The A.P.M., 29th Division will arrange to have representatives at each of these places.

4. MEDICAL.

A Battle Aid Post will be established in EAGLE TRENCH from Zero Hour onwards.
The Bearer Relay Post of the 87th Field Ambulance will be at REITRES FARM (U.22.c.9.2.).
A Combined Regimental Aid Post of the 4th Division will be at "THE PIG and WHISTLE" (U.28.b.4.3.)
The 4th Division Advanced Dressing Station will be at CEMENT HOUSE (U.28.c.1.3.).
Stretcher cases will be evacuated thence by wheeled stretcher or 60cm. railway train to HARROW.
The Walking Wounded Collecting Post will be at CHEAPSIDE B.17.3 with the Walking Wounded of the 4th Division.
As the wounded of the 29th Division will certainly make their way back through the 4th Division Area owing to the direction of the attack, the A.D.M.S., 29th Division will supplement the R.A.M.C. personnel of the 4th Division at all the above places by mutual arrangement with the A.D.M.S., 4th Division.

5.   ACKNOWLEDGE.

Lieut-Colonel, G.S.,
29th Division.

30th Sept. 1917.

M.

S E C R E T.   29th Division No. C.G.S.68/66A.

29TH DIVISION OPERATIONS.
Amendment to Instruction No. 19.
Administrative Arrangements.

In para. 4, line 10, for "HARROW"
                    read "SOLFERINO".

                                    Lieut-Colonel, G.S.,
                                        29th Division.

1st October, 1917.

SECRET.   29th Division No. C.G.S.72/56.

29TH DIVISION OPERATIONS.

Instruction No. 20.

Communications.

The following are the arrangements for signal communications during the forthcoming operations :-

1. TELEPHONE LINES.

One telephone line from U.23.c.05.15. to SAULES FARM, via Centre Bn. H.Q. and SIGNAL FARM. Another telephone line from Bn. H.Q. to AU BON GITE to SAULES FARM, via STRAY FARM (AU BON GITE to STRAY FARM buried).

2. AMPLIFIERS and POWER BUZZERS.

An amplifier will be installed at U.23.c.05.15. and will receive from a power buzzer at U.23.c.70.75. This power buzzer will move forward after Zero to about U.23.b.Central.

3. PIGEONS.

6 pairs of birds will be supplied to the assaulting battalion on "Y" day, also 2 pairs to the Centre Bn. and 2 pairs to the Left Bn.

4. WIRELESS.

A forward station will be established about U.22.c.Central.

5.   ACKNOWLEDGE.

Lieut-Colonel, G.S.,
30th Sept. 1917.   29th Division.

M.

SECRET.   29th Div. No. C.G.S.68/68.

29TH DIVISION OPERATIONS.
Instruction No. 21.
Counter-Attack Machine.

An aeroplane will be up continuously during daylight, from Zero onwards, whose mission will be to detect the approach of enemy counter-attacks.

Whenever this patrol observes hostile parties of 100 or more moving to counter-attack, it will drop a smoke bomb over that portion of the front to which the enemy is moving.

The Smoke Bomb will burst about 100 feet below the machine, into a white parachute flare, which descends slowly leaving a long trail of brown smoke about one foot broad behind it.

ACKNOWLEDGE.

A.T. Mills Capt.

Lieut-Colonel, G.S.,
29th Division.

3rd October, 1917.

M.

S E C R E T.   29th Division No. C.G.S.37/64.

29TH DIVISION OPERATIONS.

With reference to para 1 of 29th Division Order No 157, the date of the attack will be

October 4th.

ACKNOWLEDGE.

Ack. BM 116

C.P. Fuller.
Lieut-Colonel, G.S.,
29th Division.

2nd October, 1917.

Copies to :-

```
    5      "Q".
    6      C.R.E.
    7      C.R.A.
  8-9      86th Inf Bde.
 10-11     87th Inf Bde.
 12-13     88th Inf Bde.
   14      Offr i/c Sigs.
   15      1/2 Monmouths.
   16      A.D.M.S.
   17.     A.P.M.
   18.     D.M.G.O.
   19      XIV Corps.
   20      4th Div.
   21      Guards Div.
   22      29th French Div.
   23      9th Squad R.F.C.
```

S.

S E C R E T.   29th Division No. C.G.S.67/65.

29TH DIVISION OPERATIONS.

Reference 29th Division Order No. 157, para 1,

Zero hour will be _____

ACKNOWLEDGE.

Zero hour will only be communicated to those directly concerned.
It must not be mentioned in telegrams, or over the telephone, whether in code or otherwise.

C.P. Fuller.
Lieut-Colonel, G.S.,
29th Division.

3rd October, 1917.

S.

SECRET.   29th Division No. I.G.94/20.

War Diary

86th Inf. Bde.
87th Inf. Bde.
88th Inf. Bde.

As far as is known the troops opposite us are as follows :-

(1) From NEY WOOD northwards - 18th Division.

Order of Battle N. to S.   85th I.R.
                            31st I.R.
                            86th Fus. R. (who wear a monogram in red on a white shoulder strap).

Recruited from ALTONA and SCHLESWIG-HOLSTEIN.

(2) From NEY WOOD southwards - 208th Division (?).

Order of Battle N. to S.   65th R.I.R.
                            25th I.R.
                            185th R.I.R.

The distinguishing marks of these Regiments, worn on the left arm in white braid are :-

25th I.R.   185th R./I.R.   65th R.I.R.

Recruited from the RHINE and BADEN Districts.

Our Divisional Sector crosses one regiment of the 18th Division on our left and 1 regiment and part of another of the 208th Division on our right.

It is probable that the 208th Division has been relieved, possibly by the 40th (Saxon) Division, the regiments of which are the 104th I.R., 134th I.R. and 181st I.R. These would wear the Saxon Cockade (white - green - white).

It is possible also that the 16th Division has relieved the 208th Division, the regiments of this Division are 28th I.R., 29th I.R. and 68th I.R., and it is recruited from the RHINE District.

C.J. Fuller
Lieut-Colonel, G.S.,
29th Division.

3rd October, 1917.

S E C R E T.   29th Division No. C.G.S. 57/70a.

Amendment to 29th Division Order No. 159.

Reference Map 1/10,000 LANGEMARCK.

1.   In para 4 (c) and in line 17 of the Location Table issued with the above Order,

    for "SAULES FARM – U.25.b.3.2"

   read "VULCAN CROSSING – U.27.c.40.55"

2.   In line 5 of the Location Table,

    for "U.8.c.5.5."

   read "B.8.c.5.5."

                                            Lieut-Colonel, G.S.,
8th October, 1917.   29th Division.

S.

SECRET

REFERENCE BROEMBEEK MAP 1/10,000

30-9-17

SECOND OBJECTIVE
FIRST OBJECTIVE
DIVISIONAL BOUNDARY

FIRST OBJECTIVE
DIVISIONAL BOUNDARY

4th DIV.
29th DIV.

LINE OF POSTS
LINE OF DEPARTURE

3rd Battle of Ypres -
4 Oct 1917

Brigade Major
    86th Infy Bde.

Herewith report on operations carried out by this battn: on the 4th October at LANGEMARCK.

Please let me have a copy of this back when finished up for the War Diary.

                        E.W.B. Carleton Capt
7/10/17   a/adjt 1st RDF.

HQ 29 Division
            Passed to you please,
a copy has been made & sent to
87th Bde.

9/X/17
                        Robt Gulan
                    Staff Capt 86 Bde

Brigade Major
            86th Infantry Bde.

On the night of the 3/4th October the 1st RDF relieved the 16th Mids Regt in the right of sector of the Divisional front. The two leading Coys for the Assault Y Coy on the right and Z Coy on the left moved straight into EAGLE TR and put out covering posts. The section T.M Battery formed up behind Y Coy and behind them again was the flanking detachment 16th Middlesex Regt T.M Battery. W Coy who were to be in Support during the Assault were lined up in shell holes to the left rear of the T.M Battery section and X Coy in Reserve were behind W in shell holes.

The objectives of Coys were as follows - Z Coy to capture post at 45 K on the STADEN Railway - and GOED TER VESTEN Fm & dig on a line from approximately U17 d 03 to U18 d 05 - Y Coy on the right to capture CHINESE Ho & the four block houses at U 18 c 4 6 & to reach the line U 18 c 6 7 to U 18 d 38 digging on the line from the latter point to join up with Z Coy at U 18 d 05. W Coy were to move behind the leading Coy & consolidate a line approxim.

from U17 d 70 to U 18 C 4 0. X Coy to move into EAGLE TR immediately the leading three coys had got clear of it. Flanking detachment 16th Lnds were to cover the right flank during the advance & upon Y Coy reaching their objective to dig in at approx. at U.18.d.15.9 ready to beat off any counter attack threatening from that direction. The forming up of the battn was carried out very quietly and effectively. The night was dark & no movement could be seen by the enemy. There was very little shelling through the night & though the enemy shelled slightly more heavily about 5 am as is his daily custom in that region the coys had very few casualties. Immediately upon relief of 16th Lnds Regt coys proceeded to draw their battle stores from the dumps in the vicinity. Sandbags, flares, SOS rockets alone were taken up by coys together with one days ration & an iron ration. Tools &ca & Lewis Guns were brought up in advance of the battn. & dumped near GREEN MILL where coys picked them up on their way from camp to the line.
The chief stores drawn from the dumps were bombs & SAA. In addition Coys had in their possession large quantities of tape.

By Zero less one hour all coys were in their correct positions. Some hot tea in petrol tins which were wrapped round in ~~straw~~ hay & put into packs had been brought up by mules with coys as far as the junction of HUNTER SWITCH & the mule track & this was greatly appreciated by the men with a half tot of rum.

The Barrage appeared to open half a minute too soon on the right but came down punctually on our front to time. All ranks praise the accuracy & volume of the barrage though several admit that they were wounded by getting too close under it. It is interesting to note here that it ~~is~~ was extremely difficult at that hour to ascertain the line of the barrage after the first lift.

~~Before~~ Immediately the barrage came down the two leading coys who had left their posts out & strengthened them gradually as zero approached dashed out ~~under~~ & got as close to ~~it~~ barrage as possible moving in lines of sections. The remaining bodies all came forward and maintained the same formation.

W Coy were the first to report their objective taken & notified Battn HQ as that Y Coy was making good progress. A party of W Coy however overstepped the objective & moved up behind Y Coy eventually taking up a position about the four blockhouses at U18C 4.6.

Z Coy captured T GOED TER VESTEN Fm & took sixteen prisoners & also captured K 45 with two m. guns & fifteen prisoners. Twenty other prisoners were captured in shell holes between these two points. At K 45 however the Z Coy's post was under heavy M.G. fire from across the BROENBEEK & as the enemy post they were occupying had been very much blown in they left the post & consolidated in a shell hole 12 yards South of it. This gave this new post the advantage of having the old enemy wire in front of them as an obstacle.

No information could be obtained from Y coy all of whose Officers had become casualties & whose Coy Sergt Major had been killed. By a personal reconnaissance however carried out by the Intelligence Officer they were seen to be on their objective & consolidating being in touch with the Seaforth Highlanders of the 4th Division on the right.

About 1.30 pm a small local counter attack came from the direction of KORTEBEEK Fm & the Seaforth Highrs seeing the gap between certain portions of Y Coys flank & the enemy dubbling forward at once commenced to go back taking with them that part of Y Coy nearest themselves. The counter attack however was easily beaten off & the Seaforths returning swung too much over to the right taking with them the party of Y Coy of whom no news has since been heard.

About five pm however the Warwickshire Regt coming up to support the Seaforth Highrs noticing the gap caused in our line by the Centre which had remained firm & details on the right which had swung over too much to that flank sent over one coy to occupy that the gap. Throughout the afternoon the coys were subjected to fairly heavy enemy shelling but they had dug themselves in well and did not have excessive casualties.

At dusk that evening two platoons of 1st KOSB, came in to EAGLE TR to reinforce our Reserve Coy now only two platoons strong - one platoon having been sent up to reinforce the centre coy consolidating the line approx: U17c84 — U18d24 & digging a support line approx: at U.18.d.0.1.

About 9.30 pm one coy 2nd R Irs relieved X Coy in EAGLE TR & this coy was sent forward to reinforce the very thin line of Y Coy consolidating a line from the four blockhouses along the Green line to point 38. This line was dug in rear of the Warwicks as it was considered likely that the latter regt. being out of their area might be ordered to withdraw at any moment thus leaving the most important position uncovered & leaving a way open for an enemy counter attack which would come at this point of anywhere & would very dangerously expose 19 Metre Hill – the key of the position.

The night of the 4th was calm – the next morning opened very clear & there was considerable aerial activity. The country however was in a very wet condition owing to the continuous drizzle of rain on the day of the 4th & the somewhat heavier showers during the night. About 1 pm the enemy shelling became heavy & there was continuous rifle & m.g. sniping by the enemy from the BROEMBEEK line. X Coy however succeeded in pushing posts well out to within 50x of the BROEMBEEK to maintain better observation of enemy movements.

During the night of the 5th there was heavy enemy shelling and owing to the relieving battn. not knowing the locality & guides staying the relief was not complete till 2 am and the battn. returned to L TOW CAMP. Total casualties for the tour were —

	Officers	O. Rs.
Missing	2	25
Wounded	7	103
Killed	—	21

One Officer of those wounded is remaining with unit.

Communication was difficult through the day of the Assault. Telephone wires to Brigade HQrs were continually being cut & remained useless for long periods. Signalling by Lamp was fairly successful but is dependent on weather conditions. Telephone lines to the forward troops could not be maintained & were at once severed when repaired.

A forward Signals station together with a relay runner post & Battn forward HQrs were established in EAGLE TR, but as the region between EAGLE TR & Battn HQrs was in LANGEMARCK was more heavily shelled than any other area – the Signal Station in EAGLE TR was of little use though it provided a good relay runner post. Pigeons were not satisfactory as the hours during which they can be used are necessarily limited on days when there is a mist and they are also apparently useless at night. Communication by runner was the most satisfactory, although casualties hampered this. Communication is the greatest problem. Wireless messages were not picked up.

The best medical arrangements were satisfactory. The Regimental aid post was in EAGLE TR: & all cases from the leading Coys were brought there & sent on to the "Pig & Whistle". Any delay that was caused was due to the extraordinary heavy casualties amongst RAMC personnel who had to pass through LANGEMARCK on their journeys & this place was continually shelled.

The liaison with the flanks was not being satisfactory but as the HdQrs of the Battns in the assault on the right being close to our own forward battn Hd Qrs there was no great apprehension as regards the situation. The flanking detachment 16th Lncs Regt suffered heavily in casualties & no message of any sort was received from them throughout the 4.5th. They probably found themselves among elements of the 4th Div: in the same manner as certain details of our Y Coy did.

The supply of ammunition grenades etc were satisfactory. Coys used the two dumps in EAGLE TR during & after the assault & every effort was made to fill up these dumps from those at Battn HdQrs & at REITRES Fm. The latter place however receives more than adway

attention from the enemy artillery.
During the assault the men carried the
following Bombers   4 bombs &
          R. Grenadiers 4 R. Grenades
          Riflemen   170 Rounds.
          Lewis Guns   32 magazines per gun.
          4 Sandbags per man
          50% Shovels.
The leading waves of the leading Coys
were however more lightly ~~clad~~ dressed than
the rear waves.
One point which has not been stated
however was the communication with
the Artillery. There was a liaison Officer
with Battn hdqrs & all requests made
to the Artillery for fire at various points were
at once carried out.
In conclusion it is interesting to note that the
enemy was completely taken by our surprise
when our attack was launched. This is
borne out by the fact that many of them were
captured with their boots off (they nearly all had
two pairs in their possession) – also their shelters
had blankets & waterproof sheets & some were caught
inside them. There was a great quantity of beer,
cigars and rum in dugouts shelters & shell holes were
organized by erecting uprights & covering them for half the diameter
with boarding – rabbit wire & earth on top.

7/10/17   G.W.B. Paulson Capt & adjt
                              1st R. Dublin Fusiliers

REPORT ON OPERATIONS CARRIED OUT BY

1st Bn. ROYAL DUBLIN FUSILIERS ON THE

4th OCTOBER, 1917 AT LANGEMARCH.

On the night of the 3rd/4th October the 1/Royal Dublin Fusiliers relieved the 18th Middlesex Regt in the right sector of the Divisional Front. The two leading Companies for the assault Y Coy on the right and Z Coy on the left moved straight into EAGLE TRENCH and put out covering posts. The section Trench Mortar Battery/formed up behind Y Coy and behind them again was the flanking detachment 16/Middlesex Regt. W Coy who were to be in Support during the assault were lined up in shell holes to the left rear of the Trench Mortar Battery section and X Coy in Reserve were behind W in shell holes.

The objectives of Companies were as follows :- Z Coy to capture post at 45 K on the STADEN Railway and GOED TER VESTEN FARM and dig on a line from approximately U.17.d.9.5. to U.18.d.9.5.- Y Coy on the left right to capture CHINESE HOUSE and the four blockhouses at U.18.c.4.6. and to reach the line U.18.c.6.7. to U.18.d.3.8. digging on the line from the latter point to join up with Z Coy at U.18.d.0.5. W.Coy were to move behind the leading Coy and consolidate a line approximately from U.17.d.7.0. to U.18.c.4.0. X.Coy to move into EAGLE TRENCH immediately the leading three Companies had got clear of it. Flanking detachment 16/Middlesex Regt were to cover the right flank during the advance and upon Y Coy reaching their Objective to dig in at approximately at U.18.d.1.5. ready to beat off any counter attack threatening from that direction.

The joining up of the Battalion was carried out very quietly and effectively. The night was dark and no movement could be seen by the enemy. There was very little shelling through the night and though the enemy shelled slightly more heavily about 5.0 a.m. as is his daily custom in that region the Companies had very few casualties. Immediately upon relief of 18/Middlesex Regt Companies proceeded to draw their battle stores from the dumps in the vicinity. Sandbags, flares, S.O.S. Rockets alone were taken up by Companies together with one days ration and an iron ration. Tools and Lewis Guns were brought up in advance of the Battalion and dumped near GREEN MILL where Companies picked them up on their way from camp to the line. The chief stores drawn from the dumps were bombs and S.A.A. and in addition Companies had in their possession large quantities of tape.

By Zero less one hour all Companies were in their correct positions Some hot tea in petrol tins which were wrapped round in Hay and put into packs had been brought up by mules, with Companies as far as the junction of HUNTER SWITCH and the Mule Track and this was greatly appreciated by the men with a half tot of rum.

The Barrage appeared to open half a minute too soon on the right but came down punctually on our front to time. All ranks praise the accuracy and volume of the barrage though several admit that they were wounded by getting too close under it. It is interesting to note here that it was extremely difficult at that hour to ascertain the line of the barrage after the first lift.

Immediately the barrage came down the two leading Companies who had left their posts/ons and strengthened them gradually as Zero approached dashed out and got as close to barrage as possible moving in lines of sections. The remaining bodies all came forward and maintained the same formation.

W. Coy were the first to report their objective taken and
notified Battalion Headquarters that Y Coy was making good
progress. A party of W Coy however overstepped the objective
and moved up behind Y Coy eventually taking up a position
about the four Blockhouses at U.18.c.4.6. Z Coy captured
T GOED TER VESTEN FARM and took sixteen prisoners and also
captured K 45 with two Machine Guns and fifteen prisoners.
Twenty other prisoners were captured in shell holes between
these two points. At K 45 however Z Comapnies post was under
heavy Machine Gun fire from across the BROEMBEEK and as the
enemy post they were occupying had been very much blown in
they left the post and consolidated in a shell hole 12 yards
South of it. This gave this new post the advantage of having the
old enemy wire in front of them as an obstacle.
No information could be obtained from Y Coy all of whose
Officers had become casualties and whose Company Sergeant
Major had been killed. By a personal reconnaissance however
carried out by the Intelligence Officer they were seen to be
on their objective and consolidating being in touch with the
Seaforth Highlanders of the 4th Division on the right.
About 1-30 p.m. a small local counter attack came from the
direction of KORTEBEEK FARM and the Seaforth Highlanders seeing
the gap between certain portions of Y Companies flank and the
enemy dubbling forward to it commenced to go back taking with
them that part of Y Coy nearest themselves. The counter attack
however was easily beaten off and the Seaforths returning swung
too much over to the right taking with them the party of Y Coy
of whom no news has since been heard.
About 5-0 p.m. however the Warwickshire Regt coming up to support
the Seaforth Highlanders noticing the gap caused in our line by
the centre which had remained firm and details on the right
which had swung over too much to that flank sent over one Coy
to occupy the gap. Throughout the afternoon the Companies were
subjected to fairly heavy enemy shelling but they had dug
themselves in well and did not have excessive casualties.
At dusk that evening two platoons of 1st K.O.S.B's came in to
Eagle Trench to reinforce our Reserve Coy now only two platoons
strong one platoon having been sent up to reinforce the Centre
Coy consolidating the line approximately U.17.c.8.4.- U.18.d.2.4.
and digging a support line approximately at U.18.d.0.1.
About 9-30 p.m. one Coy 2/Royal Fusiliers relieved X Coy in
EAGLE TRENCH and this Coy was sent forward to reinforce the
very thin line of Y Coy consolidating a line from the four
blockhouses along the Green Line to point 38.
This line was dug in rear of the Warwicks as it was considered
likely that the latter Regiment being out of their area might
be ordered to withdraw at any moment thus leaving the most
important position uncovered and leaving a way open for an
enemy counter attack which would come at this point if anywhere
and would very dangerously expose 19 METRE HILL the key of the
position.
The night of the 4th was calm - the next morning opened very
clear and there was considerable aerial activity. The country
however was in a very wet condition owing to the continuous
drizzle of rain on the day of the 4th and the somewhat heavier
showers during the night.
About 1-0 p.m. the enemy shelling became heavy and there was
continuous rifle and Machine Gun sniping by the enemy from the
Broembeek. X Coy however succeeded in pushing posts well
out to within 50 yards of the BROEMBEEK to maintain better
observation of enemy movements.

During the night of the 5th there was heavy enemy shelling and owing to the relieving Battalion not knowing the locality and guides straying the relief was not complete till 2-0 a.m. and the Battalion returned to ETON CAMP.

Total casualties for the tour were :-

	Officers.	Other Ranks.
Missing	2	26
Wounded	7	103
Killed	-	21

One Officer of those wounded is remaining with Unit.

Communication was difficult through the day of the assualt telephone wires to Brigade Headquarters were continually being cut and remained useless for long periods. Signalling by lamp was fairly successful but is dependent on weather conditions. Telephone lines to the forward troops could not be maintained and were at once severed when repaired.

A forward Signals Station together with a relay runner post and Battalion forward Headquarters were established in EAGLE TRENCH, but as the region between EAGLE TRENCH was and Battalion Headquarters in LANGEMARCK was more heavily shelled than any other area the Signal Station in EAGLE TRENCH was of little use though it provided a good relay runner post. Pigeons were not satisfactory as the hours during which they can be used are necessarily limited on days when there is a mist and they are also apparently useless at night. Communication by runner was the most satisfactory although casualties hampered this.

Communication is the greatest problem. Wireless messages were not picked up.

The Medical arrangements were satisfactory. The Regimental Aid post was in EAGLE TRENCH and all cases from the leading Companies were brought there and sent on to the "PIG & WHISTLE".

Any delay that was caused was due to the extraordinary heavy casualties amongst R.A.M.C. personnel who had to pass through LANGEMARCK on their journeys and this place was continually shelled. The Liaison with the flanks was not very satisfactory but as the Headquarters of the Battalions in the assault On the right being close to our own forward Battalion Headquarters there was no great apprehension as regards the situation. The flanking detachment 16/Middlesex Regiment suffered heavily in casualties and no message of any sort was received from them throughout the 4th/5th. They probably found themselves among elements of the 4th Division in the same manner as certain details of our Y Coy did.

The supply of ammunition grenades etc., were satisfactory.

Companies used the two dumps in EAGLE TRENCH during and after the assault and every effort was made to fill up these dumps from those at Battalion Headquarters and at REITRES FARM. The latter place however receives more than ordinary attention from the enemy artillery.

During the assault the men carried the following :-

Bombers	4 bombs.
Rifle Grenadiers	4 R.Grenades.
Riflemen	170 Rounds.
Lewis Guns	32 Magazines per gun.

4 Sandbags per man. 50% Shovels.

The leading waves of the leading Companies were however more lightly dressed than the rear waves.

One point which has not been stated however was the communication with the Artillery. There was a Liaison Officer with Battalion Headquarters and all requests made to the Artillery for fire at various points were at once carried out.

- 4 -

In conclusion it is interesting to note that the enemy was completely taken by suprise when our attack was launched. This is borne out by the fact that many of them were captured with their boots off (they nearly all had two pairs in their possession) also their shelters had blankets and waterproof sheets and some were caught inside these. There was a great quantity of beer cigars and rum in dugouts and shelters and shell holes were organized by erecting uprights and covering them for half the diameter with boarding-rabbit wire and earth on top.

                                              Sd/ G.W.B.TARLETON.
                                                  Capt. & Adjt.,
7/10/17.   1st R. Dublin Fusiliers.

S E C R E T. Copy No. 4

29TH DIVISION ORDER NO. 158.
-o-o-o-o-o-o-o-o-o-o-o-o-o-o-o-o-o-

Ref. attached map
1/10,000 LANGEMARCK
          BROEMBEEK
1/20,000 28 N.W.

October 3rd, 1917.

1. Para. 11 of 29th Division Order No. 157 is cancelled.

2. On the night 5th/6th October, the front held by the XIV Corps will be organised into three Division fronts, 4th Division on the Right, 29th Division in the Centre, and the Guards Division on the Left.
The following reliefs will therefore be carried out on this night :-

(1) 3rd Guards Bde. will relieve the 87th Bde. in the line from U.17.c.3.3. to the left of the Divisional front (junction with 29th French Division).

(2) 4th Division will relieve the 1/R. Dub. Fusiliers (att. 87th Bde.) from the Right of the Divisional front (dependent on forthcoming operations) to U.17.d.20.15.

(3) 1 Bn. 87th Bde. will relieve the 1/R. Dub. Fusiliers and 1/K.O.S.B. from U.17.d.20.15. to U.17.c.3.3. H.Q. Bn. at SPRING FM. U.22.c.05.12.

3. G.O.C. 3rd Guards Brigade will relieve G.O.C. 87th Brigade at SAULES FARM on evening of the 5th instant at an hour to be arranged between the Brigadiers concerned, and at this hour the G.O.C. 87th Brigade will reopen his H.Q. at VULCAN CROSSING (U.27.c.45.55).

4. G.O.C. 29th Division will hand over command of the portions of the line taken over by the 3rd Guards Bde. and 4th Division, to G.O.C. Gds. Div. and G.O.C. 4th Div. at 10 a.m. on 6th instant, and on completion of the relief on night of 5th/6th respectively.

5. On the 6th instant, the 86th Brigade will move from the present Intermediate Area to the new Intermediate Area, and on the 7th instant the 88th Brigade will move from the present Reserve Area to the new Reserve Area (see Location Table).

6. Reliefs will be carried out in accordance with attached Relief Table, details being arranged between Bdes. concerned.

7. The new boundaries of the Division will be as shewn on the attached map.

/8.

- 8 -

8. MACHINE GUNS.

O.C. M. Gun Coys. will arrange for the relief of their M. Guns as follows :-

(a) <u>On night 5th/6th.</u>
8 guns 3rd Gds. Bde. M. Gun Coy. will relieve 8 guns 87th M. Gun Coy. in forward area. 1 gun 87th M. Gun Coy. will relieve 1 gun of 227th M.G. Coy. at MARTINS MILL. The 3 guns of 87th M. Gun Coy. on the Railway will remain in position.

(b) <u>On night 6th/7th.</u>
4th Gds. M. Gun Coy. will relieve the 3 guns of 227th M. Gun Coy. on WIJDENDRIFT Road and 4 guns of 227th M. Gun Coy. at SIGNAL FARM.

(c) <u>On night of 5th/6th.</u>
A M. Gun Coy. 4th Division, will relieve 4 guns 86th M. Gun Coy. on front to be handed over to the 4th Division.

(d) The Div. M. Gun Officer will arrange for the move of the 227th M. Gun Coy. to WHITE MILL (B.14.d.8.8.) on the 7th instant.

9. All trench stores, maps and photos will be handed over between units.

10. Intervals of 200 yards will be kept between Companies and between Bns. and transport.

11. 1 Officer and 3 L.G. detachments of 4/Coldstream Gds. (Pioneer Bn.) will take over the Anti-Aircraft positions for the defence of Field Artillery from 1/2nd Monmouths (Pioneers) on 5th instant.

12. C.R.E. and A.D.M.S. will arrange details of moves of Field Companies and Field Ambulances respectively with the Cs.R.E. and As.D.M.S. of Guards and 4th Division respectively.

13. Moves of all units not mentioned in these orders will be arranged by the A.A. & Q.M.G.

14. Completion of reliefs will be reported to these Headquarters, which will remain at ELVERDINGHE CHATEAU.

15. ACKNOWLEDGE.

C.P. Fuller
Lieut-Colonel, G.S.,
29th Division.

Issued at 1 p.m.

Copies					
1 - 4	G.S.	17	A.P.M.	27	14th Corps.
5	"Q"	18	D.M.G.O.	28	Gds. Div.
6	C.R.A.	19	I.A.D.O.S.	29	4th Div.
7	C.R.E.	20	I.A.I.V.S.	30	Area Commdt.
8 - 9	86th Bde.	21	SAA Sec. DAC		B. Div. Area.
10 - 11	87th Bde.	22	227th M.G. Coy.	31	1/Guernsey L.I.
12 - 13	88th Bde.	23	Camp Commdt.	32	29 Foen
14	Off. i/c Sigs.	24	Div. Train.		
15	1/2nd Mons. R.	25	S.S.O.		
16	A.D.M.S.	26	29th I.S.C.		

MARCH TABLE ISSUED IN CONJUNCTION WITH 20TH DIVISION O.O. No 15.

Serial No.	Date.	Unit.	From.	To.	Take over from. New Camp.	Relieved by.	Time of starting. Camps to be clear by 2.0 p.m.
1.	5th	1/2 Mons.	BURKE and HAMPTON.	PARRY CAMP H & A.18.a.6.7.	New Camp.	4/Cold.Gds (Pioneers)	Camps to be clear by 2.0 p.m.
2.	5th	1/R Dub Fus.	Right Front Line.	ETON.	—	1 Bn. 87th Bde.	—
3.	5th	1 Bn.87th I.Bde.	Bde Support.	Right Front line. H.Q.at SPRING Fm. U.22.c.05.12.	1/R Dub Fus. H.Q. at LANGEMARCK.	—	—
4.	5th	1 Bn. 87th I.Bde.	Bde Support (present area)	Bde Support CANAL BANK (from C15c04 to C.7.c.0.6) to LANGEMARCK.	4th Div.	—	Any time after 5.0 p.m.
5.	5th	2 Bns 87th Inf Bde.	Centre and L.front line.	Bde Support (present area) CHARTERHOUSE WHITE MILL.	—	2 Bns 3rd Gds Bde. & 1 Bn 87th Bde (see Ser.No 3.)	—
6.	5th	2 Bns 88th Inf Bde.	ABEINGLY & DULWICH.	CARIBOU & CARDOEN.	4th Div.	2 Bns 3rd Gds Bde.	Camps to be clear by 2.0 p.m.
7.	5th.	H.Q. 87th Inf Bde.	SAULES Fm.	VULCAN CROSSING.	—	H.Q. 3rd Gds Bde.	—
8.	6th.	88th Inf Bde (less 2 Bns)	Present Support Area (ZONNEBLOOM ETON)	New Support Area (see attd Location table)	Units of 4th Div.	Adv Parties 1st Gds Bde.	Camps to be clear by 2.0 p.m.
9.	6th	1 Bn 87th Inf Bde.	CHARTERHOUSE.	New Area Bde Support PARROT CAMP I. B.15.d.0.5	—	Adv Party -Gds Bde.	3.0 p.m.
10.	7th	88th Inf Bde.	Present Res. Area.	New Reserve Area. (see attached Location table.)	Units of 4th Div.	2/Gds Bde.	Camps to be clear by 2.0 p.m.

Location Table issued in conjunction with 29th Div. Order No.158.

Div. H.Q.   ELVERDINGHE CHATEAU.   B.14.b.15.15.

Bde. in Line. H.Q.   VULCAN CROSSING.   U.27.c.45.55.
   A. Bn.   SPRING FARM.   U.22.c.05.15.
   B. Bn.   Between LANGEMARCK
                   and CANAL (inclusive)
                   PARROY Camp I.   B.16.d.0.5.
   C. Bn.   WHITE MILL.   B.14.d.8.8.
   D. Bn.   Line.   Line and WHITE MILL.
   M.G. Coy.

Support Bde.   CARIBOU CAMP.   A.11.d.8.7.
   A. Bn.   "   "
   B. Bn.   CARDOEN   "   A.18.b.1.8.
   C. Bn.   ROUSSEL   "   A.13.a.25.65.
   D. Bn.   HARROW   "   B.7.d.8.5.
   M.G. Coy.   COPPERNOLLE "   A.16.b.6.9.

Res. Bde.   DUBLIN CAMP.   A.11.c.4.5.
   A. Bn.   "   "
   B. Bn.   DRAGON   "   A.15.b.5.8.
   C. & D. Bns.   DRAGON WOOD.   (A.10.c.2.0.
                                            (A.16.a.3.7.
   M.G. Coy.   COPPERNOLLE CAMP.   A.16.b.6.9.

1/2nd Mons. (Pioneers) 2 Coys. PARROY Camp.   B.16.c.9.5.
                                   II
                       1 Coy.   A.18.a.6.7.

1/Guernsey L.I.   STOKE.   F.5.d.5.8.

227th M.G. Coy.   WHITE MILL.   B.14.d.9.8.

Details all Bdes.   BEDFORD.   A.12.d.60.55.

-o-o-o-o-o-o-o-o-o-o-o-o-o-

S E C R E T.   29th Div. No. C.G.S.67/68.

Amendment to 29th Division Order No. 158.
-o-o-o-o-o-o-o-o-o-o-o-o-o-o-o-o-o-o-o-o-o-o-o-o-o-o-

Para. 8 Machine Guns is cancelled and the following substituted :-

(a) On night of 4/5th Barrage Guns Groups A & B (MONTMIRAIL FARM) return to former positions.

4 guns 227th M.G. Coy. return to SIGNAL FARM.

4 guns 227th M.G. Coy. and 4 guns 86th M.G. Coy. withdraw from the line.

(b) Night of 5/6th. 4th Gds. M.G. Coy. will relieve :-

3 guns 227th M.G. Coy. at WIJDENDRIFT.
4 guns   "   "   at SIGNAL FARM.

1 gun 227th   "   will remain at LANGEMARCK STN.
In addition O.C. 227th M.G. Coy. will arrange to put 1 gun in MARTINS MILL and 2 guns in LANGEMARCK Church.

(c) Night of 5/6th. A M.G. Coy. of 4th Division will relieve the 2 guns of 86th M.G. Coy. with liaison detachment.

2 guns 86th M.G. Coy. at U.23.A.6.3. will be withdrawn.

87th M.G. Coy. will take over the 2 guns 86th M.G. Coy. in forward position on Rly. with 1 gun from MONTMIRAIL FARM and 1 gun from U.23.A.5.9.

(d) Night of 6/7th. 8 guns of 3rd Gds. M.G. Coy. will relieve 8 guns of 87th M.G. Coy. in Forward Area.

The 4 guns 87th M.G. Coy. on Rly. will remain in position.

(e) D.M.G.O. will arrange for the move of the 227th M. Gun Coy. to Camp at WHITE MILL on 6th instant. Present camp to be vacated by 2 p.m. 6th instant.

ACKNOWLEDGE.

4th October, 1917.

Lieut.Colonel, G.S.,
29th Division.

To all recipients of 29th Division Order No. 158.

S E C R E T.

ADMINISTRATIVE ORDER NO. 18.

Reference 29th Division Order No. 158 of 3rd September 1917, as amended.

1. TRANSPORT.

The following will be the position of Brigades and Machine Gun Companies Transport Lines on moving into the new Area.

Brigade in the Line (87th Brigade)

Transport of Brigade Group, less Field Company and Field Ambulance, will be at A.18.b.9.3., near DROMORE CORNER. This site is now unoccupied.
The present lines near MICHEL FARM will be cleared by 2 p.m. 5th instant.

Brigade in Support (88th Brigade) less M.G.Company, Field
Company and Field Ambulance, on the DE WIPPE - DROMORE CORNER Road.
Bde. H.Q.......... CARIBOO CAMP, A.11.d.9.7.
One Battalion.................. A.18.b.1.2.
Two Battalions .... A.18.a.8.9.
One Battalion .... A.11.d.9.7.

These Lines will be empty at 12 noon on 6th instant, - Present Lines to be cleared by that time.
Machine Gun Company Lines will be at COPPERNOLLE, A.16.b.5.9., on the east of POPERINGHE CANAL, which is now unoccupied.

Brigade in Reserve (86th Brigade)

Transport of Brigade Group, less Machine Gun Company, Field Company and Field Ambulance will be opposite "G" Camp at, A.16.a.5.3.
These Lines will be clear by 10 a.m. on the 7th inst., present lines to be vacated by 12 noon on that date.
The Machine Gun Company Lines will be at COPPERNOLLE, A.16.b.5.9., on the west of POPERINGHE CANAL. These Lines are now unoccupied.

The Transport of No. 227 Machine Gun Company will be in the stabling West of CORNISH CROSS - A.10.d.0 5.95.
These Lines will be clear by 2 p.m. on the 6th inst., by which time the present lines will be vacated.

Companies of Divisional Train will be located as follows:-
No. 1 Company.......... present Camp A.2.d.9.9.
No. 2 Company.......... present Camp BARNES FARM
H.Qrs & No. 3 Company... PATERS FARM A.9.a.7.4.
No. 4 Company.......... BALDWIN FARM A.3.a.0.1.

The Mobile Veterinary Section will move to INTERNATIONAL CORNER on the 6th instant, to the stabling at A.9.a.2.2.

P.T.O.

(2)

A.D.M.S., A.D.V.S., D.A.D.O.S. and Divisional Ordnance Store, D.B.O., the Employment Company, and Transport of Signal Company and Divisional Headquarters will be located at DRAGON CAMP.

Details of all three Infantry Brigades will be in BEDFORD CAMP.

HOUNSLOW CAMP will be vacated by 12 noon on 5th inst.

Captain DOWLING with Headquarters at ELVERDINGHE CHATEAU, has been appointed Area Commandant Left and Centre Division Areas.

Tentage required to establish all Camps will be drawn from Area Tent Store, ELVERDINGHE CHATEAU; amount of tentage to be drawn and date of drawing will be notified to Brigades and Units from Divisional Headquarters by wire.

2. HUTTING SECTIONS will be transferred from Left Division to Centre Division Area as follows:-

86th Brigade Section on 7th instant to Camp in DRAGON WOOD for work on Brigade Transport Lines of Reserve Brigade.
87th Brigade Section to Camp, ELVERDINGHE CHATEAU, on 6th instant, for work on Forward Brigade Transport Lines, etc.
88th Brigade Section to Details Camp, BEDFORD, on 6th instant, for work on Intermediate Brigade Transport Lines.

Progress Reports on work done in Left Division Area to be rendered to the C.R.E., 29th Division.

3. DIVISIONAL GRENADE DUMP will remain at GOUVY FARM, B.11.a.7.5. and will be shared with Guards Division.

Brigade Dumps are at REITRES FARM, U.22.d.1.1., and LANGEMARCK, U.22.d.9.1. The latter Dump will require augmentation as a considerable amount has been lost by shell fire. Three hundred boxes of S.A.A. have been dumped at SPRING FARM, U.22.c.3.2., and will be taken over by the Brigade in the Line.

4. TOOLS, AMMUNITION & GRENADES on Battalion and Brigade Establishment will be taken with Units on transfer and will not be handed over.

5. DIVISIONAL R.E. BATTLE DUMP, will be at VULCAN CROSSING.

6. MEDICAL.
Field Ambulance Headquarters at BLEUET FARM, and Advanced Dressing Stations at BOESINGHE CHATEAU and GREEN HILL, and the Regimental Aid Post at RUISSEAU FARM will be shared with Guards Division. A new Regimental Aid Post will be established at REITRES FARM, and that at the "PIG & WHISTLE" will be shared with 4th Division.

7. BATHS.
The Bath at BOX CAMP will be handed over to the Guards Division.

8. **DIVISIONAL THEATRE** will remain at ONDANK, where Divisional Baths and Divisional Canteen Officer will be quartered.

9. **SALVAGE.** The Divisional Salvage Company will work from the WIDJENDRIFT ROAD back to the CANAL; but all Units in this Area, including Artillery, will assist in getting the ground clean as rapidly as possible. For this purpose a Divisional Dump will be established at VULCAN CROSSING, U.27.c.4.6., and marked with a sign-board. The clearing of this Dump to the Corps Dumps at RUGBY and ELVERDINGHE will be done by the Divisional Salvage Officer as far as possible by tram line.

Forward of the WIDJENDRIFT - LANGEMARCK Road the Brigade in the Line will be responsible for salvage, and Brigade Dumps will be established at the points where pack transport is met by the ration parties. The 87th Brigade will report places selected for these Brigade Dumps, and mark them with notice boards to be obtained from Divisional Salvage Officer. Salvage from the Forward Area will be taken by empty returning pack transport to the Forward Brigade Transport Lines near DROMORE CORNER and collected from there by the Divisional Salvage Officer.

L H Abbott

Lieut. Colonel,
A.A. & Q.M.G., 29th Division.

4-10-17.

S E C R E T.

29th Division No. G.A.S.67/69.

4

Reference 29th Division Order No. 153. Following amendments will be made to March Table.

1. Serial No. 6 is cancelled.
2. Serial Nos. 8 and 10 will now read as below.
3. Serial Nos. 6A and 10A are added.

Serial No.	Date.	Unit.	From.	To.	Take over from	Relieved by.	Time of starting
8	6th	88th Inf.Bde. (less 1 Bn.)	Present Reserve Area.	New Support Area (vide Location List)	Units of 4th Div.	Adv. parties 3/Gds. Bde.	Camps to be clear by 2 p.m.
6A	6th	88th M.G.Coy. 88th T.M.Bty.	WELLINGTON	COPPENOLLE CAMP A.16.b.8.9.	New Camp.	2nd and 3rd Gds. Bde. T.M.Btics.	Camps to be clear by 12 noon.
10	7th	88th Inf.Bde.	Present Support Area.	New Reserve Area (vide Location List)		1st Gds. Bde.	Camp to be clear by 2 p.m.
10A	7th	1 Bn. 88th Bde.	Present Reserve Area.	HARROW (New Support Area).	1/Lan. Fus. 86th Bde.	1 Bn. 2nd Gds.Bde.	Camp to be clear by 2 p.m.

NOTE. Times of starting to be arranged between 86th and 88th Bdes.

ACKNOWLEDGE.

4th October, 1917.

To all recipients of 29th Division Order No. 153.

A.T. Miller Capt

Lieut-Colonel, G.S.,
29th Division.

S E C R E T.   Copy No. _____

29TH DIVISION ORDER NO. 160.
-o-o-o-o-o-o-o-o-o-o-o-o-o-o-o-o-o-o-

Refce. Objective Map,   7th October, 1917.
issued with Instruction
No.22, and tracing attached.

1.   The attack on the enemy's position is to be renewed by the XIV Corps, in conjunction with the Corps to the North and South, on a date and at an hour Zero to be notified later.

2. (a)   The attack is to be carried out by the 4th Division on the Right, the 29th Division in the Centre, and the Guards Division on the Left.

   (b)   The attack will be made in three bounds :-
The first bound to the GREEN DOTTED line (1st Objective).
The second bound to the BLUE DOTTED line (2nd Objective), and the third bound to the GREEN line (3rd Objective).
      The objectives, and boundaries between Divisions and Brigades are shown on the map, already issued with 29th Division Instruction No. 22.

   (c)   The 12th Infantry Brigade (4th Division, with H.Q. at U.29.a.6.7.) will be on our right, and the 1st Guards Brigade (Guards Division, with H.Q. at CAPTAINS FARM (U.26.b. 25.65.) will be on our left.

3. (a)   The 29th Division will attack with the 86th Inf. Bde. (H.Q. at AU BON GITE, U.28.b.2.0.) on the right, and the 88th Inf. Bde. (H.Q. at MARTINS MILL, U.22.c.4.5.) on the left. The 87th Inf. Bde. will be in Divisional Reserve.

   (b)   One battalion will be employed by each of the 86th and 88th Inf. Bdes. for the capture of the first and second objectives, and a second battalion for the capture of the third objective. A third battalion will be held by each Brigade to act as a counter-attack battalion, (vide para. 10) and also for use in the further operations detailed in para. 12.

   (c)   The troops for the assault will be assembled at Zero in their Brigade Areas, East of the STEENBEEK. The orders for the concentration march are being issued separately.
      The fourth battalion of the 88th Inf. Bde. will be stationed on the CANAL BANK. The fourth battalion of the 86th Inf. Bde. will not be employed for these operations. The 87th Inf. Bde. will remain in their Camps, ready to move at half an hours notice.

4.   Brigades will arrange to maintain a garrison in their front line, until the third objective has been secured, when the garrison may be moved forward.

5.   The attack will be made under cover of :-

   (a) A creeping barrage.
   (b) A standing barrage.
   (c) A back barrage of 6" Hows. and 60pdrs.
   (d) A distant barrage of heavy Hows. and 60pdrs
   (e) A machine gun barrage.

/ The

The artillery barrage maps will be issued shortly to all concerned. The creeping barrage will open 150 yards (approx.) in front of the RED line, shewn on the map issued with Instruction No. 22; no troops will be in front of this line at ZERO. (sic)

There will be pauses of approximately 45 minutes on both the GREEN and BLUE IOTTED lines. As a signal for the troops to advance, the protective barrage on these lines will become intensive six minutes before it begins to creep.

The final protective barrage will be placed 300 yards beyond the GREEN line.

6. The dispositions and tasks of the Machine Guns have been issued in 29th Division Instruction No. 23.

Each Brigade will leave two Machine Guns in the original front line for its protection. Orders for the eventual disposal of the barrage guns will be issued by these Headquarters, through the Div. M.G. Officer.

7. (a) In the advance against each objective, the Right and Left Brigades will keep a "liaison detachment" of half a company and two machine guns echeloned in rear of their right and left flanks respectively, to fill any gaps that may occur on the outer flanks of the Division.

(b) Adequate mopping-up parties will be organised in rear of each assaulting wave, and all enemy dug-outs or strong points, situated between the objective and protective barrage will be dealt with as soon as the lift of the barrage permits.

(c) In the event of a unit on either flank of the Division, or within the Division, being held up, adjoining units will not check their advance, but will follow the barrage closely and will detail a party to protect their exposed flank.

(d) In the event of the battalions detailed for the first two objectives being held up, before reaching their second objective, the rear battalions will not become involved in the attack until arrangements have been made by Divisional Headquarters to bring back the barrage, and make a fresh attack. This does not however preclude the rear battalions from clearing up a local situation, by detaching a company to turn the flank of the position.

(e) Should the creeping barrage be brought back, and another attack ordered, the signal to the troops that the barrage is about to advance will be 4 minutes intense fire at 4 rounds per gun per minute. When a barrage starts again after being brought back, there will be no fire within 150 yards of the flank of the advance of any troops, who have gone forward.

8. To ensure liaison with the flank Divisions, Brigades will tell off special parties to get into touch with flanking Divisions as follows :-

    4th Division   at   MILLERS HOUSES, V.13.a.3.4.
                              WATER HOUSE, V.13.b.1.8.
                              V.7.d.8.5.

    Guards Division at   BEAR COPSE, U.17.c.8.9.
                              U.17.b.7.9.
                              U.12.c.6.8.
                              Road at U.12.b.35.70.
                              U.6.d.90.25.

/ Liaison

- 3 -

Liaison points between Brigades will be established at -

    KORTEBEEK FARM, U.18.a.75.20.
    U.12.d.2.0.
    TRANQUILLE HOUSE, U.12.d.80.55.
    V.7.a.40.15.

9. The objectives, when captured will be consolidated, and the lines strengthened with the machine guns, placed at the disposal of Brigades for this purpose, vide Instruction No. 23. When the consolidation is nearing completion, the troops will be reformed and organised in depth, ready to meet counter-attacks. A strong point will be established in the neighbourhood of the Railway Crossing at U.12.d.6.9, and a garrison for this point told off in advance.

10. Counter-attacks may be expected along the Corps front during the operations. Each Brigade will detail a battalion (vide para. 3(b)) to meet counter-attacks by immediate counter-attacks. This battalion should be assembled after the capture of the second objective on the far side of the BROEMBEEK, and should act on the initiative of its Commander without reference to Brigade Headquarters.

11. Four Tanks will be operating in the XIV Corps Area, but independently of the infantry attack. These Tanks will move forward from the neighbourhood of POELCAPPELLE at ZERO, along the POELCAPPELLE - les 5 CHEMINS Road. Two of these Tanks, on arrival at CONDE HOUSE, operate towards BERTHIER HOUSE. The remaining two, having if necessary cleared up the situation at TRANQUILLE HOUSE, will cross the Railway and operate towards EGYPT HOUSE.

Infantry should on no account wait for the Tanks, but should follow the barrage closely.

12. (a) There is a probability of a complete breakdown of the enemy's opposition.

Brigades will therefore be prepared to advance with their "Counter-attack" battalions at ZERO plus 9 hours to the PURPLE DOTTED and PURPLE lines, shewn on the attached tracing.

(b) The signal for the advance will be intensive fire on the protective barrage at the above hour, mingled with smoke shells from one gun in each battery.

(c) The advance will be made under a creeping barrage, moving at the rate of 100 yards in four minutes. Artillery barrage maps for this advance will be issued shortly.

There will be a pause of 45 minutes on the PURPLE DOTTED line.

(d) The advance will be carried out as follows :-
Patrols of one section each will advance under cover of the barrage to the following points :-

PURPLE DOTTED line.
    (DYCK FARM
    (Huts at V.2.c.4.2.
    (Huts at V.1.d.7.6.
    (Forked Roads at V.1.a.5.1.

PURPLE line.
    (DAVOUST FARM (V.2.d.35.90.)
    (Rail Crossing at V.2.a.9.1.
    (COLBERT Cross Roads.

/ These

- 4 -

These patrols will be supported at a distance of 50 yards by a platoon, and the remainder of the company will follow 100 yards in rear of the platoon.

(e) The lines will be consolidated by a series of strong points, special attention being paid to the extended left flank, which is particularly vulnerable to a counter-attack.

13. Arrangements will be made to relieve the two leading battalions by two battalions of the 17th Division, on the night of the attack (Z/Z plus 1 night). It is also probable that on that night the two rear battalions will be withdrawn.

14. A Contact aeroplane will fly over the Divisional front at :-

Zero plus 1 hr. and 20 mins.
Zero plus 2 hrs. and 45 mins.
Zero plus 4 hrs. and 30 mins.
At 12 noon, and subsequently as ordered by Corps H.Q.

RED flares will be lit by the leading troops, only when demanded by the Contact Aeroplanes either :-

(a) By Klaxon Horn.
(b) By a series of White Lights.

The necessity for lighting flares will be impressed on all concerned, and sufficient flares for this purpose will be issued to the attacking troops, and to any reserves likely to be employed. As far as possible flares should be lighted in rows of three.

Each Brigade and Battalion Headquarters will be marked by ground sheets of authorised shape, with the code letters of the unit laid out with white strips alongside. These letters should be 9 feet in depth.

Signalling to aeroplanes will be done by panels.

15. An aeroplane will be up continuously during daylight from Zero onwards, whose mission will be to detect the approach of enemy counter-attacks. Whenever this patrol observes hostile parties of one hundred or more moving to counter-attack, it will drop a smoke bomb over that portion of the front to which the enemy is moving.

The smoke bomb will burst about 100 feet below the machine, into a white parachute flare, which descends slowly leaving a long trail of brown smoke about 1 foot broad behind it.

16. The S.O.S. Signal will be a succession of S.O.S. Rifle Rockets, each bursting simultaneously into four Red Lights.

17. Watches will be synchronised from Divisional Headquarters as soon after 12 noon and 6 p.m. on " Y " Day as possible, by a Divisional Staff Officer. On no account are watches to be synchronised by telephone.

/ 18.

18.   Divisional Headquarters will remain at ELVERDINGHE CHATEAU.

19.   ACKNOWLEDGE.

                                        P. Fuller
                                Lieut-Colonel, G.S.,
                                    29th Division.

Issued at   / a.m.

        Copies 1 - 5   General Staff.
                 6   "Q".
                 7   C.R.A.
                 8   C.R.E.
             9 - 15   86th Inf. Bde.
            16 - 17   87th Inf. Bde.
            22 - 27   88th Inf. Bde.
                28   Off. i/c Sigs.
                29   1/2nd Monmouths.
                30   1/R. Guernsey L.I.
                31   A.D.M.S.
                32   A.P.M.
                33   D.M.G.O.
                34   XIV Corps.
                35   Guards Division.
                36   4th Division.
                37   17th Division.
                38   227th M.G. Coy.
                39   9th Squadron R.F.C.

M.

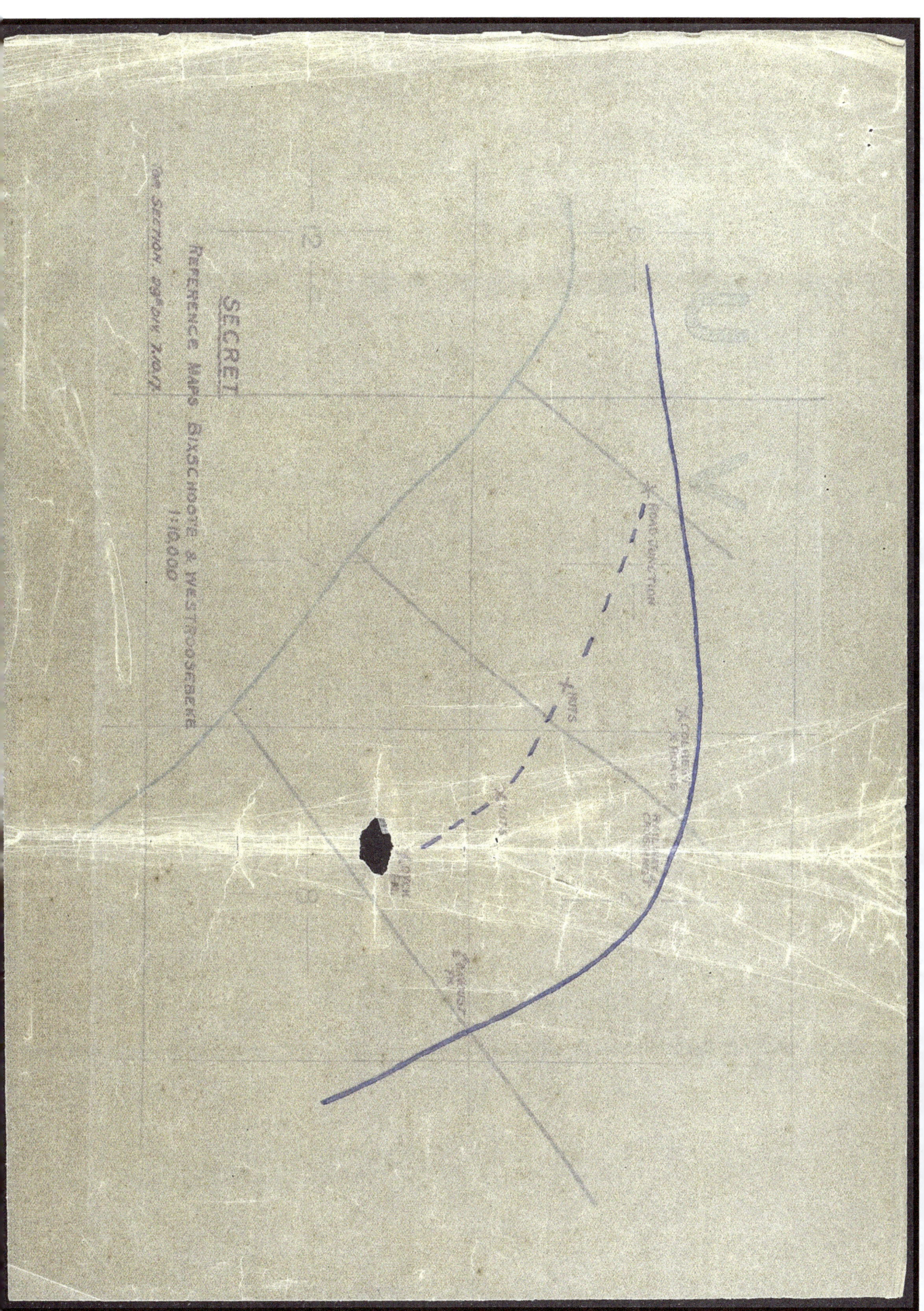

TRACKS.

SECRET.
29th Div. No. C.G.S.75/34.

REFERENCE 29TH DIVISION ORDER NO.160 DATED 7/10/17.
-o-o-o-o-o-o-o-o-o-o-o-o-o-o-o-o-o-o-o-o-o-o-o-o-o-o-o-o-o-

Herewith Tracing of existing and proposed duckboard tracks.

A.T. Milne Capt

7th October, 1917.

Lieut-Colonel, G.S.,
29th Division.

To all recipients of 29th Division Order No. 160.

SECRET.   29th Division No. C.G.S.67/71.

ADDENDUM NO. 1 TO 29TH DIVISION ORDER NO. 160.
-0-0-0-0-0-0-0-0-0-0-0-0-0-0-0-0-0-0-0-0-0-0-0-0-0-0-0-

1.   Add at end of para. 12 (b) the following :-

     "Should this signal not be given, there will be
     no advance."

2.   Add at end of para. 12 (c) the following :-

     "The barrage will become intense four minutes
     before the infantry advance from the PURPLE DOTTED
     line."

3.   In last para. of para. 12 (d),

         For "a distance of 50 yards"

         Read "a distance of 100 yards",

     and For "follow 100 yards in rear"

         Read "follow 150 yards in rear".

4.   Add at end of para. 12 (d) the following :-

     "Tanks will support this operation, but will
     act independently".

5.   With reference to para. 5, herewith map shewing
Artillery Barrage Lifts.
     It should be noted that the rate of barrage to the first
objective, and from the second to the third objective is 100
yards in 6 minutes, as previously notified in para. 7 of
Instruction No. 22.
     From the first objective (GREEN DOTTED line) to the
second objective (BLUE DOTTED line), however, the rate of the
barrage will be 100 yards in 8 minutes.

6.   ACKNOWLEDGE.

                                      Lieut-Colonel, G.S.,
7th October, 1917.   29th Division.

     To all recipients of 29th Division Order No. 160.

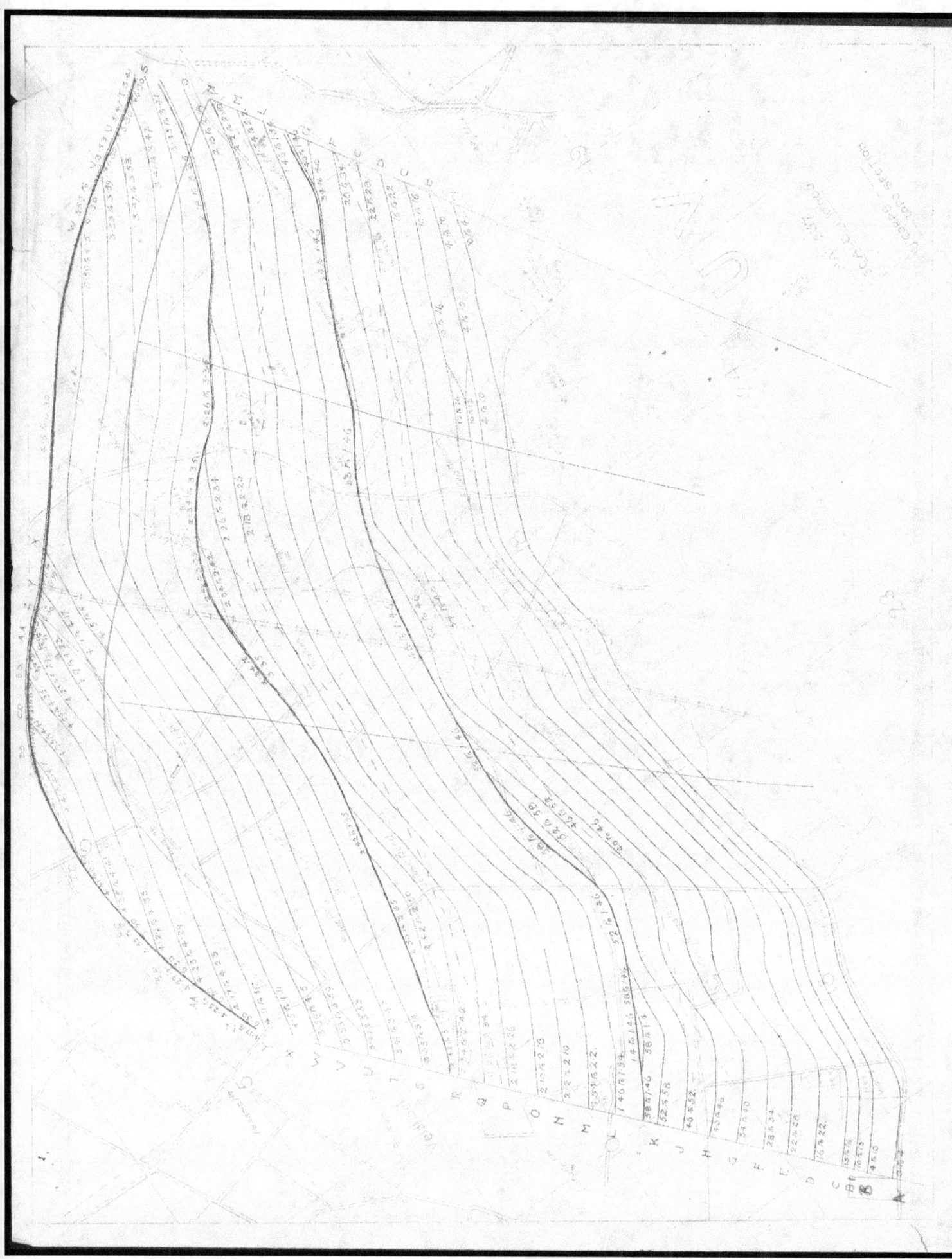

SECRET.   29th Division No. C.G.S.68/69.

29TH DIVISION OPERATIONS.

Instruction No.22.

1.   On account of the success of the operations on October 4th, a further advance will be carried out very shortly, in order to extend the front in a North-Easterly direction.

2.   It is intended that the XIV Corps shall attack as follows :-

    The 4th Division on the right.   Headquarters at WELSH FARM.
    The left of the 4th Division will be at U.18.d.40.50.

    29th Division in the centre.   Headquarters at ELVERDINGHE CHATEAU.

    The left of the 29th Division will be at U.17.c.40.50.

    Guards Division on the left.   Headquarters at ZOMMERBLOOM CABARET, rear Headquarters at "J" CAMP.

3.   The boundaries and objectives of the 29th Division are given on the attached map, and also the inter-brigade boundary.

4.   The attack will be carried out by the 86th Inf. Bde. on the right, and the 88th Inf. Bde. on the left.   The 87th Inf. Bde. will be in Divisional Reserve.

5.   The advance will be made in three bounds.

    The first bound to the DOTTED GREEN line.
    The second bound to the DOTTED BLUE line.
    The third bound to the GREEN line.

The proposed date for this attack has been communicated separately to all immediately concerned.

6.   The attack will be covered by the usual artillery and machine gun barrages.   The line on which the creeping barrage will open is shewn on the attached map.

7.   The creeping barrage will probably advance as follows :-

    From 0 to 0 + 4 on the opening barrage line.
    From 0 + 4 to 0 + 10 on a line 100 yards beyond the opening barrage line, to enable the crossing of the BROEMBEEK to be effected.
    From 0 + 10 onwards, the barrage will advance in lifts of 50 yards, and at the rate of 50 yards in 3 minutes.

8.   Brigades will report at what places and on which targets they propose to thicken the creeping barrage with Stokes Mortars.

9.   A composite battalion, composed of two Companies of 1/2nd Monmouths (Pioneers) and two Companies of 1st Guernsey Light Infantry, will be camped at PARROY II CAMP and placed at the disposal of the Chief Engineer, XIV Corps, for work on

/ forward

- 2 -

forward roads from Zero day onwards. Orders for the move of the 1st Guernsey Light Infantry will be issued later.

10. There are indications of German exhaustion, and the Commander-in-Chief proposes therefore to exploit the advance to the GREEN line to the full, if opportunity offers.
Attacking Brigades will therefore be prepared to continue their advance up to the RED line but not beyond, on Zero or Zero plus one day, should the enemy show signs of weakening.

11. The 86th and 88th Inf. Brigades will forward their proposals in detail for the operation, detailed in paras. 3 and 4, to these Headquarters by 6 p.m. to-morrow the 6th instant.

12. The following is the proposed programme of moves, to get the troops into their assembly positions by the morning of "Z" day :-

Night of 7th/8th.

87th Inf. Bde. (2 Bns.) relieved on the right of the Division front by one Bn. (1/Lancs. Fus.) 86th Inf. Bde., and on the left of the Division front by one Bn. (4/Worcesters) 88th Inf. Bde.
One Bn. (Newfoundland) 88th Inf. Bde. in support in the CANAL Bank and forward.
87th Inf. Bde. H.Q. at VULCAN'S CROSSING relieved by 88th Inf. Bde. H.Q.

Night of 8th/9th.

86th Inf. Bde. with H.Q. at AU BON GITE take over right sector, and 88th Inf. Bde. with H.Q. at MARTIN'S MILL retain command of left sector of Division front.

13. ACKNOWLEDGE.

Lieut-Colonel, G.S.,
29th Division.

5th October, 1917.

Copies to :-
    86th Inf. Bde.   A.D.M.S.
    87th Inf. Bde.   A.P.M.
    88th Inf. Bde.   D.A.G.O.
    C.R.A.   XIV Corps.
    C.R.E.   Guards Division.
    Off. i/c Sigs.   4th Division.
    1/2nd Monmouths.   "Q".
    1/Guernsey L.I.

M.

SECRET.   29th Division No. C.G.S.61/10.

29TH DIVISION OPERATIONS.

Instruction No. 23.

Machine Gun Scheme.

1.   The Machine Guns of the Division for the attack will be allotted as follows :-

   For Consolidation - 16 guns.

       2 sections Bde. M.G. Coy. with each Bde.

   For Barrage - 20 guns.

       3 sections 227th M.G. Coy.
       1 section   86th M.G. Coy.
       1 section   88th M.G. Coy.

2.   From the 2 sections allotted each Brigade -

   2 guns will be left in original front line.
   2 guns will be employed with each liaison detachment on the flanks of attack.

3.   Barrage Guns will be divided in 3 groups as follows :-

   Group A.   1 section 227th M.G. Coy. at REITRES FARM.

   Group B. (1 section 227th M.G. Coy.) about U.23.a.1.6.
             (1 section 88th M.G. Coy.)

   Group C. (1 section 227th M.G. Coy.) about U.23.a.6.3.
             (1 section 86th M.G. Coy.)

   On completion of Barrage, Groups B and C will move forward to general line North Bank of BROMBEEK in U.17.B. and U.18.A. Group C will not move forward until Group B is reported in position.

4. AMMUNITION.
   The following S.A.A. will be in position by midnight 8th/9th :-

   With Group A.   10 belts per gun = 10,000
                     2,000 rds. S.A.A.   2,000

                                          12,000

   With Group B.   15 belts per gun = 30,000
                     20,000 rds. S.A.A.   20,000

                                          50,000

   With Group C.   15 belts per gun = 30,000
                     20,000 rds. S.A.A.   20,000

                                          50,000

5. FIRING.
   Barrage table attached shows, lines of fire, targets, and rates of fire.

/ 6.

6. **COMMUNICATION.**
Communication will be by runner.
Headquarters of D.M.G.O. and Group Commanders will be notified later.

7. **ACKNOWLEDGE.**

A.T. Mills Capt.
Lieut-Colonel, G.S.,
for 29th Division.

6th October, 1917.

Copies to :-
"Q".
C.R.A.
C.R.E.
86th Inf. Bde.
87th Inf. Bde.
88th Inf. Bde.
Off. i/c Sigs.
1/2nd Monmouths.
A.D.M.S.
A.P.M.
D.M.G.O.
227th M.G. Coy.
14th Corps.
4th Division.
Guards Division.
17th Division.

S E C R E T.   29th Division No. I.G.93/132.

LOCATIONS - 29TH DIVISION
Midnight 7th/8th October, 1917, including moves in progress.

Ref 1/40,000 Map, Sheet 28, except where otherwise stated.

Unit.	Location	Map Reference.	Rear H.Q. or Transport Lines.
Div H.Q.	ELVERDINGHE CHAT.	B.14.b.15.15.	DRAGON CAMP A.15.b.5.8
H.Q. Div Arty.	-"-		
15th Bde R.H.A.	WOOD HOUSE.	C.2.c.30.65.	B.7.b.4.7.
17th Bde R.F.A.	-"-		B.7.b.4.4
D.T.M.O.		A.12.b.6.9.	-
D.A.C.(less S.A.A.Sect)		A.12.a.8.2.	-
S.A.A.Sect D.A.C.		A.6.d.Central.	-
H.Q. R.E.	ELVERDINGHE CHAT.	B.14.b.15.15	-
455th W.R.Fld Coy.	-"-	B.14.b.8.1.	A.11.a.5.4.
497th (Kent) Fld Coy.	-"-	B.14.b.9.1.	A.11.a.5.4.
510th (London) Fld Coy	-"-	B.14.a.9.5.	A.11.a.3.4.
86th Inf Bde H.Q.	ZOMERBLOOM.	B.8.c.5.5.	)
2/Roy Fus.	ROUSSEL.	A.13.a.25.65.	)
1/Lancs Fus.	R.FRONT LINE.) LANGEMARCK)	20/U.23.c.05.15.)	A.16.b.9.3.
16/Midd'x Regt.	HARROW	B.7.d.8.5.	)
1/R.Dub Fus.	DRAGON WOOD.	A.10.c.6.2.	)
86th M.G.Coy.	Line & COPPERNOLLE	A.16.b.6.9	A.16.b.5.9
86th T.M.Batty.	Line.		-
87th Inf Bde H.Q.	DRAGON CAMP.	A.15.b.5.8.	)
2/S.W.B.	WHITE MILL.	B.14.d.8.8.	)
1/K.O.S.B.	DRAGON WOOD.	A.9.d.9.3.	) A.16.a.5.3.
1/Border Regt.	DUBLIN.	A.11.c.4.5.	)
1/R.Innis Fus.	CARDOEN.	A.18.b.1.8.	)
87th M.G.Coy.	COPPERNOLLE.	A.16.b.6.9.	A.16.b.5.9
87th T.M.Batty.	DRAGON CAMP.	A.15.b.5.8.	-
88th Inf Bde H.Q.	VULCAN CROSSING	20/U.27.c.40.55.	A.11.d.9.7.
4/Worcs Regt.	L. FRONT LINE) SPRING FARM.)	20/U.22.c.05.15	A.10.a.8.9.
2/Hants Regt.	PARROY I.	B.16.d.0.5.	"
1/Essex Regt.	CARIBOU	A.11.d.8.7.	A.18.b.1.2.
1/Nfld Regt.	CANAL BANK.	C.13.c.	A.11.d.9.7.
88th M.G.Coy.	Line & COPPERNOLLE	A.16.b.6.9.	A.16.b.5.9.
88th T.M.Batty.	Line.		-
1/2 Monmouths (P)	PARROY II.	B.16.c.9.5.	-
1/Guernsey L.I.	STOKE.	27/F.5.d.5.0.	-
227th M.G.Coy.	WHITE MILL.	B.14.d.8.8.	A.10.d.05.95.
H.Q.& No.3 Co.Div Train.	PETERS FARM	A.9.a.7.4.	-
No.1 Coy Div Train		A.2.d.9.9.	-
No.2 -"-	BARNES FARM.	A.3.d.5.9.	-
No.4 -"-	BALDWIN FARM.	A.3.a.0.1.	-
29th D.S.C.	P.3 Area.	27/F.1.b.2.9.	-
87th Fld Amb.	BLUET FARM.	B.10.c.3.4.	-
88th -"-	WORMHOUDT		-
89th -"-		19/X.30.c.Central.	-
Mob Vet Sect.	INTERNATIONAL) Corner)	A.9.a.2.2.	-
Details,all Bdes.	BEDFORD.	A.12.d.60.55.	-
Railhead.	INTERNATIONAL) CORNER.)	A.2.d.	-

8th October, 1917.

Captain,
for Lieut-Colonel, G.S.,
29th Division.

SECRET.   Copy No. 4

Appen IV

29TH DIVISION ORDER NO. 159.
-o-o-o-o-o-o-o-o-o-o-o-o-o-o-o-o-o-o-o-

Ref. Map 1/10,000 BROEMBEEK.
1/20,000 28.N.W.   October 6th, 1917.

1. Following amendment has been made to 29th Division Order No. 158 and issued to all concerned :-
"Para. 2 sub-para. 2 is cancelled. 1/R. Dub. Fus. 86th Bde. will be relieved on night 5th/6th by 2/South Wales Borderers and 1 Company 1/R. Innis. Fus. 87th Bde. on the Divisional front, which will extend from present Right to U.17.c.3.3."

2. Serial numbers 8 to 10 (both inclusive) of March Table issued in conjunction with 29th Division Order No. 158 are cancelled.
29th Division No. C.G.S.67/69 dated 4th October (amendment to 29th Division Order No. 158) is also cancelled.

3. Moves will take place in accordance with the attached amended March Table.

4. (a) On the night 7th/8th the Divisional front will be divided into 2 Brigade Sectors, the 1/Lanc. Fus. (86th Bde.) taking over the Right Sector from the 2/S.W.B. (87th Bde.) and the 4/Worcester Regt. (88th Bde.) taking over the Left Sector from the 2/S.W.B. (87th Bde.).

   (b) The new Divisional boundaries and boundary between Bdes. is shewn on map issued with 29th Division Instruction No. 22.

   (c) G.O.C. 88th Inf. Bde. will relieve the G.O.C. 87th Inf. Bde. at SAULES FARM on the night 7th/8th and will assume command of both Sectors of the Divisional front.

5. Details of the relief will be arranged between Bdes. concerned. For purposes of this relief and for future movements RAILWAY STREET is allotted to the 88th Inf. Bde. and the PILCKEM - AU BON GITE Road to the 86th Inf. Bde.

6. On completion of the relief the location of units will be as shewn in attached Location Table.

7. Troops and transport moving by road to maintain 200 yards between Companies and transport.

8. Completion of reliefs to be reported to these Headquarters.

9. ACKNOWLEDGE.

A.T. Miller Capt
for Lieut-Colonel, G.S.,
29th Division.

Issued at 10 am

Copies 1 - 5 G.S.   15 Off. i/c Sigs.   22 SAA Sec.   29 Gds. Div.
        6   "Q".   16 1/2nd Mons. R.   23 227 M.G.Coy.
        7   CRA.   17 ADMS.   24 Camp Comdt.   30 4th Div.
        8   CRE.   18 APM.   25 Div. Train.
        9 - 10 86th Bde. 19 D.M.G.O.   26 S.S.O.
       11 - 12 87th Bde. 20 I.A.P.O.S.   27 29th I.S.C.   31 Area Comdt. B. Div. Area.
       13 - 14 88th Bde. 21 I.A.V.S.   28 14th Corps.
       32 1/Guernsey L.I.

March Table issued in conjunction with 29th Division Order No. 159.

Date.	Unit.	From.	To.	Take over from.	Followed by.	Time of starting.
5th	H.Q. 88th Bde. 4/Worc. R. 1/Essex R. 1/R.F.L.D. 2/Hants. } 88th T.M. Bty. }	A.5.a. DE WIPPE H. Camp HERLIN DUBLIN	CARIBOU ROUSSEL CARIBOU CARDOEN PARROY I.	New Camps and 4th Div.	Adv. parties 2nd Gds. Bde.	Camps to be clear by 2 p.m.
5th	1/Border Regt.	FOREST AREA CHARTHOUSE	COPPERMOLLE DUBLIN	2/Hants. 88th.	Adv. parties 1st Gds. Bde.	As arranged between Bdes.
5th	88th M.G. Coy. 86th T.M. Bty.	WELLINGTON	COPPERMOLLE	New Camp	2nd and 3rd Gds. Bde. T.B. H.Q. 86th Bde.	Camp to be clear by 12 noon.
7th	H.Q. 87th Bde. 2/S.W.B.	MAULES FARM Front Line	DRAGON CAMP WHITE MILL	1/K.O.S.B. 87th	4/Worc. R. 88th 1/Lan. Fus. 86th	Camp to be clear by 1 p.m.
	1/K.O.S.B.	WHITE MILL	DRAGON WOOD	New Camp	1/K.O.S.B. 87th	As arranged between Bdes.
	1/R. Innis. Fus.	CANAL BANK	CARDOEN	1/RFLD. 86th	1/RFLD. 86th	
7th	4/Worc R. } 87th 1/RFLD. 86th }	ROUSSEL CARDOEN	Left Front Line CANAL BANK	2/S.W.B. 87th 1/R. Innis. Fus.	2/R. Fus. 86th 1/R. Innis. Fus.	As arranged between Bdes.
	1/Lan. Fus. 1/R. Dub. Fus.	HARROW ETON	Right Front Line DRAGON WOOD	2/S.W.B. 87th New Camp	16/Middx. 86th 1st Gds. Bde.	Not before 1 p.m. Camp to be clear by 3 p.m.
	2/R. Fus.	ABBINGLY	ROUSSEL	4/Worc. 88th	1st Gds. Bde. }	Camps to be cleared by 2 p.m.
	16/Middx.	DULWICH	HARROW	1/Lan. Fus. 88th	1st Gds. Bde. }	16/Middx. to bivouac at HARROW until vacated by 1/Lan. Fus.

LOCATION TABLE Night 7th/8th.

-o-o-o-o-o-o-o-o-o-o-o-o-o-o-o-o-o-o-o-o-o-

Div. H.Q.	ELVERDINGHE CHATEAU.	B.14.b.15.15.
Rear H.Q.	DRAGON Camp.	A.15.b.5.8.
86th Inf. Bde. H.Q.	ZOMMERBLOOM.	U.8.c.5.5.
1/Lan. Fus.	Right Front Line.	H.Q. U.23.c.05.15.
1/R. Dub. Fus.	DRAGON WOOD.	A.10.c.6.2.
2/Roy. Fus.	ROUSSEL.	A.13.a.25.65.
16/Middx. Regt.	HARROW.	B.7.d.8.5.
86th M.G. Coy.	LINE and COPPERNOLLE.	A.16.b.6.9.
86th T.M. Bty.	LINE.	
87th Inf. Bde. H.Q.	DRAGON Camp.	A.15.b.5.8.
2/S.W.B.	WHITE MILL.	B.14.d.8.8.
1/K.O.S.B.	DRAGON WOOD.	A.9.d.9.3.
1/Border Regt.	DUBLIN.	A.11.c.4.5.
1/R. Innis. Fus.	CARDEN FARM.	A.18.b.1.8.
87th M.G. Coy.	COPPERNOLLE.	A.16.b.6.9.
87th T.M. Bty.	DRAGON Camp.	A.15.b.5.8.
88th Inf. Bde. H.Q.	SAULES FARM.	U.25.b.3.2.
4/Worcester Regt.	LEFT FRONT LINE.	H.Q. U.22.c.05.15.
2/Hampshire Regt.	PARROY I.	B.16.d.0.5.
1/Essex Regt.	CARIBOU.	A.11.d.8.7.
1/N.F.L.D.	CANAL BANK.	C.13.c.0.4. - C.7.c.0.6.
88th M.G. Coy.	LINE and COPPERNOLLE.	A.16.b.6.9.
88th T.M. Bty.	LINE.	
227th M.G. Coy.	WHITE MILL.	B.14.d.8.8.
1/2nd Mons. (Pioneers)		
2 Coys.	PARROY II.	B.16.c.9.5.
1 Coy.		A.18.a.6.7.
1/Guernsey L.I.	STOKE.	F.5.d.5.8.
Details all Bdes.	BETFORD.	A.12.d.60.55.

-o-o-o-o-o-o-o-o-

S E C R E T.   29th Division No. C.G.S. 67/70a.

Amendment to 29th Division Order No. 159.

Reference Map 1/10,000 LANGEMARCK.

1.   In para 4 (c) and in line 17 of the Location
Table issued with the above Order,

   for "SAULES FARM - U.25.b.3.2"
   read "VULCAN CROSSING - U.27.c.40.55"

2.   In line 3 of the Location Table,

   for "U.8.c.5.5."
   read "B.8.c.5.5."

                                                  Capt
                                        Lieut-Colonel, G.S.,
8th October, 1917.   29th Division.

S.

S E C R E T. Copy No. 4

29TH DIVISION ORDER NO. 162.
-o-o-o-o-o-o-o-o-o-o-o-o-o-o-o-o-o-

8th October, 1917.

1.   The 29th Division will be relieved by the 17th Division in the Centre Sector of the XIV Corps front, commencing on the 9th October, relief to be completed by 6 a.m. on the 11th October.

2. (a)   The 86th and 88th Inf. Bdes. will be relieved by the 51st Inf. Bde. in the line on the nights of the 9/10th October, and 10/11th October, in accordance with the attached march table "A" and location table "B". Details of relief will be arranged between Brigadiers concerned.

(b)   The G.O.C. 86th Inf. Bde. will hand over the command of his sector to the G.O.C. 88th Inf. Bde. on the morning of the 10th instant, and 86th Inf. Bde. H.Q. will entrain on that morning, vide March Table "A".

(c)   The 87th Inf. Bde. will entrain on the 9th as shewn on march table "A".

3.   The 29th Division on relief will be accommodated as follows :-

   86th Inf. Bde. Group - Proven No. 5 Area.
   87th Inf. Bde. Group - Proven No. 1 Area.
   88th Inf. Bde. Group - Corps Staging Area No. 1.

4.   During the process of relief, all units will be under the tactical command of the Brigadiers, in whose areas they may be.

5.   The C.R.E. and A.D.M.S. will arrange details of movements of Field Coys. and Field Ambulances with the C.R.E. and A.D.M.S. of the 17th Division, respectively.

6.   The Divisional M. Gun Officer will arrange for the moves of M.G. Coys. in accordance with march table "A" attached. The barrage machine guns will be relieved by the 17th Division on the night of 9/10th.

7.   Troops entraining will arrive at the station exactly half an hour before the train is due to start, and not earlier.

8.   Details at BEDFORD CAMP will rejoin their battalions prior to entraining.

9.   Moves of units not mentioned in these orders will be arranged by the A.A. & Q.M.G.

10.   Completion of relief in the front system will be notified to this office in B.A.B. Code.

11.   Troops moving by road will preserve the following intervals :-

/ West

West of the POPERINGHE - PROVEN road :-
500 yards between battalions and columns of
similar length.

East of the POPERINGHE - PROVEN road :-
200 yards between Coys. and columns of
similar length.

12. Divisional Headquarters will close at ELVERDINGHE CHATEAU at 8 A.M. on Thursday 11th October at which hour the command of the line will pass to the G.O.C, 17th Division. Divisional Headquarters will reopen at PROVEN Central Camp.

13. ACKNOWLEDGE.

C.P. Fuller
Lieut-Colonel, G.S.,
29th Division.

Issued at 10 p.m.

```
Copies  1 - 5   G.S.
            6   "Q".
            7   C.R.A.
            8   C.R.E.
         8A- 9  86th Inf. Bde.
        10 - 11 87th Inf. Bde.
        12 - 13 88th Inf. Bde.
           14   Off. i/c Sigs.
           15   1/2nd Monmouths.
           16   A.D.M.S.
           17   A.P.M.
           18   D.M.G.O.
           19   D.A.D.O.S.
           20   D.A.D.V.S.
           21   S.A.A. Sect. D.A.C.
           22   227th M.G. Coy.
           23   Camp Commdt.
           24   Divl. Train.
           25   S.S.O.
           26   29th D.S.C.
           27   1/Guernsey L.I.
           28   XIV Corps.
           29   4th Divn.
           30   17th Divn.
           31   Guards Divn.
           32   Area Commdt. B. Div. Area.
           33   Town Major, PROVEN.
```

M.

LOCATION TABLE "D".

Unit.	Camp.	Map Location.
29th Divn. H.Q.	PROVEN Central Camp.	27/F.7.b.5.1.
86th Inf. Bde. H.Q.	POONA	27/E.17.b.1.9.
2/Roy. Fus.	PERSIA	27/E.16.c.8.5.
1/Lan. Fus.	PATIALA	27/E.12.c.2.6.
16/Middx. Regt.	PERA	27/E.16.a.8.5.
1/R. Dub. Fus.	PALMA	27/E.18.d.2.5.
86th M.G. Coy.	PARANA	27/E.17.d.1.2.
86th T.M. Bty.	PRETORIA	27/E.17.a.4.2.
87th Inf. Bde. H.Q.	POUNDON	27/F.15.d.1.7.
2/S.W.B.	POODLE	27/F.8.b.3.3.
1/K.O.S.B.	PITCHCOTT	27/F.9.c.7.8.
1/R. Innis. Fus.	PRATTLE	27/F.15.d.1.4.
1/Border Regt.	PIDDINGTON	27/F.16.b.2.9.
87th M.G. Coy.	PILCH	27/F.15.b.8.8.
87th T.M. Bty.	PRESTWOOD	27/F.14.d.0.7.
88th Inf. Bde. H.Q.	SERINGAPATAM	19/X.28.d.5.3.
4/Worc. Regt.	SARAWAK	19/X.29.c.7.3.
2/Hants. Regt.	SUTTON	27/F.10.b.6.5.
1/Essex Regt.	SUEZ	19/X.29.d.3.1.
Newfoundland Regt.	SWINDON	19/X.29.c.9.4.
88th M.G. Coy.	SASKATOON	19/X.29.c.3.8.
88th T.M. Bty.	SELKIRK	19/X.29.a.1.4.
455th (W.Rid.) Fd.Coy.	PUTLOWES	27/F.10.a.5.2.
497th (Kent) Fd.Coy.	PATAGONIA	27/E.17.d.7.5.
510th (London) Fd.Coy.	SALEM	19/X.29.c.2.1.
87th Field Ambce.	PRIORY	27/F.10.c.8.6.) when
88th Field Ambce.	SINGAPORE	19/X.29.c.4.3.) ordered
89th Field Ambce.	PANAMA	27/E.14.c.8.5.) by A.D.M.S.
227th M.G. Coy.	P.5 Area	27/F.13.d.2.6.
1/2nd Monmouth Regt. (Pioneers)	PARROY (until relieved)	B.16.c.9.5.
1/Guernsey Light Infty.	STOKE	F.5.d.1.6.

MARCH TABLE ISSUED IN CONJUNCTION WITH 29TH DIV O.O. No.162.

Ser. No.	Date.	Unit.	From.	To.	Relieved by.	Time of starting.	Route.	Remarks.	Transport by road not to arrive at Camp before.
1.	9th.	2/SWB.87th.	WHITE HILL. B14.d8.6	P.1 Area.	D/51.Adv. party.	9 a.m.	No.1 train from ELVER-DINGHE to PROVEN.		11.0 a.m.
2.	9th	1/R Innis Fus.87th.	CARDOEN A.18.b.1.3.	P 1 Area.	C/50 Adv. party.	12 noon	No.2 Train from ELVER-DINGHE to PROVEN.		2.0 p.m.
3.	9th	1/KOSB 87th.	DRAGON CAMP	P 1 Area.	D/50	3.30 PM	No.3 Train from INTER-NATIONAL CORNER to PROVEN.	D/50 arrive DRAGON CAMP 12 noon. 1/KOSB 87 to close up un-til leaving for INTERNATIONAL CORNER Station.	5.30 p.m.
4.	9th.	1/Border Regt 87th.	DUBLIN A.11.c.4.5.	P 1 Area.	A/50 Adv party. H.Q.50th Bde Adv party.	6 P.M.	No.4 Train from ELVER-dinghe to PROVEN.	See note at end of table.	8.0 p.m.
		87th Bde HQ	CARIBOU A.11.d.8.7	P 1 Area.					
		37th M.G.Co.	COPPERNOLLE A.16.b.6.9	P 1 Area					
5.	9th	1/Essex 88th.	CANAL BANK	S 1 Area.	C/51.	8 pm.	No.5 Train from ELVER-DINGHE to INTERNATIONAL CORNER.	C/51 arrive CANAL BANK 4.0 P.M. 1/Essex to close up until leaving for train.	No res-triction.
6.	9th/10th.	4/Worc Rgt 88th.	Left Support	HARROW B.7.d.3.5	B/51.	-	-	See Serial No.8.	do.
7.	9th/10th.	1/Lancs Fus.86th.	Right Support.	ROUSSEL B.13.a.25.85	A/51	-	-	See Serial No.9.	do.

Ser. No.	Date.	Unit.	From.	To.	Relieved by.	Time of starting.	Route.	Remarks.	Transport not to arrive at Camp before
8.	10th	4/Worc 38th	HARROW	S 1 Area	D/50 Adv party.	9.30 a.m.	No.7 train from ELVERdinghe to INTERNATIONAL CORNER.	4/Worc 38th detrain and 1/R Dub Fus 38th entrain at INTERNATIONAL CORNER.	do.
		1/R Dub Fus. 227 M.G. Coy. 86 & 88 details.	DRAGON CAMP Lino. COPPERFOLLE	P 5 Area P 5 Area P 5 Area S 1 Area		10 a.m.	No.7 train from INTERNATIONAL CORNER to P.OVER.		
9.	10th	1/Lancs Fus 86th Kent F.Co H.Q.36th H.Q.36th Linn.	ROUSSEL ELVERDINGHE " "	P 5 Area P 5 Area P 1 Area P 1 Area	B/52.	12.30 p.m.	No.8 train from ELVERDINGHE to PROVEN.		do.
10.	10th/ 11th.	D/38th C/36th	Left Support M.Support.	S 1 Area P.5 Area	D/81 G/51	5.0 a.m. 11th inst	No 10 train from ELVERDINGHE to INTERNATIONAL CORNER & PROVENTIONAL	Bn to rendezvous at the Stn ELVERDINGHE. Train will stop at INTERNATIONAL CORNER for 1/Mfld to detrain.	do.
11.	10/11	B/38.	Left Support HALNOE.		B/51.			See Ser.No.13	do
12.	10/11	A/36	M.Support.	ROUSSEL	A/51.			See Ser.No.13.	do
13.	11th.	B/38th A/36th London Fd.Coy. 38th H.Q. 36th)H.G. 38th)Gos. Line.	HARROW ROUSSEL ELVERDINGHE Front Line Gos. Line.	S 1 Area P 5 Area S 1 Area S 1 Area P 5 Area S 1 Area	B/51. A/51. 51st Bde H.Q.	11 a.m.	No.11 train from ELVERDINGHE to INTERNATIONAL CORNER and PROVEN.	Troops to rendezvous at ELVERDINGHE Stn. Train will stop at INTERNATIONAL CORNER for troops of 38th Bde Group to detrain.	do.

Notes. 1. The moves of B'ns of 87th Bde will necessitate double banking in the new camps in P.I area, for approximately the following hours,— 2/S.W.B.5 hrs. 1/K.O.S.B. 2½ hrs. 1/Innis Fus 5 hrs. 1/Border Regt 2 hrs.

M.C. BARRAGE TABLE.

Group.	No of Barrage.	Zero Time.	Target.	Rate of fire.
A. 4 guns 227 M.G.Coy. LEITRES Fm.	1.	0 - +4	NAMUR CROSSING.	1 Bolt in 4 mins.
	2.	+4 - +10.	NAMUR CROSSING to 44 K.	1 Bolt in 4 mins.
	3.	+10 - +15.	44 K to extreme range.	1 Bolt in 4 mins.
B. 4 guns 83 M.G.Coy. 4 guns 227 M.G.Coy Railway U.2?.a.1.6.?	4.	+15 to +20.	U.12.c.9.3 - U.12.d.5.4.	1 Bolt in 4 mins.
	5.	+20 to +40	CAIRO HOUSE - U.12.d.35.95.	1 Bolt in 10 mins.
	6.	+40 to +1.40.	V.1.c.0.0. - V.7.a.5.6.	1 Bolt in 10 mins.
4 guns 86 M.G.Coy. 4 guns 227 -"- U.23.a.6.3.	4.	+15 to +20.	U.12.d.7.5. - V.7.c.2.0.	1 Bolt in 4 mins.
	5.	+20 to +40.	TAUBE Fm. - V.7.d.1.5.	1 Bolt in 10 mins.
	6.	+40 to +1.40.	V.7.b.2.3. - V.7.d.7.9.	1 Bolt in 10 mins.

SECRET.   29th Division No. C.G.S.61/10A.

ADDENDUM NO. 1 TO INSTRUCTION NO. 23.
-o-o-o-o-o-o-o-o-o-o-o-o-o-o-o-o-o-o-o-o-o-o-

Add Para. 8.

On completion of the 3rd Barrage, Group A will become Divisional Reserve. O.C. 227th M.G. Coy. will detail 8 pack animals to be kept in waiting to move these guns and ammunition forward if required.

Officers Commanding 88th and 86th M.G. Coys. will each detail 8 pack animals to be kept in waiting to move groups B and C forward respectively, should the advance mentioned in 29th Division Order No. 160, para. 12, take place. These groups will be prepared to move forward, on receipt of orders, to positions from which they can form a protective barrage in front of the PURPLE line. These positions will be on the general line PASCAL FARM - CONDE HOUSE.

Officers Commanding Groups B and C will notify G.Os.C. 88th and 86th Inf. Bdes. respectively, when these groups are in position and these Groups will then be at the disposal of their respective Brigades to be employed as required.

BARRAGE TABLE.

Amended times.

No. of Barrage.	Zero Time.
1	0 to 0.4
2	0.4 to 0.10
3	0.10 to 0.20
4	0.20 to 0.40
5	0.40 to 1.50
6	1.50 to 2.30

Rate of fire will be 1 belt in 10 minutes, except at the following times when 1 belt in 4 minutes will be fired :-

0 to 0.20
1.46 to 1.50
2.26 to 2.30

ACKNOWLEDGE.

                                                G.T. Miller Capt
                                                for
                                                Lieut-Colonel, G.S.,
                                                29th Division.

7th Oct. 1917.

Copies to all recipients of 29th Division Instruction No. 23.

M.

S E C R E T   29th Division No. A/2311.

29th DIVISION OPERATIONS.

Instruction No. 24.

Administrative Arrangements.

1. **AMMUNITION.**

    Two main Brigade Ammunition Dumps have been formed, the Right Brigade near SKREIBOOM, U.23.Central, the Left Brigade at SPRING FARM, U.22.c.3.4.

2. **PRISONERS OF WAR**

    The Divisional Collecting Post will be at IRON CROSS, C.3.a.8.5.
    Corps Collecting Post will be at CACTUS PONTOON.
    The A.P.M., 29th Division, will take over prisoners at IRON CROSS with M.M.P. Personnel.

3. **STRAGGLERS' POSTS.**

    The A.P.M., 29th Division, will establish Stragglers' Posts at VULCANS CROSSING and IRON CROSS.

4. **MEDICAL.**

    The Divisional Collecting Post for walking wounded will be at Railhead, HANLEY, C.3.Central.
    The Advanced Dressing Station for walking wounded will be at CEMENT HOUSE, U.28.c.1.2.
    Both the above will be shared with 4th Division.
    Field Ambulance Relay Posts are established at SPRING FARM, REITRES FARM, U.22.d.9.2., and the "PIG & WHISTLE", U.28.b.4.3., and further relays will be pushed forward during operations to the neighbourhood of NAMUR CROSSING, U.18.a.4.7. and OLGA HOUSES, U.18.b.6.2.
    Extra personnel for clearing the battle-field will be held in readiness for use under Lieut. MacNICOL, Divisional Burials Officer, as under:-

    Artillery T.M.Personnel .... 50 N.C.O's & men
    Each Inf. Brigade from drummers etc....... 50   "   "

                    Total 200

    Time and place of rendezvous will be notified from "Q" Office, by wire, to Staff Captain, Royal Artillery and Rear Infantry Brigade Headquarters.

5. **TRANSPORT.**

    The S.A.A. Section, 29th Divisional Ammunition Column, will hold 72 Pack Animals, with pack saddles and crates, in readiness under an Officer on Zero Day, for use in emergency.
    An orderly will be detailed to report to "Q" Office, ELVERDINGHE CHATEAU, on Zero Day, at 10 a.m.

                                                      P.T.O.

The 87th Brigade Pack Transport (in reserve) will also be held in readiness to supplement the 1st Line Transport of the 86th and 88th Brigades, if required.

6. VETERINARY.

The 18th Mobile Veterinary Section will be at DE WIPPE CABARET.

7. RATIONS.

On Zero Day, troops on, and east of, the Canal Bank will carry the unexpired portion of the current day's ration and one extra day's ration, as well as the Iron Ration.

7-10-17.

Lieut. Colonel,
A.A. & Q.M.G., 29th Division.

SECRET.   29th Division No. O.G.S.72/60.

29TH DIVISION OPERATIONS.

Instruction No. 25.

Communications.

1. **TELEPHONE and TELEGRAPH.**
    The main Divisional Route runs to VULCAN CROSSING via WOOD HOUSE. The lines up to WOOD HOUSE are buried. At VULCAN CROSSING a forward Divisional Office will be established. From this forward office 3 pairs of cable run to each of the Brigade Headquarters at AU BON GITE and MARTINS MILL respectively. In each case 2 pairs will be used for telephone calls and the third for Fullerphone. There will be a lateral line between MARTINS MILL and AU BON GITE. The forward exchange at VULCANS CROSSING will carry a liaison line to the right and left artillery groups at TUFFS FARM and WOOD HOUSE respectively.

2. **VISUAL.**
    The Central Div. Visual Station will be established at VULCAN CROSSING. The right brigade will establish visual stations as follows :-
    AU BON GITE, LANGEMARCK CHURCH and at U.23.B.6.2. The stations at AU BON GITE and LANGEMARCK CHURCH will work direct to the Central Visual Station. The LANGEMARCK CHURCH Station will transmit messages from EAGLE TRENCH and will be manned by Signallers, detailed by O.C. Divl. Signals.
    The left brigade will establish visual stations at MARTINS MILL and U.23.a.4.9. Both these stations will work direct to the Central Visual Station.
    Messages from the Right Sector will be answered by 3 dots and those from the Left Sector by 3 dashes.
    All these stations will be established by 5 p.m. on "Y" day.

3. **WIRELESS.**
    One wireless station will be established at AU BON GITE. Should the Right Brigade move forward this station will accompany the Headquarters. The station now at VULCAN CROSSING will remain. Both stations will work to a Directing Station at BOESINGHE. Messages thence by telephone to Div. Headquarters.

4. **AMPLIFIERS.**
    Amplifiers will be installed at U.23.b.6.2. and U.23.a.4.9. These amplifiers will receive from Power Buzzers, which will accompany the troops of the attacking units, and will work eventually from the vicinity of CONDE HOUSE and PASCALL FARM.

5. **PIGEONS.**
    8 pairs of pigeons will be supplied to each of the attacking Brigades on "Y" day.

6. **D.R.L.S.**
    All sealed packets will be delivered from the Division to the advanced office at VULCAN CROSSING, and thence to Brigades by runners. Times of departure of D.Rs. from Headquarters will remain as at present.

7. A signal officer will be at VULCAN CROSSING onwards from 6 p.m. on "Y" day to regulate all signal traffic.

8. ACKNOWLEDGE.

                                                         C.F. Fuller.
                                                    Lieut-Colonel, G.S.,
                                                         29th Division.

7th Oct. 1917.

SECRET.   Copy No.

29TH DIVISION ORDER NO. 161.
-o-o-o-o-o-o-o-o-o-o-o-o-o-o-o-o-o-

Ref. 1/10,000 LANGEMARCK,
     1/20,000 28 N.W.   October 7th, 1917.

1.   Reference 29th Division Order No. 160 the march to assembly positions will be carried out in accordance with the attached march table.

2.   Two hundred yards interval will be maintained between companies.

3.   Troops moving "up" will in all cases take precedence over troops moving "down".

4.   ACKNOWLEDGE.

                                        Lieut-Colonel, G.S.,
Issued at   29th Division.

        Copies 1 - 5 General Staff.
               6   "A".
               7   C.R.A.
               8   C.R.E.
             9 - 15   86th Inf. Bde.
            16 - 21   88th Inf. Bde.
            22 - 23   87th Inf. Bde.
               24   Off. i/c Sigs.
               25   1/2nd Monmouths.
               26   1/R. Guernsey L.I.
               27   A.D.M.S.
               28   A.P.M.
               29   D.M.G.O.
               30   XIV Corps.
               31   Guards Division.
               32   4th Division.
               33   17th Division.
               34   227th M.G. Coy.
               35   9th Squadron R.F.C.

M.

MARCH TABLE ISSUED IN CONJUNCTION WITH O.O. NO 161.

Serial No.	Date.	Unit.	From.	To.	Time.	Route.	Remarks.
1.	Y/Z night	2/R.Fus. 86th.	ROUSSEL	FORWARD AREA.	To leave Camp at 5.30 p.m.	ELVERDINGHE - DAWSON'S CORNER B.22.c.8.7 - CHEAPSIDE B.17.b.9.1 -CACTUS PONTOON-O.7.d.15.35 -duckboard track as far as C.8.a.8.5 -Switch road to C.2.b.7.4 - IRON CROSS - LANGEMARCK.	
2.	Z day	16/Middx 86th.	HARROW.	Area about PILCKEM.	Leave Camp at 2.0 a.m.	ELVERDINGHE - WHITE HOPE CORNER -CACTUS PONTOON - thence as above to PILCKEM.	
3.	Y/Z night.	1/Hfld Regt. 83th.	CANAL BANK.	FORWARD AREA.	To be clear of B.12.a75.05. by 10.0 p.m.	CACTUS PONTOON - CROSS ROADS B.12.d.3.4 - RAILWAY ST. B.12.a.75.05 - RAILWAY St.	
4.	Y/Z night	8/Harts Regt. 83th.	PARROY I.	FORWARD AREA.	Leave Camp at 9.15 p.m.	Road Junct B.22.b.7.1 - CHEAPSIDE B.17.b.9.2 - CROSS ROADS B.12.d.30.35 - RAILWAY St. B.12.a.75.05 - RAILWAY St.	
5.	Y/Z night	1/Essex Regt. (less 2 Coys).	CARIBOU	CANAL BANK (C.13.c.0.4 - C.7.c.0.6.)	NOT to arrive WHITE HOPE CORNER before 11.15 p.m. To be in position by 2.0 a.m.	DROMORE CORNER A.13.d.3.8 - ELVERDINGHE - WHITE HOPE CORNER -BOESINGHE - CACTUS PONTOON - CANAL BANK.	

S E C R E T.   29th Division No. C.G.S.67/74.

"Q",   Off. i/c Sigs.
86th Inf. Bde.   1/2nd Monmouths.
87th Inf. Bde.   A.D.M.S.
88th Inf. Bde.   A.P.M.
C.R.A.   227th M.G. Coy.
C.R.E.   D.M.G.O.
- -

Reference para. 1 of 29th Division Order No. 160.

The hour of Zero will be _____

This hour will only be communicated to those whom it immediately concerns and will under no circumstances be sent over the telephone either in code or clear.

ACKNOWLEDGE by wire.

A.T. Mills Capt

Lieut-Colonel, G.S.,
29th Division.

8th Oct. 1917.

M.

SECRET.   29th Division No. C.G.S.65/240.

29TH DIVISION WARNING ORDER.
-o-o-o-o-o-o-o-o-o-o-o-o-o-o-o-o-

                                      12th October, 1917.

1.   The 29th Division (less Artillery) accompanied by one Divisional Supply Column will be transferred from XIV Corps to Third Army on 15th, 16th, 17th October, under orders which will be issued later.

2.   The Divisional Supply Column and other motor vehicles will move by road.
        The remaining troops mentioned in para. 1 will move by rail.
        Arrangements for the above movements will be notified later.

3.   Entraining stations for the above moves will be HOPOUTRE and PESELHOEK.
        Any restrictions as to routes to entraining stations will be issued later.

4.   The 29th Divisional Artillery will be transferred to Third Army at a later date, under orders to be issued separately.

5.   ACKNOWLEDGE.

                                      Lieut-Colonel, G.S.,
                                          29th Division.

Issued at _____

Copies to :-
    "C".   D.A.D.O.S.
    C.R.A.   D.A.D.V.S.
    C.R.E.   S.A.A. Sec. D.A.C.
    86th Inf. Bde.   227th M.G. Coy.
    87th Inf. Bde.   Camp Commdt.
    88th Inf. Bde.   Divl. Train.
    Off. i/c Sigs.   S.S.O.
    1/2nd Monmouths.   29th D.S.C.
    A.D.M.S.   XIV Corps.
    A.P.M.   1/Guernsey L.I.
    D.M.G.O.   Area Commdt. PROVEN.

M.

"C" Form.
MESSAGES AND SIGNALS.

Army Form C 2123.
(In books of 100).

No. of Message........

Prefix........ Code........ Words........
Charges to Collect
Service Instructions

Received From: OCO
By: Hodgson

Sent, or sent out At............m To............m By............

Office Stamp

Handed in at CAR .... Office 11.57 m. Received 12.20 a m.

TO 29 Divn

Sender's Number	Day of Month	In reply to Number	AAA
9731			

Forecast wind SW 40 to 40 mph changing to west 45 to 55 mph with very severe squalls wet at first then fairer intervals with passing showers milder visibility indifferent becoming very good again wind midnight SW 35 mph 4 am west 40 mph

FROM PLACE & TIME: Fifth Army.

"C" FORM.
MESSAGES AND SIGNALS.

Army Form C. 2123.
(In books of 100)

No. of Message........

Prefix......Code......Words......	Received.	Sent, or sent out.	Office Stamp.
£ s. d.	From... Cco	At........m.	
Charges to Collect	By... Whs	To........	
Service Instructions		By........	

Handed in at......9D......Office 6.30 m. Received 6.40 m.

TO 29 Div

*Sender's Number.	Day of Month.	In reply to Number.	AAA
G201	9th		

12 Bde Drop report 6.10 am that enemy barrage opened at zero plus 4 on LOUIS FARM line aaa It was very ragged aaa No news of our own troops or signs of prisoners at present

FROM PLACE & TIME 4 Div 6.15 am

* This line should be erased if not required.

"O" Form. Army Form C.2123
MESSAGES AND SIGNALS. No. of Message........

TO: Felix

Sender's Number	Day of Month	In reply to Number	AAA

88th
Inf. report that 50
prisoners proceeding down Rly
6.15 am are now being
Through by Telephone to
Front.

6.15 A.M.

FROM PLACE & TIME: Felix ford

"C" FORM. Army Form C. 2123.
(In books of 100.)

MESSAGES AND SIGNALS. No. of Message..........

Prefix....Code....Words....	Received	Sent, or sent out.	Office Stamp.
£ s. d.	From... V3	At.........m.	-9 X 17
Charges to Collect	By 10pm	To.........m.	
Service Instructions by Visual	By		

Handed in at.........Office.......m. Received.......m.

TO Felix G.

* Sender's Number.	Day of Month.	In reply to Number.	AAA

Tapes were laid by
2.0pm hostile shelling along
railway from 10.30 pm onwards
counter batteries were informed
at 12.30 am FLINT men going
up in good order

(W.T
1.50/am)

FROM   Flag.
PLACE & TIME

* This line should be erased if not required.

"C" FORM.
MESSAGES AND SIGNALS.
Army Form C. 2123.
(In books of 100.)

Prefix	Code	Words 14	Received OCO From WKse By	Sent, or sent out At To By	Office Stamp

Charges to Collect

Service Instructions

Handed in at OCO ... Office 6.20 a.m. Received 6.25 a.m.

TO 29th Div

Sender's Number G66	Day of Month 9	In reply to Number	AAA

Morning report aaa Considerable intermittent hostile shelling during the night increasing towards dawn aaa Otherwise nothing to report aaa Addsd 5th Army reptd all concerned

FROM PLACE & TIME 14th Corps 6.7a.m.

"O" Form
MESSAGES AND SIGNALS.

Army Form C 2123.
(In books of 100).

TO: Felix

Sender's Number	Day of Month	In reply to Number	AAA
4C321	9		
1	Officer	417	JR
and	45	OR	417
171st	172nd	JR	passed
here	6.30 am		captured
by	Nfld	soon	after
crossing	Broombeek		
171-1152	172 - 39 Div		7.5 AM
	227		
417 -			

FROM PLACE & TIME: Felix Park 6.40 am

"C" FORM.
Army Form C. 2123.
MESSAGES AND SIGNALS.

Prefix... Army... Code... Words... 24 Received From... Code By... Wks

Handed in at... GD... Office 6.30 a.m. Received 6.4? a.m.

TO 29th Div

Sender's Number: GBH66 Day of Month: 9

1st Bde Report their leading troops over the BROENBEEK and prisoners coming back

6.46 am

FROM PLACE & TIME   Gds Div 6-15 am

"O" Form
MESSAGES AND SIGNALS.
Army Form C 2123.
(In books of 100).
No. of Message...........

| Prefix....Code....Words.... £ s. d. | Received Prefix........ By........ | Sent, or sent out. At ....m. To .... By........ | Office Stamp. |

Charges to Collect
Service Instructions

Handed in at............Office........m. Received........m.

TO: *Redox*

Sender's Number	Day of Month	In reply to Number	AAA
		Objective reported taken	
		at least	
one	Battalion	further on at	
Batt	all	than Division	
from	727	Drew post	
Rept	all	flag 88th	
well	over	Baker took over	
Tango	Excellent and	O be	
going well			
		6·45 A.m	

FROM PLACE & TIME: Front 6·21 a.m

This line should be erased if not required

"C" Form.
MESSAGES AND SIGNALS.

Army Form C 2123.
(In books of 100).

No. of Message...........

Prefix...... Code...... Words...... 4 W 95 / 50

Received From VC Wks

Sent, or sent out. At ...... m To ...... By ......

Office Stamp. 9 X 17

Charges to Collect

Service Instructions **Urgent VC**

Handed in at............ Office............ m. Received............ m.

TO Felix

Sender's Number	Day of Month	In reply to Number	AAA
JC 222	9		

of 86 Bde report trouble from M guns in pascal farm, but hows have been turned on to that point aaa Lancs Fus Casualties estimated 50

9.10 AM

FROM Felix
PLACE & TIME Forward Ian

"C" FORM.
MESSAGES AND SIGNALS.

Prefix	Code	Words 36	Received. From OCD Mason By	Sent, or sent out. At To By	Office Stamp.
Charges to Collect					
Service Instructions YDR					
Handed in at			Office 6.45 m.	Received 7.16 m.	

TO 29 Divn

Sender's Number	Day of Month	In reply to Number	AAA
JS202	9		

12. Bde reports 6.45 am aaa Deserter 417 Rgt 227 Div captured aaa About 30 prisoners coming in regiment unknown aaa Barrage continues between LANGEMARCK and Attacking troops.

FROM PLACE & TIME 4th Divn 6.55 am

"O" Form
MESSAGES AND SIGNALS.

Army Form C 2123.
(In books of 100).

No. of Message..........

Prefix... Code... Words...	Received From... By...	Sent, or sent out. At .... m To .... By	Office Stamp.	
Charges to Collect				
Service Instructions				

Handed in at............ Office............ m. Received............ m.

TO: Felix

Sender's Number	Day of Month	In reply to Number	AAA
Wounded	NCO	of	FROWN
writes he		was	hit
just	before	reaching	second
objective	immediately		S.
of	Rly	about	1500
yds	from	jumping off	
line	aaa	FROWN	was
then	going	strong	aaa
above	NCO	reached	FRUIT
HQ	9.15	am	aaa
FRUIT	reports	2	machine
guns	reached	first	objective
and	moving	forward	to
second	8.15 am		
			10.55 am

FROM PLACE & TIME: Felix Forward 9.30 am

"O" Form.
MESSAGES AND SIGNALS.

Army Form C 2123.
(In books of 100).
No. of Message..........

Prefix	Code	Words	Received From / By	Sent, or sent out. At / To / By	Office Stamp
	XD	47	OCO Mason		

Charges to Collect
Service Instructions: OCO

Handed in at .... Office 10.30 a.m. Received 10.41 a.m.

TO 29 Div PAKKOH FARM

Sender's Number	Day of Month	In reply to Number	AAA
474	9.		

Contact patrol 8.20 am shows approximate line as follows LANDING FARM — COMPROMIS FARM — WATER HOUSE — TRANQUILLE HOUSE — Railway crossing NW of TRANQUILLE HOUSE — U12 Central — U12 A1.1 — VEE Bend — U11 C9.7 — U11 A7.0 — U11 A5.2 — U10 B4.7 AAA added 5th Army repts all concerned

10.43 am

FROM 14th Corps
PLACE & TIME 10.2 am

"C" FORM.
MESSAGES AND SIGNALS.
Army Form C. 2123.

Prefix SM Code Words 33
Received from: OCO Mason
Handed in at: 7. CH Received 7.14

TO: 29th Divn

Sender's Number: SC 468
Day of Month: 4

Observer at Vulcan Farm reports infantry were seen on 1st objective at Z. Plus 45" both divns in touch and carrying parties now seen going forward

7.20 AM

FROM PLACE & TIME: Gds Divn 6.4 am

"C" Form
MESSAGES AND SIGNALS.

Army Form C. 2123
(In books of 100.)

Prefix ...... Code ...... Words 65

Service Instructions. OMO

TO: 29th Divn

*Sender's Number	Day of Month	In reply to Number	AAA
573	9		

Aeroplane patrol reports as follows aaa 6.50 am to 8.5 am area POELCAPPELLE along road to namur crossing along railway to SCHAAP BALIE VIJFWEGEN to WESTROOSEBEKE aaa no enemy movement or concentration seen in our behind this area aaa 7.10 am large fire at Dump V2A8.4 aaa no EA seen along front aaa aaa all concerned.

FROM PLACE & TIME: 14 Corps 9-35am

"C" Form
MESSAGES AND SIGNALS.

Army Form C.
(In books of 100.)
No. of Message..........

Prefix.......... Code........ Words 34

Received From: OCo By:

Sent, or sent out At..........a.m. To.......... By..........

Office Stamp

Charges to collect

Service Instructions. YDR

Handed in at.......... Office 9.20 m. Received 10-3 m.

TO 29 Div

*Sender's Number: GS212
Day of Month: 9
In reply to Number: —
AAA

FOO reports timed 7-35 am second attack progressing favourably aaa Enemy barrage shortened considerably but not very intense aaa later report dated 9-12 am states many large fires seen behind enemy's lines.

10.6 am

FROM PLACE & TIME Duke av 9-20 am

"C" Form
MESSAGES AND SIGNALS.

Army Form C. 2123

Handed in at HRZ **Office** 9.5 a.m. **Received** 9.40 a.m.

TO 29 Divn

Day of Month 9

AAA

Prisoners of 3 477th IR captured in POELCAPPELLE aaa 1st Bn relieved 10 Bavarian IR on nig 5/6th aaa Bavarians believed to be in reserve aaa all 4 Coys of 1st Bn 477th IR in front line aaa coy trench strength said to be 130 to 150 aaa Addsd Duke reptd 14 Corps. Intelligence foley Ocean.

FROM PLACE & TIME IO Duke 9 a.m.

"O" Form.
MESSAGES AND SIGNALS.

Army Form C 2123
(In books of 100).

No. of Message..........

Prefix....Code....Words....	Received	Sent, or sent out.	Office Stamp
£ s. d.	From........	At........m	
Charges to Collect	By.........	To........	
Service Instructions		By.........	

Handed in at SOJ ....Office........m. Received 9.28 a.m.

TO: 29th Divn.

| Sender's Number | Day of Month | In reply to Number | AAA |
| GG 474 | 9 | | |

8.5 am Observer reports our troops now consolidating dotted blue line in touch with right and left Divisions AAA Enemy barrage on STEENBEEK and BROENBEEK valley lighter now Two or three hundred prisoners coming in 8.15 am carrying parties now reaching 2nd objective no sign of hostile activity

FROM
PLACE & TIME

Gds Div
9.10 am.

"C" F MESSAGES AND SIGNALS.

Army Form C.2121
(In books of 100.)

Prefix ... Code ... Words 35

Received From OCD By mason

Sent, or sent out At ... m. To ... By ...

Service Instructions. OCD

Handed in at ... Office 9·15 a.m. Received 9·30 a.m.

TO 29 Divn

Sender's Number: Z 5253
Day of Month: 9
AAA

Corps on our left have taken prisoner of 138 Regt 42 Div from RUSSIA aaa 43 Div in process of relieving 18 Div aaa Addsd Divns

9·40 a.m.

9·40 a.m.

FROM PLACE & TIME
Fourteenth Corps
9·10 a.m.

"C" Form
MESSAGES AND SIGNALS.

Army Form C. 2121
(In books of 100.)
No. of Message...........

Prefix........ Code........ Words 28
Received From OCO By Dawson
Sent, or sent out At........m. To........ By........
Office Stamp

Charges to collect
Service Instructions. YDR

Handed in at........ Office 9.15 a.m. Received........m.

TO 29 Divn

*Sender's Number	Day of Month	In reply to Number	AAA
55211	9	—	

Nothing further from DROP. aaa Observers report FRUIT am going forward well aaa Add 14 Corps repl all Concerned

9-40 AM

FROM PLACE & TIME Duke Adv. 9·10a

* This line should be erased if not required.

"C" Form
MESSAGES AND SIGNALS.

Army Form C. 2123
(In books of 100.)

No. of Message..........

Prefix	Code	Words	Received	Sent, or sent out	Office Stamp
			From...1.00	At.........m.	
Charges to collect			By.........	To.........	
Service Instructions.				By.........	
			Y.D.R.		

Handed in at.......... Office.........m. Received.........m.

TO 29 Divn

*Sender's Number	Day of Month	In reply to Number	A A A
GS 209	9		

Verbal report from FOO timed 6.15 am states DROP gained first objective easily aaa All going well aaa prisoners coming in in large numbers aaa aaa added 14 Corps reply All concerned.

FROM PLACE & TIME Duke 8.45 am

"C" Form
MESSAGES AND SIGNALS.

Army Form C.2123
(In books of 100.)

No. of Message.

Prefix AW Code JHR Words 55
Charges to collect
Service Instructions.

Received From OCO By Lee

Sent, or sent out At To By

Office Stamp

Handed in at SR7 Office 0741 m. Received 0728 m.

TO	Intelligence 29 Divn.

*Sender's Number	Day of Month	In reply to Number	AAA
	9th		

Prisoners of 417th IR 441st IR state the 227th Divn relieved 6th Bavarian div. last night aaa 417th IR captured near Railway aaa 441st IR Believed to be on their left aaa location of 477th IR unknown aaa addsd Duke repd 14th Corps intelligence to lia ocean and 5th army

FROM PLACE & TIME	IO Duke 7.35 a.m

"C" Form.
MESSAGES AND SIGNALS

Army Form C 2123.
(In books of 100).

Prefix	Code	Words 75	Received	Sent, or sent out.	Office Stamp
	£ s. d.		From RO	At ... m.	
Charges to Collect			By ...	To ...	
Service Instructions				By ...	

Handed in at RO .... Office ..... m. Received ..... m.

TO 29th Divn

Sender's Number	Day of Month	In reply to Number	AAA
G 258	9		

Prisoners taken this morning 31 IR 85 IR 18 Div and 417 IR 441 RIR 477 IR — 227 Div AAA Order of battle north to South as given above AAA Coys of Regts of 227 Div appear to have had a strength exceeding 100 in line AAA fighting quality of 227 Div described as poor AAA Added fifth army I. Repld Flank Corps and all Divns

FROM Fourteenth Corps
PLACE & TIME 11·10 a.m.

"C" Form.
MESSAGES AND SIGNALS.

Army Form C 2123.
(In books of 100).
No. of Message.........

off aaa Have organised details of FROG and FROWN and sent them up to reinforce aaa Touch appears to be maintained with left but not with right aaa message ends aaa FRUGAL are in front of EAGLE TRENCH and have not been used aaa

FROM PLACE & TIME: Felix Forward 12.15 pm

"C" Form.
MESSAGES AND SIGNALS.

Army Form C 2123.
(In books of 100).

Prefix. Code. Words 13
Received From: VC
By: 4
Sent, or sent out.
Office Stamp

Charges to Collect
Service Instructions

Handed in at VC Office 12.35 Am. Received 13.30 m

TO Felix

Sender's Number	Day of Month	In reply to Number	AAA
GC 334	9th		

Following from FRUIT begins aaa following from FROWN timed 10.40 am from Olga houses begins aaa situation appears very obscure we are not beyond 2nd objective aaa FROG and FROWN are reported to have lost the barrage aaa FROWN went up to reinforce aaa on left of second objective are about 50 of FROWN reported to be in TAUBE FARM aaa FROWN and FROG on their right very mixed up aaa enemy counter attacked on second objective but was driven

FROM PLACE & TIME 1.40 pm

				SIGNALS.	No. of Message.........
......Code........Words......		Received	Sent, or sent out.		Office Stamp
£	s.	d.	From................	At ....m	
Charges to Collect			By	To	
Service Instructions				By	
....					

Handed in at..Office.............m. Received.................m.

TO

Sender's Number	Day of Month	In reply to Number	AAA

off aaa Have organised details of FROG and FROWN and sent them up to reinforce aaa Touch appears to be maintained with left but not with right aaa message ends aaa FRUGAL are in front of EAGLE TRENCH and have not been used aaa

FROM PLACE & TIME Felix Forward 12.15 pm

"O" Form. Army Form
MESSAGES AND SIGNALS. No. of Messa

Prefix...... Code...... Words...... Received from...... Sent or sent out. At......m Office Stamp
Charges to Collect By...... To......
Service Instructions Priority By...... 30
Handed in at...... Office......m. Received......m.

TO: Felix

Sender's Number	Day of Month	In reply to Number	AAA
9/225	9		

Do not try and push beyond Thine REQUETE FM LANDING FM WATER HO aaa maintain that line and fill gap reported by air observer between REQUETE FM and LANDING FM aaa added DROP reped OCEAN FELIX DOZEN DUST

FROM: DUKE
PLACE & TIME: 1.15 pm

"C" Form
MESSAGES AND SIGNALS.

Army Form C.2121

Prefix: LK Code: Words: 42
Received From: OCR By: man
Service Instructions: YDR Priority
Office: 7.47 a Received: 8.0 a.m.

TO 29 Divn

Sender's Number: GS206 Day of Month: 9

DROP reports 7:20 am aaa Begins aaa Prisoners captured by FELIX still coming in aaa No news from our front aaa Prisoners state 227 Div relieved 6 BAV. Div in line last night aaa Ends.

FROM PLACE & TIME: 4 Divn 7.45 am

"C" Form
MESSAGES AND SIGNALS.

Army Form C. 2121
(In books of 100.)

No. of Message..........

Prefix.......... Code SHW 61 Words..........
Received From: OCO
By: Mason

Sent, or sent out At..........m. To..........By..........

Office Stamp: TELEGRAPHS

Charges to collect..........
Service Instructions: OO

Handed in at.......... Office 7.43 a.m. Received 7.52 a.m.

TO: 29th Divn

*Sender's Number	Day of Month	In reply to Number	AAA
G68	9	—	

Situation 7.10 am still uncertain aaa all three Divs report prisoners aaa Right divn can give no definite information of their progress aaa fairly well confirmed reports from centre and left Divs that first objective is reached but further confirmation required aaa French progressing satisfactorily aaa addsd 5th Army repto All concerned

7-55 A

FROM PLACE & TIME: 14th Corps 7-30a

"C" Form
MESSAGES AND SIGNALS.

Army Form C. 2121
(In books of 100.)

No. of Message...........

| Prefix | Code F.d. | Words HH | Received From R By West | Sent, or sent out At .... m. To .... By | Office Stamp |

Charges to collect

Service Instructions.

Handed in at .... 6.7 .... Office .... 6.32 m. Received .... 7.3 .... m.

TO Felix

*Sender's Number	Day of Month	In reply to Number	AAA
15MV17H	9.		

R. Fus report everything going well aaa Prisoners coming down aaa guards down appear well over Hoemheek aaa Hardly any german barrage aaa Froglands report at least 200 prisoners passed Battn HQ aaa 1st objective now reported definitely taken

7.25 A

FROM PLACE & TIME   Fruit 6.30

*This line should be erased if not required.

"C" Form.
MESSAGES AND SIGNALS.

Army Form C 2123
(In books of 100).
No. of Message......

Prefix....Code....Words....	Received	Sent, or sent out	Office Stamp
£ s. d.	From............	At ....m	
Charges to Collect	By............	To	
Service Instructions		By	
Priority BS		12.5 pm	12.25 pm

Handed in at............Office............m Received............m

TO: Felix

Sender's Number	Day of Month	In reply to Number	AAA
BM 144	9		

From	Brigade	Major	U 23 B.4.5
Col	Stephens	has	60
men	at	TAUBE	FARM
aaa	He	has	~~ho~~ 50
men	with	him	at
OLGA	aaa	In	touch
with	codfisher	on	left
but	not	in	touch
with	right		
			12.33 pm

FROM PLACE & TIME: Front

"O" Form.
MESSAGES AND SIGNALS.

Army Form C 2123.
(In books of 100).

TO: 29th Divn

Sender's Number: R259
Day of Month: 9

Following from Fifth Army begins AAA 10.30 am small bodies of troops one behind the other look like sections moving south west on road in Sqt M Troops moving south west from STADEN D22d AAA Ten motor transport from HOOGLEDE to OOSTNIEUWKERKE moving very fast AAA Info AAA Guards 4 and 29 Div

12.20p

FROM PLACE & TIME: Fourteenth Corps 11.25 am

"C" Form. **MESSAGES AND SIGNALS.**			Army Form C 2123 (In books of 100). No. of Message......
Prefix......Code......Words...... £ s. d. Charges to Collect Service Instructions 2a dds Trinity	Received From............... By...............	Sent, or sent out. At ....m To .... By...............	Office Stamp
Handed in at BM Office 10.45 m Received 12.5 m			

TO: .... klr

Sender's Number	Day of Month	In reply to Number	AAA
BM 143	9		
Battalion	for	further	Objectives
established	OLGA	HOUSE	aaa
No	further	news	addressed
DROP	reptd	FLAG	
			(12.12pm)
FROM PLACE & TIME	Trinity		

* This line should be erased if not required

"O" Form.

MESSAGES AND SIGNALS.

No. of Message......

Prefix... Code...... Words...... Received... Sent, or sent out... Office Stamp.

Charges to Collect
Service Instructions

Handed in at......OCO......Office 11.5..m. Received 12.09..m.

TO 29th Div

Sender's Number	Day of Month	In reply to Number	AAA
676	9		

At 10 am observer suggests advance had not progressed beyond second objective AA Another aeroplane is going up to obtain confirmation AA Added 5th Army reptd all concerned

12.12 pm

FROM
PLACE & TIME

14th Corps
11.11 am

"O" Form.
Army Form C 2123.
(In books of 100).

MESSAGES AND SIGNALS.

Prefix...... Code..... Words......
Charges to Collect
Service Instructions Priority
Handed in at ...... Office ...... m. Received ...... m.

TO. 29 Div

Sender's Number: PJ 218 Day of Month: 9 AAA

Situation at 9 am from staff officer near front line AAA line appears to run Landing Farm – Compromise Fm – Huts between Water Ho and Miller Houses aaa no further reports of our right up to date AAA Enemy in front with M.G. opposite not serious but heavy shelling on leading troops AAA Ends

FROM PLACE & TIME: Duke Adv 11.40 am

"C" Form.
Army Form C.2123.
MESSAGES AND SIGNALS.

Handed in at H.Q. Office 11.07 m. Received 11.49 m.

TO: 29 Div

Sender's Number	Day of Month	In reply to Number	AAA
GS216	9		

No further news from our Front MA down on right report mg fire from NOBLES FARM and HELLS FARM

FROM PLACE & TIME: Drake Adv 11 am

"C" Form.
MESSAGES AND SIGNALS.

Army Form C 2121
(In books of 100).

TO	29 Divn

Sender's Number	Day of Month	In reply to Number	AAA
AG 257	9		

Following from Fifth Army begins AAA Inner patrol 10.15 area HOUTHULST Forest Westroosebeke Passchendaele all roads clear flying at 1500 feet AAA End AAA Aadsd Divisions

FROM PLACE & TIME: Fourteenth Corps 11·0 am

"O" Form.
MESSAGES AND SIGNALS.
Army Form C 2123.
(In books of 100).

No. of Message..........

Prefix.... Code........ Words.......
Charges to Collect
Service Instructions

Handed in at......CO........Office 11.34 m. Received 11.52 m.

TO 29th Divn

Sender's Number: SA56
Day of Month: 9

Following from Fifth Army begins. Air reconnaissance 9.15 am DIXMUDE road running north south through HOUTHULST FOREST and WESTROSE HOOGLEDE Road clear AA AA activity much above normal in HOUTHULST FOREST AAA Ends AAA Added Divns

11 am

FROM: 14 Corps
PLACE & TIME: 10.45 am

"C" Form.
MESSAGES AND SIGNALS.

Army Form C 2.
(In books of 100).

No. of Message...........

Prefix...... Code ..M.G.. Words ..131..

Received From ..V.C..
By ..H..

Sent, or sent out.
At .... m
To .... m
By ....

Charges to Collect

Service Instructions ..M.C..

Handed in at ..M.C.. Office ..12.35.. m   Received ..13.30.. m

TO Felix

Sender's Number	Day of Month	In reply to Number	AAA
GC 334	9th		

Following from FRUIT begins aaa following from FROWN timed 1040 am from Olga houses begins aaa situation appears very obscure we are not beyond 2nd objective aaa FROG and FROWN are reported to have lost the barrage aaa FROWN went up to reinforce aaa on left of second objective are about 50 of FROWN reported to be in TAUBE FARM aaa FROWN and FROG on their right very mixed up aaa enemy counter attacked on second objective but was driven

FROM
PLACE & TIME

V.40m

Army Form C 2123
"C" Form.
MESSAGES AND SIGNALS.

Prefix	Code	Words	Received From	Sent, or sent out At	Office Stamp
			YC		
Charges to Collect			By M	To	
Service Instructions				By	
Handed in at YC			Office 12.53 m	Received 13.39 m	

TO: Felix

| Sender's Number | Day of Month | In reply to Number | AAA |
| YC 335 | 9 | | |

Officer of FROWN wounded on 2nd objective states counter attack was at 8.30 am and consisted of 200-300 men aaa it was allowed to approach to within 200 yds of our lines and was then driven back

1.40 pm

FROM PLACE & TIME: Felix Forward
12.50 pm

"C" Form.
MESSAGES AND SIGNALS.
Army Form C 2123
(In books of 100).

No. of Message......

| Prefix... Code... Words 33 | Received From VC By H | Sent, or sent out. At ......m To ......By | Office Stamp |

Charges to Collect
Service Instructions

Handed in at VC Office 10.08 .m. Received 12.02 .m.

TO: **Felix**

| Sender's Number | Day of Month | In reply to Number | AAA |
| GC 330 | 9th | | |

Frog reported on second objective aaa no times given aaa wounded officer reports first going strong for third objective aaa was hit on second objective

12.10 pm

FROM
PLACE & TIME

Felix Forwd
9.55 am

* This line should be erased if not required

"A" Form
MESSAGES AND SIGNALS.

Army Form C. 2121
(in pads of 100).

TO	Felex G		

Flag Hdqrs is are	at	MARTINS
MILL	all	wires	are
cut.			

4.43 a.m.
9.10.17

From: Flag
Place:
Time:

S A McPaxton Capt

"C" FORM.
MESSAGES AND SIGNALS.

Prefix ... Code ... Words 30

Service Instructions: Priority

Handed in at: BHQ

TO: Felix

*Sender's Number	Day of Month	In reply to Number	AAA
BM 138	9th		

Prisoners of 477 regt. at present passing HQrs aaa Estimated 300 prisoners passed these HQrs aaa FRUGAL ~~report~~ start to move at 8am

12-20pm

FROM PLACE & TIME: Trent 7.50am

"C" FORM.
MESSAGES AND SIGNALS.

Army Form C. 2123.
(In books of 100.)

No. of Message................

| Prefix.... Code.... Words.... | Received. From...... By...... | Sent, or sent out. At.......m. To........ By...... | Office Stamp. |

Charges to Collect

Service Instructions
BG priority

Handed in at............... Office 11.18 m. Received 11.53 m.

TO Felix

*Sender's Number.	Day of Month.	In reply to Number.	AAA
Bm 142	9		

It is reported by
a walking wounded I/1/R
of FROWN that frog
have got second objective
aaa walking wounded of
FROWN report troops well up
to barrage near second objective
aaa our forward station now
in

FROM Frank
PLACE & TIME 9.45 am   12.20 p

*This line should be erased if not required.

"O" FORM.
MESSAGES AND SIGNALS.

Army Form C. 2123.
(In books of 100.)
No. of Message..................

| Prefix...... Code...... Words...... | Received. From...Trent... By...Watson... | Sent, or sent out. At......m To......m By...... 8a | Office Stamp. |

Charges to Collect
Service Instructions BG

Handed in at............ Office............m Received............m

TO Felixe

*Sender's Number.	Day of Month.	In reply to Number.	AAA
BM137	9th		

Walking wounded of 4/7 regt coming past Bde HQ aaa FROWN report bosche opposite us relieved last night

Confirmation

12.20pm

FROM
PLACE & TIME   Trent
7.25a

"C" FORM.
MESSAGES AND SIGNALS.

Army Form C. 2123.
(In books of 100.)

Prefix....Code....Words....	Received.	Sent, or sent out.	Office Stamp.
£ s. d.	From............	At............m.	
Charges to Collect	By...............		
Service Instructions		To...............	
By priority		By...............	

Handed in at................Office 0824 m. Received 0827 m.

TO Felix

*Sender's Number.	Day of Month.	In reply to Number.	AAA
Dm 139	9		

wire from EAGLE TR to FROG HQ broken aaa no more news yet

Confirmation

12.20pm

FROM PLACE & TIME Fruit 8.15am

† This line should be erased if not required.

"A" Form.
MESSAGES AND SIGNALS.

Army Form C. 2121

Appendix VIII

TO: FELIX

Sender's Number: GC 332   Day of Month: 9th

2	Coy	FLAME	reported
Consolidating	on	secured	objective
about	U 16 c 5.6	at	8.12 am
aaa	strength	2	Officers
12	OR	aaa	but
yet	in	touch	with
flanks	aaa	messages	received
by	FLAG	and	pushed
K	FLAME	aaa	up
T. Down	Established	OLGA	HOUSES
9.30 am			

From: FELIX Fowd.
Time: 10.30 am.

"O" FORM.
MESSAGES AND SIGNALS.

Army Form C. 2123.
(In books of 100.)

Prefix... AM... Code... Words... 37

From: Trink
By: Watson

Handed in at... B.4... Office... Received... 7.50...

TO Felix

Sender's Number	Day of Month	In reply to Number	AAA
BM 136	9th		

Frog report everything going well aaa Left Company report Boshe running away from them aaa Lots more prisoners coming in aaa FROWN report flanks Bde appear to be going strong

12-20 pm

FROM PLACE & TIME: Trink 7.20 am

Attach to diary

Army Form C. 2118.

Appendix VIII

WAR DIARY
or
INTELLIGENCE SUMMARY
(Erase heading not required.)

Instructions regarding War Diaries and Intelligence Summaries are contained in F.S. Regs., Part II. and the Staff Manual respectively. Title Pages will be prepared in manuscript.

Date	Hour	From Whom Received	Summary of Events and Information	Action Taken	Remarks and references to Appendices
Oct. 9th.	6-15	R.A. Telephone.	No shelling of STEEN BEEK. Right Enemy barrage from REITRES Fm to ALOUETTE. 45 prisoners 17', 172, 417.		
	6-15	VULCAN.	88th report 50 prisoners on Rly –		
	6-45	86th	1st Obj. reported taken. at least 100 prisoners at HQ 1/Lanc Fus. Prisoners from 227. Div. 441 Regt. 88th reported point well. over the BROEMBEEK. Barrage Excellent. All forward toll.	XIV Corps. Sobs +4th Dv informed. G110650. RA by telephone –	
	7-5.	VULCAN	Officer 417th Regt. 445 OR 417, 171, 172. passed 6-30 am. Captured by NFLD soon after crossing BROEMBEEK.		
	7-10	VULCAN	86th report trouble from M.G. POESAT Fm but Howrs turned on.	RA informed	
	7-15.	Guards Telephone.	Reported on 1st Objective. Observer report Guards Right in touch with 29th Dn –		
	7-20	Guards Dn	Observer at VULCAN reports infantry on 1st objective at 2 + 4.5. Both Dvs in touch.		

2449 Wt. W14957/M90 750,000 1/16 J.B.C. & A. Forms/C.2118/12.

WAR DIARY
or
INTELLIGENCE SUMMARY

(Erase heading not required.)

Army Form C. 2118.

Instructions regarding War Diaries and Intelligence Summaries are contained in F. S. Regs., Part II. and the Staff Manual respectively. Title Pages will be prepared in manuscript.

Place	Date	Hour	From whom Received	Summary of Events and Information	Remarks and references to Appendices
		7.50	Corps I.G.S.S	Aeroplane at 6.40 A.m. report LT 16 whole of GREEN DOTTED Line gained along Corps front, and of 6th Brand	
		8.3.	4th Div.	12th Bde. 7.20 A.m. Prisoners captured by 26th Div still coming in. No news from front. Prussian slide 227th Div relieved 6 Brass in line last night.	
		8.30	Corps	2nd Army reported to have gained their first objective.	
		8.45	1st Div.	Prisoners of 47th I.R. 441st Inf Regt Staff 227th Div. relieved 6th Div. Padkym 417th I.R. Captured near Railway - 441st relieved Div in the ground left sector of 417th unknown.	

ACTION TAKEN

2449 Wt. W14957/M90 750,000 1/16 J.B.C. & A. Forms/C.2118/12.

Army Form C.

WAR DIARY
or
INTELLIGENCE SUMMARY
(Erase heading not required.)

Instructions regarding War Diaries and Intelligence Summaries are contained in F.S. Regs., Part II. and the Staff Manual respectively. Title Pages will be prepared in manuscript.

Place	Date	Hour	From Whom Received	Summary of Events and Information	Action Taken	Remarks and references to Appendices
		8.45	29(D)" (Forward Telephone)	5 officers & 130 O.Rs passed Prisoners Cage at 8am. No enemy Barrage – Brandhoek on fire – found on the right – B2.H. O.T.O. Bn of OLGA HOUSES. HANTS 9 mins found on Right to EAGLE TR. NFLD Being seen going up to go through 2nd objective.		
		8.55	B.G.G.S. Corps Telephone.	18th Corps Reporting through POELCAPELLE.		
		9.00	Telephone	Guards Division reporting on 2nd Objective.		
		9 am	4th Div.	44th Regt relieved 13th Bav. 47th Regt had 4 Coys in front line. Coy munich strength 125. 8 prisoners of Guy Bnd'n. Officer says there are old & expert comm'l attack By 227th Div. but by comm'l attacking troops units of whom are unknown.		
		9.20	4th Division	Verbal Report from F.O.O at 6.15 am states 12 Infy Bde. passed two objectives easily - all going well - prisoners coming in in large numbers.		
		9.40	4th Div.	Observers report 88th Bde going forward well.		
		9.40	XIV Corps.	Corps on right have taken prisoners from 135th Regt 42nd Div. from Russia. 234 Div. in process of relieving 18th Division.		
		9.45	4th Div.	Prisoners of 477th & 478th Regt captured in POELCAPELLE. 10th battle relieved 10th Bavarian J.R. on night of 5/6". Bavarian open relieved 10th in trenches. All 4 Coys of 1st Batt. 477th Regt in front line. Coy strength said to be 130-150.		

Army Form C. 2118.

WAR DIARY
or
INTELLIGENCE SUMMARY

(Erase heading not required.)

Instructions regarding War Diaries and Intelligence Summaries are contained in F. S. Regs., Part II. and the Staff Manual respectively. Title Pages will be prepared in manuscript.

Place	Date	Hour	From whom Received	Summary of Events and Information	Remarks and references to Appendices
				ACTION TAKEN.	
		9.45	Guards Div:	8.05 am Drawn upon on troops now consolidating behind new line. In touch with R + L divisions. Enemy barrage on STEENBEEK + BROEMBEEK LIGHT. Saw a three hundred persons coming in. At 6.15am carrying parties carrying ZEEDactive. Noise of hostile activity.	
		9.55	29th Div: Forward	Message received from 4 Division that N.F.L.D. Dmy Hqrs.	
		9.58	"	Casualties reported on 2nd Objective.	
		10 am	"	H.Q. 116th Bde.is moving to OLGA HOUSES - Artry passing VULCAN CROSSING at 9.45 am. H.Q. Hants moved to LEOPARD TR: No information from 2nd objective.	
		10.10.	4th Div.	F.O.O. upon 0.7 7.35 States 2nd attack proceeding favourably. Enemy barrage consequently shortened but not very intense. Later report about 9.42. States many large fires seen behind enemy lines.	
		10.12.	Air Corps.	Aeroplane patrol upon no enemy concentration or movement seen in or behind area POELCAPELLE along road to NAMUR CROSSING - along railway to SCHAAP BAILIE - VIJFWEGEN - WESTROSEBEEK between 6.50 + 8 am. At 7.10 large fire at dump V.8.a.8.4. No E.A. seen along front.	
		10.20.	Intelligence 25th Div. Telephone.	Prisoners belong to 417, 441, 477th (R) Regt. Found at Genn reported lost.	

Army Form C. 2118.

WAR DIARY
or
INTELLIGENCE SUMMARY

(Erase heading not required.)

Instructions regarding War Diaries and Intelligence Summaries are contained in F. S. Regs., Part II. and the Staff Manual respectively. Title Pages will be prepared in manuscript.

Place	Date	Hour	From whom Rec'd.	Summary of Events and Information	Remarks and references to Appendices
		10:30	29th Bde. Fwd. Telephone	88th Bde message from 2 Coy Worcestrs 2 Sp 12 O.R. left A&T in touch with Hawkes on second objective. Timed 8.12 am.	
		10:30	"	H.Q. 2nd R. Fus. moved to OLGA H2 at 9.30 am.	
		10:50	Map	Shewing troops still on 2nd Obj — unaffected. Observer. 2nd plane sent up.	
		11:5	XIV Corps	2/4th Army reports — Patrol reports @ at 11.15 am Bavarians were HOUTHOULST FOREST — WESTROSEBEEKE — PASSCHENDALE. Flying at 1500 feet.	
		11:15	88th Bde Telephone	Report from Worcestrs as follows — Consolidation going on well. 2nd Objective reached. Now going up to inspect by 4th MANUR is good). Advance on final objective appears good — no of our planes. SKIP over at PASCAL Fm. Enemy planes active shots shelling heavy but wild. Timed 9.40.	
		12:00	4th Div.	No fur news from front. 11th Div. report M.G. fire from NOBLES Fm + HELLS Fm.	

Army Form C. 2118.

WAR DIARY
or
INTELLIGENCE SUMMARY
(Erase heading not required.)

Date	Hour	From whom Received	Summary of Events and Information	Remarks and references to Appendices
	12.12	86th Bde	Battn. for further objective established at OLGA H.Q.	
	12.12	XIV Corps	Observer at 10 am reports Odrama had not proceeded beyond second objective. Awaiting acceptance in going up to obtain confirmation.	
	12.10	29th Div Forward (Telephone)	2nd R. Fus at OLGA H.Q. at 10.40 am. Situation obscure — we are not beyond 2nd objective. Lanc. Fus & R. Fus reported taken on the barrage. R Fus went up to reinforce. So B. 2nd R Fus are on left of the 2nd objective & report they are in TAUBE Pt. Lanc. Fus & R Fus on their right very mixed up. Enemy counter-attacked on 2nd objective but was driven off. Details B R Fus & Lanc Fus have been organised & sent up to reinforce. Touch appears to be maintained with the left but not with the right.	
	12.05	86th Bde (Telephone)	16th buds are in front of EAGLE TR. They have not been employed. Bde H.Q. has gone up & will probably be back in EAGLE TR very shortly. Bgde orders in touch with EAGLE TR. by telephone.	
	12.30	29th Div. Intelligence (Telephone)	7 Officers & 237 O.Rs passed through Dura collecting village. They appear above heart.	

Army Form C. 2118.

WAR DIARY
or
INTELLIGENCE SUMMARY
(Erase heading not required.)

Place	Date	Hour	From whom Received	Summary of Events and Information	Action Taken	Remarks and references to Appendices
		12.30	Guards Divn.	F.O.O's & pigeon messages from 3rd Grenadier Guards. (Correction) that GREEN LINE final objective was Cap'd up to scheduled timings and is being consolidated.		
		12.30	XIV Corps.	No X.T. 259 movement of enemy troops.		
		12.40	Artillery (Telephone).	Report F.O.O. spot that general divn of enemy in 2nd Objective. Counter attack by enemy was reported at 10.40.		
		13.05	29/12 Divn Forward (Telephone).	Message from N.F.L.D. to 86th Bgde reads "Have captured 3rd Objective – very heavy shelling – Established H.Q. at PASCAL Fm – Please send up S.A.A."		
		13.10	29/15 Divn Forward	Lancs Fus reported on 2nd Objective, no Essex Essex, wounded Officer Reports N.F.L.D. going strong on the 3rd Objective was hit on Second objective.		
		14.15	86/15 July Bgde (Telephone)	Report from OLGA HOUSES that enemy are massing at V.7 cent. TURENNE X – ARGLE POINT.	Artillery informed.	

WAR DIARY
or
INTELLIGENCE SUMMARY

(Erase heading not required.)

Army Form C. 2118.

Date	Hour	Summary of Events and Information	Remarks and references to Appendices
14/10	XIV Corps.	Aeroplane reports there is now line BREWERY in POELCAPELLE - HELLES Xrd - V.14.c.4.8. - Thence a gap to LANDING Fm V.13.b.7.1. - Thence to SENEGAL Fm V.7.d.4.1. - to TAUBE Fm V.7.a.6.0. - Thence to railway at V.7.a.6.9. Thence along final objective. Heavy counter attack in neighbourhood of V.7.b.4. forced that portion of attack to lose the barrage. Divisions will there consolidate ground now held. 4th Div will close gap between REQUETTE Fm. & Bavarian pierre 600.	
14/10	S.B. Forward.	Following message picked up by wireless "Situation at present vague - attack held up at MIDDx ? Houses. Three are now cleared and attack appears to be progressing. Bn HdQrs MILLERS Ho. & Bavarian Couralli 120-150. From 12th Bde."	

Army Form C. 2118.

WAR DIARY
or
INTELLIGENCE SUMMARY
(Erase heading not required.)

Instructions regarding War Diaries and Intelligence Summaries are contained in F. S. Regs., Part II. and the Staff Manual respectively. Title Pages will be prepared in manuscript.

Place	Date	Hour	From whom Rec'd.	Summary of Events and Information	Action Taken	Remarks and references to Appendices
		15:00	86th Bde	Counter attack beaten off.		
		15:40	Guards Div	Report that Right Bde reports enemy tracking on A5ing at COLBERG CROSS ROADS		
		16:35	XIV Corps	Fifth army report at 1:55 pm two bodies of troops about 300 in all on DIXMUDE Rd P19.a.9.c. Direction uncertain but probably South. Otherwise no road movement seen in area STADEN – HOOGLEDE – ROULERS – MOORSLEDE.		
		16:45	88th Bde	"new form of raiders" report front line runs approx: U.6.d.8.0. to V.7.a.4.0. – V.7.a.0.1. with posts in front of TAUBE HOSPITAL is held by enemy, we are in touch with 1st Bde on left and with 2nd R. Fus on right.		
		17:00	Intelligence 29th Div	7/Ws 295 ORs through Div: collecting cage. There are known to be more working up been 160 enemy		

2449 Wt. W14957/M90 750,000 1/16 J.B.C. & A. Forms/C.2118/12.

Army Form C. 2118.

WAR DIARY
or
INTELLIGENCE SUMMARY

(Erase heading not required.)

Instructions regarding War Diaries and Intelligence Summaries are contained in F. S. Regs., Part II. and the Staff Manual respectively. Title Pages will be prepared in manuscript.

Date	Hour	From whom Received	Summary of Events and Information	Remarks and references to Appendices
				Action Taken.
	17.45	XIV Corps	Message reads "Division will consolidate line shown on map dropped at 4 pm and will also gain by patrols tonight all ground possible up to the line LANDING F^m - WATER H^o - SENEGAL F^m - TAUBE F^m. A strong second line will be made along the road from POELCAPPELLE to den 5 Chemins.	
11.4.46	18.10	Guards Divn	Situation 5 pm - we hold GREEN LINE throughout including Strong Point at U.11.a.6.8. from which prisoners were taken. Enemy reported active in K.1.a. Heavy Enemy shelling of 2nd Objective.	
	18.25	Guards Div	Report 4 battns of enemy moving in extended order from direction of COLBERT CROSS ROADS:	R.A. informed also 86th Bgde.
	18.25	R A XIV Corps	Instructions to artillery to shoot frequently tonight all roads & railways in vicinity of SCHAAP BAILIE between STADEN-DREYE-BEKE & HOOTHOULST FOREST. Also to concentrate bursts after every two hours on same area through night.	

2449 Wt. W14957/M90 750,000 1/16 J.B.C. & A. Forms/C.2118/12.

Army Form C. 2118.

WAR DIARY
or
INTELLIGENCE SUMMARY

(Erase heading not required.)

Instructions regarding War Diaries and Intelligence Summaries are contained in F.S. Regs., Part II. and the Staff Manual respectively. Title Pages will be prepared in manuscript.

Place	Date	Hour	From whom Received	Summary of Events and Information	Remarks and references to Appendices
				Action Taken	
		19.45	XIV Corps.	Our troops has been driven back from 200 – 300ˣ – Contact patrol shows line now running V.13.d.7.1. – V.13.d.3.6 – COMPROMIS F^m – V.13.a.8.7 – V.17.c.9.0 – V.7.c.3.3 – V.7.C.3.7 – Railway at V.7.a.2.6 – V.1.c.6.0 – Angle point – 5 chemins – U.5.d.8.3 – U.10.6.3.9 – U.11.a.7.8. – U.5.c.3.0.	
	10/5	04.30	88th Bgde	Situation unaltered. Quiet.	
	"	5.30	88th Bgde.	Australians relieved two coys of 8th Worcesters on 1st Objective. Remaining coys digging in on approximately the same line. Two coys of Worcesters on 2nd objective relieved by two coys S. N.F.L.D.	
	"	7.30	88th Bgde.	Barrage timed 5.40 am from N.F.L.D. to 88th Bgde roads from line runs approx: TRANQUILLE H^o – EGYPT H^o road. Fen? tried in touch with Puschino Aud grades. Enemy patrol captured near Bⁿ H.Q. by 8th Warwicks Cazuallies on 8th ? 9 OR's 0 Pars.	

Army Form C. 2118.

SECRET. 29th Division No. C.G.S.65/240.

29TH DIVISION WARNING ORDER.
-o-o-o-o-o-o-o-o-o-o-o-o-o-o-o-o-o-o-

12th October, 1917.

1.　　The 29th Division (less Artillery) accompanied by one Divisional Supply Column will be transferred from XIV Corps to Third Army on 15th, 16th, 17th October, under orders which will be issued later.

2.　　The Divisional Supply Column and other motor vehicles will move by road.
　　　　The remaining troops mentioned in para. 1 will move by rail.
　　　　Arrangements for the above movements will be notified later.

3.　　Entraining stations for the above moves will be HOPOUTRE and PESELHOEK.
　　　　Any restrictions as to routes to entraining stations will be issued later.

4.　　The 29th Divisional Artillery will be transferred to Third Army at a later date, under orders to be issued separately.

5.　　ACKNOWLEDGE.

　　　　　　　　　　　　　　　　　　Lieut-Colonel, G.S.,
Issued at　11.45　　　　　　　　　　29th Division.

Copies to :-
"C".　　　　　　　　　　D.A.D.O.S.
C.R.A.　　　　　　　　　D.A.D.V.S.
C.R.E.　　　　　　　　　S.A.A. Sec. D.A.C.
86th Inf. Bde.　　　　　227th M.G. Coy.
87th Inf. Bde.　　　　　Camp Commdt.
88th Inf. Bde.　　　　　Divl. Train.
Off. i/c Sigs.　　　　　S.S.O.
1/2nd Monmouths.　　　　29th D.S.C.
A.D.M.S.　　　　　　　　XIV Corps.
A.P.M.　　　　　　　　　1/Guernsey L.I.
D.M.G.O.　　　　　　　　Area Commdt. PROVEN.

M.

SECRET   29th Division No. 2014/2.

1. The following orders and instructions are issued regarding the move of by rail of the 29th Division (less Artillery).

2. Time table and order of entrainment attached. Approximate length of journey seven hours.

3. The A.P.M. will make the necessary arrangements to control traffic on the road approaches to the entraining Stations, and no troops or transport should be allowed to enter the Station Yards until the R.T.O. is ready.

4. (a) All trains consist of 1 Officers carriage: 17 flat trucks: 30 covered trucks.
   (b) (i) Each flat truck will take an average of 4 axles.
       (ii) Each covered truck will take 6 H.D. Horses, or 8 L.D. Horses or Mules., or 40 men.
   (c) No personnel or stores will be allowed in the brake vans at each end of the train, or on the roofs of the trucks. No covered trucks should be used for baggage as it restricts space available for personnel.

5. The transport of Infantry Battalions will arrive at entraining stations 3 hours and personnel 1½ hours before the departure of the train.
   Other Units will arrive complete 3 hours before the departure of the train.

6. (a) The following fatigue parties are required at entraining stations:-

   At PESELHOEK

   87th Brigade will detail 1 Company from 1st Border Regiment to load Nos. 1, 2, 3, and 4 Trains.

   88th Brigade will detail 1 Company from 1st Newfoundland Regiment to load trains from No. 5 to 11 inclusive.

   The Royal Guernsey Light Infantry will be responsible for the loading of their own train.

   At HOUPOUTRE.

   87th Brigade will detail 1 Company, Royal Inniskilling Fusiliers, to load trains Nos. 1, 2, and 3, and the Company of Royal Inniskilling Fusiliers travelling by No. 7 train will be detailed to load trains from No. 4 to No. 7 inclusive.
   The 86th Brigade will detail 1 Company Royal Dublin Fusiliers, to load trains Nos. 8 to 11 inclusive.
   The Monmouth Regiment will be responsible for the loading of their own train.
   These parties will report to the R.T.O. at entraining stations three hours before the departure of the first train they have to load.

P.T.O.

(b) The following fatigue parties will be required at detraining stations.

AT SAULTY.

The 87th Brigade will detail 1 Company 1st K.O.S.B. to unload trains Nos. 1, 2, 3, and 4.

The 88th Brigade 1 Company, 4th Worcester Regiment, to unload Trains Nos. 5 to 11 inclusive.

The Royal Guernsey Light Infantry will be responsible for unloading train No. 12.

AT BEAUMETZ.

The 87th Brigade will detail 1 Company South Wales Borderers to unload trains Nos. 1, 2, 3, and 4.

The 86th Brigade will detail 1 Company 2nd. Royal Fusiliers to unload trains Nos. 5, 6, and 7, and 1 Company of 16th Bn. Middlesex Regiment to unload trains Nos. 8 to 11.

The Monmouth Regiment will be responsible for unloading train No. 12.

7. Brigades will detail an Officer to remain at the entraining station until the last train of the Brigade Group is ready to be despatched. He will report to the R.T.O. three hours prior to the departure of the first train and render all necessary assistance.

An Officer will also be detailed to remain at the station until the detraining of the Brigade Group is complete. He will also report to R.T.O. at Detraining Station immediately on arrival.

8. A complete marching out state showing the numbers of men, horses, G.S., limbered G.S., and 2 wheeled wagons and bicycles should be sent down with the transport of every unit, so that accommodation in the train can be checked by the R.T.O. at the beginning of the entrainment.

9. Supply and baggage wagons will accompany <u>their own Units in every case.</u>

10. The entrainment of all units must be completed half an hour before the time of departure of train.

11. Breast ropes for horse trucks must be provided by the Units themselves: ropes for lashing vehicles on the flat trucks will be provided by the railway.

12. Pickets must be provided at all stops for each end of the train to prevent troops leaving.

13. All doors of covered trucks and carriages on the right-hand side of the train, when on the main line, should be kept closed.

LMAcock

Lieut. Colonel,
A.A. & Q.M.G., 29th Division.

Entrain PESSIMOUK.
Detrain - Sewth (Resund?)

No. of Train.	Unit.	Date.	Time of Departure.
1.	1st K.O.S.B., less 1 Coy., 1 Cooker & team	15th	14-30
2.	87th Bde. H.Q., 87th M.G.Co., 87th T.M.B., 87th Bde. Signals. 1 Coy., 1 Cooker and team, 1st K.O.S.B.	15th	18-20.
3.	No. 227 M.G.Co. 87th Field Ambulance.	15th	22-30
4.	1st Border Regt., less 1 Co., 1 Cooker and team.	16th	2-30
5.	4th Bn. Worcester Regt.	16th	6-30
6.	2nd Bn. Hampshire Regt.	16th	10-20
7.	88th Brigade H.Q., 88th M.G.Co., 88th T.M.B., 88th Brigade Signals. 1 Coy. 1st Border Regt., 1 Cooker and team.	16th	14-30
8.	1st Bn. Essex Regt.	16th	18-20

Entrain LOUPOUTHE.
Detrain Resund

No. of Train.	Unit.	Date.	Time of departure.
1.	2nd Bn. S.W.Bords.	15th	12-25
2.	H.Q., Div. R.E. No. 455th (W.Riding) Field Co.		
3.	No. 3 Co. Div. Train.	15th	16-45
	1st Bn. R.Inn. Fus., less 1 Co., 1 Cooker & team.	15th	20-35
4.	29th Div. H.Q. H.Q. and No. 1 Sect. Div. Signals. ½ Employment Co.	16th	0-45
5.	2nd Bn. Royal Fusiliers	16th	4-45
6.	1st Bn. Lancashire Fusrs.	16th	8-35
7.	86th Brigade H.Q., 86th M.G.Co., 86th T.M.B. 86th Brigade Signal Co. 1 Coy. Royal Innis. Fus., 1 Cooker and team.	16th	12-25
8.	16th Bn. Middlesex Regt.	16th	16-45

PTO

Entrain PESELHOEK.
Detrain

No. of train.	Unit.	Date	Time of departure.
9.	H.Q. Div. Train. No. 4 Coy. Div. Train. No. 510th .: (London) Field Coy.	16th	22-30
10.	88th Field Ambulance. 18th Mobile Veterinary Sect. 1 Coy. Royal Guernsey Light Infantry, 1 Cooker, 1 team. ½ Employment Co.	17th	2-30
11.	1st Newfoundland Regt.	17th	6-30
12.	Royal Guernsey Light Infantry less 1 Coy., 1 Cooker and team.	17th	10-20

Entrain HOUPOUTRE.
Detrain

No. of train.	Unit.	Date	Time of departure.
9.	No. 497 (Kent) Field Co. No. 2 Coy. Div. Train.	16th	20-35
10.	89th Field Ambulance. 1 Coy. Monmouth Regt, 1 Cooker and team.	17th	0-45
11.	1st Royal D.Fus.	17th	4-45
12.	1/2nd Monmouth Regt., less 1 Coy. 1 Cooker and team.	17th	8-35

Appendix X

SECRET.   Copy No. 4

29TH DIVISION ORDER NO. 163.
-o-o-o-o-o-o-o-o-o-o-o-o-o-o-o-o-

Map Ref. 1/20,000, 28 N.W.
         1/20,000, 27 N.E.   October 14th, 1917.

1.   The 29th Division (less Artillery) will be transferred from FIFTH ARMY to the THIRD ARMY.

2.   Moves will be carried out by train on 15th, 16th and 17th instant. Train arrangements and billets on arrival will be issued later.

3.   Troops will entrain at HOUPOUTRE (L.17.d.) and PESELHOEK (A.26.b.).

4.   Routes to Entraining Stations.

   (a) Troops for HOUPOUTRE.

          PROVEN - POPERINGHE Road.

   (b) Troops for PESELHOEK.

          INTERNATIONAL CORNER - Road Junction A.20.d.

5.   The Divisional Supply Column and other motor vehicles will move by road under orders to be issued later.

6.   The 29th Divisional Artillery will be transferred to the THIRD ARMY at a later date, under orders to be issued separately.

7.   ACKNOWLEDGE.

                                     Lieut-Colonel, G.S.,
                                         29th Division.

Issued at

Copies to :-
   Nos. 1 - 5 G.S.   20 D.A.D.O.S.
         6   "Q".   21 D.A.D.V.S.
         7   C.R.A.   22 S.A.A. Sect. D.A.C.
         8   C.R.E.   23 227th M.G. Coy.
       9 - 10 86th Bde.   24 Camp Commdt.
      11 - 12 87th Bde.   25 Divl. Train.
      13 - 14 88th Bde.   26 S.S.O.
         15   Off. i/c Sigs.   27 29th D.S.C.
         16   1/2nd Lons.   28 XIV Corps.
         17   A.D.M.S.   29 1/Guernsey L.I.
         18   A.P.M.   30 Area Commdt. PROVEN.
         19   D.A.G.O.

B.

Reports on

Operations

Miscellaneous

SECRET.   29th Division No. C.G.S.72/62.

86th Inf. Bde.
88th Inf. Bde.
87th Inf. Bde.
C.R.A.
----

1.   All troops should be reminded of the importance of lighting flares, when asked for by a contact aeroplane. Should flares not be available, troops should signal to the aeroplane by waving their arms or handkerchiefs, and thus facilitate very greatly the task of the observer.

2.   All troops should also be reminded that the signal from the infantry to a tank, that a tank is wanted, is as follows :-   Helmets placed on the end of fixed Bayonets, and raised straight above the head.

A.T.Miller Capt

                                     Lieut-Colonel, G.S.,
7th October, 1917.   29th Division.

Copies down to Company Commanders.

M.

SECRET.   29th Division No.C.G.S.56/20.

NOTES FOR COMPANY COMMANDER.
-o-o-o-o-o-o-o-o-o-o-o-o-o-o-o-o-o-o-

1. Present fighting efficiency of the Battalion.

2. Task in view. Where difficulty may be expected.

3. How to deal with above
    - (a) Close to barrage.
    - (b) Use of rifle grenades, Lewis guns, and smoke grenades.
    - (c) A Flank to be turned. Signals to sections.
    - (d) Determination to get there.

4. Compasses. Direction Bearing - Set Compass.

5. Every man to know what to do.

6. Smoke in Barrage to denote 1st Objective.

7. Consolidation
    - (a) Connect up with Flanks.
    - (b) Covering parties.
    - (c) Dig in. Dont crowd.
    - (d) Tell off men to light flares (3).
    - (e) Prepare for counter-attack (Right Flank).

8. Action of Supports and Reserve.

9. S.O.S. Signals - practice.

10. Arrange guides with tape for relief.

11. Rum and Hot food.
    Cleaning of Arms.
    March discipline.

12. No Barrage; no attack of PURPLE line.

13. Counter-attack Battalion.

14. Patrol followed by Platoon at 100 yards followed by Company at 150 yards.

29th Divn. HdQrs.

7th Oct. 1917.

SECRET. Ha Deay 29th Division No. I.G.103/19.

XIV Corps.

In reply to your No. G.136/1 of 10/10/17, para. 1.

1.   The 29th Division was engaged in the fighting in the ARRAS sector from April 13th - June 3rd, when it was taken out of the line until June 29th, on which date it took over a sector of the line N. of YPRES.

The battle casualties incurred by the Division during the ARRAS operations were 278 Officers and 5744 Other Ranks, and the sick wastage 28 Officers 822 Other Ranks, a total of 6892.

2.   The state of training when the Division took over the line on September 22nd was ~~fair~~ *good*, but the training of the Officers left room for considerable improvement. Since September 22nd numerous casualties have been incurred, and fresh drafts have been received, and a period of training is desirable to restore the Division to its previous fighting efficiency.

3.   Reinforcements now on their way to join the Division, and which have been accumulating at the Corps Reinforcement Depot, total 85 Officers 1614 Other Ranks. The strength of the infantry now present with the Division is 389 Officers 10,464 Other Ranks (excluding Pioneers). This total includes a fresh Battalion (1st Guernsey Light Infantry), who have not yet been in action or held trenches.

4.   Battle Casualties incurred by the Division during the last two months in the course of operations N. of YPRES amount to 206 Officers 4530 Other Ranks. The sick evacuated during this period totalled 44 Officers 860 Other Ranks. Total 5640.

5.   The first period of operations in this sector, i.e. June 29th - July 21st was spent in holding the line during the temporary withdrawal of the 38th Division, in preparing the trenches and accumulating stores for this Division,

/ who

- 2 -

who were to carry out active operations in that sector. The casualties incurred during this period amounted to about 1000.

From August 8th to August 29th the Division was in the Left Sector of the Corps front and took part in the attack on August 16th.

From September 22nd to October 11th the Division held the Left, and subsequently the Centre Sectors of the Corps front and carried out attacks on October 4th and 9th.

The total wastage in the Division for the six months from April 10th to October 10th amounts to :- 644 Officers 13,792 Other Ranks, this does not include Casualties in the Divisional Artillery, R.E. or Pioneer Bn.

6. **29th Divisional Artillery.**

The 29th Divisional Artillery were in action in the ARRAS Sector from about April 1st to June 22nd when they were withdrawn from the line.

The Battle Casualties during this period were 40 Officers and 327 O.R. and the Sick wastage 6 Officers and 227 Other Ranks.

They remained at rest until June 30th when they marched to YPRES and came into action on July 15th. In action from July 15th to August 30th when they were withdrawn to wagon lines until September 15th, on which date they again came into action and are still in the line.

7. The training whilst in rest has been elementary but much good work was done with signallers. The present state of training is fair.

8. The number of Reinforcements received during the last two months is 27 Officers 408 Other Ranks. The present strength including D.A.C. is 92 Officers and 2350 Other Ranks.

9. Battle Casualties incurred in the course of operations N. of YPRES amount to 27 Officers and 429 Other Ranks, and the Sick wastage to 16 Officers and 325 Other Ranks. Total 797.

10. **Divisional Engineers.**

All three Field Companies went into the line with

/ the

- 3 -

the Division on August 7th and worked continuously in the line until August 26th when they were withdrawn to rest.

On September 6th, 510th (London) Field Company went forward and worked on forward roads under C.E., XIV Corps until 14th September, 1917, when they returned to rest area.

All three Field Companies were working in the forward area whilst the Division was in the line from September 20th, 1917, to October 11th, 1917.

12. The state of training is good.

13. The number of reinforcements recently received is 3 Officers and 39 Other Ranks. The present strength is 24 Officers 635 Other Ranks.

14. The Battle Casualties during the period August 7th to October 11th, 1917, amount to 3 Officers and 48 Other Ranks.

15. Pioneer Battalion.

The Battalion last returned to the line on 19th September.

The present state of training of the Bn. is fair.

The number of reinforcements lately received is 8 Officers and 112 Other Ranks, and the present strength of the Bn. is 47 Officers and 1067 Other Ranks.

The Battle Casualties incurred during the last two months amount to 4 Officers and 94 Other Ranks, and the Sick wastage to 2 Officers and 57 Other Ranks.

(Sgd) Beauvoir de Lisle.
Major-General,
Commanding 29th Division.

15th October, 1917.

M.

Period 7th August, 1917 to 11th October, 1917.

| Unit. | Reinforcements. | | TOTAL. | Casualties. | | | | | TOTAL. |
	Officers.	O.R.		Killed. O.R.	Wounded. O.R.	Wounded. O.R.	Wounded at duty. O.R.	Wounded at duty. O.R.	
Headquarters.	-	1	1	-	-	-	-	-	-
455th Field Co.	-	8	8	-	-	-	5	-	3	8
497th Field Co.	1	16	17	-	2	1	19	-	-	22
510th Field Co.	2	14	16	-	1	2	10	-	8	21
TOTAL.	3	39	42	-	3	3	34	-	11	51

War Diary

29th Division No. G.G.S. 70/54.

VI Corps.

Reference to your G.473 of the 13th October, the following notes are submitted.

(a) In all cases troops were assembled in the open. Jumping off trenches were not used. Previous to the attack the frontage of the leading Companies was taped out and an arrow was placed in the centre of the tape to mark the direction of the advance. The tape should be laid at right angles to the line of advance. Company markers should be sent forward to mark the flanks of Companies on the tape and protective patrols sent out in advance to keep off enemy patrols or to give warning of counter-attacks. Attacking troops should be moved up in close formation on to the tapes, each Company extending along the tape to its marker thus avoiding overlapping or gaps. When attacking troops are new to the country great care is necessary when moving up to assembly positions. All duckboard tracks, etc. should be piquetted under the supervision of officers or else tapes raised well off the ground should be used to mark the line of approach to the assembly tapes. A single strand of wire on screw picquets proved of great value where tapes were not procurable. Tapes should be labelled every 500 yards shewing the destination in each direction. If possible they should be made broader and of cheaper material than the present issue. Ropes were used for the crossing of the BROEMBEEK and proved of great assistance. The ground was very heavy and waterlogged and ropes assisted the men who fell into the mud.

(b) Leading waves should be as lightly equipped as possible: hence the importance of moving forward dumps of fighting necessities is increased.

170 rounds of S.A.A. is as much as a man can carry, but more ammunition is required after the objective has been reached. This must be brought up by fresh troops from the rear.

Every N.C.O. and man except the Nos. 1 and 2 of Lewis Gun teams should carry a pick or shovel.

Additional Machine Gun belts carried in the haversack proved useful, they can be filled with ammunition collected from casualties.

The number of rifle grenades and bombs laid down in S.S.135 proved sufficient. The Hales rifle grenade was of doubtful value owing to its very local effect in wet ground.

It is suggested that carrying parties should always be detailed to follow up assaulting Battalions with S.A.A., water and rations, assembling in rear of the rearmost wave and moving forward when the assaulting troops reach the objective or at about Zero plus 4 hours. All movement backwards from the objective to dumps is to be deprecated.

Pack animals in the case of one Brigade proved of the greatest value. On Z day the ground was reconnoitred for mule tracks and tapes laid to the Advanced Bn. H.Q. and on Z plus 1 Night, animals were able to get up to Bn. H.Q. taking up stores and ammunition without difficulty.

/ (c)

(c) All but leading waves should keep in Artillery formation as long as possible.

Bns. should be trained in advancing under a barrage in lines of half platoons or sections moving in file at short interval so as to cross shell torn country without getting mixed up. This formation lessens casualties, lends itself to better direction and better control of sections by those in command.

(d) On gaining the objective a proportion of Lewis Guns should be pushed well forward into shell holes to cover the consolidation. Thus used they proved of the greatest XXXXX use in helping to break up counter-attacks. Quickness of decision and readiness to take advantage of fleeting opportunities are what is most required from Lewis Gunners. The greatest difficulty experienced was to keep the guns clean and a good cover which can be quickly removed is necessary.

(e) These are best dealt with by rushing them in the first instance and only trying to work round them if this fails. Vital necessity of troops being taught that if they keep close to a heavy barrage opposing infantry will be so dazed that Pill boxes will fall easy victims to a determined advance.

In almost every case Lewis Gun and rifle fire were used to engage the hostile Machine Guns whilst bombers moving round the flanks attacked in rear. Garrisons in nearly every case surrendered as soon as attacked in rear. In some cases 20 rounds from a 3" Stokes Mortar were found sufficient to induce surrender.

One Stokes Gun was carried with each Battalion.

(f) Ground flares were found most satisfactory.

(g) A covering party of Lewis Guns was always sent forward in shell holes to cover the work of consolidation. Strong points were then established in positions previously arranged and troops in rear disposed in depth, rear posts covering the gaps in front. Once established posts were wired, enemy's trenches turned over and work of connecting up posts commenced.

(h)   (i) Standing barrage.
      (ii) S.O.S. line of Artillery and Machine Guns.
      (iii) Lewis Gun and Rifle Grenade posts.
      (iv) Stokes Mortars and Machine Guns.

(i) In addition to the Guns used for M.G. barrage, Mobile Guns were attached to the assaulting Battalions and went forward with the supporting waves at once taking up positions on the line of consolidation. On several occasions these guns proved invaluable in helping to break up the enemy counter-attack. Pairs of Guns were also attached to flanking parties detailed to move on either flank of the Division in order to close any gaps which might occur. These guns proved exceedingly useful and on one occasion effectively closed a gap of 500 yards which occurred.

(j) (1) Telephone communication to Bn. H.Q. from Bdes. was frequently interrupted by shell fire but lines were always repaired and the interruption was seldom for long.

(2) Power Buzzers were not satisfactory.

(3) Lucas Daylight Signalling lamp proved useful, but men require a good deal more training in the use of it.

(4) Pigeons were satisfactory but only limited numbers can be carried.

(5) Runners. By far the most satisfactory means of communication. Frequent relay posts are most necessary as the work is very exhausting.

(6) Observation posts pushed well forward from Bn. H.Q. and connected by telephone and runner orderlies were found most satisfactory.

(k) The S.O.S. signal was not satisfactory on the whole. Owing to the numerous coloured lights used by the enemy it was found difficult to distinguish the S.O.S. and frequent false alarms occurred. It was found necessary to have a chain of observers at relay posts with S.O.S. rockets to repeat the Signal to Brigade H.Q.

(Sgd) L. H. Moore, Lt.Col.,

for Major-General,

Commanding 29th Division.

25th October, 1917.

III			
C/S 72/57		Restriction in Use of Telephones in Forward Areas	1.10.17
IV			
S 94/20		Information regarding German Regiments Opposite the Div	3.10.17
C/S 72/62		Flares for Contact Aeroplanes	7.10.17
C/S 56/20		Notes for Coy Comdrs	7.10.17
C/S 56/22		Notes of 29 Div Confce at Basseux	18.10.17
C/S 78/25		Formation of Div Depot Bn	20.10.17
S 29/11		Winter Sports Competitions	20.10.17
—		Agenda of Lecture by M.G. Sir Beauvoir de Lisle, KCB, DSO at VI Corps Sch	23.10.17

War Diary.

29th Division No. C.G.S.56/22.

29th Divisional Conference - BASSEUX 18th October, 1917.
(Brigadiers and Commanding Officers attending).
-o-o-o-o-o-o-o-o-o-o-o-o-o-o-o-o-o-o-o-o-o-o-o-o-o-o-o-

1. Probable plans. Leave.

2. Improvement of Billets. Amusement for Troops.
   Assistance to Farmers. Bed mats. Clipping.

3.   Preliminary Training.
   (1) Method of Instruction :- Explanation - Demonstration - Execution - Repetition.
   (2) Personal smartness, bearing, marching and handling of arms. Dismiss those who attain standard. Saluting. Refer to orders on subject.
   (3) Guards. Uniformity. Fall in with closed ranks. Usual mistakes.
   (4) Brigade Group Ceremonial Parade when ready for inspection. Massed Bands. Presentation of Decorations.

4.   Training of Specialists.
   (1) Bombers and Machine Gunners to practice with German weapons. Scouts, snipers. Camouflage suits.
   (2) Musketry Course. Field Firing.

5.   Trench Warfare.
   (1) Divisional Trench Standing Orders.
   (2) Field Engineering.
   (3) Rapid construction of Strong Points.
   (4) Rapid wiring.
   (5) System of Defence of Battalion.
        Piquet Line. Line of Observation.
        Support Line. Line of Resistance.
        Reserve Line.
   Analogy of Trench System to Outpost System.

             Line of Observation.

             Line of Resistance.

             Reserve Line.
       Bn. H.Q.

6.   Raids.
   (1) Platoon Raids.
   (2) Company Raids.
   (3) Battalion Raids.
       Essentials for success.
       Determination.
       Practice over marked trenches.
       Wire destroyed.
       Direction by tape.
       Flank Guards.
       Covering fire by Artillery and Trench Mortars.

/ P.T.O.

7. Battalion Exercises, to be submitted to Brigadiers prior to being carried out.

8. Battalion Conferences prior to Schemes.

9. Reconnaissance of ground before preparation of schemes.

10. Organise system of questions to test the value of the training i.e. Brigadiers to question Company Commanders, Commanding Officers to question Platoon Commanders, and Company Commanders to question Section Leaders.

11. Make the period of training a happy time, short strenuous times followed by sport and amusement.

29th Division H.Q.

War Diary

86th Inf Bde.
87th Inf Bde.
88th Inf Bde.
Major J.S. HODDING, 2/Roy.Fus.
O.C. Corps Reinforcement Camp.
"Q"
C.R.E.

29th Division CGS.78/25.

---

1. Consequent upon the training of all reinforcements now being undertaken by Corps, the VI Corps Reinforcement Camp consisting of a H.Q. Staff and Depot Bn. from each Division in the Corps has been formed about ½ mile S.W. of ACHIET LE PETIT on the ACHIET LE PETIT – MIRAUMONT ROAD.

2. The 29th Division Depot Bn. will be formed forthwith consisting of the reinforcements for the Division now at the Camp and establishments as laid down in Tables "A" and "B" attached.

3. The Battalion will be accommodated in C. Camp and will be organised in 3 Companies, one Company being affiliated to each of the Infantry Brigades of the Division.

4. Major J.S. HODDING, 2/Royal Fusiliers, is appointed Commanding Officer. He will be responsible for the general training of all reinforcements for the Division.
   The O.C. Corps Reinforcement Camp is responsible for the general supervision and administration of all Depot Battalion Camps and for the allotment of training facilities in the neighbourhood.

5. The Officers and N.C.Os. enumerated in Tables "A" and "B" (less those referred to in para 6), will join the Corps Reinforcement Camp on a date to be notified later.
   Arrangements for transport will be notified later.

6. The O.C., Adjutant, R.S.M. and Q.M.S. will proceed to the Camp on Monday 22nd instant.
   The C.R.E will detail 1 R.E. Officer and 12 Sappers to accompany this party to assist in the erection of huts, construction of ranges etc, and the laying out of the camp generally.

7. One G.S. Wagon and one Water cart (as a temporary measure) will be detailed by "Q" to proceed to the Camp on the 22nd instant reporting to O.C. Depot Bn. on arrival.

8. Names of permanent Staffs and Instructors will be forwarded to this office as soon as possible.

9. Each Brigade party will take with them 8 dixies. Until the arrival of the BOLLEZEELE Depot Bn. Stores by rail, no facilities exist for Officers Messes other than the Mess Tent furniture and cook house.

20th Oct. 1917.

Table "A".

(a) Depot Battalion H.Q.

Consisting of	To be found by
1 Commanding Officer	86th Bde. (Major J.S.HOTBLAG, 2/Roy. Fus.)
1 Adjutant & Quartermaster	87th Bde.
1 O.S.R. (A.S.R.)	88th Bde.
1 Sergt. (C.R.S.)	86th Bde.
1 Clerk (Orderly Room Sgt.)	87th Bde.
1 Clerk (Lance Cpl.)	88th Bde.
1 Sgt. (Master Cook)	86th Bde.
5 Privates (Cooks)	
(1 Butcher	87th Bde.
(1 Officers Mess	88th Bde.
(1 Sgt's Mess	86th Bde.
(1 Mens Cookhouse	87th Bde.
(1 Mens Cookhouse	88th Bde.
1 Shoemaker	86th Bde.
1 Tailor	87th Bde.
1 N.C.O. for Officers Mess	88th Bde.
1 Waiter for Officers Mess	86th Bde.
1 Waiter for Sgt's Mess	87th Bde.
1 Batman	88th Bde.
1 Batman	86th Bde.

(b) Depot Company H.Q.

To be found by each Brigade.

1 Company Commander.
1 C.S.M.
1 C.Q.M.S.

(c) To be found by Div. Employment Coy.

10 O.R. for camp duties.

-o-o-o-o-o-o-o-o-o-

Table "B".

Instructional Staff for Depot Battalion.

Subject.	To be found by					
	86th		87th		88th	
	Off.	N.C.O.	Off.	N.C.O.	Off.	N.C.O.
Musketry.	-	1 Sgt. 1 L/Cpl.	-	1 Sgt. 1 L/Cpl.	-	1 Cpl. 1 L/Cpl.
Bombing.	-	1	-	1	-	1
X Lewis Gun.	-	1	1	1	-	1
P.T. & B.F.	-	-	-	-	1	-
		C.S.M. MARTIN Army Gym. Staff.				
Gas.	-	1	-	1	-	1

X   1 Lewis Gun will accompany each Brigade party.

War Diary.

29th Division No. G.S.29/11.

Reference VI Corps Winter Sports Programme.

It has been decided to amend the above programme to facilitate the participation in the Sports of the Divisional Troops.

The Competition will be carried out by the three Brigade Groups to which will be attached units of Divisional Troops. The latter have been attached to nearest Brigade Groups as under :-

86th Brigade Group.	87th Brigade Group.	88th Brigade Group.
H.Q. 86th Inf. Bde.	H.Q. 87th Inf. Bde.	H.Q. 88th Inf. Bde.
2/Roy. Fus.	2/S.W.B.	4/Worcester Regt.
1/Lan. Fus.	1/K.O.S.B.	2/Hants. Regt.
16/Middx. Regt.	1/R. Innis. Fus.	1/Essex Regt.
1/R. Guernsey L.I.	1/Border Regt.	1/Newfoundland Regt.
86th M.G. Coy.	87th M.G. Coy.	88th M.G. Coy.
86th T.M. Bty.	87th T.M. Bty.	88th T.M. Bty.
455th Fd. Coy. R.E.	87th Field Ambce.	88th Field Ambce.
497th Fd. Coy. R.E.	510th Fd. Coy. R.E.	89th Field Ambce.
227th M.G. Coy.	Mob. Vet. Sect.	
Divisional Train.	Div. H.Q. troops.	
Divl. Supp. Col.	& Signal Coy.	

Lieut-Colonel, G.S.,
29th Division.

21st October, 1917.

Copies to :-
"Q".
86th Inf. Bde.
87th Inf. Bde.
88th Inf. Bde.
C.R.E.
A.D.M.S.
Off. i/c Sigs.
29th Divl. Train.
29th Divl. Supply Col.
Mob. Vet. Sect.
227th M.G. Coy.
Camp Commdt. 29th Div. H.Q.

M.

War Diary.

SOME LESSONS FROM RECENT OPERATIONS AT YPRES
by
Major-General Sir Beauvoir de Lisle, K.C.B., D.S.O.
-o-o-o-o-o-o-

1. Introduction.

2. Preliminary Measures. Communications. Depots. Camps. Artillery. Trench Dumps.

3. Work necessary in a Divisional Sector. Porterage. Assembly Trenches. Artillery.

4. Starting Line should be perpendicular to general direction. Forming up on tapes. Difficulties. Discovery by enemy.

5. The Assembly. Control Posts on the routes.

6. The hour for attack. Advantage of dawn.

7. The initial attack on a Trench System. The increased difficulty of subsequent attacks.

8. The advantage of attaching Bombardment Groups to Division.

9. Causes of the initial attack being easier than subsequent advances. Adequate Artillery Preparation. Practise over facsimile trenches. All know what to do.

10. Subsequent attacks. Semi-open warfare. Necessity of training in initiative.

11. Method of training for semi-open warfare. Battalion Exercises - Demonstrations. Interrogation of Company Commanders. Constant Conferences.

12. Circulars to Company Commanders :- Close up to Barrage. Capture of defended posts. Turning a flank. Stokes Gun. Position of Battalion H.Q. Consolidation. How to meet a counter-attack.

13. Counter-attack Battalions. Written orders to these.

14. Ammunition Supply. Flanking Parties.

15. Runner Relay Posts and Stretcher Bearer Relay Posts. Treatment of Wounded.

16. Guiding Tapes. Duck boards. Tracks. Roads.

17. Stokes Guns in Barrage and during advance.

18. Laying of white direction tapes followed by Duck Board Tracks and Mule Tracks.

19. Determination and bravery essential, and deserving of every assistance.

VI Corps School.

23rd October, 1917.

-o-o-o-o-o-o-o-o-

Training Instructions
& Schemes

C.

Locations.

War Diary

S E C R E T.   29th Division No. I.G.93/153.

CHANGES IN LOCATIONS - 29TH DIVISION
6 p.m. 30th October, 1917.
-o-o-o-o-o-o-o-o-o-o-o-o-o-o-o-o-o-o-o-o-o-o-o-

Reference Disposition and Movement Report No. 11a. (29th Division No. I.G.93/149) dated 27th October, 1917, for Nos. 46 - 49

read

46.	V/29	M.T.M. Battery	VAULX	57c/C.26.a.9.1.
47.	X/29	M.T.M. Battery	PATRICIA	57c/B.9.a.5.6.
48.	Y/29	"	"	"
49.	Z/29	"	"	"

Capt.
for Lieut-Colonel, G.S.,
30th October, 1917.   29th Division.

Copies to all recipients of Disposition and Movement Report No. 11a
- -

E.

Hardcary

S E C R E T.   29th Division No. I.G.93/149.
DISPOSITION AND MOVEMENT REPORT No. 11a.
29TH DIVISION.
At 6 p.m. 27th October, 1917.

Unit No.	Unit.	Position of H.Q. at 6 p.m.
1.	Div. H.Q.	BASSEUX
2.	H.Q. Div. Arty.	RANENCOURT
3.	15th Bde. R.F.A.	ORVILLE
4.	17th Bde. R.F.A.	AUTHIEULE
5.	D.A.C.	AMPLIER
6.	D.T.M.O.	CAUMESNIL
7.	S.A.A. Section D.A.C.	AMPLIER
8.	L.C.R.A.	SOREL LE GRAND
9.	455th (W.R.) Fd. Coy. R.E.	BLAIRVILLE
10.	497th (Kent) " " "	GOUZEAUCOURT 57C/T.5.B.
11.	510th (London) " " "	" 57C/R.31.D.3.2.
12.	1/2nd Monmouth Regt. (P)	XVIII Corps Area.
13.	227th M.G. Co.	HENDECOURT.
14.	Mob. Vet. Section.	BASSEUX
15.	29th Div. Emplyt. Coy.	BASSEUX
16.	H.Q. Div. Train.	BLAIRVILLE 51C/X.4.d.2.1.
17.	No. 1 Coy. Div. Train.	SARTON
18.	No. 2 " " "	HENDECOURT
19.	No. 3 " " "	BAILLEULVAL
20.	No. 4 " " "	BIENVILLERS
21.	29th Div. Supply Col.	BEAUMETZ
22.	87th Field Ambce.	BAILLEULMONT.
23.	88th " "	BIENVILLERS
24.	89th " "	LA CAUCHIE
25.	H.Q. 86th Inf. Bde.	BLAIRVILLE 51C/R.34.d.4.3.
26.	2/Royal Fus.	" 51C/X.4.d.4.1.
27.	1/Lan. Fus.	" 51C/X.11.c.3.7.
28.	16/Middx. Regt.	HENDECOURT 51C/X.17.a.3.5.
29.	1/R. Guernsey L.I.	BLAIRVILLE 51C/X.11.c.2.7.
30.	86th M.G. Coy.	" 51C/X.4.d.1.1.
31.	86th T.M. Bty.	" 51C/X.4.d.1.1.
32.	H.Q. 87th Inf. Bde.	BAILLEULMONT.
33.	2/S.W.B.	BELLACOURT
34.	1/K.O.S.B.	BAILLEULVAL
35.	1/R. Innis. Fus.	"
36.	1/Border Regt.	BAILLEULMONT
37.	87th M.G. Coy.	BELLACOURT
38.	87th T.M. Bty.	BAILLEULMONT
39.	H.Q. 88th Inf. Bde.	POMMIER
40.	4/Worcester Regt.	BERLES AU BOIS
41.	2/Hampshire Regt.	BIENVILLERS
42.	1/Essex Regt.	POMMIER
43.	1/Newfoundland Regt.	BERLES AU BOIS
44.	88th M.G. Coy.	BIENVILLERS
45.	88th T.M. Bty.	POMMIER
46.	V/29 M.T.M. Bty.	CAUMESNIL
47.	X/29 M.T.M. Bty.	"
48.	Y/29 " "	"
49.	Z/29 " "	"

Capt.
for Lieut-Colonel, G.S.
29th Division.

27th October, 1917.

War Diary

SECRET.   29th Division No. I.G.93/147.

      Reference Disposition and Movement Report No. 2 (29th Division No. I.G.93/138) dated 18th October, for Nos. 2 - 8, 10 and 11

  read

2.	H.Q. Div. Arty.	CHATEAU HARENCOURT
3.	15th Bde. R.F.A.	ORVILLE.
4.	17th Bde. R.F.A.	AUTHIEULE.
5. & 7.	D.A.C.	ALPLIER.
6.	D.T.M.O. and T.Ms.	CAUBESNIL.
8.	H.Q. R.E.	SOREL LE GRAND.
10.	497th (Kent) Fld. Coy.	FINS.
11.	510th (London) " "	SOREL LE GRAND.

                                            Lieut-Colonel, G.S.,

26th October, 1917.   29th Division.

Copies to all recipients of Disposition Report No. 2.

War Diary

S E C R E T.   29th Division No. I.G.93/138B.

CHANGES IN LOCATIONS - 29TH DIVISION
up to 6 p.m. 21st October, 1917.
-o-o-o-o-o-o-o-o-o-o-o-o-o-o-o-o-o-o-o-

Unit No.	Unit.	Position of H.Q. at 6 p.m.
7.	S.A.A. Section D.A.C.	XIV Corps Area.
9.	455th (L.R.) Fd. Coy. R.E.	COURCELLES LE COMPTE.
24.	89th Field Ambulance.	LA CAUCHIE.

21.10.17.

Capt.
for Lt-Col. G.S., 29th Divn.

Copies to all recipients of Disposition and Movement Report No. 2.

SECRET.   29th Division No. I.G.93/138C.

Reference Disposition and Movement Report No. 2
(29th Division No. I.G.93/138) dated 18th October, for No. 21
read -

21. 29th Div. Supply Column.   BRAUMETZ.

21.10.17.

Capt.
for Lieut-Colonel, G.S.,
29th Division.

To all recipients of Disposition and Movement Report No. 2.
- -

War Diary

S E C R E T.　　　　　　　　　　29th Division No. I.G.93/138A.

　　　Reference Disposition and Movement Report No. 2 (29th Division No. I.G.93/138), dated 18th October, for Nos. 40 and 41 <u>read</u> :-

　　40.　　4/Worcester Regt.　　　BERLES AU BOIS.
　　41.　　2/Hampshire Regt.　　　BIENVILLERS.

　　510th (London) Field Coy. R.E. has moved to LAHERLIERE.

　　　　　　　　　　　　　　　　　　　W.U. Croome
　　　　　　　　　　　　　　　　　　　Capt.
　　　　　　　　　　　　　　for Lieut-Colonel, G.S.,
18th October, 1917.　　　　　　　　29th Division.

Copies to all recipients of Disposition and Movement Report No. 2.

War Diary

SECRET. 29th Division No. I.G.93/138.

DISPOSITION AND MOVEMENT REPORT NO. 2.

29TH DIVISION.

Period 6 p.m. 18.10.17. to 6 p.m. 19.10.17.

Unit No.	Unit.	Position of H.Q. at 6 p.m.	Proposed destination.
1.	Div. H.Q.	BASSEUX	
2.	H.Q. Div. Arty.	)	
3.	15th Bde. R.H.A.	)	
4.	17th Bde. R.F.A.	) XIV Corps Area.	
5.	D.A.C. (less SAA Sec.)	)	
6.	D.T.M.O.	)	
7.	S.A.A. Section D.A.C.	FICHEUX	
8.	H.Q. R.E.	BASSEUX	
9.	455th (W.R.) Fd.Coy.RE.	BLAIRVILLE	
10.	497th (Kent) -"-	"	
11.	510th (London) -"-	BIENVILLERS	LAHERLIERE
12.	1/2nd Monmouth Regt.(P)	XIV Corps Area.	
13.	227th M.G. Coy.	HENDECOURT	
14.	Mob. Vet. Sect.	BASSEUX	
15.	29th Div. Empl yt. Coy.	"	
16.	H.Q. Div. Train.	BLAIRVILLE	
17.	No. 1 Coy. Div.Train.	XIV Corps Area.	
18.	No. 2 " " "	HENDECOURT.	
19.	No. 3 " " "	BAILLEULVAL	
20.	No. 4 " " "	BIENVILLERS	
21.	29th Div. Supp. Col.	WAILLY	
22.	87th Field Ambce.	BAILLEULMONT	
23.	88th " "	BIENVILLERS	
24.	89th " "	HENDECOURT	
25.	H.Q. 86th Inf. Bde.	BLAIRVILLE	
26.	2/Royal Fus.	"	
27.	1/Lan. Fus.	HENDECOURT	
28.	16/Middx. Regt.	BLAIRVILLE	
29.	1/Guernsey L.I.	"	
30.	86th M.G. Coy.	"	
31.	86th T.M. Bty.	BAILLEULMONT	
32.	H.Q. 87th Inf. Bde.	BELLACOURT	
33.	2/S.W.B.	BAILLEULVAL	
34.	1/K.O.S.B.	"	
35.	1/R. Innis. Fus.	BAILLEULMONT	
36.	1/Border Regt.	BELLACOURT	
37.	87th M.G. Coy.	BAILLEULMONT	
38.	87th T.M. Bty.	BAILLEULMONT	
39.	H.Q. 88th Inf. Bde.	POMMIER	
40.	4/Worcester Regt.	BIENVILLERS	
41.	2/Hampshire Regt.	BERLES AU BOIS	
42.	1/Essex Regt.	POMMIER	
43.	1/Newfoundland Regt.	BERLES AU BOIS	
44.	88th M.G. Coy.	BIENVILLERS	
45.	88th T.M. Bty.	POMMIER	
46.	1/R. Dub. Fus.	BEAUMETZ	to 16th Div. 19th Oct.

18th October, 1917.

W.H. Croome
Capt.
for Lt-Col. G.S., 29th Divn.

SECRET.   29th Division No. C.G.S.67/79.

Addendum to 29th Division Order No. 163.
- - - - - - - - - - - - - - - - - - - -

    Divisional Headquarters will close at PROVEN at 10.0 A.M. on 16th October and will reopen at the same hour at RASSEUX.

A.T. Milla. Capt

Lieut-Colonel, G.S.,
29th Division.

14th October, 1917.

To all recipients of 29th Division Order No. 163.

S E C R E T.   29th Division No. I.G.93/132a

AMENDMENT TO LOCATIONS - 29TH DIVISION.
Midnight 7th/8th October, 1917.

Reference 1/40,000 Map, Sheet 28.

37th Inf Bde.H.Q.   CARIBOU   A.11.d.8.7.

G.T. Milla Capt.

for Lieut - Colonel, G.S.,
7th October, 1917.   29th Division.

S.

S E C R E T.   29th Div. No. I.G.93/125.

CHANGES IN LOCATIONS - 29TH DIVISION

up to Midnight 3rd/4th October, 1917.
-o-o-o-o-o-o-o-o-o-o-o-o-o-o-o-o-o-o-o-o-o-o-o-

Ref. 1/40,000 map, sheets 20 and 28.

Div. Advanced/H.Q.)		
H.Q. Div. Arty.)	ELVERDINGHE	28/B.14.b.15.15.
C.R.E.)	CHATEAU.	
D.M.G.O.)		
Rear Div. H.Q.	J. Camp.	28/A.8.b.2.6.
86th Inf. Bde.		
16/Middx. Regt.	DULWICH.	28/B.8.c.6.9.
1/R. Dub. Fus.	Right Front Line, LANGEMARCK.	20/U.23.c.05.15.

[signature]
Capt.

for Lieut-Colonel, G.S.,

2nd October, 1917.   29th Division.

M.

War Diary

S E C R E T.   29th Div. No. I.G.93/124.

CHANGES IN LOCATIONS - 29TH DIVISION

up to Midnight 2nd/3rd October, 1917.
-o-o-o-o-o-o-o-o-o-o-o-o-o-o-o-o-o-o-o-o-o-

Reference 1/40,000 Map, sheets 20, 27 and 28.

87th Inf. Bde.

2/S.W.B.	CHARTERHOUSE.	28/B.9.c.8.5.
1/K.O.S.B.	CENTRE FRONT LINE.	20/U.22.c.05.15.
1/Border Regt.	LEFT FRONT LINE.	20/U.21.a.6.3.
1/R. Innis. Fus.	WHITE MILL.	28/B.14.d.8.8.

1/Guernsey L.I.   STOKE.   27/F.5.d.5.8.

Capt.

for Lieut-Colonel, G.S.,

1st October, 1917.   29th Division.

M.

D.

Summaries

War Diary

29th Division No. I.G.106/60.

29TH DIVISION INTELLIGENCE SUMMARY
6 a.m. 30th Sept. to 6 a.m. 1st Oct. 1917.
-o-o-o-o-o-o-o-o-o-o-o-o-o-o-o-o-o-o-o-o-o-o-o-

I. PATROLS.

(a) An officers patrol left our lines at U.17.c.35.00. and proceeded in a north-easterly direction along the railway for a distance of about 400 yards.
Sounds of wiring were heard about U.17.d.15.40. and U.17.c.95.45. An enemy patrol was observed moving in a south-westerly direction along the railway, turning off about U.17.c. 95.40. Our patrol opened fire but no results could be observed. It would appear that the enemy have a post S. of the railway about U.17.d.10.40. and a post under construction about U.17.c.95.45. Our patrol was frequently sniped at from the left.

(b) A patrol went out from U.16.d.00.85. and patrolled Westwards along the BROEMBEEK to U.16.c.2.9. No bridges were discovered. The Banks of the stream were swampy, and there are numerous pools of water up to 8 feet wide. The ground on the North bank appeared badly cut up but dry. Wire was noticed at intervals on the North bank, but did not seem to form a serious obstacle anywhere. An enemy M.G. was firing from blockhouse at U.16.c.85.90, and a sniper from U.16.c.90.90.

(c) & (d) Two officers patrols examined the BROEMBEEK on the night of the 30th. No practicable crossing was found. Patrols were fired on from enemy post at U.16.Central and from blockhouse in NEY WOOD.

II. ENEMY ACTIVITY.

(a) Movement. At 11 p.m. 30 of the enemy were seen moving across the open from U.17.d.2.5. and disappearing behind the bank at U.17.d.4.2. They were engaged by our rifle fire.
A party of 50 enemy was seen about U.18.c.0.0. They were dispersed by rifle fire from our post at U.23.b.6.5. making off in a northerly direction. It was thought that a relief was taking place from the unusual amount of movement. A patrol was sent to investigate this (Report not yet to hand).
Movement was seen just East of t' GOED TER VESTEN FARM.
20 of the enemy were seen moving towards the BROEMBEEK from NEY WOOD at 8 p.m. last night.

(b) Artillery.
LANGEMARCK, CANNES FARM, DENAIN FARM and WIJDENDRIFT were lightly shelled yesterday forenoon.
In the afternoon the vicinity of MARTINS MILL and REITRES FARM were heavily shelled.
Our rear approaches and battery positions were heavily shelled from 7 p.m. till 9 p.m.
The WOOD HOUSE - SAULES FARM line was intermittently shelled throughout the night with gas, and H.E. up to 5.9's.

/ (c)

- 2 -

(c) <u>Aircraft.</u>

Much activity during the period. On all possible occasions E.A. were engaged by our M.Gs.

Enemy formations up to 15 machines were noted during the day.

1 E.A. flying low fired M.G. at our trenches in the afternoon.

Our back areas and camps were bombed during the night. Our M.Gs. engaged E.A. which were visible in searchlight beams or in the moonlight.

(d) <u>Machine Guns.</u>

A hostile M.G. was firing from the direction of NEY CROSS ROADS on CANNES FARM.
U.17.d.70.15. - suspected M.G.

<u>Sniping.</u>

U.16.a.9.9. - sniper active.
U.17.d.70.55. - sniper reported.

(e) <u>Trench Mortars.</u>

An enemy T.M. was active last night on our left front and support line - location doubtful.

III. ENEMY WORK.

<u>Front and Support Lines.</u>

U.17.d.15.40.)
) Sounds of enemy wiring reported.
U.17.c.95.45.)   (patrol report).

U.16.c. - isolated lengths of wire along northern bank of BROEMBEEK reported: not forming serious obstacle. (patrol report).

IV. <u>ENEMY DISPOSITIONS.</u>

U.16.c.85.90. - blockhouse occupied: M.G. active
                                    (patrol report).

1st Oct. 1917.

A.M.Simpson, Lieut.
for Lieut-Col. G.S., 29th Division.

M.

29th Division No. I.G.100/61

29TH DIVISION INTELLIGENCE SUMMARY
6 a.m. 1st October to 6 a.m. 2nd October, 1917.

I. PATROLS.

(a) An officers patrol left our lines at U.15 central and proceeded towards NEY COPSE. On reaching U.15.b.5.4. the patrol was sniped at from the blockhouse at U.15.b.48.49. - NEY COPSE. Rifle grenades were also fired from the same point.

Duckboards were observed to cross the BROEMBEEK at U.15.b.50.45. for about 12 yards then turning at right angles and running N.W. on the opposite bank of the stream in front of the blockhouse. Sounds of hammering were heard near NEY COPSE. It is thought that with existing means of crossing, the passage of the BROEMBEEK would be slow owing to the large number of shell holes full of water that mark the course of the stream.

(b) A N.C.O's. patrol left our trench at U.16.c.22.55, reaching the BROEMBEEK at U.16.c.25.90, and proceeding along the stream to U.16.c.95.85.

A few of the enemy were seen to leave the partially damaged blockhouse at U.10.c.20.95, move along about 30 yards eastwards and jump down into a trench or organised shell hole. Men were also seen in pairs moving down from the ridge to a point about U.16.c.55.98. Movement was also seen about U.16.a.90.15.

Following are the salient points of this reconnaissance (b).

1. The stream along the portion examined U.16.c.25.90. to U.16.c.95.85. is 4 yards wide. The ground on our side is fairly dry and easy to move over.

2. No bridges were seen.

3. No wire was observed, but pairs of pickets in echelon 4 ft. high and 3 ft. apart were seen at regular intervals of 15 yards. The line of pickets was about 5 yards N. of the stream and continued along the whole portioned examined.

II. ENEMY ACTIVITY.

(a) Movement. Two men carrying sacks were seen to enter the blockhouse in NEY COPSE about 1.30 p.m.

Two men were seen to run along for some distance during our shelling of U.18.c.0.0.

Twelve of the enemy were seen to leave a trench about U.24.a.2.5. and take cover in shell holes in front during our shelling.

(b) Artillery. As for the previous period enemy artillery was fairly quiet during the morning and afternoon increasing towards evening, when approaches and region of WIJDENDRIFT and STEENBEEK were kept under fire.

/ Bursts

Bursts of H.E. intermixed with Gas shells fell on the WOOD HOUSE - SAULES FARM line during the night.

The WIJDENDRIFT Road and the STEENBEEK were heavily shelled between 4.30 a.m. and 6.45 a.m. this morning from the HOUTHULST FOREST Group. Shells used, chiefly 5.9's.

(c) Aircraft. Very active between 9 a.m. and 10.30 a.m.
E.A. flew over our lines at a low altitude on three occasions. They were driven off by our rifle and M.G. fire.
Throughout the day small patrols of E.A., and enemy night bombing planes were engaged by our M.Gs.

(d) Machine Guns.

NEY COPSE - enemy M.G. active during the night.

Sniping.

U.15.b.4.8. - suspected snipers post.

(e) Trench Mortars.
Enemy T.M. located near blockhouse in NEY WOOD at U.16.a.2.0.

(f) Signal Lights.
Lights breaking into orange stars sent up from enemy lines seemed to precede a lengthening of range.
2 E.A. flying over our lines between 9 a.m. and 10.30 a.m. dropped red and green lights which burst into numerous red and green stars.

III. ENEMY WORK.

BLOCKHOUSES U.18.c.4.5. (Special Report)

Four Blockhouses marked on Map, only two visible. Left hand one either a small one or the end of a rectangular one (probably the former). Hole in side visible, partly covered by willow tree. Blockhouse otherwise badly damaged and roof appears to be strengthened with logs on top. The top left hand corner was knocked off by shell at 11.25 a.m. to-day.
Right hand Blockhouse rectangular in shape, with longer sides facing N.E. and S.W. It has been hit many times, roof and south corner especially being damaged. At 11.25am. to-day shell hit side facing N.W. and blew a tree over which was leaning against it. At about 10.45 a.m. 4 shrapnel shells burst round them. Between 11.20 a.m. and 11.45 a.m. about 20 H.E. shells burst round about. Hits as above reported, most other shells going beyond them.
To S.E. of larger Blockhouse (and double the distance from it than the smaller one is) there is a low dugout, with only roof of logs covered with a heap of earth visible. From its position this is possibly the remains of the Southernmost of the 4 Blockhouses marked on map. If that

/ is

- 3 -

is so, the third one is destroyed, and its presumed site shows signs of something having been blown to pieces. No signs of life.

U.18.c.3.6. - No blockhouse visible but much debris and broken elephants.

U.17.d.97.02. and U.23.b.90.95. - no blockhouses visible at these points.

t' GOED TER VESTEN FARM - No signs of life among rubble and concrete slabs. There appears to be a roof of a blockhouse intact facing S.W.

LAUDETBEEK - continuous breastwork 100 yards eastwards along S. bank from North side of t' GOED TER VESTEN FARM. Gap at U.17.d.90.08. where road crosses stream, with mound on each side: the left mound appears to be a dugout.

U.24.a.20.92. - Snipers post suspected, tree trunk seen with a hole near the ground and one about the height of a man in it. Continuous sniping from this point during night 30th Sept./1st Oct.
Yesterday our Stokes Mortars ranged on the post and only 4 shots have since been fired from this point up to Midnight 1st/2nd October.

U.17.d.85.10. - loophole in parapet just W. of mound.
Our Stokes Mortars engaged this point and boards were thrown into the air.

New Work.

Newly turned earth is visible about U.23.b.8.7.

IV. MAPS - ADDITIONAL NAME.

The following name has been allotted :-

1/10,000 Sheet, BIXSCHOOTE, 20 S.W.4:-

Building at U.22.c.05.13. - SPRING FARM.

2nd Oct. 1917.

A.M.Simpson, Lieut.
for Lt-Col. G.S., 29th Divn.

M.

War Diary

29th Division No. I.G.106/62.

29TH DIVISION INTELLIGENCE SUMMARY
6 a.m. 2nd Oct. to 6 a.m. 3rd Oct. 1917.

1. **PATROLS.**

   Patrol reports are annexed.

2. **ENEMY ACTIVITY.**

   (a) **Movement.**

   One man moving at 7 a.m. about U.18.a.1.3.
   At 1.15 a.m. enemy party was seen moving opposite Right Battalion front: on being fired on they disappeared about U.23.b.70.95.
   Two men walking across open from U.17.d.4.5. disappeared about U.17.d.4.1., 3 a.m. 2/10/17.

   (b) **Artillery.**

   Enemy artillery inactive on our front during the morning and early afternoon, except for intermittent shelling of LANGEMARCK all day.
   In the afternoon the enemy counter-batteries were active, especially South of the STADEN Railway.
   At night the forward area and communications were less shelled than usual. The WOOD HOUSE - SAULES FARM line was again shelled with all calibres up to 5.9 - both gas and H.E. - but less heavily than usual.

   (c) **Aircraft.**

   Activity of E.A. over forward areas somewhat greater than usual. In the early morning E.A. flew frequently at low altitudes over whole area back to the STEENBEEK, firing with M.Gs. on suitable targets.
   They were fired on by our Machine Guns and rifles without observed effect. In the evening large enemy formations appeared but no air fighting was observed though our aircraft were active over enemy lines.
   About 7 p.m. an aeroplane of unknown nationality fell in flames in HOUTHULST FOREST, N. of the sector.
   Bombs were dropped near SIGNAL FARM, WOOD 15 and BOESINGHE, also for the first time as far forward as WIJDENDRIFT.

   (d) **Machine Guns.**

   An enemy M.G. fired on a patrol from blockhouse at U.16.d.60.65. (NEY CROSS ROADS) - patrol report.

   Sniping.

   Sniping from points U.17.d.8.0. and U.23.b.9.1. has ceased since our T.M. fire on those points yesterday.

   (e) **Trench Mortars.**

   At 6.5 a.m. four small T.M. bombs dropped behind our trench at U.23.a.7.9.

   (f) **Signal Lights.**

   At 10.30 p.m. several rockets bursting into two golden stars were seen to go up from about U.16.d.9.9. without apparent result.

   / III.

III. ENEMY WORK.

(a) Blockhouses.
(1) U.18.c.4.5. - special report in yesterday's summary confirmed by further observation.

(2) U.18.a.5.6. - 2 blockhouses badly damaged - one low with roof covered with earth.

(3) U.12.d. 15.20. - 1, also badly damaged.

(4) U.18.a.6.4. - only top visible, with broken edges.

(b) New Work.
Enemy party seen laying tape at U.23.b.8.7. (where fresh earth was observed yesterday) - patrol report.
About U.17.d.8.6. trench which appeared fairly new - patrol report.

Capt.

3.10.17.   for Lt-Col. G.S., 29th Divn.

M.

PATROL REPORT.

Division.	Strength of Patrol.	Time and date.	Objective or task.	Remarks & Information.
29th.	Two Scouts FRUGAL.	3 a.m 2.10.17.	To find a possible approach to the trench at U.17.d.4.1.	Scouts got out about 50x - fired at from N.E. unable to proceed. Two enemy were soon walking across upon from direction of U.17.d.4.5. and disappeared about U.17.d.4.1.
	2/Lieut PHILPOTTS and 4 O.R. (FRUGAL)	2 a.m. 2.10.17	To reconnoitre CHINEESE HOUSE and t' GOED ter VESTEN FARM.	Patrol passed on right of CHINEESE HOUSE without recognising it; fired at from the North, proceeded as far as U.25.b.70.95. - fired at from both N.E. and N.W. - unable to proceed - moonlight very bright - no enemy seen or posts located.
	2/Lieut JENKINS and 4. O.R. (FRUGAL)	Midnight 23/10/17.	To reconnoitre CHINEESE HOUSE.	Left point U.25.b.25.55 at midnight CHINEESE HOUSE was found to be occupied. Patrol then moved forward to U.23.b.5.9. From this point a party was seen in the direction of U.23.b.6.7. Party was laying tape. At this moment patrols attention was distracted by M.G. fire and 3 bombs at U.23.b.30.95 on their other flank and on going forward direction was temporary lost and a swamp encountered which was apparently the South of GOED TER VESTEN FARM. Patrol extricated itself from swamp and nothing further was seen - returned at 0130 The position of party with tapeis same place where new earth was reported thrown up in yesterdays Observer's Report.

29th.	Captain FEATHERSTONE (IMUGAL)	12.15 p.m. to 12.45 p.m. 2.10.17.	To reconnoitre STADEN Railway and ground to the South of it.	An Officer went out from our front line at 12.15 p.m. along the hedge on the South side of STADEN Railway for about 500 yards. No signs of the movement of enemy patrols, such as tracks or footmarks could be seen in the mud. At A.17.d.7.5 there was a little wire along the hedge, also running East across the hedge. About 40 yds further N.E. there was a trench which appeared fairly new. To the right only 100 yds of ground could be seen with the top of the ruins of GOED TER VESTEN Farm showing above the dip in the ground. Returned to our lines 12.45 p.m.
	1 Officer and 2 O.R.	11.50 p.m. 2.10.17.	To examine BLOEMBEEK and approaches from HEY CROSS ROADS to a point 500 yds to the right along the stream.	Within 40 yds of the stream at HEY CROSS ROADS the ground was very marshy; further to right ground was much drier and stream 8 to 10' broad at a point 100 yds to right of HEY CROSS ROADS. At U.17.c.2.7. stream is 6' wide and shell holes are full of water for 20 yards this side of stream. An enemy M.G. fired from Concrete dugout at HEY CROSS ROADS.

War Diary

29th Division No. I.G.106/63.

29TH DIVISION INTELLIGENCE SUMMARY
6 a.m. 4th to 6 a.m. 5th October, 1917.
-o-o-o-o-o-o-o-o-o-o-o-o-o-o-o-o-o-o-o-o-o-o-

I. As a result of yesterday's operations our line now runs :- U.18.d.3.8. - U.18.c.8.8. - U.18.c.3.6. - U.17.d.65.35. - U.17.d.15.40. - BEAR SUPPORT - with posts at 45K and U.17.d.2.6.

II. PATROLS. Two of our patrols examined the BROEMBEEK. Reports are annexed.

III. ENEMY ACTIVITY.

(a) Movement. At about 2 p.m. yesterday during our shelling 15 of the enemy were seen to run from U.16.b.3.2. towards GRUYTERSZALE FARM.

3 of the enemy were seen to leave the trench at U.16.a.1.5. and move off in a north-easterly direction; they appeared to be wounded.

Between 3 and 4 p.m. on our shelling blockhouse at U.16.a.95.12. a number of the enemy without caps were seen to run from the spot and take cover in shell holes. 8 of the party were hit and left lying and our snipers accounted for some others.

(b) Artillery.

At 6.5 a.m. yesterday morning enemy artillery showed great activity; front and support lines and the STEENBEEK were heavily shelled until midday.

About 1.10 p.m. heavy shelling re-commenced and continued intermittently until 10 p.m. Battery positions in rear were heavily shelled all day.

A few lachrymatory shells were fired during the afternoon.

Enemy shelled his own lines at U.16.a.60.15. from 12.30 p.m. till 1.30 p.m.

Enemy's field guns seemed much nearer during the night.

Fire principally came from the HOUTHULST Group: calibre chiefly 5.9's and 77 mm.

Light Signals.

Enemy S.O.S. which went up at 6.2 a.m. consisted of 2 Red and 2 Green lights. "Golden rain" rockets were persistently sent up from U.16.a.60.15. apparently to call for lengthening of range.

(c) Aircraft.

Enemy activity slight.
2 E.A. flew over our lines in U.17.d. at 9.25 a.m. but were driven off by Lewis Gun fire.

(d) Machine Guns.

An enemy M.G. was active at intervals from NEY WOOD.
U.17.c.20.80.)
U.17.c.90.90.) M.Gs. reported active.

(e) Trench Mortars.

Enemy T.Ms. fired on PANTHER TRENCH from U.16.c.95.95. at 3.45 p.m. yesterday.

/ IV.

IV. ENEMY WORK.

Front and Support Lines.

U.15.b.9.2. - sounds of enemy wiring party heard.
(ground observer)

V. BROEMBEEK.

U.16.c.50.87. to U.16.c.70.85. - sides of stream marshy and stream pitted with shell holes. Water deep in places.

U.16.d.1.8. to NEY CROSS ROADS - stream 4 to 8 feet wide with broken trees and duckboards scattered across.

Bridges.

(a) U.16.d.20.75. - mat bridge.

(b) U.16.c.50.90. - broken stone bridge; could be easily repaired.

VI. IDENTIFICATIONS.

6th Bavarian Division.

    13th Bav. I.R. - N.E. LANGEMARCK.
    10th Bav. I.R. - E. LANGEMARCK.
                  (prisoners)

VII. ENEMY ORDER OF BATTLE.

All the prisoners examined gave the order of battle N. to S. as :-

    6th Bav. I.R.
    13th Bav. I.R.
    10th Bav. I.R.

5th Oct. 1917.

                        A.W. Simpson, Lieut.
                       for Lieut.-Colonel, G.S.,
                            29th Division.

M.

PATROL REPORT.

Div.	Strength of Patrol.	Time and Date.	Objective of Patrol.	Remarks and information.
29th.	1 Officer and 4 O.R. Lt. STEEL. 2/Coldstream Gds.	10.30 p.m. 2nd October 1917.	Reconnaissance of BROEMBEEK between U.13.d.1.3 and NEW CROSS ROADS.	The BROEMBEEK between U.13.d.1.3 and NEW CROSS Roads is from 4 to 6 feet wide, with broken trees and Duckboards scattered across the stream. There is a mat laid across at U.13.d.20.75. No enemy rifle or machine gun fire was experienced along the whole portion examined. No enemy wire was visible on opposite bank of stream.
29th	1 Officer and 2 O.R. 2/Lt GASH.	8.0 p.m. to 9.15 p.m. 3rd Oct.1917.	To reconnoitre BROEMBEEK and examine condition of any bridges seen, and report on condition of stream for crossing.	Patrol left our lines at U.13.c.4.5 and reached the BROEMBEEK at U.13.c.30.37 and proceeded along the South bank to U.13.c.70.85. The sides of the stream are marshy and pitted with shell holes. The water is deep in places. Patrol reports matting would be unsatisfactory for crossing- patrol thinks night be of use, but duckboards and stakes suggested are best method. There is a broken stone bridge at U.13.c.50.90 which could be easily mended. There is a double plank bridge at U.13.c.70.35 in good condition.

War Diary

29th Division No. I.G.106/64.

29TH DIVISION INTELLIGENCE SUMMARY

6 a.m. 5th to 6 a.m. 6th October, 1917.

-o-o-o-o-o-o-o-o-o-o-o-o-o-o-o-o-o-o-o-o-

I. PATROLS.   Patrol reports have not yet been received.

II. ENEMY ACTIVITY.

  (a) Movement.   No enemy movement was observed.

  (b) Artillery.   Enemy fairly active.

    Areas just behind our front line, and the neighbourhood of SPRING FARM were intermittently shelled.

    Our routes and approaches were kept under fire throughout the night.

    Shells chiefly employed 4.2 cm. and 77 mm.

  (c) Aircraft.   Enemy activity below normal.

  (d) Machine Guns.   Enemy M.Gs. still reported active from direction of BEAR COPSE. Our T.Ms. engaged the suspected positions at 3 a.m. this morning.

III. INFORMATION FROM OTHER SOURCES.

  Light Signals.   (From XIV Corps Summary of 4/10/17.)

    A captured document shows that the following light signals will come into use on the 5th October at 3 p.m. on the front of the 6th Bavarian Division :-

    GREEN .... Barrage.
    RED .... Destructive Fire.
    YELLOW .... Lengthen Range.

6th October, 1917.

                              A.M. Simpson, Lieut.
                              for Lt-Col. G.S., 29th Divn.

War Diary

29th Division No. I.G.106/65.

29TH DIVISION INTELLIGENCE SUMMARY
6 a.m. 6th to 6 a.m. 7th October, 1917.
-o-o-o-o-o-o-o-o-o-o-o-o-o-o-o-o-o-o-o-o-

I. PATROLS.

(a) A N.C.O's patrol left our advanced post at U.17.d.35.55 and proceeded along the railway to the BROEMBEEK at U.17.d.65.92, thence along this stream to U.18.c.22.88. There appears to be no crossing where the railway meets the BROEMBEEK, and no bridge could be located along the length of stream examined.
 The BROEMBEEK between U.17.d.65.92 and U.18.c.22.88. has no regular width or form but has the appearance of a marsh surrounded by flooded shell holes.
 A sniper fired across the railway from the direction of BEAR COPSE.
 About 100 yards N.E. along the railway in front of the post - U.17.d.35.55 - there are several small dumps of stick bombs.

(b) A patrol of 4 O.R. reconnoitred the BROEMBEEK between U.17.d.30.65. and U.17.c.60.70. No enemy were encountered South of the BROEMBEEK. The breadth of the stream is irregular varying from 6 to 10 feet. There are no practicable crossings and much marshy ground, occasionally swept by M.G. fire from the higher ground N. of the BROEMBEEK.

(c) A patrol went out from U.17.c.60.60. and along the BROEMBEEK to the railway. Talking was heard on the other side of the stream. No crossing could be located.
 Two emplacements were observed in BEAR COPSE. One seems to have fresh earth thrown over it, the other appears to be slightly damaged.
 A track runs along the W. side of the Copse thence along the edge of the BROEMBEEK for about 10 yards eastwards where it is lost to view.
 At U.17.c.65.85, four planks have been thrown across the stream.
 A few strips of trench with a little wire in front can be seen just below the crest of the hill.
 There are numerous pickets along the crest but the state of the wire is not known.
 A large mound can be seen at U.17.b.5.5, this is presumed to be a dug-out.

II. ENEMY ACTIVITY.

(a) Movement.
 Enemy were seen to run into a trench or organised shell holes just N. of BEAR COPSE.
 One of the enemy was seen carrying a Machine Gun just in front of our post at U.17.d.70.55, this morning. He was fired at but made off leaving the M.G. behind, which we took.

/ (b)

- 2 -

(b) Artillery.

Hostile fire was much below normal on forward areas during the day.

One 77mm. gun and one 10cm. how. fired on the STEENBEEK and on LANGEMARCK in the afternoon.

About 6.30 a.m. a H.V. battery fired on our back areas from direction of HOUTHULST.

Hostile fire increased during the night, the approaches to the STEENBEEK receiving most attention. It is thought that the guns used were brought forward during the night and returned at dawn.

The French shelled HOUTHULST very heavily yesterday. Three dumps were exploded about U.6.a. and a large fire caused at U.5.a.

(c) Aircraft.

Two E.A. flew very low over our lines in U.15, 16, 17 from 6 p.m. to 6.30 p.m. last night. They were engaged by our M.Gs.

(d) Machine Guns.

Since our T.Ms. engaged the suspected enemy M.G. positions near BEAR COPSE no enemy M.G. fire has been encountered from that direction.

III. ENEMY WORK.

Front and Support Lines.

U.17.d. - small dumps of wire and stakes have been discovered N. of the BROEMBEEK.

U.17.a.3.6. - suspected O.P.

U.17.a.5.4. - sniper reported.

IV. ENEMY DISPOSITIONS.

U.17.b.65.45. - enemy post suspected.

U.17.a.9.1. - enemy dug-outs reported about this point.

7th October, 1917.

M.

Lieut.
for Lieut-Colonel, G.S.
29th Division.

Army Form W.3091.

Cover for Documents.

Nature of Enclosures

War Diary,
November
1917

Notes, or Letters written.

General Staff

29th Division.

WAR DIARY

GENERAL STAFF

29TH DIVISION

FOR

THE MONTH OF

NOVEMBER 1917

VOLUME XXXIII.

Army Form C. 2118.

Instructions regarding War Diaries and Intelligence Summaries are contained in F.S. Regs., Part II. and the Staff Manual respectively. Title pages will be prepared in manuscript.

WAR DIARY

~~INTELLIGENCE SUMMARY~~

(Erase heading not required.)

Place	Date	Hour	Summary of Events and Information	Remarks and references to Appendices
			NOVEMBER, 1917.	
BASSEUX	1st		3rd Army Commander visited G.O.C. G.O.C. presented medals to 88th Brigade. G.O.C.'s lecture to 86th Brigade in afternoon. G.S.O.2 to "Q" conference at 3rd Corps H.Q.	
	2nd		G.O.C. visited 88th Brigade training.	
	3rd		G.O.C. and G.S.O.I to conference at 3rd Corps H.Q.	
	4th		Tank demonstration near BOISLEUX AU MONT.	
	5th		G.O.C.'s lecture to 87th Brigade at BAILLEULMONT.	
	6th		G.O.C. and G.S.O.I to 3rd Corps Area for reconnaissance. Spoilt by weather.	
	7th		G.O.C. and G.S.O.I to conference at 3rd Corps H.Q.	
	8th		Wet. G.O.C. conducted Indoor Tactical Exercise with officers of 87th Inf. Bde.	

Army Form C. 2118.

WAR DIARY

~~INTELLIGENCE SUMMARY~~

(Erase heading not required.)

Place	Date	Hour	Summary of Events and Information	Remarks and references to Appendices
	9th		G.O.C. reconnoitred training area with a view to Divisional Tactical Exercise. Final of 86th Brigade Football. 16/Middlesex Regiment v 1/Royal Guernsey Light Infantry. Won by 16/Middlesex Regiment 6 - 0. G.O.C. conducted Indoor Tactical Exercise with officers of 86th Brigade.	
	10th		G.O.C. and G.S.O.I to conference at 3rd Corps H.Q. G.O.C. conducted indoor Tactical Exercise with officers of 88th Brigade.	
	11th		G.O.C.'s conference of Brigadiers of 87th and 88th Brigades at Divisional Headquarters.	
	12th		86th Brigade Tactical Exercise.	
	13th		87th Brigade Tactical Exercise.	
	14th		88th Brigade Tactical Exercise.	
	15th		Divisional Tactical Exercise. Commander-in-Chief present. Warning Order to move on 17/18th - C.G.S.67/81.	Appen: I Appen: II

Instructions regarding War Diaries and Intelligence Summaries are contained in F. S. Regs., Part II. and the Staff Manual respectively. Title pages will be prepared in manuscript.

Army Form C. 2118.

WAR DIARY
INTELLIGENCE SUMMARY.
(Erase heading not required.)

Instructions regarding War Diaries and Intelligence Summaries are contained in F. S. Regs., Part II. and the Staff Manual respectively. Title pages will be prepared in manuscript.

Place	Date	Hour	Summary of Events and Information	Remarks and references to Appendices
	16th		Preparations for entrainment to 3rd Corps Area.	
BASSEUX & MOISLAINS	17th		Entrainment at BOISLEUX AU MONT. Divisional Headquarters from BASSEUX to MOISLAINS (5 miles North of PERONNE). Brigades at HAUT ALLAINES and MOISLAINS. (O.O.164 & 165)	Appen. III & IV
	18th		Brigades moved by march route after dark to FINS, SOREL and EQUANCOURT. Divisional Headquarters remained at MOISLAINS. (O.O.166)	Appen. V
	19th		March to assembly area carried out without a hitch and all in position by 5.0 A.M. Divisional Headquarters to SOREL with Advanced Headquarters at QUENTIN MILL, GOUZEAUCOURT. (O.O.168)	Appen. VI
QUENTIN MILL & SOREL.	20th		Z day. Zero hour 6.20 A.M. See special account of operations. (O.O.167)	Appen. VII

Army Form C. 2118.

WAR DIARY
~~INTELLIGENCE SUMMARY~~

Instructions regarding War Diaries and Intelligence
Summaries are contained in F. S. Regs., Part II.
and the Staff Manual respectively. Title pages
will be prepared in manuscript.

(Erase heading not required.)

Place	Date	Hour	Summary of Events and Information	Remarks and references to Appendices
	24th		Orders issued for a further operation by 86th and 87th Brigades to complete capture of the MASNIERES - BEAUREVOIR Line. This attack was ultimately cancelled. (O.O.169)	Appen. VIII
	25th		G.O.C. visited Brigade H.Q. in the line.	
	26th		G.S.O.I ~~xxxxx~~ visited front line.	
	27th		G.S.O.2 visited front line of Left Brigade.	
	28th		G.S.O.3 visited front line of Right Brigade. 87th Brigade relieved 88th Brigade in LEFT Sector of Divisional front. (O.O.170)	Appen. IX
	29th		Hostile Artillery more active. Rumours during the afternoon of an enemy concentration on right flank of the Corps.	
	30th		German attack (included in Diary for December).	

11th December, 1917.

J.H. ~~[signature]~~
Lieut-Colonel, G.S.
29th Division.

APPENDICES.
-o-o-o-o-o-o-o-

Appendix A comprises :-

I.   29th Div. Order G.S.37/31 for Div. Tactical Exercise.

II.   29th Div. Warning Order - move from BASSEUX Area.

III. 29th Div. Order No. 164 - move from BASSEUX Area.
IV. 29th Div. Order No. 165 - move from BASSEUX Area.

V.   29th Div. Order No. 166 - move to Reserve Area.

VI. 29th Div. Order No. 168 - move to Assembly Area.

VII. 29th Div. Order No. 167 - Attack on 20th November.

VIII. 29th Div. Order No. 169 - Attack of ridge North of MASNIERES.

IX. 29th Div. Order No. 170 - relief of 88th Bde. by 87th Bde.
                                                             in the Left Sector.

Appendix B comprises :-

Various Instructions for the Operations of

20th November and following days.

29th Div. No. C.G.S.51/136 - message of congratulation

from Commander-in-Chief.

Appendix C comprises :-

29th Division Intelligence Summaries

23/11/17. to 29/11/17. both dates inclusive.

Also Location Lists.

Appendix D comprises :-

Report on Operations carried out by 29th Division

near CAMBRAI on November 20th, and following days.

                                                                   (Map attached)

-o-o-o-o-o-o-o-o-o-o-

War Diary

Appen A
mentioned in Diary

Operation Orders.

SECRET

Copy No. 4

29TH DIVISION OPERATION ORDER NO. G.S.37/31.

Reference Map issued with
No. 3 Tactical Exercise.

November 14th, 1917.

1.   The attack by the X Corps on the enemy's system of trenches between BERLES AU BOIS and BELLACOURT will take place tomorrow at an hour Zero to be notified later.

2.   As soon as the 1st objective is completely in our hands the Brigades of the 29th Division will be ordered to advance as follows :-

<u>86th Inf. Bde.</u> to Q.33 covered by an Advanced Guard with vanguard at point X in the first objective.

<u>87th Inf. Bde.</u> to W.4 and 5 covered by an Advanced Guard with vanguard at point Y in first objective.

<u>88th Inf. Bde.</u> to W.10 covered by an Advanced Guard with vanguard at point Z in first objective.

<u>227 M.G.Coy.</u> to Football Ground BAILLEUX.

3.   When the 2nd objective has been completely captured, Brigades will be ordered to advance as follows :-

<u>86th Inf. Bde.</u> will seize the high ground about the GRANGE in X.3.b., pushing forward detachments to the CANAL in X.9. They will be responsible for forming a defensive flank to the North East, consolidating the line X.9.c.1.7. to X.2.d.1.7., and will endeavour to assist by their fire the attack of the 87th Inf. Bde. on RANSART.

<u>87th Inf. Bde.</u> will attack RANSART from the West and seizing the bridge over the CANAL at X.9.c. will push forward and establish themselves on the high ground, consolidating the line X.20.central-X.15.a.2.0. - X.9.c.1.7. (junction with 86th Inf. Bde.).

<u>88th Inf. Bde.</u> will attack MONCHY AU BOIS from the North and seizing the bridge over the CANAL at W.29.d. will push forward and establish themselves on the high ground, consolidating the line E.6.d.4.2. to X.25.a.7.1.

4.   During the advance Brigades must protect their own flanks and connection between Brigades will be maintained by detached units to ensure that all ground is properly searched.

5.   During consolidation patrols will be sent to ADINFER WOOD, ADINFER and BLAIRVILLE with definite questions to answer.

6.   Each Brigade will at all times maintain a Battalion in Reserve to act as Counter-attack Battalion.

2.

7. After consolidation the defence of the new position will be arranged in depth, the line of observation and the line of resistance being in front of the crest of the spur and the Reserve line in rear. Special works as Bridgeheads will be prepared and strongly wired.

8. A Contact Aeroplane will fly over the Divisional front at 1-0 p.m. Troops will light flares only when called for, either by Klaxon Horn or Very Lights. Divisional and Brigade Headquarters will be marked by the authorised ground sheets, and communication to the aeroplane will be either by shutter or lamp.

9. Divisional Headquarters will remain at BASSEUX with a Forward Report Centre at the Tin Huts about W.12.b.90.25. (on L'ALOUETTE - RANSART ROAD).

10. ACKNOWLEDGE.

Lieut-Colonel, G.S.,

29th Division.

Copies to :-

86th Inf. Bde.
87th Inf. Bde.
88th Inf. Bde.
227th M.G.Coy.
Officer i/c Signals.
59th Squadron R.F.C.
O.C., Mech. Sch., WAILLY.
D..G.O.

SECRET

No 4

Routine Order No. G.S.37/30
by
Major-General Sir Beauvoir de Lisle, K.C.B., D.S.O.
-o-o-o-o-o-o-o-o-o-o-o-o-o-o-o-o-o-o-o-o-o-o-o-o-o-o-o-

Ref. 1/20,000 51 C S.E.   Nov. 14th, 1917.

86th Inf. Bde.   1. The troops as in margin will parade tomorrow to carry
87th Inf. Bde.   out the Third Tactical Exercise already issued.
88th Inf. Bde.   Dress. Fighting Order but without ammunition.
227th M.G.Coy.

2. Brigades will be formed up by 10.30 a.m. as under :-

   86th Inf. Bde.   In square Q.36. with vanguard at the
                     point X - Brigade H.Q. Q.36 central.

   87th Inf. Bde.   In square W.4. & 5., but west of the
                     track BASSEUX - L'ALLOUETTE with
                     vanguard at point Y - Bde. H.Q.
                     W.4.b.3.0.

   88th Inf. Bde.   In square W.10. with vanguard at point Z.
                     Brigade H.Q. W.10.b.9.0.

   227th M.G.Coy.   Football ground BASSEUX.

3. O.C. Div. Sig. Coy. will connect these H.Q. by
telephone with Div. H.Q. As Brigade H.Q. moves forward
O.C. Div. Sig. Coy. will maintain communication.

4. No formed body of troops will be East of the
BERLES - BELLACOURT Road after 10.30 a.m., until orders
have been received from Div. H.Q. for the advance to
commence.

                                    J.H. Moore

                                    Lieut-Colonel, G.S.,

                                    29th Division.

       Copies to :-
                    86th Inf. Bde.
                    87th Inf. Bde.
                    88th Inf. Bde.
                    227th M.G.Coy.
                    Off. i/c Sigs.
                    59th Squadron R.F.C.
                    O.C. Mech. Sch. WAILLY.
                    D.A.G.O.

SECRET Appx III

Copy No. 4

29TH DIVISION ORDER NO.134.

Reference Map, 1/100,000 LENS
                    AMIENS

1. 29th Division (less Artillery and R.E. and Pioneer Bn) will move from its present area by rail and road on nights 16/17th, 17/18th.

2. (a) Move of personnel will be by rail in accordance with time table which has already been issued by the A.A.& Q.M.G. Times of starting and routes to station will be notified later.
    (b) All transport will move by road commencing 13th inst. in accordance with attached March Tables "A" & "B".

3. All marching will take place between the hours of 4.p.m. and 7.a.m.

4. 1 Copy of Restriction as to Movement in IV.Corps Area is issued herewith. These restrictions are to be strictly adhered to.

5. Groups of transport will be placed under the command of Brigade Transport Officers or Senior Transport Officer, who will be responsible for carrying out the instructions contained in this order.

6. Billets in BAPAUME will be obtained on application to Town Major - (see para 9 attached, Restrictions to Movements).

7. ACKNOWLEDGE.

A.T. Miller
Capt
for Lieut-Colonel G.S.
29th Division.

16th November 1917.

P.T.O.

Issued at 1 a.m.

Copies 1 - 5 G.S.
       6   Q.
       7   86th Bde
       8   87th Bde
       9   88th Bde
      10   Off. i/c Sigs.
      11   1/2nd Monmouths.
      12   A.D.M.S.
      13   A.P.M.
      14   D.A.G.O.
      15   D.A.D.O.S.
      16   D.A.D.V.S.
      17   227th M.G?Coy.
      18   Camp Commandant.
      19   Div.Train.
      20   S.S.O.
      21   29th D.S.C.
      22   IV Corps
      23   VI Corps
      24   Town Major BAPAUME.

SECRET.

Restrictions as to Movement.

With a view to enforcing the strictest march discipline the following arrangements will be adhered to :-

1. Intervals of 200 yards will be maintained between Batteries, Sections of Divisional Ammunition Columns, Companies, Transport of Battalions, and similar units.
In bus or lorry movements a five minutes interval between each group of 6 vehicles will be maintained.

2. No double banking will anywhere be permitted.

3. All units except a column consisting entirely of mechanically propelled vehicles, will observe the regulation clock hour halts.

4. In the event of a vehicle breaking down, it will be at once be cleared off the road.

5. An officer will march in rear of each Battery, Section D.A.C., Company or similar unit.

6. A free passage for traffic movement in the opposite direction will be kept.

7. On arrival at destination main traffic routes must be cleared.

8. A guide from the Town Major, BAPAUME, will meet each unit which is to be billetted in BAPAUME at the road junction, H.27.a.6.2. (sheet 57 C) as it arrives and lead it straight to its destination.

9. The starting point for all units leaving ARRAS will be the bridge over the railway at G.29.c.6.6. (sheet 51 B 1/40,000).

10. The completion of all moves to IVth Corps area will be reported direct to IVth Corps Headquarters.

11. Troops are not to be informed of their destination until arrival in IVth Corps Area.

H.Q.IVth Corps.,
8th Novr., 1917.

(Sd) W.C.EADY, Capt., G.S.,
for Brigadier General,
General Staff, IVth Corps.

March Table for TRANSPORT 15/17th November. Table "A"

SECRET

Item.	Unit.	From.	To.	Route.	Restrictions.
1.	Transport of 86th Bde. Group. H.Q. 86th Bde. 4 Battalions. 86th M. Gun Coy. 227th M. Gun Coy. 89th Field Amb. No. 2 Coy. Train.	BLAIRVILLE and HENDECOURT.	BAPAUME.	HENDECOURT – BOISLEUX AU MONT – BOISLEUX ST. MARC – Main ARRAS – BAPAUME Road.	Not to enter BOISLEUX AU MONT before 7 p.m. to be clear of the Main ARRAS – BAPAUME road by 1.30 a.m.
2.	Transport of 88th Bde. Group. H.Q. 88th Bde. 4 Battalions. 88th M. Gun Coy. 88th Field Amb. No. 4 Coy. Train.	POMMIER, BERLES & BIENVILLERS.	BAPAUME.	HANNESCAMPS – BUCQUOY – ACHIET LE PETIT – ACHIET LE GRAND – BIHUCOURT – BAPAUME.	Head of column to leave BIENVILLERS at 6.0 p.m. To be across level crossing at ACHIET LE GRAND by 11 p.m. Not to enter BAPAUME before 12 midnight. To be clear of ARRAS – BAPAUME Road by 1.30 a.m.
3.	Transport of Div. H.Q. Mob. Vet. Sec.	BASSEUX	BAPAUME	BASSEUX – BELLACOURT – RANSART – ADINFER – AYETTE – ABLAINZEVELLE – ACHIET LE GRAND – BIHUCOURT – BAPAUME.	Head of column to leave BASSEUX at 5.45 p.m. Not to arrive level crossing before 11.15 p.m. and to be clear of same by 11.30 p.m. To be clear of ARRAS – BAPAUME Road by 1.30 a.m.

SECRET

Item.	Unit.	From.	To.	Route.	Restrictions.
4.	Transport of 87th Bde. Group:- H.Q. 87th Bde. 4 Battalions. 87th M. Gun Coy. 87th Field Amb. No. 3 Coy. Train.	BAILLEULMONT - BAILLEULVAL - BELLACOURT.	BAPAUME	BASSEUX - BELLACOURT - RAMSART - ADINFER - ALETTE - ABLAINZEVELLE - ACHIET LE GRAND - BIHUCOURT - BAPAUME.	Head of column to arrive BASSEUX 8.15pm. Not to arrive level crossing before 11.45pm. To be clear of ARRAS - BAPAUME Road by 1.30am.

March Table for TRANSPORT 17/18th November.   Table "B"

SECRET

Item.	Unit.	From.	To.	Route.	Restrictions.
5.	86th Bde. Group.	BAPAUME.	HAUT-ALLAINES.	BAPAUME - BOUCHAVESNES - MOISLAINS.	Not to leave BAPAUME before 4 p.m. Not to enter MOISLAINS before 8.15 p.m.
6.	87th Bde. Group.	BAPAUME.	HAUT-ALLAINES.	As in Item No. 5 thence HAUT-ALLAINES.	To follow in rear of 86th Bde. Group.
7.	Div. H.Q. Group.	BAPAUME.	MOISLAINS.	BAPAUME - BOUCHAVESNES - MOISLAINS.	To follow in rear of 87th Bde. Group.
8.	88th Bde. Group.	BAPAUME.	MOISLAINS.	As in Item No. 7.	To follow in rear of Div. H.Q. Group.

Times of starting to be arranged between Officers in charge of Transport Groups.

SECRET

29th Division No. G.G.S.67/81.

29TH DIVISION WARNING ORDER.

Ref. 1/40,000 map, sheet 51c.

1. The 29th Division (less Artillery, R.E. and Pioneer Bn.), will move by rail from its present area on the night of the 17th/18th.

2. Entraining Station will be BOISLEUX AU MONT: destination and details of train arrangements will be notified later.

3. No horses, baggage or transport vehicles will be taken on the trains for this movement: orders for the march of transport by road will be issued in due course. All baggage will be reduced to a minimum.

4. ACKNOWLEDGE.

W. G. Wyrne Capt
for Lieut-Colonel, G.S.,
29th Division.

15th November, 1917.

Copies 1 - 4	G.S.	11 Off. i/c Sigs.	18 VI Corps.
5	"Q"	12 1/2nd Monmouths.	19 D.A.D.O.S.
6	C.R.A.	13 A.D.M.S.	20 D.A.D.V.S.
7	C.R.E.	14 A.P.M.	21 Camp Commdt.
8	86th Inf Bde.	15 D.M.G.O	22 Div Train.
9	87th Inf. Bde.	16 227th M.G. Coy.	23 S.S.O.
10	88th Inf Bde	17 III Corps.	24 29th Div. S.C.

SECRET

Moves of Personnel 17/18th

Table "G"

Item.	Unit.	From.	To.	Route.	Restrictions.
1.	Div. H.Q.	PERONNE.	MOISLANS.	PERONNE – ETRICOURT Road.	Not to enter HAUT ALLAINES till 7.30 p.m.
2.	88th Bde. Group.	PERONNE.	MOISLANS.	– do –	To follow in rear of Div. H.Q.
3.	87th Bde. Group.	PERONNE.	HAUT-ALLAINES.	– do –	–
4.	86th Bde. Group.	PERONNE.	HAUT-ALLAINES.	– do –	March to be complete by 7.0 a.m. 18th instant.

SECRET Appen IV

Copy No. 4

29th DIVISION ORDER NO.165.

Reference Map 1/100,000. LENS.
AMIENS.

1. Reference 29th Division Order No.164 dated 16th November 1917 para 2(a) and Instructions for Entrainment issued under Instructions No.5 dated 15th November 1917.
Personnel marching to entraining station on 17/18th inst may do so by any route convenient, time of starting being regulated by the time of arrival at Entraining Station as laid down and the observation of normal halts and distances.

2. It is possible that troops of another Division will be using the BEAUMETZ - RANSART - ADINFER Road. The interval of 200 yards maintained between companies will enable companies of this Division to cross the above road between companies of the other Division.

3. On detrainment, troops will march to billets, groups being disposed as follows :-

    Div. H.Q.   MOISLANS (5 miles N. of PERONNE)
    86th Bde Group. HAUT-ALLAINES (3 miles N. of PERONNE)
    87th Bde Group. HAUT-ALLAINES
    88th Bde Group. MOISLANS.

4. These movements will be carried out with distances of 100 yards instead of 200 yards between Companies and Columns of equivalent length.

5. Moves will take place in accordance with attached March Table "C"

6. Div. H.Q. will close at BASSEUX at 2 P.M. on 17th inst and will reopen at the same hour at MOISLANS.

7. ACKNOWLEDGE.

Lieut-Colonel G.S.
29th Division.

Issued at 3 P.M.

16th November 1917.

Copies	1 - 4	G.S.	16	227th M.G.Coy
	5	Q.	17	Camp Comdt.
	6	86th Bde.	18	Div. Train.
	7	87th Bde.	19	S.S.O.
	8	88th Bde.	20	29th D.S.C.
	9	Off. i/c Sigs	21	IV Corps.
	10	1/2nd Mon. R.	22	VI Corps.
	11	A.D.M.S.	23	Town Major BAPAUME
	12	A.P.M.		
	13	D.M.G.O.	24	D.A.A.G.
	14	D.A.D.O.S.	25	40th Division.
	15	D.A.D.V.S.		

SECRET

Moves of Personnel 17/18th   Table "C"

Item.	Unit.	From.	To.	Route.	Restrictions.
1.	Div. H.Q.	PERONNE.	MOISLANS.	PERONNE - ETRICOURT Road.	Not to enter HAUT ALLAINES till 7.30 p.m.
2.	88th Bde. Group.	PERONNE.	MOISLANS.	- do -	To follow in rear of Div. H.Q.
3.	87th Bde. Group.	PERONNE.	HAUT-ALLAINS.	- do -	-
4.	86th Bde. Group.	PERONNE.	HAUT-ALLAINS.	- do -	March to be complete by 7.0 a.m. 18th instant.

Copy No. 4

29TH DIVISION ORDER NO. 166.
-o-o-o-o-o-o-o-o-o-o-o-o-o-o-o-o-

Ref. 1/100,000 AMIENS & VALENCIENNES. November 17th, 1917.
1/40,000 57 C. and 62 C.

1. 29th Division (less Artillery, R.E. and 1/2nd Monmouths Pioneer Bn.) will move from the ALLAINES - MOISLANS Area to Reserve Area on the night 18/19th in accordance with the attached March Table "D".

2. Locations in the Reserve Area will be as follows :-

Div. H.Q.	MOISLAINS (no change).
86th Bde. Group. (less No. 2 Coy. Train)	EQUANCOURT.
87th Bde. Group. (less No. 3 Coy. Train)	FINS.
88th Bde. Group. (less No. 4 Coy. Train)	SOREL.
1st Line Transport.	W.13.b. (Sheet 57c).
Div. Train.	V.29.a. (Sheet 57c).

3. (a) Coys. of the Div. Train will march with their respective Brigade Groups branching off on arrival at Div. Train Lines at V.29.a. on main NURLU - FINS Road.

   (b) All 1st Line Transport (less cookers and water carts) will concentrate in 1st Line Transport Lines in W.13.b. Any transport required to draw rations and stores from sidings enumerated in 29th Division Instructions No. 2 (Administration) para. 7(d) must be returned to Transport Lines W.13.b. as soon as work is completed.

4. Brigades should have representatives at the points where their Company of the Div. Train and their 1st Line Transport branch off to ensure that there is no delay and no blocking of the road.

5. The above movements will be carried out with distances of 100 yards instead of 200 yards between Companies and columns of equivalent length.

6. Completion of move will be notified by wire to these H.Q.

7. Div. H.Q. will remain at MOISLAINS.

8. ACKNOWLEDGE.

Issued at 7 a.m.

A.T. Miller. Capt.
Lieut-Colonel, G.S.,
29th Division.

P.T.O.

Distribution of 29th Division Order No. 166.

```
Copies 1 - 4    General Staff.
       5        "Q".
       6        86th Inf. Bde.
       7        87th Inf. Bde.
       8        88th Inf. Bde.
       9        Off. i/c Sigs.
      10        1/2nd Monmouths.
      11        A.D.M.S.
      12        A.P.M.
      13        D.M.G.O.
      14        D.A.D.O.S.
      15        D.A.D.V.S.
      16.       227th M.G. Coy.
      17        Camp Commdt.
      18        Div. Train.
      19        S.S.O.
      20        29th D.S.C.
      21        III Corps.
      22        6th Division.
      23        12th Division.
      24        20th Division.
      25        6th Motor Machine Gun Battery.
      26        Capt. Quill.
```

Moves of Infantry 18/19th November, 1917.   Table "D".

Unit.	From.	To.	Route.	Restrictions.
88th Bde. Group. H.Q. 88th Bde. 4 Battalions. 88th M.G. Coy. 88th T.L. Bty. 88th Field Amb. No. 4 Coy. Train	MOISLAINS	SOREL LE GRAND	MOISLAINS - NURLU - FINS - Road junction W.13.b.2.9 - SOREL LE GRAND.	Tail of column to be clear of MOISLAINS by 5.45 p.m. Head of column not to enter FINS till 7.15 p.m.
86th Bde. Group. H.Q. 86th Bde. 4 Battalions. 86th M.G. Coy. 86th T.M. Bty. 89th Field Amb. No.2 Coy. Train 227th M.G. Coy.	HAUT-ALLAINES	EQUANCOURT	HAUT-ALLAINES - MOISLAINS - NURLU - FINS - EQUANCOURT.	Tail of column to be clear of HAUT-ALLAINES by 7.50 p.m. Head of column not to enter MOISLAINS before 7.0 p.m.
87th Bde. Group. H.Q. 87th Bde. 4 Battalions. 87th M.G. Coy. 87th T.M. Bty. 87th Field Amb. No.3 Coy. Train	HAUT-ALLAINES	FINS	HAUT-ALLAINES - MOISLAINS - NURLU - FINS.	Head of column to leave HAUT-ALLAINES at 8.30 p.m.

SECRET

Copy No. 4

29TH DIVISION ORDER NO. 168.

18th November, 1917.

1. With reference to 29th Division Order No. 167 dated 18th November, 1917, the assembly march on Y/Z night will be carried out in accordance with the attached March Table "E".

2. An amended tracing showing the sub-division of the area was issued to all concerned on 15th instant, under this office No. O.G.S.68/79.

3. Special attention is to be paid to the following points :-

   (I) ABSOLUTE SILENCE AND NO LIGHTS.

   (II) STRICT PUNCTUALITY and adherence to times in March Table.

4. The track from W.4.A.0.5. to road junction Q.23.C.8.4. which will be used by the 86th Brigade Group, will be picquetted by a platoon of the Corps Cyclists (under 2/Lt. ORFORD) in pairs at intervals of about 150 yards. One man from each pair will pass the head of each Battalion on to the next pair and so on.

   This track should be reconnoitred tomorrow, if not already done, by daylight by representatives of 86th Inf. Bde.

5. Arrival of Brigade Groups, R.E., and 6th M.M.Gun Battery in Assembly positions will be reported to Div. H.Q. ST. QUENTIN MILL by telephoning the word NORMAL or by runner.

6. Distances of 100 yards will be maintained between companies and similar units West of the Daylight line.

7. ACKNOWLEDGE.

A.T. Miller Capt

Lieut-Colonel, G.S.,
29th Division.

Issued at 11 p.m.

Copies			
1 - 4	G.S.	13	A.D.M.S.
5	"Q".	14	D.M.G.O.
6	86th Inf. Bde.	15	227th M.G. Coy.
7	87th Inf. Bde.	16	III Corps.
8	88th Inf. Bde.	17	6th Division.
9	C.R.A.	18	12th Division.
10	C.R.E.	19	20th Division.
11	Off. i/c Sigs.	20	6th Motor M.G. Battery.
12	1/2nd Monmouth R.	21	2nd Bde. Tanks.
		22	O.C. Platoon Corps Cyclists.

M.

Assembly March Y/Z Night.   Table "E".

Item.	Unit.	From.	To.	Route.	Restrictions.
1.	87th Bde. Group H.Q. 87th Bde. H.Q. 4 Battalions 87th M.G. Coy. 87th T.M. Bty. 1 sect. 510th Field Coy. Bearers 87th Field Amb.	FINS	Assembly Area about R.19.c. & Q.30.	FINS - Cross Roads at W.4.a.0.5. - GOUZEAUCOURT thence by road junction Q.30.d.2.8. or Q.30.d.8.7.	Head to pass Road junction V.12.b.5.0. at 1.20 a.m. Tail of column to be clear of FINS by 2.20 a.m. and to be clear of Road junction Q.30.c.Central by 3.40 a.m.
2.	88th Bde. Group H.Q. 88th Bde. H.Q. 4 Battalions 88th M.G. Coy. 88th T.M. Bty. 1 sect. 510th Field Coy. Bearers 88th Field Amb.	SOREL LE GRAND	Assembly Area about Q.29.c. & d. Q.35.a. & b.	SOREL LE GRAND - Road junction W.15.b.2.9. - Cross Roads at 2.25 a.m. HEUDICOURT W.15.Central Not to arrive at Road junction W.15.c.Central d.9.8. - REVELON F. - Road junct. Q.33.c.Central - thence into Area.	Head of column to pass Road junct. W.15.b.2.9. at 2.25 a.m. Not to arrive at Road junct. Q.36.c.Central before 3.50 a.m. to be clear by 5.0 a.m.
3.	89th Bde. Group H.Q. 89th Bde. H.Q. 4 Battalions 89th M.G. Coy. 89th T.M. Bty. 1 sect. 510th Field Coy. Bearers 89th Field Amb. 327th M.G. Coy.	EQUANCOURT	Assembly Area about Q.23. Q.29.a. & b.	EQUANCOURT - FINS - Cross roads W.4.a.0.5. - thence by track to QUEENS CROSS Q.23.d.4.4. - thence by track to Road junction Q.23.c.6.4. thence into assembly area.	Not to enter FINS before 2.30 a.m., to be clear of FINS by 3.40 a.m. To be clear of Cross Roads W.4.a.0.5. by 4.20 a.m.
4.	497th Fd.Coy.RE 455th Fd.Coy.RE 510th Fd.Coy.RE (less 3 secs)	SOREL NURLU	Assembly Area about Q.34.c. & d. Q.35.c. & d.	FINS - Cross Roads W.4.a.0.5. - thence into Assembly Area.	Head of column to pass Road junct. V.12.b.5.0. at 3.50 a.m. To be East of Cross Roads W.4.a.0.5. by 4.40 a.m.
5.	8th M.M. Gun Battery.	AIZECOURT LE BAS	Assembly Area about N.5.a. & b.	LIERAMONT - Road junction V.26.a.1.5. - SOREL LE GRAND - Cross Roads W.15.b.3.9. - HEUDECOURT - Cross Roads W.15 Central 0.5. - Assembly Area.	To arrive at Cross Roads W.4.a.0.5. at 4.40 a.m. To be East of Cross Roads W.4.a.0.5. by 5.0 a.m.

Identification Trace for use with Artillery Maps.

NOTE.—(1) These traces are intended to facilitate the communication of information as to the position of targets, which have been located on a squared map.
(2) The squares on this trace are 500 yards in length on the 1/10,000 scale, 1,000 yards in length on the 1/20,000 scale, and 2,000 yards in length on the 1/40,000 scale.
(3) The squares on the trace are fitted to the squares of the map showing the targets, which are then drawn on the trace. Sufficient letters and numbers must also be added to enable the recipient to place the trace in the correct position on his own map. A little detail may also be traced, but this is not essential. The name and scale of the map to which the trace refers must be always given. The trace can be used for the 1/10,000, 1/20,000, or 1/40,000 scale.

G.S.G.S. 3088.

Tracing taken from Sheet_____

of the 1:_____ map of_____

Signature_____ Date_____

Copy No. 4

29TH DIVISION ORDER NO. 187.

Ref. Map issued with
Instruction No. 1.   18th November, 1917.

1. On the date known as Z day, the IIIrd Corps and the IVth Corps on its left will attack. Zero hour will be notified. This operation will be carried out in five phases.

1st Phase. The attack of the German first and second lines of defence by the 12th Division on the right, 20th Division in the Centre, 6th Division on the left, and 29th Division in Reserve.

2nd Phase. On the capture of the German second (BROWN) line the 29th Division will pass through the leading Divisions as follows :-

The 88th Brigade with one section 510th Field Coy. R.E. and the bearer division 88th Field Ambulance attached, will force the crossing of the ST. QUENTIN CANAL at MASNIERES assisted by tanks and will seize and consolidate the MASNIERES - BEAUREVOIR line from G.27.B. to the MASNIERES - CAMBRAI Road G.20.B. inclusive, and will be protected on its right flank by the 59th Brigade x ..   , 20th Division, which will form a defensive flank from M.8.b. through M.2.d. and b. to the road junction G.26.d.1.5.

x Brig-Gen. HYSLOP, D.S.O.

The 87th Brigade with one section 510th Field Coy. R.E. and bearer division 87th Field Ambulance attached, will force the crossings of the Canal East of MARCOING, and assisted by tanks seize and consolidate the MASNIERES - BEAUREVOIR line from the MASNIERES - CAMBRAI Road G.20.b. exclusive to the Canal at L.12.c.

The 86th Brigade with one section 510th Field Coy. R.E. and bearer division 89th Field Ambulance attached, with the assistance of tanks will capture and consolidate a position from the Canal in L.12. through L.11.d. and c. North of NINE WOOD to PREMY CHAPEL Hill where its left flank will be protected by the 18th Brigade (Brig-Gen. CRAUFURD) of the 6th Division. On attaining the above line success will be exploited by strong patrols.

3rd Phase. Three Divisions of Cavalry will pass through the 29th Division. The 5th Cav. Div. followed by 2nd Cav. Div. at MASNIERES and MARCOING working to the East and North-East, and the 1st Cav. Div. moving on NOYELLES and CANTAING to the North, with one Regiment moving East of the Canal. Roads and bridges are to be kept clear to ensure the passage of the Cavalry is not impeded.

4th Phase. As soon as the above mentioned position is consolidated by the 29th Division, and sufficient Cavalry have passed over to screen the further advance, the 88th Brigade will push forward to G.23.Central

/and

and consolidate a position across the top of the
spur back to the bridge on the Canal at G.34.c.0.9.
leaving two battalions to hold the BEAUREVOIR line.
The 87th Brigade will send one battalion to hold
and consolidate the Northern and Eastern fringe of
RUMILLY, and a second battalion to the knoll in
G.2. and 3. keeping two battalions in the BEAUREVOIR
line.

        In support of the above movements the Brigade
of the 20th Division holding the line from N.2.d. to
MASNIERES will move forward and establish themselves
on the BONAVIS - CREVECOEUR ridge. A second Brigade
of the 20th Division will move to MASNIERES.

        The 86th Brigade will then be relieved by the
6th Division and will come into Reserve in MARCOING
or East of that village and be ready to follow up
the Cavalry at dawn on Z plus 1 day.

5th Phase.   At dawn on Z plus 1 day the Cavalry will continue
its advance to the East and North-East and a defensive
flank will be formed by the IIIrd Corps as follows :-

        The 20th Division will hold the Eastern approaches
to CREVECOEUR and as far North as the track in
H.19.a.

        The 86th Brigade moving at 6.15 a.m. will take
over and consolidate a defensive position from the
track in H.19.a. along the Eastern slope of the spur
in H.13.c. and a. and H.7.c. as far North as LA BELLE
ETOILE knoll in B.25c. exclusive.

        The 87th Brigade will move to NIERGNIES G.6.
and will consolidate the knoll LA BELLE ETOILE
inclusive, and the Northern slopes of the spur running
to the West as far as A.28.Central, leaving a detachment on the knoll G.2. and 3.

        The 88th Brigade will move to a position about
G.11.Central ready to operate as required.

        Div. H.Q. will remain at QUENTIN HILL during
Z day and on Z plus 1 day will move forward to a
position about RUMILLY, which will be notified to
Brigades later.

2.   Brigades will assemble in their allotted area on
Y/Z night by Zero - 2 hours.

3.   At Zero the leading battalions of each Infantry
Brigade, preceded by small Advanced Guards, will take over the
present front line from the 20th and 6th Divisions as under :-

88th Bde. from R.14.d.9.7. to the Sunken Road in R.8.d. (incl.)
H.Q. FUSILIER ALLEY R.14.d.5.1. approx.

87th Bde. from Sunken Road in R.8.d. (excl.) to R.7.b.9.0.
H.Q. R.14.a.9.9. approx.

86th Bde. from R.7.b.9.0. to R.7.a.0.5.
H.Q. R.13.a.2.7. approx.

4.   As soon as the second objective (BROWN LINE) has
been captured and orders received from Divisional H.Q. to
"Move".

        The 88th Inf. Bde. will move via the LA VACQUERIE

/ valley

- 3 -

valley, and crossing the BROWN LINE about square L.35. will attack LASNIERES from the South-West and will continue the attack consolidating the line as laid down in para. 1, Phase 2.

The 87th Inf. Bde. will move via the Eastern slopes of the COUILLET WOOD valley, and crossing the BROWN LINE about square L.34. will attack MARCOING from the South, and will continue the attack consolidating the line as laid down in para. 1, Phase 2.

The 86th Inf. Bde. will cross the BROWN LINE in square L.27. and will attack and capture NINE WOOD consolidating the RED LINE from the Wood to the Canal. They will be responsible for forming a defensive flank to the North, and will assist by their fire the attack of the 87th Inf. Bde. on MARCOING from the South-West.

5. The attached tracing shews the dividing lines between Brigades.

6. The advance of each Brigade will be covered by one Brigade of Field or Horse Artillery as under :-

88th Inf. Bde. by 15th Bde. R.H.A. firing from positions about R.5.c.

87th Inf. Bde. by 17th Bde. R.F.A. firing from positions about L.33.b.

86th Inf. Bde. by 16th Bde. R.H.A. firing from positions about L.32.d.

The orders for the advance of this Artillery will be issued by Div. H.Q. as soon as the BROWN LINE has been captured.

7. Four tanks are allotted to each Infantry Brigade but troops will in no case wait for the tanks if by so doing their advance is likely to be retarded. The positions at which these tanks will be picked up will be notified later.

8. A Contact Aeroplane will fly over the Corps front at
    Zero plus 45 mins.
    Zero plus 2 hrs. 15 mins.
    Zero plus 3 hrs.
    Zero plus 3 hrs. 30 mins.

and subsequently as ordered.

9. Watches will be synchronised by a Staff Officer from Div. H.Q. at 9.30 a.m. and 12.30 p.m. on Y day.

10. Divisional H.Q. will be established at QUENTIN MILL R.31.d.1.3. at 4.30 p.m. Y/Z night.

11. ACKNOWLEDGE.

Issued at 1.30 am

Lieut-Colonel, G.S.,
29th Division.

Distribution of 29th Division Order No. 167.

```
Copies 1 - 4    General Staff.
         5      86th Inf. Bde.
         6      87th Inf. Bde.
         7      88th Inf. Bde.
         8      C.R.A.
         9      C.R.E.
        10      "Q".
        11      Off. i/c Sigs.
        12      1/2nd Monmouths.
        13      A.D.M.S.
        14      D.M.G.O.
        15      227th M.G. Coy.
        16      III Corps.
        17      6th Division.
        18      12th Division.
        19      20th Division.
        20      2nd Bde. Tanks.
        21      6th Motor M.G. Battery.
```

29th Division No. C.G.S.87/85.

"G".
86th Inf. Bde.
87th Inf. Bde.
88th Inf. Bde.
C.R.A.
C.R.E.
Off. i/c Sigs.
A.D.M.S.
A.P.M.
227th M.G. Coy.
1/2nd Monmouth Regt.
- -

With reference to para. 1 of 29th Division Order No. 167, Z day will be 20th November, 1917.

ACKNOWLEDGE by wire.

November, 1917.

Lieut-Colonel, G.S.,
29th Division.

29th Division No. C.G.S.67/86.

"Q".
86th Inf. Bde.
87th Inf. Bde.
88th Inf. Bde.
C.R.A.
C.R.E.
Off. i/c Sigs.
A.D.M.S.
A.P.M.
227th M.G. Coy.
1/2nd Monmouth Regt.   6th Motor M.G. Battery.

Reference para. 1 of 29th Division Order No. 167.

The hour of Zero will be **6.20 A.M. 20th NOVEMBER**

This hour will only be communicated to those whom it immediately concerns and will under no circumstances be sent over the telephone either in code or clear.

ACKNOWLEDGE by wire.

A.T. Miller
Capt

Lieut-Colonel, G.S.,
29th Division.

19th November, 1917.

6 Units
89th Field Ambce.
No 2. Coy. Train.
M. Brigade Signals.   ack.
227 M.G Co.   CgS.
19th Nov. 1917.

SECRET.

Third Army No. G.S.56/154.

III Corps.
IV Corps.
Cavalry Corps.
Tank Corps.

Adv.G.H.Q.   )
G.O.C., R.A.   ) For information.
3rd Bde. R.F.C.)

OPERATION G.Y.

1. The Army Commander wishes all ranks to understand that the element of surprise is the key note of the operations of the III and IV Army Corps.

2. If this is attained and we are successful in over-running the enemy's line of defence, a unique opportunity for the Cavalry action becomes possible. This action may have a most far reaching effect, not only on the local situation, but on the course of the war.

3. Attacking Divisions must realise that the boldest action is required during the first two days. Hesitation and waiting for support may enable the enemy to recover from his first surprise and delay the advance of the Cavalry.

4. It is with supreme confidence that the Army Commander leaves the issue in the hands of all ranks of his command.

Louis Vaughan

Major-General,
General Staff, Third Army.

17th November 1917.

Copies to:- 'Q'.
C.E.
A.D.G.T.III.

Secret No. C.G.S. 67/91

86th Inf. Bde.
87th Inf. Bde.
88th Inf. Bde.
----

1.   Reference para. 7 of 29th Division Order No. 167, the 4 tanks for each Infantry Brigade will assemble in NO MANS LAND immediately in front of the Sector of our present front line allotted to each Infantry Brigade under para. 3 of above order.

2.   The two wireless tanks referred to in para. 5 of 29th Division Instruction No. 4 will assemble -

   One with the 4 tanks of the 88th Brigade.
   One with the 4 tanks of the 86th Brigade.

   These wireless tanks will remain with the H.Q. of these Brigades.

                                        Lieut-Colonel, G.S.,
18th November, 1917.   29th Division.

M.

War Diary.   Appendix VIII   SECRET

Copy No. 4

29TH DIVISION ORDER NO. 169.

Ref. 1/10,000 Map RUMILLY.   24th November, 1917.

1. The Division will attack the ridge North of MASNIERES on a date and at an hour Zero to be notified later; the objective being from the MILL House G.21.B.3.2. along the German trench to the CAMBRAI Road G.20.B.½.8½. thence in a westerly direction to G.20.A.1.9.

2. The attack will be made by the 86th Brigade on the right and the 87th Brigade on the left. The MASNIERES - CAMBRAI Road will be the dividing line between Brigades and will be inclusive to both Brigades.

3. A Heavy Artillery bombardment will be directed on the southern portion of RUMILLY to destroy it and on the houses on the CAMBRAI Road North of our present position. Destructive shoots will also be directed against occupied enemy's trenches within and close to the area to be attacked.

4. The attack will be made under cover of

   (a) A creeping barrage.
   (b) A standing barrage.
   (c) A creeping machine gun barrage.
   (d) A standing Stokes Gun barrage of all three batteries.
   (e) A standing Heavy Artillery barrage.

   The ground on the flanks will be dealt with by Artillery from 20th Division on the right and the 6th Division on the left.

5. The creeping barrage will fall at Zero on a line 100 yards in front of our position and will move at the rate of 50 yards in 2 minutes until it reaches a line 200 yards in advance of the objective where it will remain for one hour. This line will be the S.O.S. line if required. Until the objective is reached the rate of fire will not be less than 4 rounds a minute.

6. Mopping-up parties will be detailed to search all ground gained.

7. As soon as the advance is launched supporting troops with machine guns will move up into our front line and garrison it. A flank detachment of 2 machine guns and one company will be posted on the right flank of the 86th Brigade.

8. A contact aeroplane will fly over at Zero plus ½ hour. Flares will be lighted when called for. Troops not lighting flares should always wave their helmets to contact aeroplane.

9. A map shewing the objective and tracings shewing Artillery and Machine Gun barrages, are attached.

10. ACKNOWLEDGE.

Issued at 5 p.m.

J.H. Moore
Lieut-Colonel, G.S.,
29th Division.

Copies 1 - 4 G.S.   10 88th Inf. Bde.   16 III Corps.
       5 "A"   11 Off. i/c Sigs.   17 6th Div.
       6 C.R.A.   12 1/2nd Monmouths.   18 12th Div.
       7 C.R.E.   13 A.D.M.S.   19 20th Div.
       8 86th Inf. Bde. 14 D.M.G.O.   20 No. 6 M.G. Bty.
       9 87th Inf. Bde. 15 227 M.G. Coy.

War Diary.

SECRET

Copy No. 4

29TH DIVISION ORDER NO. 170.
-o-o-o-o-o-o-o-o-o-o-o-o-o-o-o-o-o-

27th November, 1917.

1. (a) On the night of 28th/29th November, the 87th Brigade will relieve the 88th Brigade in the Left Sector of the Divisional front.

   (b) All details of relief will be arranged direct between Brigadiers concerned.

   (c) Command will pass to B.G.C. 87th Brigade on completion of relief.

2. All trench stores, maps and aeroplane photographs will be handed over on relief.

3. On relief the 88th Brigade will be accommodated in MARCOING.

4. Completion of relief will be reported to Div. H.Q.

5. ACKNOWLEDGE.

Lieut-Colonel, G.S.,
29th Division.

Issued at 5 p.m.

Copies 1 - 4   G.S.   14   D.A.G.O.
       5   "Q".   15   227th M.G. Coy.
       6   C.R.A.   16   D.A.D.O.S.
       7   C.R.E.   17   D.A.D.V.S.
       8   86th Inf. Bde. 18   Div. Train.
       9   87th Inf. Bde. 19   S.S.O.
      10   88th Inf. Bde. 20   A.P.M.
      11   Off. i/c Sigs. 21   III Corps.
      12   1/2nd Monmouths. 22 6th Div.
      13   A.D.M.S.   23   20th Div.

M.

SECRET

Copy No. 8

29TH DIVISION ORDER NO. 171.
=o=o=o=o=o=o=o=o=o=o=o=o=o=o=

29th November, 1917.

1. (a) On night of 30th Nov./1st Dec. two Battalions 88th Inf. Bde. will relieve two Battalions 86th Inf. Bde. in the Right Sector of the Divisional front.
Battalions of 88th Inf. Bde. will come under the Command of B.G.C. 86th Inf. Bde. On relief Battalions of 86th Inf. Bde. will be withdrawn to MARCOING coming under the Command of B.G.C. 88th Inf. Bde.

   (b) On night of 1st/2nd December remainder of 88th Inf. Bde. will relieve the remainder of 86th Inf. Bde.

2. All details of relief will be arranged direct between B.G.C. 86th and 88th Infantry Brigades, but relieving Battalions will not leave MARCOING before 4.30 p.m. on each night.

3. Command of the Right Sector will pass to B.G.C. 88th Inf. Brigade on completion of relief.

4. All trench stores, maps and aeroplane photographs will be handed over on relief.

5. Completion of relief will be reported to Div. H.Q.

6. ACKNOWLEDGE.

BMO 36
28/11/17

J. H. Moore
Lieut-Colonel, G.S.,
29th Division.

Issued at 11-15 a.m.

Copies 1 - 4 G.S.
     5 "Q"
     6 C.R.A.
     7 C.R.E.
     8 86th Inf. Bde.
     9 87th Inf. Bde.
    10 88th Inf. Bde.
    11 Off. i/c Sigs.
    12 1/2nd Monmouths.
    13 A.D.M.S.
    14 D.A.G.O.
    15 227th M.G. Coy.
    16 D.A.D.O.S.
    17 D.A.D.V.S.
    18 Div. Train.
    19 S.S.O.
    20 A.P.M.
    21 III Corps.
    22 6th Div.
    23 20th Div.

Appen B

Instructions

SECRET.   29th Division No. C.G.S.68/71.

29TH DIVISION OPERATIONS.

Instructions No. 1.

Ref. 1/20,000 map, Special Sheets
GOUZEAUCOURT and NIERNES attached.

1.   The information and orders in this and subsequent instructions are only to be communicated to those immediately concerned.

2.   On a date and hour Zero to be notified later, an attack is to be carried out by the III Corps in conjunction with the Corps on the Left. Subsidiary attacks and feints are to be carried out by Corps along the remainder of the Third Army front.

3.   The object of the operation is, with the assistance of Tanks, to break the enemy's defensive system between the CANAL de ST. QUENTIN at BANTEUX and the CANAL DU NORD (not shewn on map) West of HAVRINCOURT, and to pass the cavalry through the gap thus made with a view to operating in a N.E. direction.

4.   The success of the operation is entirely dependent on our ability to seize the crossings over the Canal de ST. QUENTIN at MASNIERES and MARCOING, break through the enemy's last line of defence the MASNIERES - BEAUREVOIR line and pass the cavalry through before the enemy can bring up his reserve divisions to counter attack.

5.   Secrecy is therefore essential for success and the most careful precautions regarding it must be taken.

6.   The line opposite the frontage referred to above is held by the enemy as follows :-

From BANTEUX to WELSH RIDGE.   2 Inf. Regts.(9th Res. Div.)
From WELSH RIDGE to HAVRINCOURT.   3 Inf. Regts.(54th Div.)

Each Regiment has two Battalions in the outpost and front line and a resting Bn. in rear.
The resting Battalions are situated as follows :-

9th Res. Div.   One Bn. each at LES RUES des VIGNES and CREVECOEUR.

54th Div.   One Bn. each at RUMILLY, MARCOING, and NOYELLES.

The 204th Div. is North of HAVRINCOURT.

All these three Divisions have been engaged in the recent fighting in FLANDERS.

7.   The attached map shews the Corps boundaries, boundaries between divisions and the objectives. The capture of the RED Line is the object of the 1st day's operations.

/ 8.

- 2 -

8. The capture of the BLUE and BROWN lines will be carried out by the 12th Division on the Right, the 20th Division in the Centre, and the 6th Division on the Left. There will be no preliminary bombardment and no wire cutting by artillery, except in one or two places, prior to Zero. The attack will be made under the protection of an outpost line of Tanks, followed by a wave of Tanks, and with the assistance of standing artillery and smoke barrages which will lift from objective to objective as the attack progresses. 72 Tanks have been allotted to the 12th Division, 60 to the 20th Division, and 72 to the 6th Division.

9. The 29th Division will be in Reserve and will be used for the capture of the RED line, its flanks being protected during the advance as follows :-

RIGHT FLANK. By an extension of the right flank of the 12th Division to about M.2.d.9.7. and a prolongation of this flank to the Road Junction at G.26.b.3.0. by a Brigade of the 20th Division. This Brigade is to seize the MASNIERES bridge, if unoccupied, and to form a bridge head there until relieved by the 29th Division.

LEFT FLANK. By a Brigade of the 6th Division holding the line from PREMY CHAPEL to L.19.b.6.4. where they connect with the 51st Division attacking on the Right of the Corps on our Left.

The 20th Division is also to push patrols forward from the BROWN Line to the Canal bridges at L.24.c.8.5. and L.23.d.9.3. and occupy them, and the 6th Division is to patrol towards the outskirts of MARCOING.

10. The 29th Division will assemble in the area marked on the map on Y/Z night. Assembly will be completed by Zero minus 2 hours.

11. As soon as the assaulting troops have left our trenches, the present front line from R.14.d.9.7. to R.7.a.0.5. will be taken over by Brigades as follows :-

By 88th Inf. Bde. from R.14.d.9.7. to the Sunken road in R.8.d. (incl.)

By 87th Inf. Bde. from Sunken Road in R.8.d. (excl.) to R.7.b.9.0.

By 86th Inf. Bde. from R.7.b.9.0. to R.7.a.0.5.

Brigades will be responsible for reconnoitring routes forward from Assembly positions.

12. On receipt of orders to move, the advance of the Division from the above line will be carried out as follows :-

(a) The 88th Inf. Bde. moving via the LA VACQUERIE valley and crossing the BROWN Line in about square L.35. will attack MASNIERES from the South-West and, crossing the Canal, will push forward and establish themselves in the RED Line to the North and East of that village.

/ (b)

- 3 -

(b) The 87th Inf. Bde. moving via the Eastern slopes of the COUILLET WOOD valley and crossing the BROWN Line in about square L.34. will attack MARCOING from the South and seizing the bridges over the Canal in squares L.23.b. and c. will push forward and establish themselves in the RED Line in approx. squares L.13.b. and L.14.c.

(c) The Junction between these Brigades will be the MASNIERES - CAMBRAI Road inclusive to 88th Brigade.

(d) The 86th Inf. Bde. will cross the BROWN Line in square L.27. and will attack and capture NINE WOOD and the RED Line from the wood to the river ESCAULT. They will be responsible for forming a defensive flank to the North and will endeavour to assist with their fire the attack of the 87th Inf. Bde. on MARCOING from the South.

13. Four Tanks will be allotted to each Infantry Brigade. They will assemble with the Brigades to which they have been allotted on Y/Z night and will be used as a screen behind which the advanced guard will move. These tanks will be marked as shewn in Appendix 1. In addition to the above as soon as the BROWN Line has been captured, 10 Tanks, from those allotted to the 20th Division will be pushed forward to MASNIERES and 20 Tanks from those allotted to the 6th Division into MARCOING to assist in the capture of those villages and the RED Line. These Tanks will be working independently of Brigades.

14. The advance of the Division will be covered by the Divisional Artillery assisted by one Brigade R.H.A. and Heavy Artillery. The Field Artillery will follow the Division by three special routes, which will be notified later, to positions about R.5.c., R.3.b., and L.32.d. respectively. The leading battery of each Brigade will probably be required to move forward as soon as the BLUE Line has been captured.

One section 181st Tunnelling Coy. R.E. consisting of 1 Officer and 40 O.R. will accompany each of these Brigades of Artillery in order to clear the wire and prepare crossings over the trenches to enable the guns to advance rapidly.

15. One Field Coy. R.E. will be held in readiness to proceed, on receipt of orders, to MASNIERES and one Field Coy. R.E. to MARCOING for the repair or reconstruction of the bridges over the Canal de ST. QUENTIN.

Extra pontoons for this purpose will be placed at the disposal of the C.R.E. by the C.E. III Corps.

16. All objectives when gained will be consolidated immediately and the defences strengthened by Vickers guns disposed as far as possible chequerwise and in depth. The defence will be re-organised in depth and each Brigade will detail one Battalion to act as counter attack Battalion for the purpose of meeting hostile counter attacks.

17. On the capture of the RED Line the cavalry will pass through the gap in the enemy's defences and operate towards the N.E.

The following roads are reserved for the use of the cavalry and are on no account to be used by troops of the Division until the cavalry have passed through.

(a) GOUZEAUCOURT - BARRICADE (R.21.d.3.4.) LA VACQUERIE - R.5.central (DOUGLAS ROAD)

(b) VILLERS PLOUICH - R.8.b.1.7. - R.3.a.15.90. - MARCOING - (KAVANAGH Road)

(c) TRESCAUT - RIBECOURT.

/ 18.

- 4 -

18. In the event of the capture of hostile guns, information should be sent immediately to the nearest Brigade Hd.Qrs. for transmission to the Artillery, giving exact locations of guns, nature of gun and whether ammunition is at hand. This information should be passed on to the nearest 6" Trench Mortar Detachment, who will arrange to send up personnel to man the gun. On no account should spare parts, sights, etc. be removed as souvenirs from captured guns.

19. An aeroplane will be up continuously from daylight onwards whose sole mission will be to detect the approach of enemy counter attacks.

Whenever this 'plane observes hostile parties of 100 or over either assembling or moving to counter attack, it will drop a smoke bomb over that portion of the front at which the enemy is moving. The smoke bomb will burst about 100 feet below the machine into a white parachute flare, which descends slowly leaving a trail of Brown smoke about 1 ft. broad behind. On seeing the above signal, artillery and machine gun barrages will be opened immediately without further orders on all hostile approaches in that vicinity.

20. A contact aeroplane will fly over the Corps front on "Z" day at hours to be notified later.

Flares will be lit by the leading troops, only when demanded by the contact 'plane either :-

    (a) By Klaxon Horn.

    (b) By a series of white lights.

The necessity for lighting flares will be impressed on all concerned, and sufficient flares for this purpose issued to the troops. If troops have exhausted their stock of flares, they should indicate their position to the aeroplane by waving their helmets.

Brigade and Battalion Headquarters will be marked by ground sheets of authorised shape, with the code letters of the unit laid out with white strips (9 feet in depth) alongside.

21. 86th, 87th and 88th Brigades will forward their proposals in detail for the operations outlined above to reach Divisional Headquarters by 6 p.m. on 13th instant.

22. ACKNOWLEDGE.

                                  Lieut-Colonel, G.S.,
                                     29th Division.

11th November, 1917.

Copies				
1 - 4	G.S.		13	A.D.M.S.
5	86th Inf. Bde.		14	D.M.G.O.
6	87th Inf. Bde.		15	227th M.G. Coy.
7	88th Inf. Bde.		16	III Corps.
8	C.R.A.		17	6th Division.
9	C.R.E.		18	12th Division.
10	"Q".		19	20th Division.
11	Off. i/c Sigs.		20	2nd Bde. TANKS.
12	1/2nd Monmouths.			

M.

S E C R E T.   29th Division No. C.G.S.68/71.

APPENDIX 1 TO 29TH DIVISION INSTRUCTION NO. 1.

MARKING OF TANKS.

Tanks working with 86th Brigade will be marked   [red/blue diamond]

Tanks working with 87th Brigade will be marked   [red/green diamond]

Tanks working with 88th Brigade will be marked   [red/white diamond]

SECRET

29th Division No. C.G.S.68/74.

Addenda and Corrigenda to 29th Division
Operations Instruction No. 1.
-o-o-o-o-o-o-o-o-o-o-o-o-o-o-o-o-o-o-o-

Para. 10 at end of para. add :-

"Brigades will select forward routes within
their Areas for the assembly of their Battalions.
The most careful marking out of these routes
is necessary and Staff Officers should be sent
forward to select them and have them marked out".

Separate orders will be issued allotting routes from
the staging area to the assembly area.   These routes will
probably be as under :-

86th) Inf. Bdes.   METZ EN COUTURE - Cross roads Q.28.D.
87th)
88th Inf. Bde.   FINS - GOUZEAUCOURT Road.

Para. 17 after the words "for the use of the Cavalry and"
insert "with the exception of (a)".

[signature]

              Lieut-Colonel, G.S.,
13th November, 1917.   29th Division.

Copies to all recipients of Instruction No. 1.
- -

SECRET

29th Division No. C.G.S.68/79.

Amendment No. 1 to 29th Division Instructions No. 1.
- -

1.   Herewith tracing shewing amended division of assembly area. Maps issued with 29th Division Instructions No. 1 will be altered accordingly.

2.   The positions of Brigade Headquarters are also marked.

3.   ACKNOWLEDGE.

[signature]

Lieut-Colonel, G.S.,
29th Division.

15th November, 1917.

Copies to all recipients of Instruction No. 1.
- -

M.

SECRET

29th Division No.C.G.S.68/81.

29th DIVISION OPERATIONS.

CORRECTION TO INSTRUCTION NO. 1.

Para. 12, Sect. (b), line 6.   For "L.13.b. and L.14.c" substitute "G.13.b. and G.14.c".

G.T. Miller. Capt.

Lieut-Colonel, G.S.,
16th Novr., 1917.   29th Division.

To all recipients of Instruction No. 1.

SECRET.   29th Division No. C.G.S. 68/73

29TH DIVISION OPERATIONS.

Instruction No. 3.

1. Concentration. Orders for the Concentration of the Division in the IIIrd Corps Area will be issued separately. According to present arrangements the Division will detrain and march to the area as under :-

Detraining area.	Staging area.	Forward area.
W/X	X/Y	Y/Z Nights.

A map shewing the Divisional staging and concentration area will be issued later.

One platoon IIIrd Corps Cyclist Battalion is being placed at the disposal of the Division on arrival in IIIrd Corps area to assist in conducting troops on arrival to their bivouac areas etc.

2. Battle H.Q. Divisional Battle H.Q. will be located at QUENTIN MILL, R.31.D.
Rear H.Q. will be shared with the 20th Division and will be located at SOREL LE GRAND.

3. Surplus Personnel. Para. 5 of 29th Division Instruction No. 2 is cancelled. Surplus personnel will be disposed as follows :-

(a) Men employed with A.D. Signals, IIIrd Corps, and detailed for Guards on Prisoners of War Cages.

(b) 70 men from each Infantry Brigade working with the 20th Division in the Back area.

(c) Two thirds of the remainder will be sent to MONDICOURT, and one third will be accommodated in the SOREL Area as soon as the Division moves forward from the Staging area.

4. S.O.S. Signals. The IIIrd Corps S.O.S. Signal during the operations will be a rifle grenade bursting into two GREEN and two WHITE Lights.
A similar S.O.S. signal will be used by the Corps on the right.
The S.O.S. signal of the Corps on the left will be a rifle grenade bursting into two RED and two WHITE lights.
The Cavalry S.O.S. Signal will be a GREEN 1" Very Light.

5. ACKNOWLEDGE.

H. Moore.
Lieut-Colonel, G.S.,
29th Division.

13th November, 1917.

Copies to all recipients of Instruction No. 1.

SECRET

29th Division No. C.G.S. 72/70

29TH DIVISION OPERATIONS.

Instruction No. 4.

Communications.

1. **Telegraph and Telephone.**

(a) Direct communication will be arranged between Advanced Divisional Headquarters and Brigades in the position of assembly, and whilst holding the original front line.
   Positions of Brigade Headquarters during these periods should be notified to O.C. Signals, 29th Division, as soon as possible, in order that the necessary communication may be arranged.

(b) When the Division moves forward, two pairs of field cable will be laid from R.14.d.95.95. in original front line (FUSILIER ALLEY) which is an existing cable head, via R.9.b. and R.4.a. and c. to about L.34.d.5.7, where the Main Divisional Visual Station and forward Exchange will be established.
   Telephone lines will be laid from this point to the respective Brigade Headquarters as soon as their position is known.
   In addition, two linemen with three miles of cable will be attached to each Brigade H.Q. on Y/Z night, by O.C. Divisional Signals.
   Each Brigade with the assistance of these linemen will lay one pair as it moves forward, under the supervision of the Brigade Signal Officer. This line will connect them direct with Advanced Divisional Headquarters.

(c) The above will be improved by erecting poled-cable routes as soon as time and circumstances permit.

2. **Visual.**

The Main Divisional Visual Station will be established about L.34.d.5.7.
   If the ground in the neighbourhood of LES RUES VERTES and MASNIERES is not visible from there, a second station will be pushed forward to L.7.b., which will transmit messages to the Main Station. 35
   The 20th Division are establishing a Visual Station about R.7.b. on HIGHLAND RIDGE, with which the 29th Division Main Station will communicate, if telephonic communication to the rear is cut off.
   Battalions should be informed of the position of the Divisional Main Station. The latter station will send forward as well as receive, while operations are in progress.
   The 87th Brigade will establish a transmitting station about L.16.c. (to the N.W. of MARCOING) to receive messages from ground in neighbourhood of G.13.a. and 14.c, and transmit them to the Main Station.
   O.C. 29th Div. Sig. Coy. will detail a Signal Officer for Visual communications, who will be in charge of the Main Visual Station, and any other Divisional Visual Station.
   Visual Signallers will be detailed as under to report to O.C. 29th Div. Signal Coy. on Y Day :-

1/2nd Monmouths	8 (incl. 1 N.C.O.)
86th Inf. Bde.)	
87th Inf. Bde.)	4 each
88th Inf. Bde.)	(incl. 1 N.C.O.)

- 2 -

3. **D.R.L.S. and Runners.**

D.R.L.S. will be by motor-cyclist to VILLERS-PLOUICH thence by Mounted Despatch Rider to Forward Exchange and Main Visual Station: thence by runners to Brigade Headquarters.

If the roads are practicable, motor-cyclist D.Rs. will proceed direct to Brigade Headquarters.

In addition, if feasible, mounted despatch riders will proceed direct to Brigade Headquarters.

The runner post at the Forward Exchange will be manned by 5 runners from each Brigade, who will report to Officer i/c Visual at Divisional H.Q. on Y day.

4. **Pigeons.**

All tanks taking part in the operations will be equipped with pigeons.

10 pairs of pigeons will be supplied to each Infantry Brigade on afternoon of Y day.

5. **Wireless.**

Two Wireless Tel. Tanks have been allotted to the Division for the purpose of Communication between forward Brigades and Advanced Divisional H.Q.

One of these Tanks will be taken forward by the 88th Inf. Bde. and the other by the 86th Inf. Bde.

The location of these Tanks will be notified later.

A Wireless station will be erected at the Forward Exchange, L.34.d.5.7, as soon after the Division moves forward as possible.

A second (Pack) station will be held in readiness at Advanced Divisional Headquarters for employment as the situation may demand.

6. ACKNOWLEDGE.

Lieut-Colonel, G.S.,
29th Division.

13th November, 1917.

Copies 1 - 4   G.S.
       5   86th Bde.
       6   87th Bde.
       7   88th Bde.
       8   C.R.A.
       9   C.R.E.
       10   227th M.G. Coy.
       11   IIIrd Corps.
       12   6th Div.
       13   12th Div.
       14   20th Div.
       15   2rd Bde. Tanks.
       16   A.D.M.S.
       17   "Q".
       18   Off. i/c Sigs.
       19   D.A.G.O.
       20   1/2nd Monmouths.

M.

Secret No. C.G.S. 68/86.

Addendum No. 1 to
29th Division Operation
Instruction No. 4.

Add new para. 6.

A dropping station for aeroplanes will be established near Advanced Divisional Headquarters, QUENTIN MILL at R.31.D.

Lieut-Colonel, G.S.,
29th Division.

19th November, 1917.

Copies to all recipients of Instruction No. 4.

M.

SECRET

29th Division No. G.A.S.29/72.

29TH DIVISION OPERATIONS.

Instruction No. 6.

Medical Arrangements prior to Zero.

1. REGIMENTAL AID POSTS.

   R.20.d.7.4.
   R.20.a.2.9.

2. RELAYS.

   R.19.d.2.8.
   R.25.a.6.2.

3. ADVANCED DRESSING STATION.

   GOUZEAUCOURT.   Q.36.d.4.9.

4. MAIN DRESSING STATION & CORPS WALKING WOUNDED.

   FINS.   V.18.c.

5.   As soon after Zero as circumstances permit RELAY POSTS will be formed at :-

   1st Relay.   (G.25.c.9.2.
                (L.28.b.central.

   2nd Relay.   (L.36.a.5.0.
                (L.34.b.8.5.

   FORWARD ADVANCED DRESSING STATION on road as in R.5.b.

   MOTOR AMBULANCE stand in R.10.b. on VACQUERIE ROAD.

6.   A tea-shop will be formed in LE VACQUERIE, and two others will be formed on convenient positions as soon as circumstances permit.

7.   The Bearer Divisions of Each Field Ambulance will assemble with their respective Brigades in the Assembly Area. Thereafter they will conform to the movements of the Brigades. The Officer in charge keeping in close touch with Brigade Staff Captain.

8.   A Party of 3 Officers and 200 men including N.C.Os, will report to O.C. 88th Field Ambulance on arrival in detraining area. They will take the current days ration with them. Parties to be found from the one ___ third of 10% proceeding to III Corps area. ~~~~~~~~~~~~~~~~~~~~~~~ They are for use as Stretcher bearers under A.D.M.S. and will be detailed from "Q" office.

9.   Regimental Stretcher bearers will be increased from 16 to 32 per battalion for the forthcoming operations. The eight extra stretchers will be issued to units in the Staging area on Y day.

                                        J.H. Moore
                                        Lieut-Colonel, G.S.,
                                        29th Division.

15th November, 1917.

To all recipients of ~~previous~~ Instructions, No. 1.

SECRET

29TH DIVISION OPERATIONS.

INSTRUCTION NO. 7.

PRISONERS OF WAR, REFUGEES, ENEMY DOCUMENTS.

1. **PRISONERS OF WAR.**

    The Divisional Cage will be at W.5.b.1.9., S.W. of GOUZEAUCOURT. Prisoners will be kept off the roads as far as possible. As soon as circumstances permit an Advanced Collecting Post will be established at VILLERS PLOUICH, where prisoners will be handed over to the M.M.P.

2. **SEARCHING OF PRISONERS.**

    All officer prisoners should be searched immediately on capture and their letters, notebooks, maps, and all other papers taken from them, and brought with them by their escorts to the Divisional Cage, and handed over to the Officer in charge for investigation by the Intelligence Officer.

    N.C.Os. and men need not be searched at once and may be allowed to retain their papers till they reach the Corps Collecting Station, but their escorts should be on the watch for any attempt on their prisoners' part to make away with any papers.

    Commanding Officers should take steps to impress on all ranks the importance of the above orders and of ensuring that all documents found on prisoners or enemy corpses or in dugouts, reach the Intelligence Officers detailed to deal with them.

3. **PRISONERS KEPT FOR WORK IN THE LINE.**

    If prisoners are kept, e.g., in order to carry down stretcher cases, it is of the utmost importance that all the prisoners captured are not so detained. A certain number must always be sent back to the Collecting Station at once, a selection being made from each regiment represented.

    Prisoners captured on or near the final objective or during unsuccessful enemy counter-attacks usually give the most useful information, and some of them should always be sent to the rear as quickly as possible.

4. **REFUGEES.**

    Any stray Refugees will be directed to VILLERS PLOUICH where there will be a post of Gendarmes, to conduct them to GOUZEAUCOURT.

5. **GERMAN GAS RESPIRATORS.**

    Specimens of the German respirator are urgently required by the Chemical Service for experimental purposes. Respirators should therefore not be taken from prisoners but the latter should be made to bring them with them to the Collecting Stations. The respirator is easily damaged by damp and should therefore not be taken out of its tin case.

    Specimens marked II II on the right of the date on the drum are particularly required.

6. **ACKNOWLEDGE.**

    F.H. Crone
    Lieut-Colonel, G.S.,
    29th Division.

15th November.

Copies to all recipients of previous Instructions No. 1
& A.P.M.

SECRET

29th Division No. C.G.S.68/80.

29TH DIVISION OPERATIONS.
Addendum No. 1 to Instruction No. 7.

Add para. 7

Cases have occurred of Prisoners retained in the forward area seizing arms and successfully assisting an enemy's counter attack. Parties of not more than 6 may be kept to carry stretchers to Advanced Dressing Station and will then be sent on to the Collecting Station and not kept in the forward area.

A.T. Miller Capt

Lieut-Colonel, G.S.,
29th Division.

16th November, 1917.

Copies to all recipients of Instruction No. 7.

M.

29th Division No. C.G.S.61/28.

29TH DIVISION OPERATIONS.

Instruction No. 9.

Employment of Machine Guns.

1. The following Machine Guns will be available :-

At the disposal of Brigadiers 86th Machine Gun Coy.
                                               87th   "   "   "
                                               88th   "   "   "
In Divisional Reserve   227th   "   "   "
                                          No. 6 Battery M.M.G.

2. As the ground is exceptionally favourable for the employment of overhead and flanking fire, Machine Guns should as far as possible be employed in sections or sub-sections under a Machine Gun Officer. The Machine Gun Officers should be allotted specific tasks and should be given freedom of action in carrying them out.

        When Machine Guns are attached to Battalions, they should be kept under the control of the Machine Gun Officer who will employ them as the Officer Commanding the Battalion requires.

3. One Machine Gun Section will be allotted to Advance Guard Battalions of each Brigade, and 1 sub-section and 1 company should form a flank detachment on the flanks of each Brigade.

4. Machine Guns working on flanks of Brigades, must know the position of Machine Guns of the next Brigade and should co-operate with them.

5. When the Final Objective has been gained, Machine Guns will be reorganised in depth. Brigades will arrange that their flank guns cross fire with the flank guns of the Brigades on their right and left.

6. One section of 227th Machine Gun Coy. will move up in rear of 88th Brigade and one section in rear of 86th Brigade. These sections will be under their section officer who will keep in touch with Brigade Headquarters. They will take any opportunity of giving covering fire to the advance and of engaging fleeting targets. They will take up Final positions about G.31 and G.32. and L.21 and L.27, respectively.

        The remaining two sections of 227th Machine Gun Coy. will move up in rear of the 87th Brigade. They will take up Final positions about L.28, L.29 and L.30.

7. The anti-aircraft defence by Machine Guns in the IIIrd Corps area is to be organised in three echelons as follows :-

(1)   Trench System, mainly by Lewis Guns.

(2)   Remainder of Forward Area back to the Daylight Line.

(3)   Throughout the Central Area for the protection of refilling points, dumps, camps, billets, etc.

/ G.O.C.

- 2 -

7. G.O.C. Brigades will organise a scheme of anti-aircraft Machine Gun Defence, from X day onwards, for the area in which they happen to be. On Z day all available Lewis and Machine Guns will engage low flying enemy aeroplanes when opportunity offers.

8. All transport will be by pack animals after leaving the Staging Area. All essential Battle Stores will be carried as far forward as possible by Pack on Z day. Officers Commanding Machine Gun Companies will arrange dumps when it is impossible to get pack transport further. These dumps will be clearly marked and left in charge of an officer who will arrange to move these dumps forward as soon as tracks permit.

9. No. 6 Battery Motor Machine Gun Service will be in General Reserve at Divisional Headquarters.

10. ACKNOWLEDGE.

F.H. Moore

Lieut-Colonel, G.S.,
29th Division.

16th November, 1917.

Copies to all recipients of Instruction No. 1.
- -

M.

SECRET

29th Division No. G.G.S. 62/76.

86th Inf. Bde.
87th Inf. Bde.
88th Inf. Bde.
227th M.G. Coy.
A.D.M.S.
O.C. Divl. Train.
"Q".
A.P.M.

----

1. Following instructions are issued with a view to maintaining secrecy during coming operations.

2. The attached tracing shews the division of the Corps Area into the three following Zones :-

  (I) Front Zone in front of the daylight line and under direct observation of hostile O.Ps.

  (II) Central Zone where movement and roads can be observed by hostile balloons on fine days.

(III) Back Area. which can only be observed by hostile aircraft.

3. In the front zone movement by day in the open will be restricted to the following :-

  (I) No party to exceed 2 men.

 (II) Parties of 2 to move at 100 yards distance.

(III) Working parties not exceeding 10 may proceed to the front line at intervals of 100 yards, by the special routes selected by the 20th Division.

4. In the Central Zone, on a "clear day" all movement by day will be restricted to the following :-

  (I) No party to exceed 32 foot men and 16 mounted men.

 (II) All parties to move in single file along the edges of metalling. No troops to move in the centre of roads.

(III) Intervals of 100 yards between parties and convoys - convoys to be limited to 10 vehicles.

5. "Clear Days" will be notified from these H.Q. On ordinary dull days the restrictions applicable to the Back Area only will apply.

6. In the Back Area, movement will be subject to the following restrictions at all times :-

    Parties of men and transport not larger than the equivalent of one Company at intervals of 200 yards.

/ 7.

- 2 -

7. On foggy days traffic will be permitted, subject to the same restrictions as are in force in the Central Zone on clear days (vide para. 4 above), in the forward area up to but not in front of the following line :-

N.E. edge of BEAUCAMP - VILLERS PLOUICH Road - Railway thence to FLAG Ravine R.26.Central - R.33.Central - X.3.Central - X.9.Central - X.14.Central.

8. Concentration. (I) All units going into the Central Area (vide attached map) must occupy existing accommodation until properly camouflaged accommodation has been made: tents, or new camouflaged accommodation, will on no account be put up for the purpose.

(II) The number of horses and vehicles brought into the Central Area is to be restricted to the very lowest number essential for the cooking and equipment of the men. Every endeavour will be made to keep this down to one quarter of the normal establishment of a Division, so as to enable the existing standings to suffice during the Concentration period.

(III) Horses will be watered, and water carts filled, in the morning and evening during the first and last hours of daylight and not during the day.

9. From the time of arrival in the new area onward, all troops in the Forward and Central Zones will be strictly confined to billets by day. Troops in villages must be kept off the roads. Those in camouflaged shelters must remain strictly under camouflage throughout the whole day.

10. Fires and Lights. Will be subject to the following restrictions :-

In the Forward Area no fires by night whatever except in cookers. By day fires will be limited to 1 per Platoon and special precautions taken to ensure that they are not allowed to smoke.

In the Central Area fires will be restricted at night to cookers.

Attention is directed to III Corps G.O.5963 of November 9th 1917, attached.

11. ACKNOWLEDGE.

Lieut-Colonel, G.S.,
29th Division.

15th November, 1917.

M.

SECRET

III Corps General Staff.
G.O.5963, November 9th, 1917.

1. The following instructions and orders regarding use of lights at night will be brought into operation from this date until further notice.

2. (a) No fire or light is to be lighted in any camp, bivouac, hut or shelter unless the light is screened from ground and aerial observation.

 (b) All cooking for troops in the open will be done in cookers only and not in open fires, unless these are properly screened.

 (c) Electric torches, when used to aid movements, must only be flashed, and not used as a continuous light.

 (d) No lights will used on any vehicles in the area except motors and lorries for which special instructions are issued below.

3. Motor and Lorry Lights.

Motors and lorries will use their side lights in the area as far as the Daylight Line, where they will extinguish all lights.

Motor headlights will be extinguished in the central area, i.e. on a line EQUANCOURT Cross Roads - N.E. ends of NURLU and LIERAMONT.

No completely open headlights are permitted - the upper quarter of the headlight glass will be painted black or red.

4. In every unit Officers and N.C.O's. will be specially detailed to patrol their lines periodically during the night

... to ...

to see that no lights are showing.

The A.P.M's. of the Corps and Divisions will also visit camps.

5. Arrangements are being made for a balloon or aeroplane to be up at night, whose sole duty will be to locate and report naked lights.

Brigadier-General,
General Staff,
III Corps.

H.Q., III Corps.
9th November, 1917.

DISTRIBUTION :-

6th Division	...	27 copies.
12th Division	...	27 copies.
20th Division	...	27 copies.
29th Division.	...	27 copies.
A.P.M., III Corps.	...	5 copies.
C.E., do.	...	5 copies.
G.O.C., R.A.	...	5 copies.
G.O.C., H.A.	...	25 copies.
Q.	...	2 copies.
41st Balloon Sec.	...	1 copy.
59th Sqn. R.F.C.	...	1 copy.
Camp Cmdnt.	...	1 copy.
Tank Corps	...	25 copies.
Area Commandant:-		
FINS	...	2 Copies.
SOREL	...	2 copies.
NURLU	...	2 copies.
HEUDICOURT	...	2 copies.
HAUT ALLAINES	...	2 copies.
ETRICOURT	...	2 copies.
EQUANCOURT	...	2 copies.
GOUZEAUCOURT	...	2 copies.
No 6 M.M.G. Battery		2 copies.
3rd Corps Cyclist Bn.		4 copies.

29th Division No. C.G.S.55/65.

29TH DIVISION OPERATIONS.

Instruction No. 10.

CODES and CIPHERS.

1. **For Wireless Sets.**

    Instructions regarding the cipher to be used are being communicated to Officer i/c Signals.

2. **B.A.B. Code.**

    Not to be used in front of our present front line. No B.A.B. Code Books are to be taken into action. To ensure this they should be collected at H.Q. of Units on Y day or earlier.

3. **Station Code Calls.**

    The station code calls issued with this office No. C.G.S.55/57 on the 14th instant will be taken into use from Zero onwards.

    Copies of station code calls of this Division are being sent to all Divisions in III Corps, the flanking Division of the IV Corps and Cavalry Divisions.

    Officer i/c Signals will communicate to all Signal officers the code calls of troops outside the Division with which they will be concerned.

4. Fresh code names for all units will shortly be issued. These will be used in the Text of messages in the Danger Zone.

5. **Playfair.**

    This will be used for messages in cipher from Brigades to Divisional H.Q. The G.H.Q. cipher key word issued to Brigades under this office I.G. No. 55/64 of today, will be utilised for this, and all messages in Playfair cipher will begin and end with the letter K.

6. ACKNOWLEDGE.

                                            F. H. Moore
                                            Lieut-Colonel, G.S.,
                                                29th Division.

16th November, 1917.

Copies to all recipients of Instruction No. 1 excluding
    IIIrd Corps, 6th, 12th and 20 Divisions and 2nd Bde. Tank Corps.

M.

29th Division No. C.G.S.68/82.

29TH DIVISION OPERATIONS.
Instruction No. 11.
Employment of R.E.

1. The Divisional R.E. will rejoin the Division on Y day.

2. One section R.E. will be attached to each of the three Infantry Brigades from 4 p.m. on Y day, and will assemble with their respective Brigades on Y/Z night. During the advance they will form part of the Advanced Guard of each Brigade to assist in clearing obstacles etc.

3. The remainder of the Field Companies will be in Divisional Reserve. They will assemble on Y/Z night in the area allotted to them (vide tracing issued with Amendment No. 1 to 29th Divisional Instructions No. 1).
As soon as the Division has been ordered to advance from our present front line they will move to VILLERS PLOUICH under the orders of the C.R.E. in readiness to act as laid down in 29th Division Instructions, para. 15.

4. ACKNOWLEDGE.

Lieut-Colonel, G.S.,
29th Division.

16th November, 1917.

Copies to all recipients of Instruction No. 1.

SECRET

Secret No. C.G.S.68/84.

Amendment to 29th Division Operation
Instruction No. 11.
-o-o-o-o-o-o-o-o-o-o-o-o-o-o-o-o-o-o-

Para. 3 is cancelled. The following will be substituted :-

Para 3. The remainder of the Field Companies will be in Divisional Reserve. They will assemble on Y/Z night in the area allotted to them (Vide tracing issued with Amendment No. 1 to 29th Division Instruction No. 1).

As soon as the Division has been ordered to move, the 497th (Kent) and the 455th (West Riding) Field Companies R.E. will follow in rear of the 88th and 87th Infantry Brigades respectively, to act as laid down in 29th Division Instruction No. 1, para. 15.

Add new paras. 4.
One Company 1/2nd Monmouth Regiment (Pioneers) will come under the orders of C.R.E. on Y day. They will be used for the clearing of wire and the making of tracks forward from the BROWN LINE from approx. squares L.27, L.34 and L.35.

5. It is proposed on Z + 1 day to improve our communications by throwing additional pontoon bridges over the Canal West of CREVECOEUR. This work will be undertaken by the Div. R.E. under the orders of C.R.E.

Lieut-Colonel, G.S.,
18th November, 1917.   29th Division.

Copies to all recipients of Instruction No. 11.

29th Division No. C.G.S.68/83.

29TH DIVISION OPERATIONS.

Instruction No. 12.

Dress, Equipment, etc.

1.	Dress.	Battle Order.
2.	Ammunition.	One bandolier (50 rounds) will be carried per man in addition to the equipment ammunition. This extra ammunition has already been issued to Brigades.
3.	Tools.	75 per cent of the Infantry will carry a pick or shovel. 333 picks and 1000 shovels per Brigade will be issued in billets in the Staging Area. The balance will be made up from existing Brigade establishments.
4.	Flares.	One flare per man will be carried. These will be issued in the Staging Area.
5.	Bombs.	2 Mills bombs per man will be issued in billets in the Staging Area. This is dependent on the actual number allotted by III Corps to the Division.
6.	S.O.S. Grenades.	250 S.O.S. Grenades will be dumped at each Brigade Headquarters in the Staging Area.
7.	Wire Cutters.	4 Wire Cutters or breakers per section will be carried. These have already been dumped in billets in the Staging Area.
8.	ACKNOWLEDGE.	

Lieut-Colonel, G.S.,
29th Division.

16th November, 1917.

Copies to all recipients of Instruction No. 1.
- -

M.

S E C R E T.

29th DIVISION OPERATIONS.

INSTRUCTION No 13.

ADMINISTRATIVE ARRANGEMENTS.

Reference 29th Division Instruction No. 6 para. 1 and Instruction No. 2 para. 10 (d).

1. In order to ensure it being available as soon as required, the Pack Transport will move up to assembly position on Y/Z night with Brigades.

2. When the troops move forward from assembly area the pack transport will be collected by Brigades within the assembly area and as near as circumstances will permit to VILLERS PLOUICH.

3. Pack Transport will be moved forward to supply units under Brigade orders and arrangements, as and when required.

4. Forage must be carried by them for morning feed on "Z" day. Water Troughs have been erected at R.13. central.

5. Brigades must notify Divisional Headquarters "Q" as to where they collect their respective Groups of Pack Transport, in accordance with para. 2 above.

6. Pack Transport must join Brigades prior to their marching out from EQUANCOURT-FINS-SOREL to assembly Area, and movement must be carried out between 4 p.m. and 6 p.m., "Y" Day.

7. All Pack Animals must be fed and watered early on "Z" Morning, in order to be prepared to start off as soon as required by Brigades.

8. A telephone is being installed at Advanced Divisional Dump VILLERS PLOUICH, R.13.d.3.8.

Lieut. Colonel,
A. A. & Q.M.G., 29th Division.

18th November 1917.

Copies to:-

66th Brigade.
87th Brigade.
88th Brigade.
C.R.A.
C.R.E.
1/2nd Monmouths.
III Corps.

A.D.M.S.
Div. Signals.
D.A.D.V.S.
A.P.M.
General Staff.
Div. Train.

SECRET

Secret No. C.G.S.67/89.

Amendment No. 1

to

29th Division Order No. 167.
-o-o-o-o-o-o-o-o-o-o-o-o-o-o-

Page 1.   2nd Phase.   Line 4. for "497th Field Coy."
                            read "510th Field Coy."

                       Line 14. for "455th Field Coy."
                            read "510th Field Coy."

Page 2.   Line 2.   for "G.34.D.O.9."
                            read "G.34.B.O.9."

Amended

F.H. Moore
Lieut-Colonel, G.S.,
29th Division.

18th November, 1917.

Copies to all recipients of 29th Division Order No. 167.
- -

M.

SECRET

Secret No. C.G.S.67/89.

Amendment No. 1

to

29th Division Order No. 167.
-o-o-o-o-o-o-o-o-o-o-o-o-o-o-

Page 1.   2nd Phase.   Line 4.   for "497th Field Coy."
                                 read "510th Field Coy."

                       Line 14. for "455th Field Coy."
                                 read "510th Field Coy."

Page 2.   Line 2.   for "G.34.D.0.9."
                       read "G.34.B.0.9."

amended

J.H. Moore
Lieut-Colonel, G.S.,
29th Division.

18th November, 1917.

Copies to all recipients of 29th Division Order No. 167.

M.

29TH DIVISION OPERATIONS.
Instruction No. 14.

CS 6787
19.11.17

The following are the arrangements for liaison within the Division :-

(a) Major LATHOM-BROWNE, Royal Fusiliers, will be liaison officer with 86th Inf. Bde.

(b) Capt. CROOKE, G.S.O.3, 29th Division, will be liaison officer with 87th Inf. Bde. until arrival at the BROWN LINE when he will proceed to the Divisional Visual Signal Station L.34.D.5.7. to receive and forward reports to Div. H.Q.

(c) Capt. T. K. INNES, K.O.S.B. will be liaison officer with 88th Inf. Bde.

All the above officers report to the H.Q. of Brigades concerned at Zero and will take horses with them so as to be able to communicate with the Central Visual Station at L.34.D.5.7. in the event of visual or telephonic communication failing.

19th November, 1917.

Lieut-Colonel, G.S.,
29th Division.

Copies to 86th Inf. Bde.
87th Inf. Bde.
88th Inf. Bde.
Major Lathom-Browne.
Capt. Crooke.
Capt. Innes.

War Diary

Third Army No. G.14/289.
III Corps G.O.6739.
29th Div. No. C.G.S.51/136

III Corps.
----

1.   The Army Commander has the greatest pleasure in communicating the attached message, which has been received from the Field Marshal Commanding in Chief British Armies in France, for your information and communication to your Command.

2.   The message will appear in due course as an "Order of the Day".

                    (Sd) LOUIS VAUGHAN,
                          Major-General,
25.11.17.   General Staff, Third Army.

- 2 -

86th Inf. Bde.	A.D.M.S.
87th Inf. Bde.	D.A.D.V.S.
88th Inf. Bde.	D.A.D.O.S.
C.R.A.	A.P.M.
C.R.E.	Div. Train.
227th M.G. Coy.	Div. Supp. Col.
6th M.M.G. Bty.	Camp Commdt.
Off. 1/c Sigs.	"Q".
1/2nd Monmouths.	S.S.O.
D.M.G.O.	

For information.

                    A.T. Miller Capt.
                    Lieut-Colonel, G.S.,
28.11.17.   29th Division.

K.

24th November, 1917.

The capture of the important BOURLON position yesterday crowns a most successful operation and opens the way to a further exploitation of the advantages already gained.

In the operations of the Third Army during the past four days, the troops engaged were called on to advance under conditions different to anything ever attempted before. The manner in which they adapted themselves to the new conditions was in all respects admirable, and the results already gained by their efforts are of far reaching importance. Although practically all the divisions employed have already been engaged in severe and prolonged fighting this year all Arms and Services have met these fresh calls on them in a manner worthy of the highest traditions of the British Army.

In this battle the Tanks have for the first time been afforded an opportunity of working in large numbers and of showing their special value under conditions suitable to them. Without them the complete surprise gained would not have been possible and could not even have been attempted. Their performances have entirely justified the trust placed in them.

Infantry, artillery and aircraft have co-operated with the efficiency and complete devotion to duty in which they never fail.

The Cavalry has co-operated with the other Arms with excellent results.

The Royal Engineers, Signal Services, Transportation Services and the Army Service Corps and various administrative Services concerned have each in their several spheres performed most valuable work both in the rapid preparation for the attack and the concentration of troops and material, and also in the maintenance of communication, the development, extension and repair of roads and railways, and the regular supply of food, ammunition and stores of all kinds throughout our subsequent advance.

To General Sir Julian Byng and his Staff, to the Commanders and Staffs under him, and to all Arms and Services engaged in these operations my thanks and warmest congratulations are due for the manner in which they have prepared and carried through these operations and on the splendid results achieved.

I desire also to take this opportunity of expressing my obligation to the Staffs and Services of all ranks at General Headquarters of the Armies in France for the success with which they have met the severe strain imposed by the arrangements for these operations in addition to the sudden movement of troops to Italy, the operations on the Flanders front, and the many other movements and reliefs which have had to be carried out simultaneously.

The operations on the Third Army front would in all probability have mis-carried if the enemy had gained timely warning of our intentions, and a most satisfactory feature to note in connection with these operations is the complete secrecy which was maintained. For this my thanks are due to all ranks concerned.

Appen C

Intell. Summaries

and

Location Lists.

29th Div. No. I.S.106.

29TH DIVISION INTELLIGENCE SUMMARY
Period ending 6 a.m. 23.11.17.

ARTILLERY.
Enemy artillery activity has increased. The front line in left sector was registered accurately by 6 guns firing from the direction of CAMBRAI and MARCOING. MARCOING was also lightly shelled at intervals.

AEROPLANES.
Strong enemy formations appear frequently over our front and fire with machine guns on front line and parties moving in forward area. They were engaged by our A.A. machine guns.

MOVEMENT & ENEMY BEHAVIOUR.
Enemy was quiet yesterday and during the night 22nd/23rd there was little sniping or machine gun fire.
Some movement was observed about G.14.A.6.0.
Patrols report enemy mending gaps in his wire caused by tanks, and talking was heard in MASNIERES - BEAUREVOIR line in G.13. & 14.

SIGNALS.
At 4.30 a.m. a green light followed by a red light was fired twice from far in rear of enemy's line. A white light was then fired from his front line, apparently in answer.

PATROLS.

1. A N.C.O. and 3 men went N. along the MASNIERES - BEAUREVOIR road for about 50 yards and were then fired on from houses on both sides of the road. A machine gun also fired across the road.

2. Two N.C.Os. and 10 men passed through a small gap in the enemy wire in G.14.c. and lay down. They heard enemy talking and working in the MASNIERES - BEAUREVOIR line, and were convinced that the trench was held.

3. Three patrols reconnoitred the enemy line between G.14.c.2.9. and G.7.d.2.2. The front line consists of a line of dug-outs only, which are occupied. The wire in front of them is has too badly damaged by tanks and parties of the enemy were at work repairing wire. The support trench of the MASNIERES - BEAUREVOIR line has good wire in front, and the patrols could hear the garrison of the trench talking.

Capt. G.S.,

23.11.17.   29th Division.

29th Div. No. I.G.106

29TH DIVISION INTELLIGENCE SUMMARY
6 a.m. 23rd – 6 a.m. 24th Nov.

OPERATION. At 11 p.m. an attempt was made to drive the enemy out of the houses on the MASNIERES – CAMBRAI road in G.20.b. and RUMILLY SUPPORT in G.21.a. Strong opposition was encountered and the enemy had several machine guns firing from the houses and the trench. Our men withdrew suffering some casualties and the enemy were seen to come out of their trench and bayonet or shoot our wounded.

ENEMY ARTILLERY. During the greater part of the day the enemy shelled MASNIERES, LES RUES VERTES, and vicinity of the bridge at G.26.b.45.45. with field guns and howitzers.
MARCOING was also occasionally shelled.
In response to his S.O.S. at 11 p.m. he put down a heavy barrage between our front line and the MASNIERES – CREVECOEUR road, lasting for about an hour. Some 15 cm. howitzers took part in this barrage.
There was very little artillery fire after Midnight.

AIRCRAFT. E.A. flew over MASNIERES during the morning and fired into the village with machine guns. They were engaged by our aeroplanes, Machine Guns and Lewis Guns and driven off.
An aeroplane of unknown nationality fell behind enemy lines in G.3. about 3 p.m.

MACHINE GUNS. Enemy machine guns were very active between 5 p.m. and Midnight.

TRENCH MORTARS. The enemy employed T.Ms. to thicken their barrage during the minor operation last night.

SNIPERS. Enemy snipers were active during daylight but no posts were located.

MOVEMENT. Enemy were observed digging on the ridge in G.22.c. at dusk and were fired on by our Lewis Guns.
A working party was also seen about G.13.b.6.4. at 11.45 a.m.; and enemy movement has been seen in vicinity of PLOT FARM.

GENERAL. A RED light was used by the enemy as S.O.S. signal; the "Alarm" was also blown on a bugle.
GOLDEN RAIN lights were also used but no action was observed to follow.
Attitude of enemy remains generally quiet and defensive.

Capt. G.S.,
24th November, 1917.   29th Division.

29th Division No. I.S.106.

29TH DIVISION INTELLIGENCE SUMMARY
6 a.m. 24th to 6 a.m. 25th Nov. 1917.

OPERATIONS.   Nil.

ENEMY ACTIVITY.

Artillery.   MOEUVRES was shelled intermittently all day with field guns and howitzers.
At 5 p.m. the Quarry at G.20.d.9.7. was shelled for 5 minutes by a H.V. gun from behind NEUILLY.
MARCOING was more heavily shelled during the afternoon by 15cm. howitzers. The Northern part of the village was considerably damaged.
The enemy was very quiet between 2 a.m. and 6 a.m. on the right, and on the left between Morning "stand to" and 10 a.m.

Aeroplanes.   6 E.A. flew over our lines at 12 noon.
2 E.A. were also over at 2.15 p.m. and appeared to be ranging for their Artillery.
3 E.A. were over again at 2.45 p.m. but were driven off by Lewis Gun fire.
Since the arrival of our A.A. guns in MARCOING E.A. have been less active in that direction.

Machine Guns.   During the night one fired from house at G.20.b.6.6. and another from G.26.a.0.3.

Trench Mortars.   A T.M. fired occasionally from the direction of G.21.b.0.5.

Snipers.   Very active on the left of our line. One was located in house at G.20.b.7.4. Another was shot down from a tree at G.20.b.3.5.

ENEMY MOVEMENT.

Enemy were seen barricading the windows of the house at G.20.b.7.7.
Parties in full marching order were seen entering their trenches opposite our left Bn. front at dawn, and came under our Lewis Gun fire.

GENERAL.   Fires were observed behind NEUILLY in the direction of NIERGNIES, and a large explosion was observed in the vicinity of L.6.

The enemy's attitude remains defensive.

Capt. G.S.,
25.11.17.
29th Division.

29th Div. No. I.G.106

29TH DIVISION INTELLIGENCE SUMMARY
6 a.m. 25th to 6 a.m. 26th Nov. 1917.

-o-o-o-o-o-o-o-o-o-o-o-o-o-o-o-o-o-o-o-o-o-o-

1. **OPERATIONS.** Nil.

2. **HOSTILE ACTIVITY.**

   Artillery. The enemy was very active all day and night, chiefly at dawn and midday and between 11 p.m. and midnight. The shelling chiefly comes from the direction of NIERGNIES and field guns and howitzers were mainly employed though some 15cm. shells fell in the N. end of MARCOING during the afternoon.

   Aeroplanes. 1 E.A. flew over our right sector at 10 a.m., 2 p.m. and 4 p.m. at a height of 3000 feet. 2 E.A. flew high over left sector at 9 a.m.

   Machine Guns. A enemy Machine Gun was firing during the night from FLOT FARM. On the whole Machine Gun fire was much less than usual.

   Trench Mortars. Were active all night. One shell fired from the MASNIERES - RUMILLY road fell short of the houses at G.21.a.45.10. Several shells fell in the grounds of MASNIERES MARCOING Chateau G.20.d.3.1.
   T.Ms. also fired during the afternoon on the support line in the right sector and on the Quarry at G.20.d.9.6.

   Snipers. Sniping continued but no posts were spotted.

3. **ENEMY MOVEMENT.**

   About 9 a.m. a party was observed digging behind a hedge on the crest in G.21.d. 500 yards from our lines. Rifle fire was opened on them and movement ceased. Two Germans moving back at dawn near the same place were killed by Lewis Gun fire. An enemy patrol was seen about G.20.a.25.95. at 2 a.m. and one man was hit.

4. **ENEMY WORK.**

   A strong point has been located at G.20.a.4.5., apparently vacated by day and occupied at night.

5. **PATROLS.**

   (a) An officer's patrol went out at 8.20 p.m. on the 24th and examined the dug-outs about G.20.b.5.5. These were found empty. The first is 20 ft. deep, completely furnished, finished, with three entrances and accommodation for 100 men in fair comfort. The second is 20 ft. deep with two entrances and would accommodate about 60 men.

   (b) An officer's patrol left our lines at G.21.c.6.4. at 10 p.m. and again at Midnight on the night 25/26th to about G.21.c.80.45 where two recently made fire bays (10 - 15 yards long, 8 feet deep) and 2 shafts for dugouts (30 feet deep) were discovered. Position was unoccupied.

6. **ENEMY ATTITUDE** remains quiet until roused by activity on our part, e.g. shelling.

26.11.17.

Capt. G.S.,
29th Div.

29th Div. No. I.G.106/74

29TH DIVISION INTELLIGENCE SUMMARY
6 a.m. 26th to 6 a.m. 27th Nov, 1917.
-o-o-o-o-o-o-o-o-o-o-o-o-o-o-o-o-o-o-

I. At dusk yesterday 2 officers and 4 men left our lines at G.21.c.6.4, and occupied the trench discovered at G.21.c.80.45.

II. ENEMY ACTIVITY.

(a) <u>Artillery.</u> The enemy showed little activity during the night: the Canal Bank and vicinity of G.26.a.8.8. were shelled at intervals.
Our front line and MONT PLAISIR FARM were lightly shelled this morning with 77mm. and 10.5cm.
The vicinity of MASNIERES Church was shelled about 9 a.m. by 10.5cm. howitzers.
About 8.30 a.m. a few mustard gas shells were fired on our line in G.21.c.

(b) <u>Aircraft.</u> Much enemy activity over our lines, mostly at a great height.
At 2 p.m. today 6 E.A. flew high over our right battalion lines and dropped six bombs. Our Lewis Guns drove the enemy machines off.

(c) <u>Machine Guns.</u> Between 11.30 p.m. and 12.30 a.m. hostile M.Gs. opened fire on our working parties on our left front. This firing and other active M.Gs. were located in houses about G.20.b.9.8.?

(d) <u>Sniping.</u> Enemy snipers were active from houses in G.20.b.
An enemy sniper was active from the road at G.21.a.5.3.
One of our men shot an enemy sniper near FLOT FARM G.7.d.

(e) <u>Movement.</u> No enemy patrols were encountered last night.
Several of the enemy were seen on the ridge at G.22.d. about 6 a.m.
At 10 p.m. working parties of the enemy were heard in G.21.d. They were dispersed by our M.G. fire.

(f) <u>Attitude of the Enemy.</u> Only a few Very Lights were sent up from enemy lines last night.

III. <u>ENEMY WORK.</u>

New Work. Groups of enemy were observed this morning working on what appeared to be gun positions at approximately G.29.a.3.0.
There appears to be about a dozen mounds at this point and several guns were observed.
Later, the guns disappeared having probably been placed in position.

/ Strong Point

- 2 -

<u>Strong Point.</u> A strong point in the form of a "pill box" has been located at about L.12.c.95.40. about 100 yards North of the small bridge. New earth has been thrown up at this point, and the enemy has been seen carrying baulks of timber to the position.
     A M.G. has been reported firing from this point.

                                          [signature], Lieut.
                                              for Lieut-Colonel, G.S.,
                                                   29th Division.

27th Nov. 1917.

M.

29th Div. No. I.G.106.

29TH DIVISION INTELLIGENCE SUMMARY
6 a.m. 27th to 6 a.m. 28th Nov. 1917.
-o-o-o-o-o-o-o-o-o-o-o-o-o-o-o-o-o-o-o-

I. ENEMY ACTIVITY.

(a) Movement. An enemy patrol was observed last night in G.13.d. It was dispersed by our Lewis Gun and rifle fire.
Our men shot 2 of the enemy who were seen crawling out of a trench about G.13.b.4.5.
Working parties were heard digging behind enemy front line wire during the night.
When the enemy trenches were shelled by our artillery yesterday morning, a number of the enemy were seen to leave their trenches and run back. Our Lewis Guns opened fire and several of the enemy were hit.
Only a few Very lights were sent up from the enemy lines last night.
An enemy observer was seen using a telescope about G.22.d.45.05. and disappeared on being fired upon.

(b) Artillery. The enemy replied to our shelling yesterday morning with 77mm. and 4.2cm. fire on our lines, but his retaliation was light.
The Canal was intermittently shelled during the night.

(c) Aircraft. Little activity on either side.

(d) Machine Guns. Little activity during the day.
During the night, the enemy fired short bursts at our working parties.
An enemy M.G. swept the road in L.24.c. at intervals during the night, and one was active from G.22.a.0.5.

(e) Trench Mortars. The northern parts of MASNIERES were fired at with T.Ms. occasionally.

II. IDENTIFICATION.

424 Minenwerfer Co. - prisoner.

III. PRELIMINARY EXAMINATION OF ABOVE PRISONER.

Prisoner's company is normally with the 214th Division which was in the OPPY Sector some time ago and lately sustained our attack in the MOEUVRES - BOURLON Sector.
Prisoner's movements conform to the movements of the 214th Division, having been in FRESNES-les-MONTAUBAN, DOUAI (rest) and lately in FRESSIES 6 miles W.N.W. of CAMBRAI.
He had heard that his Company was going to be attached to a different division.
Along with his company he marched from FRESSIES at 10 a.m. yesterday and passed through CAMBRAI on his way into the line possibly to join the 30th Division, now in the MARCOING - MASNIERES Sector.
Prisoner, being a poor walker, had become detached from his company and had lost his way in CAMBRAI and acting on vague answers to his enquiries eventually walked into our lines on the CAMBRAI - MASNIERES road in G.20.b.
Prisoner is very stupid and can give no definite information of any kind.

                                                                              Lieut.
                                                                   for Lieut-Colonel, G.S.,
28.11.17.   29th Division.

29th Div. No. I.G.106.

29TH DIVISION INTELLIGENCE SUMMARY
6 a.m. 28th to 6 a.m. 29th Nov.1917.

1. PATROLS.

A patrol of 1 N.C.O. and 3 men patrolled the Canal from L.17.d.7.7. for a distance of 700 yards in a north-westerly direction. Nothing was seen or heard of the enemy.

11. ENEMY ACTIVITY.

(a) Movement.
Movement was frequently observed in enemy trenches near FLOT FARM in G.13.b., and several of the enemy in that vicinity were hit by our rifle fire.
An enemy working party was observed wiring his trench about G.20.b.6.8.

(b) Artillery.
Enemy shelling has been much more systematic of late. Battery positions and rear approaches were engaged during the day and night.
More attention was paid by enemy artillery to back areas - LA VACQUERIE and COUILLET Wood Valley especially.
During the night battery positions in L.22.d. and L.28.b. were shelled by 10.5 cm. hows. guns.
In the afternoon MASNIERES was shelled by 15 cm. hows.

(c) Aircraft.
A few E.A. appeared to attempt registration of our batteries yesterday but were driven off by M.G. and anti-aircraft fire.
Our A.A. guns engaged a formation of 7 E.A. and forced one down in a nose dive in the vicinity of PROVILLE.

(d) Machine Guns.
Bursts of enemy M.G. fire swept the railway in L.23.b. and the bridge over the Canal at L.23.b.2.8.
Occasional bursts of M.G. fire were fired at our working parties during the night.
An enemy M.G. was observed firing from a trench about G.13.d.6.9.

A.M.Simpson, Lieut.,
for Lieut-Colonel, G.S.,
29th Division.

29.11.17.

S E C R E T.   29th Division No. I.G.93/167.

CHANGE IN LOCATIONS - 29TH DIVISION

13th November, 1917.
-o-o-o-o-o-o-o-o-o-o-o-o-

Reference Disposition and Movement Report No. 11A
(29th Division No. I.G. 93/149) dated 27th October, 1917,
for No. 11 read :-

11. 510th (London) Field Coy. R.E.   NURLU.

[signature]
Capt.
for Lieut-Colonel, G.S.,
29th Division.

12.11.17.

War Diary

SECRET.　　　　　　　　29th Division No. I.G.93/164.

CHANGES IN LOCATIONS - 29TH DIVISION
11th November, 1917.
-o-o-o-o-o-o-o-o-o-o-o-o-o-o-o-o-o-o-o-o-o-

Reference Disposition and Movement Report No. 11a. (29th Division No. I.G.93/149) dated 27th October, 1917, for Nos. 7, 12 and 46 read :-

    7. S.A.A. Section D.A.C.   SOREL.

   12. 1/2nd Monmouth Regt.   EQUANCOURT.
        (Pioneers)

   46. V/29 Heavy T.M.   CAURESNIL.
        Battery.

                                Capt.
                      for Lieut-Colonel, G.S.,
11th November, 1917.   29th Division.

SECRET

29th Division No. I.G.93/174.

LOCATIONS - 29TH DIVISION.

No.	Unit.	7 a.m. 18th Nov.	7 a.m. 19th Nov.
1.	Div. H.Q.	MOISLAINS.	No change.
2.	H.Q. Div. Arty.	ETRICOURT.	" "
3.	15th Bde. R.F.A.	With 20th Div.	" "
4.	17th Bde. R.F.A.	With 6th Div.	" "
5.	D.A.C.	EQUANCOURT.	V.3.c.
6.	D.T.M.O. & V/29 H.T.M.B.		V.3.c.
7.	X.Y. & Z/29 M.T.M. Bties.	PATRICIA 57c/B.9.a.5.6.	No change.
8.	H.Q. R.E.	SOREL LE GRAND.	)
9.	455th (W.Riding) Fd.Coy.RE.	" " "	)
10.	497th (Kent) -"-		)
11.	510th (London) -"-	NURLU.	) No change.
12.	29th (1/1st London) Sig. Coy. RE.	MOISLAINS.	)
13.	H.Q. 86th Inf. Bde.	)	)
14.	2/Roy. Fus.	)	)
15.	1/Lan. Fus.	)	)
16.	16/Middx. R.	)	)
17.	1/R. Guernsey L.I.	) HAUT-ALLAINES.	) EQUANCOURT.
18.	86th M.G. Coy.	)	)
19.	227th M.G. Coy.	)	)
20.	86th T.M. Bty.	)	)
21.	69th Field Amb.	)	)
22.	No. 2 Coy. Train.	)	V.29.a.
23.	H.Q. 87th Inf. Bde.	)	)
24.	2/S.W.B.	)	)
25.	1/K.O.S.B.	)	)
26.	1/R. Innis. Fus.	)	)
27.	1/Border R.	) HAUT-ALLAINES.	) FINS.
28.	87th M.G. Coy.	)	)
29.	87th T.M. Bty.	)	)
30.	87th Field Amb.	)	)
31.	No. 3 Coy. Train.	)	V.29.a.
32.	H.Q. 88th Inf. Bde.	)	)
33.	4/Worc. R.	)	)
34.	2/Hants. R.	)	)
35.	1/Essex R.	)	)
36.	1/N.F.L.D.	) MOISLAINS.	) SOREL LE GRAND.
37.	88th M.G. Coy.	)	)
38.	88th T.M. Bty.	)	)
39.	88th Field Amb.	)	)
40.	No. 4 Coy. Train.	)	V.29.a.
41.	1/2nd Monmouth Regt. (Pioneers)	EQUANCOURT.	No change.
42.	H.Q. Div. Train.	MOISLAINS.	V.29.a.
43.	Mob. Vet. Sect.	MOISLAINS.	No change.
44.	226th Emplyt. Coy.	MOISLAINS.	" "

Capt. G.S.
for Lieut-Colonel, G.S.,
29th Division.

16th November, 1917.

War Diary

29th Division No. I.G.93/159.

S E C R E T.

CHANGES IN LOCATIONS - 29TH DIVISION
6 p.m. 5th November, 1917.
-o-o-o-o-o-o-o-o-o-o-o-o-o-o-o-

Reference Disposition and Movement Report No. 11a.
(29th Division No. I.G.93/149) dated 27th October, 1917, for

Nos. 10 and 16 read

10. 497th (Kent) Field Coy. R.E.   SOREL LE GRAND
                                   57c/W.13.c.

16. H.Q. Div. Train.   BERLES AU BOIS
                                   51c/W.21.central.

                                   [signature]
                                   Capt.
                                   for Lieut-Colonel, G.S.,
                                   29th Division.

5th November, 1917.

Appendix D

Report on Operations by 29th Division

on 20th November, 1917.
-o-o-o-o-o-o-o-o-o-o-o-o-o-o-o-o-o-o-o-

HEADQUARTERS,
29th DIVISION.
No. G/S 7056
Date..........

1. **Order of Battle.**

Divisional Commander.	Major-General Sir BEAUVOIR de LISLE, K.C.B., D.S.O.
86th Inf. Bde. Commander.	Brig-Gen. G.R.H. CHEAPE, M.C.
2/Royal Fusiliers.	Major J.S. HODDING.
1/Lanc. Fusiliers.	Major T. SLINGSBY, M.C.
16/Middlesex Regt.	Lt-Col. J. FORBES-ROBERTSON, D.S.O. M.C. (Border Regt.)
1/R. Guernsey L.I.	Lt-Col. H.J. de la CONDAMINE.
87th Inf. Bde. Commander.	Brig-Gen. C.H.T. LUCAS, D.S.O.
2/S. Wales Borderers.	Lt-Col. G.T. RAIKES, D.S.O.
1/K.O.S.B.	Lt-Col. C.A.G.O. MURRAY.
1/R. Inniskilling Fus.	Lt-Col. J. SHERWOOD-KELLY, C.M.G., D.S.O. (Norfolk Regt.)
1/Border Regt.	Lt-Col. A.J. ELLIS, D.S.O.
88th Inf. Bde. Commander.	Brig-Gen. H.NELSON, D.S.O.
4/Worcester Regt.	Lt-Col. C.S. LINTON, D.S.O., M.C.
2/Hampshire Regt.	Capt. K.A. JOHNSTON.
1/Essex Regt.	Lt-Col. Sir G.M.H. STIRLING, Bart. D.S.O.
Newfoundland Regt.	Lt-Col. A.L. HADOW, C.M.G.

2. **Disposition of Troops at Zero.**

86th Inf. Bde. In the area Q.23, Q.29.a. and b.

87th Inf. Bde. In the area Q.24, Q.30.a. and c.

88th Inf. Bde. In the area Q.29.c. and d., Q.35.a. and b.

Field Coys. R.E. In the area Q.34.c. and d., Q.35.c. and d.

The Assembly areas are shewn on the attached Map.

3. **Objectives.**

The task allotted to the Division was, to pass through the 20th and 6th Divisions as soon as these had captured the BROWN LINE and the 12th Division had captured the BONAVIS Plateau, force the crossings over the Canal at MASNIERES and MARCOING and, breaking through the enemy's last line of resistance the MASNIERES - BEAUREVOIR line, to enable the Cavalry to pass through the gap thus formed.

4. **Plan.**

To carry out this task successfully, it was essential that both MASNIERES and MARCOING should not only be captured, but that strong bridgeheads should be established on the Eastern side of the Canal. Both these villages are of considerable size and are some two miles apart, and it was considered that in each case one Infantry Brigade would be required.

/ Moreover

- 2 -

Moreover NINE WOOD at the Eastern edge of FLESQUIERES Ridge overlooks MARCOING from the North at a range of 1000 yards and is 100 feet above it. The capture of MARCOING was therefore dependent on the capture of this position, thus necessitating the use of my third Brigade.

No reserve of Infantry was kept in hand as I considered that being a pursuing force, extraordinary risks might be taken and the holding back of any portion of the fighting force might seriously hamper the success of the operation.

The 88th Brigade was therefore directed on MASNIERES, the 87th Brigade on MARCOING, and the 86th Brigade on NINE WOOD.

5. **Concentration.**

The Division entrained at BOISLEUX AU MONT on the night of 17th/18th November, resting for the day of the 18th at MOISLAINS.

On the following night it marched to FINS, EQUANCOURT and started at 2 a.m. on the morning of the 20th November for the Assembly position north of GOUZEAUCOURT a distance of 5 miles.

This assembly march was accomplished by 5.30 a.m. without any trouble. Routes had been previously reconnoitred and all road and track junctions piquetted to guard against loss of direction.

It will be noticed that the 3 nights prior to the attack the troops had been on the move.

6. **The Approach March.**

By the scheme the Division was not to advance until the BONAVIS Plateau and the BROWN LINE (HINDENBURG Support Line) had been gained by the 12th, 20th and 6th Divisions but as time was an important factor in a complete success, the leading Battalions of Brigades were moved at Zero into our front line which had been vacated by the above Divisions.

Further, each Brigade of this Division pushed out Advanced Guards up to the BLUE LINE as soon as this objective

/ had

had been gained, with patrols following the troops as they attacked the BROWN LINE.

It was intended that Contact Planes should drop situation reports at this H.Q. to enable me to start this Division at the earliest possible moment. The fog however made the work of contact planes impossible, and the news of the capture of the BLUE LINE of which the scheduled time was 8 A.M. did not reach this H.Q. until 9.15 A.M., 1½ hours later.

To have waited for news of the complete capture of the BROWN LINE would have so delayed the start of the 29th Division that at 10 A.M. on hearing that the troops of the 6th and 20th Divisions were well on their way to the BROWN LINE, I asked permission to take the risk and move my Brigades to their objective. At 10.15 A.M. the order was issued and was conveyed to all Units of each Brigade by Bugle Call.

The Division therefore moved off simultaneously, with the 88th Brigade on the Right directed on MASNIERES, the 87th Brigade on MARCOING, from a point due South of it, and the 86th Brigade on NINE WOOD at the Eastern end of the FLESQUIERE Ridge.

Brigades adopted a Diamond formation, with one Battalion at each point, the long axis being 1800 yards, and the short axis, parallel to the direction, 1200 yards. Each Battalion placed their four Companies in a similar formation. This formation was adopted with a view to saving time, the flanking units being in position to envelope should opposition be met by the leading Battalion acting as Advanced Guard to each Brigade. Four tanks were allotted to each Brigade and moved in advance of the Infantry Advanced Guards.

7. Narrative of the Action of the 88th (Right) Brigade.

On approaching the BROWN LINE in R.5. and L.35. hostile fire was opened from rifles and Machine Guns and 3 of the Battalions were forced to attack it. This caused a delay

/ of

of ¾ hour and accounted for over 150 prisoners. On the left the Newfoundland Battalion had some difficulty and sustained many casualties, but with their accustomed dash they broke down all opposition, using covering fire from rifles, Machine Guns and a Stokes Gun. This delay however was unfortunate as it gave time for the enemy to partially organise the defences of LES RUES VERTES. The right Battalion (4/Worcestershire Regt.) however, pushed on to its objective, the Lock in G.27.c, and got one Company across to form a Bridgehead, sending another along the eastern Canal Bank to outflank the defence. This manoeuvre was entirely successful.

A tank now endeavoured to cross the Main Iron Bridge at MASNIERES but the bridge, previously partially destroyed, gave way. No assistance from tanks could then be expected on the east side of the Canal.

Finding the leading Battalion held up at the Canal Bridge at MASNIERES, the 2/Hampshires, skilfully led by Acting Lieut-Colonel JOHNSTON, moved down to the Lock 1000 yards to the S.E. crossed there and attacked the RED Line with 2 Companies and captured these prepared trenches as far North as G.21.c.8.8. The other half Battalion was sent to attack MASNIERES from the east and gained the outskirts of the town.

The death of Lieut-Colonel LINTON, D.S.O., M.C., 4/Worcesters, left this Battalion without a leader and the Companies somewhat disorganised, but Lieut-Colonel JOHNSTON quickly took over the situation, organised the defences to the North and East as far as MONT PLAISIR FARM, and continued to press on his attack of MASNIERES until dawn of the 21st.

About 4 p.m. on the 20th a squadron of Canadian Dragoons crossed the Canal at Lock in G.27.c. and rode up over the RUMILLY Ridge.

On the left the N.F.L.D. crossed at the Lock in L.24.d. and attacked to the East gaining the gun pits in L.19 & 20,

/ but

but were unable to cross the open ground between this cover and the town.

Heavy fighting was in progress during the night but at dawn we held the town as far North as L.20.d.7.9. with the exception of a pocket in the centre. Here a number of the enemy were sheltered in the Catacombs, to which there are 7 openings. These were not captured until midday of the 21st.

8. **Narrative of the Action of the 87th (Centre) Brigade.**

The Centre Brigade marched straight on MARCOING and MARCOING Copse. In the former place the enemy hurriedly evacuated the town. The Commander General VON KEPPEL had not even time to remove his personal belongings. At MARCOING Copse, some resistance was experienced and many enemy killed in the Wood. The leading Battalion of this Brigade, 1/Kings Own Scottish Borderers marched through the town and crossed by the Railway Bridge. Only 1 tank succeeded in crossing, the others for various causes being unable to get there. The right flank Battalion, 2/South Wales Borderers, crossed at the Lock L.24. These two Battalions, as ordered, immediately prepared Bridgeheads covering the crossings, where the other two Battalions, 1/Royal Inniskilling Fusiliers on right, and 1/Border Regiment on left, passed over and advanced again at the RED LINE.

After a long advance of about a mile the attack was brought to a standstill some 300 yards behind our present line L.14.c.3.0. to the Lock at L.17.d.8.7. The RED LINE was seen to have been reinforced just before the attack of our troops, and the Machine Gun fire from it made any further advance impossible without the aid of Artillery or tanks. On the left one Company of the 1/Border Regiment gained the RED LINE in 13.a. and took 19 prisoners there, but owing to the right of the line being held up, this Company was withdrawn, retiring firing by alternate platoons. The above line was consolidated the same night.

/ The

The following day with the assistance of 9 Tanks, the 87th Brigade made another attempt to take the whole of the RED LINE, but without success. The tanks suffered from armour piercing bullets, 50 per cent of the personnel becoming casualties, and the Infantry came under heavy Machine Gun fire both from the front and from FLOT FARM where a number of guns firing indirect prevented the troops gaining the top of the ridge in L.20.a. & b.

9. **Narrative of the 86th (Left) Brigade.**

The 86th Brigade advanced without opposition to the Quarry S.W. of NINE WOOD, but here the leading Regiment (16/Middlesex Regiment) was checked. The flank Regiments however, 2/Royal Fusiliers on the right and 1/Royal Guernsey L.I. on the left, continued to push on enveloping the Wood from the S.E. and N.W. and so gaining all objectives by 1 p.m.

A Company was then sent to occupy NOYELLE and form a bridgehead on the eastern bank of the Canal. Between the R. ESCAUT and the Canal opposition was met and the troops were unable to accomplish the crossing.

10. **Counter-attacks.**

On November 21st three counter-attacks were launched against the new line of defence.

(a) At 11 a.m. a heavy attack from the N.E. was launched against the 88th Brigade by 2 Battalions which advanced in dense waves. This was caught by Artillery and Machine Gun fire and could not approach closer than 500 yards.

(b) The second attack at 1 p.m. moved S.W. against the 87th Brigade but came under heavy fire as it crossed the Support line in G.14 and did not get beyond the German front line.

(c) The third attack advanced on NOYELLE from the Wood north of the village and drove back our outposts to the southern end of the village. Reinforcements were sent down from NINE WOOD until we had 3 Companies in the village opposed to 5 Companies of the enemy. Our troops gradually drove the enemy

/ back

back, and at dusk had cleared the village except for 28 Germans who later surrendered. A relieving Battalion of the 6th Division took over the village the same night without a shot being fired. The troops of the 26th Brigade fired 200 rounds per man and expended all bombs and Stokes bombs. In the end they were fighting entirely with German weapons and ammunition.

11. General Remarks.

(1) This being the first occasion that this Division has been engaged in open warfare, it was necessary to adapt the training to the probable requirements. Fortunately the area, South of ARRAS, allotted by the VI Corps for this purpose was ideal in every way. By means of Brigade and Divisional Schemes Battalions were enabled to gain very valuable instruction. The difficulty in training Company and Platoon leaders to act correctly according to the situation and ground is far greater than training them to lead in a trench to trench attack, and the time available was inadequate. Much however was done by lectures and Brigade Exercises prepared by my General Staff.

(2) The diamond formation was found most suitable, saving time, and being less liable to casualties under shell fire.

(3) One Stokes Gun with 64 rounds was attached to each Battalion and this was found invaluable.

(4) One section Machine Guns was attached to the leading Battalion of each Brigade and a flank detachment of 2 Machine Guns and ½ Company was maintained on the flank of each Brigade, a precaution which has always proved useful.

(5) The rapidity of the advance of the 3 Brigades enabled them to gain the crossings before resistance could be organised and had it been possible to get tanks across in time before German reinforcements arrived from CAMBRAI, the success would have been even more complete. The breaking of the MASNIERES Bridge was fatal to the co-operation of the tanks.

/ (6)

(6)   A remarkable feature of these operations was the physical endurance of the troops. From 2 a.m. on the 20th November, the Division marched 10 miles to the Canal, carrying over 60 lbs. of equipment. They fought till dark on the 21st, and have since consolidated a position 5000 yards long and 1500 yards deep.

After 10 days in the line, they are certainly worn out but still capable of defence.

This remarkable performance is due to the careful attention of Regimental Officers to the comfort of the troops and to the excellent discipline in all Brigades.

I append a statement of casualties incurred by the Units engaged in this attack, prisoners and war material captured.

November, 1917.

Major-General,
Commanding 29th Division.

M.

APPENDIX "A".

Casualties of units engaged in this attack were :-

	Officers.	O.R.
KILLED	15	199
WOUNDED	50	1002
MISSING	6	309
	71	1510

Prisoners passed through Cage :-

Officers	9
O.R.	746
	755

Civilians evacuated :-

MARCOING	-	Nil.
MASNIERES	-	414
NOYELLE	-	102
		516

Material captured :-

Field Guns and Howitzers.

105mm.	4
77mm.	16

Trench Mortars.	3
Machine Guns.	42
Spare barrels.	50
Machine Gun Limbers.	6
Field Kitchens.	3
Fuel, wood.	360 tons.
Coal.	300 tons.

In addition 15 head of cattle were realeased from MASNIERES, of which 2 were killed by shell fire during evacuation.

(6202) W 11186/M1151 350,000 12/16 McA. & W., Ltd. (Est. 781) Forms/W 3091/3.   Army Form W. 3091.

Cover for Documents.

79

29th Division

Nature of Enclosures.

REPORTS
on
CAMBRAI
operations

Notes, or Letters written.

LINE GAINED BY 29TH DIVISION
ON 20TH AND 21ST NOVEMBER.
LINE REACHED BY GERMAN ATTACK
ON 30TH NOVEMBER.
LINE GAINED BY COUNTER ATTACK OF
88TH BDE WITH 2 BATTS 87 BDE ATTACHED
AND HELD TILL NIGHT DEC. 3/4. WHEN
WITHDRAWN TO BLUE DOTTED LINE
TO LINK UP WITH 6TH DIV.

Scale 1 : 20,000

Detail and Trenches revised to 24-11-17.

Report on Operations by 29th Division
on 30th November and following days.
-o-o-o-o-o-o-o-o-o-o-o-o-o-o-o-o-o-o-o-

1. **Order of Battle.**

    <u>Divisional Commander.</u>   Major-General Sir BEAUVOIR de LISLE,
                                          K.C.B., D.S.O.

    <u>86th Inf. Bde. Commander.</u>   Brig-Gen. G.R.H. CHEAPE, M.C.

       2/Royal Fusiliers.   Major J.S. RODDING.
       1/Lancashire Fusiliers. Major T. SLINGSBY, M.C.
       16/Middlesex Regiment. Lt-Col. J. FORBES ROBERTSON,
                                      D.S.O., M.C. (Border Regiment)
       1/Royal Guernsey Light   Lt-Col. A.R.S. HART SYNNOTT, D.S.O.
          Infantry.

    <u>87th Inf. Bde. Commander.</u>   Brig-Gen. C.H.T. LUCAS, D.S.O.

       2/South Wales Borderers. Lt-Col. G.T. RAIKES, D.S.O.
       1/Kings Own Scottish   Lt-Col. C.A.G.O. MURRAY.
          Borderers.
       1/Royal Inniskilling   Lt-Col. J. SHERWOOD KELLY,
          Fusiliers.   C.M.G., D.S.O. (Norfolk Regiment)
       1/Border Regiment.   Lt-Col. J. ELLIS, D.S.O.

    <u>88th Inf. Bde. Commander.</u>   Brig-Gen. H. NELSON, D.S.O.

       4/Worcestershire Regiment. Major D.C.S. CLARKE, D.S.O.
       2/Hampshire Regiment.   Capt. K.A. JOHNSTON.
       1/Essex Regiment.   Lt-Col. Sir G.M.H. STIRLING, Bart.
                                      D.S.O.
       Newfoundland Regiment.   Lt-Col. A.L. HADOW, C.M.G.

2. **Dispositions of Troops
   on morning of November 30th.**

    <u>Front line.</u>   <u>86th Inf. Bde. on the right.</u>

    16/Middlesex Regiment from the Canal at G.27.c.90.15. to
          G.21.c.8.5. with outposts at MON PLAISIR
          FARM and the Canal bridge G.28.c.25.00.
    1/Lancashire Fusiliers from G.21.c.8.5. to the
          MASNIERES - CAMBRAI Road.
    2/Royal Fusiliers in support about the SUGAR FACTORY and the
          houses in G.20.d.
    1/Royal Guernsey Light Infantry in reserve in the CATACOMBS
          in MASNIERES.

    <u>87th Inf. Bde. on the left.</u>

    1/Royal Inniskilling Fusiliers from the MASNIERES - CAMBRAI
          Road to G.13.d.8.2.
    1/Border Regiment from G.13.d.8.2. to the River ESCAUT
          L.17.b.5.2.
    2/South Wales Borderers in support in the MARCOING Bridgehead
          defences.
    1/Kings Own Scottish Borderers in Brigade Reserve in MARCOING.

    <u>88th Inf. Bde. in Divisional Reserve</u>

    in MARCOING

3. Narrative.

The Divisional Headquarters of the 29th Division was situated in the Quarry half a mile S.E. of GOUZEAUCOURT, known as QUENTIN MILL.

Early on the morning of the 30th, this spot received a few shells, one actually falling in the Quarry, severely wounding Brig-Gen. STEVENSON my C.R.A.

About 8.45 a.m. rifle fire was suddenly heard at close range from the direction of VILLERS GUISLAIN and a staff officer sent up the steps to ascertain the cause, reported that the ridge 300 yards to the South-East was held by Germans. A few men with rifles were sent up as covering party, and the personnel of Headquarters were warned to leave as quickly as possible and gain shelter in GOUZEAUCOURT. We had to run the gauntlet from rifle fire at 400 yards range, and pass through a heavy barrage of artillery between the Railway and the town, which caused a number of casualties.

On reaching the south-western part of the town, I organised a small party of about 20 rifles to defend the two 8" guns in action there.

A large number of road and railway workers and others were streaming down the road to FINS and across country, but having no arms were useless. Fortunately a Field Company R.E. of the 59th Division on the way to FLESQUIERES was met coming up the road and I ordered the officer Major ROBINSON, R.E., to take over the southern defences of the town until reinforced. I was informed later that he performed his duty most satisfactorily until reinforced by troops of the Guards Division in the afternoon.

I sent off my G.S.O.I to MARCOING to warn my Reserve Brigade there to move up to defend the right flank of the Division, and my A.D.C. to warn the Headquarters of the 6th and 20th Divisions at VILLERS PLOUICH, retaining Capt. MILLER, G.S.O.II, the only officer left to assist me. Capt. NICKALLS my A.D.C. was able to warn the 1st Line Transport of the 2/Durham L.I. and West Yorks. Regt. and under the Adjutant of the latter and the

/ Quarter

Quarter-Master of the former Battalion, all men with rifles moved up to defend the northern part of the town. This was also successfully performed. Capt. NICHALIS then proceeded to convey the situation to the other two Divisions.

Having no more troops at my disposal, I proceeded to MARCOING on foot myself, and found the situation as regards the 29th Division most satisfactory. The two Brigades North of the Canal had held their line against several counter-attacks, and the 88th Brigade in reserve at MARCOING had moved out to counter-attack the enemy who had gained the southern outskirts of MARCOING, driving back the enemy in front of them with great execution, until they linked up with the 20th Division on the right and the 86th Brigade on the left at LES RUES VERTES. Further progress was found to be impossible against the large numbers which had collected in the valley East of WELSH RIDGE.

Being assured that 29th Division were capable of defending the position they held, I returned to 6th Division H.Q. in order to convey the situation to Corps Headquarters.

Later in the afternoon I again went into GOUZEAUCOURT, then held by the 1st Guards Brigade, and assisted other troops coming up by giving them the situation.

On the morning of December 1st I moved my Headquarters to TRESCAULT, and in the afternoon recommended to the Corps that the 86th Brigade should be withdrawn from MASNIERES and LES RUES VERTES, as their position was a dangerous salient, and the troops worn out by the two days heavy fighting coming after the previous twelve days abnormal fatigue in digging the defences on a front of 5000 yards. On receiving approval from the Corps, this withdrawal was carried out after dark without the knowledge of the enemy, who continued to shell it on the morning of the 2nd until 8.30 a.m.

All wounded were evacuated and the operation was carried out in perfect order.

I wish to bring to notice of the Corps Commander the very efficient manner in which Brig-Gen. CHEAPE and the troops of the 86th Brigade, carried out the defence of these villages

/ surrounded

surrounded as they were on three sides. They beat off numerous attacks and when LES RUES VERTES was lost to the enemy it was at once regained by an immediate counter-attack.

The 87th Brigade holding MARCOING and the defences of the N.E. were relieved on the night of the 2nd/3rd December by the 16th Brigade of the 6th Division.

On the morning of December 3rd a very heavy bombardment of some hours duration was directed against the 88th Brigade South of the Canal, and on the 16th Brigade to the North of it. The left regiment of the 88th Brigade holding the drain covering the Lock in G.24.c. suffered heavy casualties from shell fire, losing 70% of its strength, and in the afternoon the enemy occupied this trench but were unable to advance further West into MARCOING Copse owing to flanking M.G. fire which had previously been arranged to cover this open space.

At 4.30 p.m. it was reported by 6th Division H.Q. that the enemy had entered MARCOING. This however was not the case, and an R.E. officer who was preparing the Railway Bridge for demolition kept me informed as to the real situation there.

During the night patrols were sent from the 87th Brigade in Reserve on HIGHLAND Ridge, every two hours to the 88th Brigade, to keep me informed of the situation from time to time. I also sent Brig-Gen. LUCAS to the 88th Brigade H.Q. to report on the situation in general. He reported that the troops of the 88th Brigade were very tired; that the two left battalions owing to heavy losses had been withdrawn into reserve and replaced by the reserve battalion; that connection with the 20th Division on the right and the 6th Division on the left had been secured; and that the Brigade was capable of holding their position for another 24 hours unless very heavily attacked.

I also wish to bring to notice of the Corps Commander the excellent arrangements made by Brig-Gen. NELSON, and the stubborn fighting qualities of the troops under his command, consisting of two battalions of the 87th Brigade and his own 88th Brigade. On reaching this area on the 6th December,

/ Brig-Gen.

Brig-Gen. NELSON collapsed from the great strain he had undergone and after being unconscious for 12 hours was sent to hospital.

4. REMARKS.

The many acts of personal gallantry and devotion to duty which were performed during this period, were only what should be expected from regular troops, but it is gratifying to notice that the three battalions raised during the war have adopted similar principles from association with regular battalions. The gallantry and devotion to duty throughout was however remarkable in that the attack on the 30th came as a complete surprise: our right flank was turned, and the situation of the Division at first appeared to be critical. In addition to this the troops were already very tired; they had had no rest since the night of November 17/18th when they entrained for this area. The next two nights were occupied in marching to the position of assembly. The 20th was occupied by a long march of ten miles, starting at 2 a.m., each man carrying his fighting equipment of over 60 lbs. The action of the 20th was fatiguing and continued throughout the night until the evening of the 21st. The Division then prepared a defensive position of 5000 yards of front, digging and wiring front support and reserve lines, with communication trenches, and placing two villages in a state of defence. By the morning of the 30th I thought that the troops had reached the limit of human endurance, and I consider that the successful operation from November 30th to the night of December 4/5th reflects the utmost credit on all the battalions concerned.

I attach reports from the three Infantry Brigades on the operations as well as reports from other sources.

10 December, 1917.

Major-General,
Commanding 29th Division.

BGS 70
with November 17

30th NOVEMBER 1917.

	8.12 a.m.	To III Corps. Situation generally quiet. Slight hostile shelling during the night.
S. end of GOUZEAUCOURT	9.10 a.m.	To III Corps. Troops South of MEAVIS are retiring before German attack. Advanced German patrols have reached as far East as Mt. CHAPEL HILL which I have evacuated. All communication to front and rear cut. Have sent up to my Division my General Staff Officer to do all they can. Formed bodies of troops urgently needed as nothing but working parties in vicinity.
	9.40 a.m.	To III Corps. Enemy now hold Railway East of GOUZEAUCOURT and advancing up the village very cautiously. Am moving my Headquarters to high ground half a mile West of the village.
	10 a.m.	To III Corps. The enemy appear to be checked at GOUZEAUCOURT which is not being held by one Company of R.F. 9th Division which I stopped for the purpose. They having gone out of GOUZEAUCOURT with advanced parties in QUEEN'S HILL and moving up towards the village. Have sent my A.D.C. to give 8th, 20th and 59th Divisions the situation and my S.O.S. to hasten to do what he can to protect my right flank. A hostile attack from the North is reported.
	10.20 a.m.	To III Corps. Enemy have cut road S.W. of METZ-AMBEZ, moving my Headquarters towards RIBECOURT to see what can be done as I can do nothing here.
	10.45 a.m.	To III Corps. GOUZEAUCOURT captured by enemy from the South at 10.15 a.m. If troops can attack enemy from direction of RIBECOURT from indications they would succeed as enemy seems in small strength and much strung out. I am on my way to 8th Division H.Q. and have stopped at this Signal Station to send this message.
6th Division A.G. VILLERS PLOUICH	11.45 a.m.	To III Corps. Have reached 6th Division H.Q. and find situation there is good. Formed Officer reports my right flank turned and enemy approaching MATTIGNY. I am moving troops country on foot to organise best defence possible under circumstances.
		From 66th Brigade timed 12.05 p.m. Situation still in hand. To hold all our line and have defensive flank on outskirts of the RUE VERTE. In touch with 20th Brigade and half brigade heads all along Canal.

From 88th Brigade. Time 11.15 a.m. Received 1.30 p.m. Our troops in LES RUES VERTES report being shelled by our own artillery.

From Gen. LUCAS. Timed 2.18 p.m. 88th Brigade report Worcestershire Regiment has advanced about 200 yards and occupied enemy trenches in front of them.

From 88th Brigade. Timed 9.47 a.m. Received 2.30 p.m. Enemy guns in action at u.8.b.

From III Corps. Timed 9.55 a.m. Received 2.30 p.m. Reorganisation of Corps front. Extract :- 29th Division will continue to be responsible for their original sector and the portion of the line from LES RUES VERTES to R.5.a.Central.

From Gen. LUCAS. Timed 1 p.m. Received 2.45 p.m. Is there any hope of reinforcements being sent up tonight? Otherwise 86th Brigade must evacuate MASNIERES. Reply urgent. (Repeated to III Corps 2.50 p.m.).

To Gen.LUCAS. Timed 3.25 p.m. I have seen the Army Commander who is most anxious to give up no ground. There is no hope of 88th Brigade being relieved tonight but will certainly be relieved tomorrow night. If you think and CHEAPE agrees that MASNIERES cannot be held you must withdraw 86th Brigade out of the line and throw back right flank of 87th to cover LOOK in 19.c. Keeping the Eastern edge of gun pits in 20.a. and throw back the left of the 88th Brigade to connect with right flank of 87th Brigade. Report your action by wireless and inform artillery supporting you. In this case send 86th Brigade to RIBECOURT and hold on to above line at all costs with remainder of Division.

To 87th Brigade. Timed 3.30 p.m. Monmouth Pioneers will reach you tonight as a reserve.

From Gen.LUCAS. Timed 11.30 a.m. Received 3.30 p.m. 88th Brigade beat off another counter-attack at 7.30 this morning but had heavy casualties. Unless they are sent a fresh battalion tonight I doubt if they will maintain their position. I have used up the troops from the bridgehead line which is now empty. 88th Brigade plus King's Own Scottish Borderers still have Hampshire Regiment in reserve. A second battalion is urgently required to hold Bridgehead line with 2 Companies and 2 Companies in reserve. Cannot move Hampshire Regiment as they may be urgently required to protect our right rear

From 86th Brigade. Received 1.29 p.m. Enemy massed Cavalry in N.3 and N.9.

From 86th Brigade. Received 1.37 p.m. They in position close in front of artillery in R.11.a. They running hard from West to East about R.12. Enemy running hard from West to East about R.12.

To III Corps. Timed 2.15 p.m. G.O.C. just returned from MARCOING. Situation appears that enemy attacked LES RUES VERTES from South-East and gained footing in that place. Left Brigade line at 12.30 p.m. was intact and in touch with Right Brigade in MASNIERES who it is thought held original line with exception of MONT PLAISIR Farm. Reserve Brigade now holding a line from LES RUES VERTES to VILLERS PLOUICH and has orders to clear LES RUES VERTES of the enemy.

To III Corps. Timed 2.30 p.m. Have just returned from MARCOING and find everything satisfactory. Heavy attack from the North beaten off. Enemy entered LES RUES VERTES from the South-East and my Reserve Brigade is now counter-attacking and has reached the line G.31.c. - L.34.c. - R.5.b. My line East of Canal intact except for post at MONT PLAISIR FARM. Suggest one Brigade 6th Division be sent to R.4. to connect my right with 29th Division. Have ordered 29th Division to give no ground.

From 86th Brigade. Received 2.31 p.m. Enemy infantry again advancing about R.12.

From 86th Brigade. Received 2.44 p.m. Enemy guns and cavalry have retired over R.7 to East. All well here.

From 86th Brigade. Received 2.50 p.m. Enemy artillery moving from LATEAU East. Enemy infantry entering LATEAU WOOD from North and East.

From III Corps. To 88th Brigade. Untimed. Fifteen Brigade through MARCOING on to Ridge at R.4 and R.9. This message was cancelled by telephone from III Corps at 2.40 p.m.

From III Corps. Timed 4 p.m. Please congratulate Gen.SHIATE and troops under him on their splendid defence of MASNIERES. Also convey to the 87th and 88th Bdes. my appreciation of their fine work to-day.

From G.S.O.I at 87th Brigade H.Q. Received 4.15 p.m. Situation 4 p.m. 87th Brigade hold original line. 88th Brigade hold original line and LES RUES VERTES also all bridges over the Canal. 88th Brigade holding line approx. L.W.s. thence along Sunken Road through L.35.b. not yet known whether in touch with 29th Division on right. 88th Brigade have been ordered to advance and endeavour to consolidate the line of the Sunken Road through L.33. G.31.a. effecting a junction with the 86th Brigade at the Cross Roads G.25.c.1.5. Brigade Major 88th Brigade wounded slight. Send up S.A.A. reinforcements badly needed.

From Gen. LUCAS. Received 12 midnight. Situation MASNIERES and MARCOING unchanged.

To III Corps.   Timed 8.10 p.m. I left GOUZEAUCOURT at 4.30 p.m. 1st Guards Brigade was holding
& 36th   Eastern fringe of the village and the enemy in apparent strength and well
57th   supplied with Machine Guns on QUENTIN Ridge. I saw every gun come into action
88th Bdes.   100 yards South of the GOUZEAUCOURT—VILLERS GUISLAIN Road where it cuts ridge.
Attack by troops of 5th Division and three tanks still West of GOUZEAUCOURT when darkness fell. Squadron 5th Calvry Division also West of village. My line intact at 4 p.m. and LES RUES VERTES in our hands.

Added. to 3 Bdes. The attack will be continued tomorrow against GONNELIEU and VILLERS GUISLAIN.
29th Division to hold on.

To 28th Bde. only. If 56th Bde. are forced out of MASNIERES they will fall back along Canal to HARGOING and will hold on to WELSH RIDGE at all costs but the operations tomorrow depend on your being able to hold your line.

From 86th Bde. Received 6.30 p.m. Have beaten off another counter attack on LES RUES VERTES. Situation otherwise unchanged. Heavy shelling from every gun at H.Q.

From Gen. LUCAS. Timed 9.40 p.m. Situation remains the same. A fair defensive flank is being established from WELSH RIDGE to LES RUES VERTES by 86th Bde. with King's Own Scottish Borderers attached. 2 Companies South Wales Borderers are filling in gap between 86th and 88th Brigades. CHEAPE says he doubts if he can hold on tomorrow without assistance but has been told to do so. NELSON's line is very much strung out. He has the 2/Hampshire Regiment in reserve but requires further help. I have now no reserve in hand. At least two battalions are required. One for CHEAPE and one for NELSON to stand a fresh attack in force. CHEAPE cannot withdraw by day.

From 36th Brigade. Received 10.30 p.m. Line intact. Heavy shelling from all sides. Have you any orders for me?

10 p.m. G.O.C. visited III Corps Headquarters.

DECEMBER 1st, 1917.

To III Corps. Timed 9.35 a.m. Very heavy enemy barrage on line GONNLIEU - LA VACQUERIE - WELSH RIDGE.

From G.S.O.I at H.Q. 37th Brigade. Timed 9.50 a.m. Situation 9.45 a.m. We hold same line as reported in my 9.40 p.m. despatch last night. Quiet night. 36th and 58th Brigades now in touch at LES RUES VERTES. 35th Brigade is in touch with 29th Division on their right. Between 7 a.m. and 7.45 a.m. enemy put down an intense barrage on HARISBIES and 36th Brigade has suffered heavy casualties from it. It is imperative that some reinforcements be sent so my last Reserves have now been put in. If no reinforcements are forthcoming it may be necessary to evacuate HARISBIES.
9.45 a.m. Divisional Headquarters shelled out of VILLERS PLOUICH and moved to TRESCAULT.

To 37th Brigade. Timed 12.10 p.m. Corps Commander says well done and congratulate all troops on splendid defence. Definite orders will be sent you before that as to your future movements. Divisional Headquarters Town Major's Office TRESCAULT.

From 36th Brigade. Received 1.30 p.m. Attack on LES RUES VERTES at 7.45 a.m. was repulsed. Situation has quietened and our position seems more satisfactory.

From 36th Brigade. Timed 7.15 a.m. Received 1.30 p.m. Very heavy enemy barrage on whole village.

From 36th Brigade. Timed 10.20 p.m. Received 1.30 p.m. Enemy in numbers in quarry G.32.d.

From III Corps Commander. Well done hang on at all costs - timed 11.55 a.m. - received 12.40 pm.

From III Corps. Timed 11.25 a.m. Received 4 p.m. Giving situation. Guards Division ordered to capture ridge from GONNELIEU to GOUCHE WOOD. 2nd Cavalry Division are moving on REVELON Ridge and Cavalry Corps are moving two Divisions towards VAUCELETTE Farm from direction of VILLERS FAUCON.

From III Corps. Timed 11.35 a.m. Received 4 p.m. If you are forced to withdraw your troops from MASNIERES do so via MARCOING. Hold WELSH Ridge (R.4 and R.9) in order to cover the withdrawal along the COUILLET Valley. You must hold on to WELSH Ridge at all costs and if forced back you must retire on HIGHLAND Ridge.

From 86th Brigade. Received 12.52 p.m. 88th Brigade driving enemy back. They are retiring through G.31 and 33. My line intact.

From 86th Brigade. Received 12.35 p.m. Holding out. They in great strength attacking us from G.31 and G.32. They are in South end of LES RUES VERTES. Have stopped three attacks from along the CAMBRAI Road. Any orders?

From 86th Brigade. Received 12.38 p.m. We are in touch with 87th at G.19.d.Central. Enemy appear to be running away from MARCOING towards 4.5%. Our line intact.

From 86th Brigade. Received 1 p.m. Still hold all bridgeheads and in touch with 87th. We hold all LES RUES VERTES. Patrol has been through copse in 4.25.a. and reports no enemy within 200 yards of copse.

From 86th Brigade. Received 1.25 h.r. LES RUES VERTES clear of enemy. Our line intact. Enemy appears to be retiring on CRUNEOURT.

From 86th Brigade. Received 1.30 p.m. Enemy massing about G.35 Central and again advancing.

From 86th Brigade. Received 1.14 p.m. Position intact. Large number of enemy behind camouflage about Cross Roads G.32.b.0.

To III Corps. Timed 4.35 p.m. Officer just returned from forward area reports:- 86th Brigade on right have beaten off eight attacks to-day.

From 86th Brigade. Received 4.51 p.m. Enemy in LES RUES VERTES but we hold all bridges as yet.

From 86th Brigade. Received 4.55 p.m. Situation critical.

From III Corps. Received 4.55 p.m. Instruct 86th Brigade under circumstances to withdraw to line West of MASNIERES in G.20.a. and c. and alter line of 88th Brigade accordingly. Convey Corps Commander's hearty congratulations to 86th Brigade on their fine performance.

To III Corps. With reference to above message timed 5 p.m. Instructions already issued but will only be carried out if absolutely necessary and both Brigadiers agreeing.

To 87th Brigade. In continuation of my message timed 3.25 p.m. this has Corps Commander's approval. Convey his heartiest congratulations to 86th Brigade on fine performance.

From Gen. LUCAS. Received 5.35 p.m. 86th Brigade report that we are being driven out of LES RUES VERTES.

To III Corps. Timed 7.15 p.m. Message just received from 87th Brigade. LES RUES VERTES retaken by 88th Brigade and 50 prisoners captured.

DECEMBER 2nd, 1917.

To III Corps and Flank Divisions. Timed 7.50 a.m. After dark last night the 86th Brigade were withdrawn from the MASNIERES Salient into reserve. The line now runs 88th Bde. from about R.5.Central along the Sunken Road in L.25.Central to L.30.Central - along the drain to lock L.24.c. which is connecting point with 87th Brigade whose line runs along Canal to houses L.19.c. then North along Eastern edge of gun pits in L.20.a. to our original front line. Enemy have persistently shelled MASNIERES all the morning and continue to do so unaware of our withdrawal.

To Gen. LUCAS. Timed 8.50 a.m. Following moves will take place after dark to-night December 2nd/3rd. 18th Brigade 6th Division will relieve 87th Brigade on that portion of the Divisional front North of the ST. QUENTIN Canal. The 88th Brigade will withdraw to area about TRESCAULT. 87th Brigade on relief will withdraw to Squares K.56., L.51, L.52. 88th Brigade will continue to hold their present line from the ST. QUENTIN Canal to junction with Division on right about R.5.a. at present the 20th Division but to-night will be the 61st Division. G.O.C. 58th Brigade will remain in command of the Divisional front.

To III Corps. Timed 9.5 a.m. Enemy reported massing in MASNIERES. Please turn on all available heavies. ?. *Redirected*

To III Corps. Timed 9.45 a.m. Enemy that was massing in MASNIERES attacked our line North of Canal about 8.30 a.m. He was successfully driven off. Please keep heavies on to MASNIERES.

From III Corps. Timed 10 a.m. All bridges over the ST. QUENTIN Canal will be prepared for demolition.

From III Corps. Timed 1.30 p.m. Giving details of reserve line to be consolidated. Extract:- 29th Division from R.7.b. to HINDENBURG SUPPORT in L.32.c.9.5.

From III Corps. Timed 4.15 p.m. Brigade of 29th Division holding the line from the Canal to the left of the 61st Division will be placed under the orders of the 6th Division on completion of the relief of the Brigades North of the ST. QUENTIN Canal by the 6th Division.

To 58th Brigade. Timed 5 p.m. You will be accommodated to-night in RIBECOURT.

From 6th Division. Instructions from Corps to take over the Battalion front South of the Canal were received too late to alter arrangements. This Battalion front will be taken over to-morrow night.

DECEMBER 3rd, 1917.   To III Corps. Timed 3.30 a.m. Reference Order No. 328, para: 12, relief complete 1.30 a.m. of troops East of Canal. 57th Brigade still have two battalions in front line attached to 88th Brigade.

11 a.m.   88th Brigade obliged to vacate RIBECOURT owing to hostile shelling. Situation on front uncertain, but eventually Corps sanctioned the move of 88th Brigade to HAVRINCOURT WOOD.

From O.C. 17th Brigade R.F.A. Attack extends from MARCOING to South. Bombardment heavy. First wave of attacking enemy caught in our barrage in C.36 and C.25 and dispersed. Keeping up strong barrage.

From G.O.C. 88th Brigade. My left very hard pressed. South Wales Borderers and Newfoundland Regiment almost wiped out by shell fire. An sending Hampshire Regiment to take their place. If enemy bombard again fear will be unable to stop infantry attack on left flank. Situation North of Canal remnants of Durham Light Infantry arrived here and Commanding Officer reported that he had been driven out of defences, also that left battalion was retiring. Enemy however did not appear to be in occupation so I ordered him back. Major WILSON is collecting men in MARCOING to send to hold defences. No reinforcements have arrived. If MARCOING is to be held assistance is wanted at once or the enemy will be in before us. If MARCOING defences fall intend to hold line L.35.a. - L.29.d. - L.29.a. - L.23.b., but cannot remain there if enemy get MARCOING. Please advise me of any action contemplated. Fresh troops badly wanted, my men being shaken by to-day's bombardment and exertions of past four days.

From III Corps. Timed 6.30 p.m. Giving details of relief of 88th Brigade by 109th Brigade.

Under instructions from Corps Gen. LUCAS proceeded to Headquarters of G.O.C. 88th Brigade to report on situation and if necessary to take over command from Gen. NELSON should the latter not be in a fit state to carry on.

From Gen. LUCAS. Timed 6.10 p.m. Present situation. A few of the 16th Brigade in MARCOING defences, remainder driven back. G.O.C. 16th Brigade now on his way with one battalion to retake or rather restore line. Left two battalions very badly out up by this morning's bombardment. My line at present runs a post of 25 men covering the Lock in L.24 and then a gap to the road in L.29.d. where this is a strong point. Enemy very close to my posts on the road in L.29.d. Message received from 16th Brigade 5.25 p.m. very holding ridge North of Canal with outposts. Have brushed aside a little initial opposition and an endeavouring to re-establish reserve line and cover both ridges but as weak.

From Gen. LUCAS. Timed 8.25 p.m. WILSON and Brigade H.Q. Going strong. WILSON is throwing back his left flank to South-West corner of MARCOING COPSE. 16th Brigade have promised to connect at this point. They were establishing line behind MARCOING only putting patrols out to the bridges. This must be stopped at all costs and a line established along west bank of Canal in front of village to join up with us. Everything wady satisfactory on this front. South Wales Borderers have been relieved by 16th Brigade and are moving back to RIBECOURT. Much regret Major GARNET, South Wales Borderers, killed.

H.Q. 88th Brigade moved to L.34.a.4.7.

DECEMBER 4th, 1917.

To III Corps. Timed 5.50 a.m. Gen. LUCAS confirms Major Wilson's report that no German ever crossed the bridges into MARCOING. At 9 p.m. last night enemy were still shelling bridges when Major WILSON examined demolition charges. 88th line runs L.29.a.2.4. to L.35.c.0.3 with Brigade H.Q. at L.34.a.4.7. WILSON confirms that parties of 70 men seen marching over bridges yesterday were our men.

To 88th Brigade. Timed 10 a.m. Orders for move to FINS.

To Brigades, Flank Divisions. Informing them of moves to take place 4th instant and night of 4th/5th. Extracts:- 86th Brigade HAVRINCOURT WOOD to FINS. 87th Brigade to SOHM. 85th Brigade on relief by 109th Brigade to assemble at Brigade Transport Camp K.36.c.Central. 227th Machine Gun Coy. to FINS.

From 88th Brigade. Timed Received 11.41 a.m. Situation quiet.

The relief of 88th Brigade by 106th Brigade was much delayed owing to a readjustment of the line ordered by the Corps having to be carried out by the 88th Brigade before relief could commence. The leading troops of the 88th Brigade did not arrive at the Brigade Transport Camp until 4 a.m. A hot meal was ready for the whole Brigade and after a short rest the march was continued to the entraining station at EQUANCOURT a distance of 6½ miles, where the Brigade rested until entraining that evening.

Advanced Divisional Headquarters closed at TRESCAULT at 3.50 a.m. and moved back to SORRL.

ARTILLERY REPORT.

29th Div. No. C.G.S. 70/79.

III Corps.

SECRET

In continuation of my C.G.S.70/73, dated 29th December 1917, I herewith send you 2 Copies of the Report from my C.R.A. of the Operations during 30th November – 3rd December 1917, as it may be of interest to you.

Brigadier-General,
30th December 1917.   Commanding 29th Division.

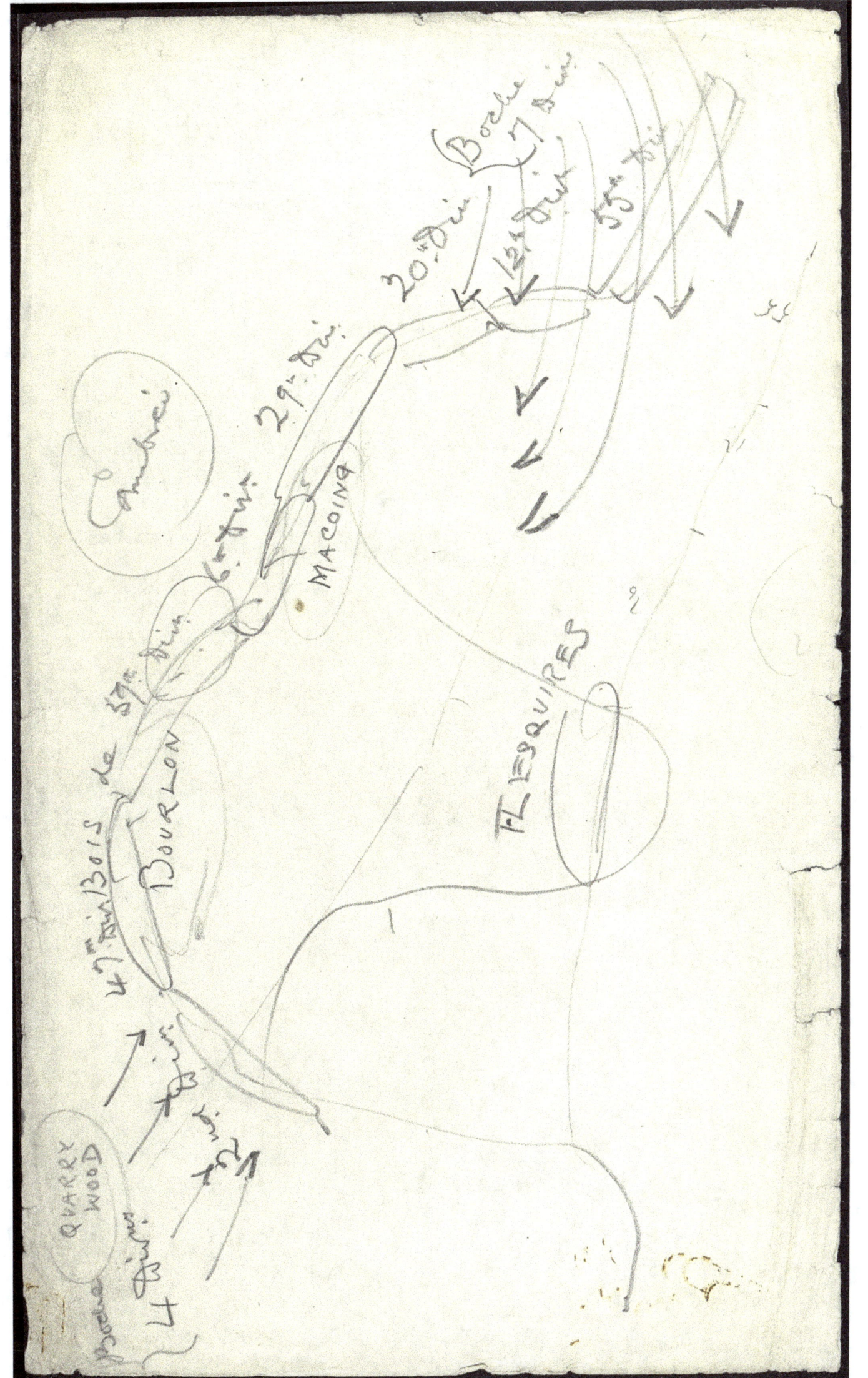

29th Divisional Artillery.

Report on Operations of 30th November 1917,

and following days.

SECRET

Reference:- 1/20,000 Map, Special Sheet.
GOUZEAUCOURT.

1.
DISPOSITIONS
ON NIGHT
29th/30th NOV.

A. On the night 29th/30th November, the field artillery supporting 29th Division consisted of 29th Divisional Artillery (15th Brigade R.H.A. and 17th Brigade R.F.A.) and 232nd (Army) Brigade R.F.A. with a total of 85 – 18-pdrs. and 12 – 4.5" Howitzers in action under the orders of the C.R.A. 29th Division.

B. The above artillery was disposed as under:-

H.Q. 29th Divl. Arty. — R.31.c.7.8.
(Brig.Genl. E.H.STEVENSON D.S.O.)

29th D.A. Signal Exchange — R.4.a.2.4.

15th Bde. R.H.A.
(Lieut.Col. E.R.HUNTE, D.S.O.)
18 – 18pdrs. 6 – 4.5" Hows.
Brigade H.Q. — R.10.a.3.6.
"B" "L" and "Warwick" Batteries) VACQUERIE VALLEY
R.H.A. & 460th(How.) Bty. R.F.A.) (R.5.d.)

17th Bde. R.F.A.
(Lt.Col. W.A.MURRAY, D.S.O.)
17 – 18pdrs. 6 – 4.5" Hows.
Brigade H.Q. — L.27.d.30.15.
13th, 26th, 92nd and D/17) COUILLET WOOD
Batteries R.F.A.) VALLEY.
(L.27.d. and
L.33.b.) with
an enfilading
section of 92
Bty. R.F.A. at
L.16.a.5.5.

232nd Army Bde.R.F.A.
(Lt.Col. T.T.GIBBONS).
18 – 18pdrs.
Brigade H.Q. — L.28.d.9.8.
"A", "B", and C/232 Btys.R.F.A. — COUILLET WOOD
VALLEY.
(L.28.b. and
L.27.d.).

C. Six – 6" Newton Trench Mortars were in position in MASNIERES and LES RUES VERTES, but only two were in action, the remaining 4 having been previously put out of action by enemy shell fire during the afternoon and evening of Nov.29th.

D. No Heavy Artillery was directly under the orders of 29th Division, but Heavy Artillery fire could be obtained by request to Heavy Artillery IIIrd Corps or by request to 63rd H.A.G. to whom a direct telephone line had been laid from H.Q., 29th D.A.

E. The 18-pdr S.O.S. line was continuous and was approximately 300 yards beyond our front line, running approximately, G.29.d.4.7. - G.28.c.8.6. - G.21.d.7.0. - G.21.b.2.1. - G.20.b.9.8. - G.14.a.9.0. - L.16.a.5.8.

 This line was covered by 15th Brigade R.H.A. on the right, 17th Bde. R.F.A. in the centre, and 232nd Army Bde.R.F.A. on the left.

2.
NOV.
30th. At 2.0 a.m. on November 30th the enemy opened heavy destructive and neutralising fire with 77 mm. guns and 105 mm and 150 Howitzers on all Field Batteries in the VACQUERIE VALLEY using H.E. and Gas Shells.

 Counter Batteries III Corps were kept informed of the situation, but their fire no way affected the severity of the shelling.

 From 4 a.m. to 7 a.m. 15th Bde.R.H.A. opened counter-preparative fire on the approaches N. of RUMILLY and on likely places of assembly.

 At 7 a.m. at the request of G.O.C. 86th Infantry Brigade the fire of 15th Bde. R.H.A. was concentrated on the area opposite and flanking MONT PLAISIR FM, and an F.O.O. was sent to MONT PLAISIR FM. to watch for any movement which might develop from the direction of CREVECOUER. This F.O.O. reported shortly after 7 a.m. that there was no sign of movement on 29th Division front, but that movement of some sort was visible in the direction of REVELON CHATEAU and at 8 a.m. reported that more decided movement could be observed round CREVECOUER, but that the exact nature of the movement could not be determined.

 By this time numerous hostile aircraft had made their appearance and 16 enemy machines were flying low, machine gunning and apparently directing fire on our batteries in VACQUERIE VALLEY who had by this time suffered heavy casualties and had had many dugouts blown in.

 Shortly after 8 a.m. an S.O.S. rocket was seen to go up on the front of the Division on our right (20th Division)

 Up to 8.10 a.m. 15th Bde.R.H.A. had been in continuous communication with Headquarters 29th D.A. by telephone through 29th D.A. forward exchange. At 8.10 a.m. all telephone lines from 29th D.A. forward exchange to H.Q. 29th D.A. were cut. Communication was not re-established as D.A.H.Q. had to be abandoned at about 8.40 a.m. and at about 9.10 a.m. was occupied by the enemy who had advanced from the direction of VILLERS GUISLAINS.

 Brigadier General STEVENSON (C.R.A. 29th Division) who had been wounded by shell fire at about 8 a.m. could not be moved from D.A.H.Q. and had to be left behind with a wounded orderly. As a result of a counter-attack by another Division General STEVENSON and the orderly were rescued early on the morning of December 1st.

 All documents etc of H.Q. 29th D.A. were at one time in possession of the enemy who apparently looked through them, but did not remove many important documents. All remaining documents were subsequently recovered.

 At about 9 a.m. more movement round CREVECOEUR was reported and it became apparent that the enemy had broken through on the 20th Division front South of the ST. QUENTIN CANAL as bodies of British Infantry retiring through 15th Brigade R.H.A. guns in VACQUERIE VALLEY and 17th Bde.R.F.A. guns in GOUZEAUCOURT WOOD VALLEY and bodies of enemy Infantry could be seen advancing over WELSH RIDGE close to 17th Bde.R.F.A. and passing through one battery of 232nd Army Bde. R.F.A. in action in L.28.b. The personnel of this latter battery had suffered heavy casualties before they withdrew with sights and breech locks. As soon as the situation became apparent 92nd and D/17 batteries of 17th Bde. R.F.A. ran their guns out of their emplacements and engaged with open sights bodies of the enemy advancing over WELSH RIDGE. Major STANFORD of 92nd Bty.R.F.A. assisting with the fire of a Lewis Gun which was in the battery position at the time, and Captain BOOTH (D.T.M.O.29th Division) assisting with the fire of a Lewis Gun which he obtained from a party of retiring Infantry of 20th Division. The fire of the remaining two batteries of 17th Bde.R.F.A. and of the two remaining batteries of 232nd Army Bde.R.F.A. was directed on large numbers of the enemy who were seen approaching MASNIERES in mass from the direction of CREVECOEUR.

-8-

At the same time Colonel BURNE commanding 15th Bde.R.H.A. with the consent of G.O.C. 86th Infantry Bde. switched off the zone he was covering on 29th Division front to cover a probable gap on the right, informing 17th and 232nd Bdes. by telephone of the action he had taken and requesting them to arrange between themselves to cover the whole of the 29th Division front without his aid. At the request of G.O.C.86th Infantry Brigade two senior officers (Majors EDEN & ST.CLAIR) were sent by O.C. 15th Bde. R.H.A. to stop the British Infantry who were retiring from BONAVIS RIDGE and to assist them to hold back the enemy while G.O.C. 86th Inf. Bde. made flank dispositions. Majors EDEN & ST. CLAIR were unable to stop the Infantry, who stated that they had been ordered to retire to the Hindenburg Support Line. This was communicated to G.O.C. 86th Inf. Bde. who ordered Colonel BURNE to hold the gap with his guns. Colonel BURNE accordingly sent out flank observers and turned on intense searching and sweeping barrage on to the line of Canal Crossings CREVECOEUR - REVELON - lock on Canal East of MONT PLAISIR Fm, where enemy cavalry and Infantry reserves were crossing.

By 9.15 a.m. all British Infantry had retired through the guns of 15th Bde. R.H.A. which were left to hold the line with no escort. By 9.30 a.m. all wires from 29th D.A. advanced exchange had been cut and at 10.30 a.m. the exchange had to be abandoned as it was practically surrounded by the enemy.

At 10.40 a.m. the advanced line of the enemy's Infantry came into full view of 15th Bde. guns. These lines of Infantry were advancing over the crest of BONAVIS RIDGE and down the valley running to the East from the gun positions, and were followed by small columns and machine gun detachments. All enemy Infantry were walking and were wearing full kits. All 18-pdr.guns of 15th Bde. engaged the advancing enemy with direct laying and succeeded in keeping them till 11.10 a.m. by which time the enemy had worked forward by sunken roads to positions within 40 yards of the guns from where they were firing kneeling at the gunners. At 11.10 a.m. O.C., 15th Bde. ordered the withdrawal of wounded and personnel with breechblocks, sights etc. to the Hindenburg Support Line. "L" Battery R.H.A. covered this withdrawal firing very steadily and rapidly and sweeping away many small columns of enemy Infantry. This action of "L" Battery R.H.A. shook up the enemy and prevented heavy casualties being inflicted on the withdrawing personnel personnel, who, laden with wounded, breechblocks, sights etc., had to withdraw up hill over some 600 yards of ground in full view of the enemy whose advanced lines were within 40 yards of "L" Battery's guns. When the personnel of the other batteries were well clear of their positions, the personnel of "L" Battery also withdrew taking with them or destroying all sight and breech blocks.

Although many men who were carrying breechblocks, sights etc. were killed or wounded, a proportion of these articles was safely brought back, and it is believed that the remainder were all destroyed or damaged beyond local repair on the spot.

At this time it was hoped that all guns might be recovered by a local counter-attack and Colonel BURNE conferred with the local Infantry O.C's urging this action. No counter-attack developed but eventually Colonel BURNE persuaded a small party of Infantry consisting of one Officer, a Lewis Gun and 20 men to accompany himself, three other R.A. Officers and 8 R.A. personnel. This party advanced almost up to the left flank of 15th Bde. guns recapturing the Brigade H.Q. and wireless station and the trench just East of this place. From the line established great execution was done and at least 150 enemy were accounted for at short easy ranges. In the meantime all maps, secret documents etc. at Brigade H.Q. were burnt. By 2 p.m. the enemy had worked round this advanced line and was throwing bombs and enfilading the line with machine guns. Ammunition also ran out, so the party withdrew to the main line of defence in the Hindenburg Support Line, where Colonel BURNE remained till dusk still hoping that a counter-attack might develop.

In the meantime 92nd and D/17th Batteries of 17th Bde. R.F.A. assisted to hold the enemy in check between HARGOING and GOUILLET WOOD, until about 11.30 a.m. when a counter-attack delivered by Infantry of 29th Division and supported by the fire of 17th Bde. R.F.A. drove the enemy back to LES RUES VERTES and established a line of defence between this latter village and the left of 29th Division in L.4.

- 4 -

The remaining two batteries of 17th Bde. R.F.A. and the two remaining batteries of 232nd Army Bde. R.F.A. continued to engage the enemy who continued to attack MASNIERES and LES RUES VERTES from the North and East. A rapid rate of fire was maintained until midday by which time the situation appeared to be again in hand.

Shortly after midday the whole of the field artillery supporting 29th Division was placed under the command of Lieut.Col. MURRAY who was informed that he must deal direct with General LUCAS who had been made responsible for the defence of the whole of the front line system held by troops of 29th Division. At this time the guns available for the defence of the line were:-

    17th Bde.R.F.A. 18 - 18pdrs. 6 - 4.5" Hows.
    232nd Army Bde.R.F.A. 11 - 18-pdrs.

and the line held by 29th Division was approximately 7000 yards in length. All idea of a continuous S.O.S. line was therefore abandoned, but reconnaissance by Battery Commanders of the front gave information by which it was possible to ascertain the dangerous points where the enemy were massing and from which further attacks might be expected. Fire was concentrated on these points which were kept under fire throughout the day.

During the afternoon, several enemy attacks developed and were met by the concentrated fire of 17th and 232nd Brigades. Several hostile batteries were seen advancing into action and were engaged. One of these batteries was put completely out of action, and on several occasions it was possible to silence other batteries which could be seen in action. Throughout the afternoon there was movement on the roads leading South and East from CREVECOEUR and South from RUMILLY. This movement was engaged and considerable disorganization of enemy troops resulted.

During the afternoon touch was established with 63rd Heavy Artillery Group South of RIBECOURT, and arrangements were made to carry out a concentrated shoot by 6" Hows. and 60-pdrs. on CREVECOEUR and RUMILLY and to shell these towns intermittently throughout the night.

Close touch was maintained by Colonel MURRAY with the Infantry in the line throughout the day, one Artillery officers being always with General LUCAS and several Artillery officers being always with the Infantry in the front line.

Replenishment of ammunition to the batteries of 17th and 232nd Brigades was carried out by man-handling trolleys along the broad guage railway running up the COUILLET WOOD VALLEY, the ammunition being obtained from 29th D.A. dump at R.14.a.0.9. and the ammunition dump at the guns was almost constantly kept up to the amounts ordered (300 rds. per 18-pdr. gun and 240 rds. per 4.5" Howr.).

During the day the ammunition expended by 17th and 232nd Batteries amounted to about 1500 rds. per battery in action, giving a total of 7500 rds. 18-pdr. and 1500 rds. 4.5" Howr. Before withdrawing from their guns 15th Bde. had expended approximately 4000 rds. 18-pdr. and 1000 4.5" Howr. The total ammunition expenditure for the day was therefore approximately 11500 rds. of 18-pdr. and 2500 rds. 4.5" Howr.

The action taken by Trench Mortar Batteries is given in Appendix "A" attached to this report.

3. No further attacks were made by the enemy during the night November
DEC. 30th/December 1st.
1st. On the morning December 1st the guns covering 29th Division front were:-

    17th Bde. R.F.A. - 17 - 18-pdrs. 6 - 4.5" Hows.
    232nd Army Bde. R.F.A. - 11 - 18-pdrs.

Practically continuous barrage fire was kept up throughout the day on the outskirts of MASNIERES village which was heavily attacked by the enemy on six separate occasions.

As 29th Division Infantry were ordered to withdraw from MASNIERES during the night December 1st/2nd, Colonel MURRAY decided to move back one battery of 232nd Army Bde. R.F.A. from L.28.b. and 92nd and D/17th Batteries of 17th Bde. R.F.A. from L.27.d. and L.33.b, as it was considered advisable not to risk the loss of any more of the few guns left in action.

The withdrawal of these batteries was successfully carried out and all guns were in action in their new positions in L.27.a. and L.26.d. by dawn on December 2nd.

The ammunition expended by 17th and 232nd Brigades during December 1st, amounted approximately to 2400 rds. 18-pdr. and 400 rds. 4.5" How., replenishment being carried out as on November 30th.

The action taken by Trench Mortar personnel is given in Appendix "A" attached to this report.

4. DEC. 2nd.
No enemy Infantry attack developed during the night Dec. 1st/2nd or on December 2nd.

On the morning of December 2nd the Field Artillery covering 29th Division was re-inforced by 5th Army Bde. R.H.A. with 10 - 18-pdr. guns. These batteries came into action early on the afternoon of Dec. 2nd astride the railway in L.21.c. and by 2 p.m. the guns available for the defence of the line were:-

    17th Bde. R.F.A.   16 - 18 pdrs.   6 - 4.5" Hows.
    232nd Army Bde. R.F.A.   11 - 18-pdrs.
    5th Army Bde. R.H.A.   10 - 18-pdrs.

During the night December 2nd/3rd, 13th and 26th Batteries of 17th Bde. R.F.A. withdrew from their positions in L.27.d. to new positions in L.27.a. and L.21.c., whilst Col. MURRAY and H.Q., 17th Bde. R.F.A. withdrew to L.31.b.

The withdrawal was successful, all guns and howitzers being removed and only about 300 rds. of ammunition per battery had to be left behind.

On the night December 2nd/3rd the command of all Field Artillery covering 29th Division on December 2nd passed to G.O.C. 6th Division.

Casualties suffered by R.A. personnel of 29th Division are given in Appendix "B" attached to this report.

APPENDIX "A".

Action of Medium Trench Mortar Batteries of 29th Division.
November 30th and December 1st 1917.

At 8.0 a.m. on 30th November, the enemy was observed advancing on MASNIERES and LES RUES VERTES. Lieut. CECIL with his one Mortar fired all ammunition available (30 rds.) at advancing enemy, destroyed his piece, and reported to G.O.C. Infantry Brigade for orders with the remainder of his personnel.

The remaining Mortar was used to fire bursts of five rounds every half hour on such parts of LES RUES VERTES as remained in the hands of the enemy, also on all targets within range as requested by G.O.C. 86th Bde. Some 100 rds. were thus fired until during final attack of the enemy at about 3.30 p.m. on Dec.1st the Mortar could not stand the strain, and, being out of action was thrown into the Canal. All remaining personnel (5 Officers 18 Other Ranks) reported to O.C. Coy. holding Canal bank and new support line, remaining there till ordered to evacuate by G.O.C. 86th Infantry Bde. at midnight December 1st/2nd when all ranks withdrew to HARGOING carrying wounded on stretchers withdrawing from there to EQUANCOURT on the morning Dec.2nd.

APPENDIX "C".

Casualties which occurred during the operations of 30th November 1917 and 1st and 2nd December 1917.

	Killed.		Wounded.		Missing.	
	O.	O.R.	O.	O.R.	O.	O.R.
Headquarters 29th Divnl. Arty.	.	1.	1.	4.	.	3.
15th Brigade RHA	-	5.	3.	34.	.	20.
17th Brigade RFA	-	.	.	2.	.	9.
29th D.A.C.	-	.	.	8.	.	2.
Trench Mortars	2	.	.	4.	.	3.
	2	6	4	52	.	37

"Complete" copy to be kept

29th Division No. C.G.S.70/73.

III Corps.

Herewith report on Operations by the 29th Division on November 30th, 1917, and following days.

On further enquiry, I learn that the German attack South of the Canal on Dec 3rd was supported by a large number of 6" trench mortars. Sometimes as many as 12 Bombs were in the air at the same time.

Beauvoir de Lisle

Major-General,
10th December, 1917.   Commanding 29th Division.

Report on Operations near MASNIERES on Nov. 30th and Dec. 1st
by 86th Brigade.
-o-o-o-o-o-o-o-o-o-o-o-o-o-o-o-o-o-o-o-o-o-o-o-o-o-o-

On the night of the 28/29th November my Brigade took over the MASNIERES Sector from the 88th Brigade. I reorganised the grouping of battalions and issued new defence orders. The 1/Lancashire Fusiliers held from the CAMBRAI Road to G.21.c.8.5. with 3 Companies in the front system and 1 in support.

The 16/Middlesex Regiment from G.21.c.8.5. to G.27.c.90.15. with outposts at MON PLAISIR FARM and Canal Bridge G.28.c.25.00. 3 Companies in front line 1 in close support.

2/Royal Fusiliers in support at, 1 Company in houses G.20.d.5.5, 1 Company in the vicinity of G.20.d.9.3. 2 Companies at SUGAR FACTORY G.27.a.2.6.

The 1/Royal Guernsey Light Infantry resting in the CATACOMBS.

8 Machine Guns in the front system, 8 4 in support and 4 resting in LES RUES VERTES.

4 6" Stokes were also under my command.

We were in touch with 87th Inf. Bde. on the CAMBRAI Road and with the 20th Division at the Canal Bridge G.28.c.25.00.

At 5 a.m. the artillery liaison officer Major BALL, R.F.A. 29th Division, reported that his batteries had been heavily shelled during the night. The battalions were at once warned to be on the alert.

The 2/Royal Fusiliers were "standing to" at their alarm posts and 2 Companies of the 1/Royal Guernsey Light Infantry were ordered to "stand to" in the CATACOMBS ready to move.

There was considerable shell fire on our lines and on the village between 7.15 and 8 a.m.

It was a misty morning but our observation post on the roof of Brigade H.Q. (CHATEAU) G.20.b.3.0. reported considerable movement on the ridge W. of CREVECOURT about 8 a.m.

At 8.40 a.m. the 16/Middlesex Regiment reported that the Brigade on our right were falling back followed by the enemy in waves. At the same time the 1/Lancashire Fusiliers and 16/Middlesex Regiment were heavily attacked.

The 2 Companies of the 1/Royal Guernsey Light Infantry were ordered across the Canal to make a defensive flank round LES RUES VERTES.

Capt. GEE (Staff Captain) at Rear H.Q. G.26.b.1.2. was warned about the retirement on our right and ordered to send a D.R. direct to 87th Brigade H.Q. MARCOING and alarm R.E. in the southern portion of LES RUES VERTES.

The 87th and 88th Brigades were warned by runner. All telephone lines were cut by shells. In the meantime there was fighting going on in LES RUES VERTES.

I then went to the Canal and hurried the 2 Companies 1/Royal Guernsey Light Infantry over the Canal to turn the Germans out of the village. Heavy rifle fire was developing on both the Lancashire Fusiliers and Middlesex Regiment fronts.

I then came back to Brigade H.Q. sent Capt. INNES to the Brigade on our left (2/South Wales Borderers) who warned them of the situation and took a platoon to man all bridgeheads W. of MASNIERES.

Capt. INNES returned and reported that the Germans were close to MARCOING.

My Staff Captain then appeared. He had been captured by the Germans in the yard at Rear H.Q. He had escaped by killing a German with his walking stick. He then organised all signallers, runners, etc. and followed by the 2 Companies of 1/Royal Guernsey Light Infantry chased the enemy out of LES RUES VERTES and established a position on the outskirts of the village. 5 dead Germans as proof of this were left in the yard at Rear H.Q. Many were slaughtered in house to house fighting and a few prisoners taken.

/ The

- 2 -

The village was all clear except for a M.G. at G.26.c.1.3. which was giving us a lot of trouble. Capt. GEE with 1 remaining orderly (4 had already been killed beside him) rushed the gun, his orderly was killed but Capt. GEE managed with his 2 revolvers to kill the crew of 8 Germans, then collected more men and turned the gun on the enemy. This absolutely cleared the village, Capt. GEE was wounded in the knee but remained on duty till the following morning when I ordered him back to MARCOING. This officer by his heroic conduct undoubtedly saved the Brigade if not the whole Division.

In the mean time the enemy had delivered three heavy attacks on the 1/Lancashire Fusiliers between the RUMILLY and CAMBRAI Road, and one on the 16/Middlesex Regiment front. These attacks did not get nearer than 100 yards and were defeated with great slaughter by rifle, Lewis Gun, Machine Gun and Trench Mortar fire.

I had sent the remainder of the 1/Royal Guernsey Light Infantry into LES RUES VERTES to help to clear the village.

I then made arrangements for all round defence.

2/Royal Fusiliers (less 1 Company) were ordered to take over the defence from lock G.27.c.5.5. to G.26.d.2.3. 1/Royal Guernsey Light Infantry 2 Companies and the 10% of all battalions, who had arrived late the night before and were billeted in LES RUES VERTES, were ordered to hold from G.26.d.2.3. to the Canal at G.19.c.5.5.

2 Companies of 1/Royal Guernsey Light Infantry in support along the Canal Bank holding the crossings from the North Bank.

1 Company of the 2/Royal Fusiliers in reserve at the Quarry G.20.d.

Both these battalions shifted their H.Q. to cellars near Canal Bridge G.20.d.3.4.

It was then reported that the 88th Brigade were driving the enemy back from MARCOING. During this day my wires were continuously being cut but I kept the wireless going sending no less than 35 wires to the Army and 25 the next day. The wireless was extraordinarily useful.

My 6" Stokes Guns under Capt. BOOTH, I placed in such a position that they shelled the Sunken Road G.32.b. where the enemy were continually massing troops. This officer was magnificent and it was largely due to him and his 6" Stokes that we kept the enemy out, at least 300 shells were fired. Unfortunately this officer was very severely wounded on the night of the 1st/2nd December, he had finished all his ammunition, thrown his guns into the Canal and was leading a party of Infantry driving the Germans out of LES RUES VERTES. A very gallant officer.

During the whole of this day, the village was shelled lightly. We patrolled the Copse G.25.a. and cleared it of enemy. They now appeared to be digging in near the MARCOING Road.

About 4 p.m. the Germans attempted to attack all sides but were easily driven off.

At 4.40 p.m. 30th I sent a message to the 87th Brigade stating that I held LES RUES VERTES and that my original front was intact and if they could push up to G.32.a. & c. we could hold on.

It was a quiet night and about 11 p.m. Capt. HAMILTON, Brigade Transport Officer, arrived with pack mules 90 boxes S.A.A. and bombs. During the day all battalions drew munitions from Rear H.Q. in LES RUES VERTES.

At 5.10 the enemy attacked LES RUES VERTES from the South and South-East but were driven off with slaughter, we were then being heavily shelled from three sides.

During the evening I received a message from Gen. LUCAS saying that our Army were to attack and re-establish the position the next morning.

I issued an order that we were to hold on at all costs. Before this I informed Gen. LUCAS that I did not think it possible to hold on another 24 hours. My position was enfiladed from all sides, enemy 77 guns were firing from three sides at a distance of only 800 yards and enfilading our trenches, especially on the 16/Middlesex Regiment front. This regiment fully deserves its name of "Die Hards" for they never gave a foot of ground the whole time.

During the morning of the 30th, Col. FORBES ROBERTSON although wounded in the right eye; held the lock at G.27.c.5.5. with his Battalion H.Q. until it was taken over by the 2/Royal Fusiliers.

This officer behaved with greatest gallantry was continuously in the front line encouraging his men, and through his splendid example they stood firm.

Although wounded he remained at duty and is still with his battalion. He visited his front line several times during the night although unable to see. He was led by the hand by his orderly. This greatly encouraged his men.

During that night we sent out patrols and got in touch with the 2/Hampshire Regiment and 2/South Wales Borderers on our right in G.23.a.

We evacuated most of our wounded along the Canal Bank.

I sent Major BALL R.F.A. back to his battery about 3 p.m., but he came back on his own initiative the next day to tell us the situation.

1st December.

On the morning of the 1st at about 7.15 the enemy bombarded us till 7.45 a.m.

A most intense barrage was followed by an attack of 8 lines of infantry. They drove in our outposts from MON PLAISIR FARM and bridge G.28.c.25.80. but everywhere else were driven back with great slaughter.

4 M.Gs. in the SUGAR FACTORY, excellently posted by Capt. ROBERTS, Machine Gun Company, had a particularly fine target enfilading the dense lines of enemy approaching LES RUES VERTES from the East. It is estimated that at least 500 Germans were downed at this point. The German Red Cross party were out during the whole of the remainder of the day working in this vicinity.

3" and 6" Stokes played a great part in the defence of LES RUES VERTES. Capt. LATHOM BROWN, 2/Royal Fusiliers, greatly distinguished himself in repelling this attack, and after the attack was repulsed reported that his line was intact after visiting and encouraging every post on the LES RUES VERTES side of the Canal.

At 10.10 a.m. the 16/Middlesex Regiment reported that the enemy was endeavouring to advance in rushes and that he was having trouble from T.Ms. and direct Field Gun fire. They established themselves in MON PLAISIR Avenue, but he had formed a block and was holding them.

Capt. CORDER, 88th T.M. Battery, did very good work on the CAMBRAI Road and kept the enemy off with a barrage.

My men were now very exhausted and I asked for reinforcements.

Just as one Company of 2/South Wales Borderers were arriving (about 2.30 p.m.) two German aeroplanes flew over LES RUES VERTES and each dropped 2 red lights.

An intense bombardment from all calibres commenced on our trenches and the village from three sides. I have been in France since September 1914 but have never experienced anything like it. From the roof of the Chateau there was nothing to be seen but dust. The whole village was wrecked.

This lasted for 1 hour 15 minutes when it gradually lifted from LES RUES VERTES but remained on MASNIERES for an extra 15 minutes. As it lifted I came out of the Chateau and heard that the Germans were on the Canal Bridge.

During this bombardment the enemy must have crept up to the outskirts of LES RUES VERTES and as it lifted rushed the houses.

There was great panic on the Canal Bank men firing wildly in every direction. I went along the bank and made the men lie down and wait, with orders not to shoot till they saw the white of a man's eye. Thence along the bank to the 16/Middlesex Regiment, having organised bridgehead defences and started barricades. I found the 16/Middlesex Regiment and 1/Lancashire Fusiliers calm and determined to hang on at all costs.

It was reported to me that Germans were crossing by the lock bridge at G.27.c.5.5. I found a platoon of 1/Lancashire Fusiliers and sent them to hold it.

In the mean time my Acting Brigade Major, Capt. INNES, had organised bridgehead defences, crossed the Canal at 26.a.8.7. with his orderly Pte. MARTIN followed by a few Guernseys placed them at

/ 26.a.5.6.

26.a.6.6., and followed by about 6 men cleared the houses on the South
bank of the river as far as the bridge. He and his orderly killed
4 and captured 5 Germans. Capt. Innes fired all his revolver
ammunition, then took a German's rifle and came back to me with the
bayonet red.

He reported to me and we organised further bombing parties
and established a barricade at g.26.D.2.9.

The Germans were easily frightened and driven back till the
village was nearly clear, but it was difficult to discriminate
between friend and foe. About 80 prisoners were captured and more
killed during these operations.

I estimate the number of Germans, at about 300 with many
Machine Guns.

Things were fairly quiet by 7 p.m.

I had reported on critical situation and stated that unless
troops came up on my right the position was untenable with exhausted
men, and prepared my scheme for retirement. I asked that a defensive
line should be formed across the Canal for me to retire through. I
also started to evacuate my wounded which was a heavy task in which
prisoners were very useful and doors etc. were used to supplement
stretchers.

7.30.p.m. Col. MOORE, G.S.O. I, 29th Division, arrived and we
arranged details of the retirement. This commenced at II p.m.

I formed Lewis Guns posts at the bridge heads and all along
my front, and a bombing post at the barricade on the CAMBRAI Road
in RUES VERTES. I then withdrew the Brigade in the following
order. (1) All troops S. of the Canal (2) The Royal Fusiliers who
had been in support and were rather widely distributed in the village,
(3) The Middlesex Regt. which was originally my right battalion
and lastly, (4) The Lancashire Fusiliers, which held the left
Brigade front and were in touch with the 87th Brigade.

This retirement was skilfully done without a sound. Every
cellar was searched before leaving and every wounded man evacuated,
some being carried on the back of a comrade. As the last platoon
of the 1/Lancashire Fusiliers retired they warned the 1/Royal
Inniskilling Fusiliers. All papers were destroyed and our Rear H.Q.
set on fire.

Our bridgehead defences were withdrawn last, and all ammunition
that we could not carry was burned or sunk in the Canal. Both the
1/Lancashire Fusiliers and 16/Middlesex Regiment coming out with
170 rounds S.A.A. and 2 bombs per man.

During the whole of this battle Capt. ROBERTS, Machine Gun
Company, controlled his guns with great skill and it was greatly
owing to his organisation that counter-attacks were repulsed.

I cannot speak too highly of the services of Lieut-Colonel
FORBES ROBERTSON. He was the hero of the defence.

Lieut-Colonel HART SYMNOT commanding the 1/Royal Guernsey
Light Infantry organised his part of the defences excellently with
Capt. WILSON, 16/Middlesex Regt., who I had attached to help him.

Certain troops holding the Southern part of LES RUES VERTES
fought with great gallantry the first day, but during the heavy
bombardment on the 2nd got demoralised and cut off so retired before
they should have done. These men were mostly 10% and drafts who
had only arrived late the night before the first attack, and had
not even joined their respective battalions but were still with Rear
H.Q. in LES RUES VERTES.

My signalling staff were continuously mending wires and it was
entirely owing to them that I kept touch with the situation, as so
many runners were knocked out.

My last men left about 7.30 a.m. and the withdrawal was
successfully carried out without a single casualty.

The behaviour of all ranks during this trying time was beyond
praise and extraordinary heavy casualties were inflicted on the enemy.
At least seven heavy attacks were beaten off.

(sd) G. R. H. CHEAPE,

Precis of Operations of 87th Infantry Brigade
November 30th to December 3rd, 1917.
-o-o-o-o-o-o-o-o-o-o-o-o-o-o-o-o-o-o-o-o-o-o-o-

On the morning of November 30th from about 7 a.m. onwards it became evident from the unusual amount of activity on our front that the enemy was preparing for action of some sort and the troops in the Front Line and Bridge head defences stood to Arms. The shelling until about 9 a.m. was confined to our front system and communication trenches and although steady was at no time heavy and as subsequent events showed was evidently intended to attract attention from the main front of attack.

At about 8.30 a.m. some patrols of the enemy attempted to debouch just North of the MASNIERES - CAMBRAI road but were promptly wiped out by our rifle and machine gun fire. At about this time the alarm was raised from our rear that the enemy could be seen swarming over WELSH RIDGE and advancing in extended order unopposed in the direction of LES RUES VERTES and MARCOING and the immediate danger of being cut off was realised. The front line was by this time more or less tranquil and the grave situation which demanded instant action had to be met by available personnel in the rear.

The first intimation that anything serious was wrong reached Brigade Headquarters at 10 a.m. and immediately an officer was dispatched to alarm and turn out the 1/Kings Own Scottish Borderers from MARCOING with orders for them to take up a position from the lock in L.24.c. to the MARCOING - LES RUES VERTES road to prevent the Germans from breaking through South of the Canal. Meantime the enemy was reported to be rapidly approaching the Sunken Road near the Brigade Headquarters and all available personnel of the H.Q. staff was promptly turned out, the alarm sounded on the bugle, and, after lining the Sunken Road a heavy fire was opened on the advancing German lines, and the H.Q. troops advancing in their turn drove back the enemy from the immediate vicinity, capturing eight prisoners.

While this was going on the 1/Kings Own Scottish Borderers were emerging from the village and observing the enemy advancing from the high ground to the South-East, their Commanding Officer moved the regiment so as to occupy the high ground on WELSH Ridge driving the enemy before them. Owing to the shell fire on the village considerable difficulty was experienced in getting the troops out of the village in any formation but immediately the outskirts of the village were cleared the counter-attack took definite shape and was pressed with vigour. The 1/Kings Own Scottish Borderers were barely clear of the village when the 88th Brigade which had also been alarmed emerged in attack formation and following close to the 1/Kings Own Scottish Borderers pressed home the counter thrust, successfully driving the Germans off the Western slopes of WELSH Ridge. The movement of the 1/Kings Own Scottish Borderers for the high ground brought them on to the right flank of the counter-attack and it was in this position that they finally came to a halt and formed a right defensive flank to the new line which had been taken up. Instructions were issued that the 1/Kings Own Scottish Borderers would come under the orders of the 88th Brigade and at 11.30 a.m. further orders were given to the 2/South Wales Borderers to send 2 Companies across the Canal to the vicinity of the East of MARCOING COPSE to fill the gap between the 86th and 88th Brigades. As the situation developed and LES RUES VERTES was reported clear of the enemy further orders were sent to the 2/South Wales Borderers to push forward their line as far as the Crucifix G.25.d.0.3. and connect up with the 86th Brigade in LES RUES VERTES.

By 9 p.m. the new dispositions were taken up and the process of consolidation was well advanced.

/ The

The night 30th/1st was quiet and the new line was consolidated. At dawn the situation was still quiet but during the morning a heavy enemy bombardment was commenced followed by an enemy attack on the LES RUES VERTES sector without result. At 2.30 p.m. another heavy bombardment was commenced on the same sector followed by an attack which continued until dusk when from observation it became clear that the flank of the LES RUES VERTES defences had been turned by the enemy, and at 4.30 p.m. orders were issued to withdraw the left flank of the 2/South Wales Borderers and fall back on the ditch in L.30.a.

Upon news being received that the turned flank had been re-established the orders to withdraw were immediately cancelled, The general situation necessitating a withdrawal altogether of the garrisons of MASNIERES and LES RUES VERTES. Orders were issued that the line of the 2/South Wales Borderers would be withdrawn as soon as the detachments of the 86th Brigade had retired and at the same time orders were issued to the 1/Royal Inniskilling Fusiliers to throw back their right flank from G.20.a.30.80. along the communication trench to L.24.a.55.40. and from there to the Canal Bank at G.19.c.15.60. The evacuation of MASNIERES was complete at 1 a.m. and by this time two Companies of the 1/Royal Inniskilling Fusiliers were in position on the new flank and one Company was in reserve in a trench at L.23.d.90.50.

Two Companies of the 1/2nd Monmouthshire Regiment were ordered to be attached to the 1/Royal Inniskilling Fusiliers and moved up to occupy trenches from the Canal Bank at G.19.c.15.60. to the road at G.19.c.0.80. The whole move was completed by 4 a.m. without molestation.

At 5 a.m. two more Companies of the 1/2nd Monmouthshire Regiment were attached to the 1/Royal Inniskilling Fusiliers to reinforce the Support Line and these also took up their position. Up till dawn the enemy were firing their flares and occasional bursts of Machine Gun fire from their original line, but at shortly after 7 a.m. the enemy were seen to be advancing in small groups from house to house in MASNIERES, and a fairly heavy fire from Machine Guns was being maintained on our position from the LES RUES VERTES copse.

Just about this time one of the evacuated strong points in Square G.20.a. was rushed by a party of about 30 of the enemy. This strong point on evacuation had been filled with wire hurdles, and the few of the enemy who succeeded in reaching it were unable to enter it and turning to retrace their steps were accounted for to a man by our rifle and Lewis Gun fire. No further attempt was made by the enemy on the new front that day, and the day and night passed more or less quietly save for steadily increasing trench mortar and machine gun fire.

The relief of the 1/Royal Inniskilling Fusiliers and the 1/Border Regiment by regiments of the 6th Division was carefully effected that night, leaving the 2/South Wales Borderers and 1/Kings Own Scottish Borderers still garrisoning their positions on the new flank.

At 9.30 a.m. on the morning of the 3rd the enemy commenced a heavy bombardment of our line concentrating on the portion of the new front along the drain in L.30.A. At 11 a.m. the enemy attacked this portion in great force and succeeded in over-running this line, which by now had ceased to exist, but did not succeed in penetrating as far back as our supports, who kept him under harassing fire, and thus prevented him from advancing further. The hostile bombardment recommenced, and heavy casualties were suffered in our Support Line, which on this sector constituted our sole defence, and was manned by every available rifle of the 2/South Wales Borderers including the personnel of the Battalion Headquarters. The fighting gradually died down and ceased almost entirely at dusk. That night the relief of the 2/South Wales Borderers now only 78 men strong was

/ effected

was effected by the 1/Hampshire Regiment.

The 1/Kings Own Scottish Borderers were relieved the next night along with the 88th Brigade and proceeded to the entraining area.

(Sd) C. H. TINDALL LUCAS,
Brigadier-General,
Commanding 87th Brigade.

In the Field.
December 9th, 1917.

Report on Operations near MARCOING on Nov. 30th and Dec. 1st
by 88th Brigade.
-o-o-o-o-o-o-o-o-o-o-o-o-o-o-o-o-o-o-o-o-o-o-o-o-o-o-o-o-o-o-

The Brigade had been at rest in MARCOING since night of 28/29th November.

On the afternoon of the 29th, during night of 29/30th, MARCOING was heavily shelled, the firing becoming intensified at daybreak on the 30th.

All wires between Brigade and battalions were cut.

Between 8 a.m. and 9 a.m. a communication was received from G.O.C. 87th Brigade to turn out 88th Brigade at once to protect the right flank of the 29th Division, the enemy having broken through. Orders were accordingly sent to all units to rendezvous E. of MARCOING. At 9.30 a.m. I received orders to report at 87th Brigade H.Q. the message arriving by runner. On arrival there, the G.S.O.I 29th Division gave me written orders as to the action - timed 10 a.m. After returning to 88th Brigade H.Q. no time was lost in collecting Brigade H.Q. and in starting for the rendezvous previously given out to battalions.

At 10.30 as H.Q. were emerging from the E. exit of MARCOING, they were met by heavy fire, and it was apparent that the enemy were considerably nearer than had been anticipated. Taking with him some dozen runners and signallers, the Brigade Major dashed forward to a mound about 100 yards off, where fire was opened upon the enemy advancing some 400 yards away. The remainder of H.Q. lined a hedge near by and opened a steady fire, being assisted by several cooks of units of the 87th Brigade.

Shortly after this, companies from different Battalions in the Brigade began to arrive on the scene, and were immediately sent forward. In my opinion it was essential to get men forward without waiting for Battalions to come up so as to seize the ridge commanding MARCOING before the enemy's main body could come up.

There was accordingly an intermingling of units: but the men went forward with magnificent dash, making good use of covering fire. The H.Q. of Battalions from the right flank were Kings Own Scottish Borderers, 2/Hampshire Regiment, 4/Worcestershire Regiment, 1/Essex Regiment and Newfoundland Regiment: the right battalion going forward with its right on Sunken Road L.28.D, L.34.B. & D, and the left battalion towards LES RUES VERTES.

There was a heavy fire from M.G. and rifles, but as soon as the lines got going, the enemy began to retire. About 25 Germans belonging to the 99th Regiment were killed in square L.29 - amongst the number being 3 officers. In the Sunken Road referred to above, several Germans were killed and 1 officer and 50 men taken prisoner.

At 1 p.m. the right had worked up near the line held by 20th Divn. and the left was making good progress towards LES RUES VERTES, while the centre was held up by fire from M.G. in L.35.B.

The enemy appeared to be holding the ridge there in strength and further progress was not possible without very heavy casualties.

Urgent calls for ammunition were received from the front, and all men left in Brigade H.Q. took it up in bandoliers.

So far during the action communication between Brigade and battalions was practically nil, the Brigade H.Q. Staff having become disorganised during the early stages, but Brigade H.Q. were established with the H.Q. of the Essex Regiment, and the Brigade Major, who was mounted, maintained communication with the left battalion and made a reconnaissance of LES RUES VERTES. I saw Commanding Officers of other battalions in the Sunken Road L.28.D.

At about 3 p.m. the Brigade Major who was returning to Rear Brigade H.Q. was wounded. Shortly after this, I reported at 87th Brigade H.Q. and explained the situation to Brig-Gen. LUCAS.

At 4.30 p.m. the 88th Brigade H.Q. were established in L.28.d.8.8., and orders were sent to units to reorganise and dig in: one Company in each Battalion to be in support, and the Hampshire Regiment to be Brigade Reserve at L.34.B.

The line selected was the best available; but on the left it was commanded by the enemy well entrenched further up the slope.

/ There

There was a shortage of tools, but by daylight there was cover for every man.

The night was quiet, both sides sending out patrols. A German patrol was dispersed by the Kings Own Scottish Borderers, who captured two prisoners. There was a shortage of water and rations on the night of the 30th.

150,000 rounds of S.A.A. were brought up during the night, and units were able to have 200 rounds a man with a good reserve.

On December 1st there was little activity. The Worcestershire Regiment advanced their line 100 yards taking two prisoners and finding 4 M.Gs., but efforts to move forward on the part of other units were met by a heavy Machine Gun fire. Small parties of the enemy had been seen moving towards LA VACQUERIE valley from the E. and our artillery searched the valley at intervals. There was constant activity on the part of M.G. and snipers.

In the evening one Company of the 2/Hampshire Regiment was sent to reinforce the 2/South Wales Borderers on our left.

On the 30th after we had driven back their leading troops, the enemy advanced against our right - in excellent order - in waves with a good interval between men. They were however enfiladed by us from the lower ground and the attack was stopped.

At about 2.30 p.m. on the 30th four horse drawn vehicles were seen near LES RUES VERTES going up LA VACQUERIE valley. It was not possible to see clearly what they were, but that evening light guns were fired at us at close range.

         (Sd) H. NELSON,
         Brigadier-General,
Dec. 2nd, 1917.   Commanding 88th Inf. Bde.

Remarks by Brigadier.

The action was a confused one owing to the suddeness of the enemy attack; and was remarkable for the extreme gallantry of all ranks who moved forward in the face of a galling fire, unsupported by artillery. The enemy fought well, standing their ground well and being killed at close quarters. They appeared to be very well equipped, their advanced troops being plentifully supplied with automatic rifles and Machine Guns.

In the pack of one officer was found a tin of Savory and Moore's meat lozenges, and a tin of cocoa tablets also from an English firm.

There was naturally much confusion amongst the artillery units near the scene of action, and I think it right to report that for several hours after the Brigade had retaken ground, there were four eighteen pounder guns, layed to cover MASNIERES, which were without any personnel whatever.

A private in the Kings Own Scottish Borderers was found firing one gun.

A 60 lb. gun is still in the road, 200 yards from these H.Q. without personnel and the dugout now in occupation of this Brigade was apparently used as H.Q. for Heavy Artillery, but no one has been here to claim the instruments and kit left behind.

There was the greatest difficulty in getting messages through between Brigade and battalions and between battalions and companies. owing to the heavy shelling of MARCOING, and battalions on their way through the village had considerable casualties.

On the afternoon of the 30th, German aeroplanes flew at a very low altitude over our troops and were not fired upon by our A.A. guns stationed in MARCOING.

Casualties 15 officers 457 other ranks killed, wounded or missing.

         (Sd) H. NELSON,
         Brigadier-General,
Dec. 2nd, 1917.   Commanding 88th Inf. Bde.

SUMMARY STATEMENT OF CASUALTIES INCURRED BY 29th DIVISION IN ACTIVE OPERATIONS S.W. OF CAMBRAI 20-11-17 TO 3-12-17 INCLUSIVE.

	Killed.		Wounded.		Missing		Total		Sick Admitted.		Sick Evacuated.	
	O.	O.R.	O.	O.R.	O.	O.R.	O.	O.R.	O.	O.R.	O.	O.R.
86th Brigade.	12	87	33	665	9	479	54	1231	5	183	5	151
87th Brigade.	5	141	32	715	8	355	45	1211	5	197	5	147
88th Brigade.	12	142	26	917	3	358	41	1417	4	152	4	99
1/2nd Monmouths.	2	16	7	98	1	58	10	172	1	12	-	10
Divisional Troops.	1	10	22	204	9	149	32	363	3	85	4	65
	32	396	120	2599	30	1399	182	4394	18	629	18	472

17th December 1917.

J.P. Sked Taplan
for Brig. General,
Commanding 29th Division.

Complete Copy
6 to kept

Army

HEADQUARTERS.
29th DIVISION
No. GS 7056
Date...........

Report on Operations by 29th Division
on 20th November, 1917.
-o-o-o-o-o-o-o-o-o-o-o-o-o-o-o-

1. **Order of Battle.**

   Divisional Commander.   Major-General Sir BEAUVOIR de LISLE,
                                 K.C.B., D.S.O.

   86th Inf. Bde. Commander.   Brig-Gen. G.R.H. CHEAPE, M.C.
   2/Royal Fusiliers.   Major J.S. HORNING.
   1/Lanc. Fusiliers.   Major T. SLINGSBY, M.C.
   16/Middlesex Regt.   Lt-Col. J. FORBES-ROBERTSON,
                                 D.S.O. M.C. (Border Regt.)
   1/R. Guernsey L.I.   Lt-Col. W.J. de la C.......

   87th Inf. Bde. Commander.   Brig-Gen. C.H.T. LUCAS, D.S.O.
   2/S. Wales Borderers.   Lt-Col. O.T. RAIKES, D.S.O.
   1/K.O.S.B.   Lt-Col. C.A.C.G. MURRAY.
   1/R. Inniskilling Fus.   Lt-Col. J. SHERWOOD-KELLY, C.M.G., D.S.O.
                                 (Norfolk Regt.)
   1/Border Regt.   Lt-Col. A.J. ELLIS, D.S.O.

   88th Inf. Bde. Commander.   Brig-Gen. H.NELSON, D.S.O.
   4/Worcester Regt.   Lt-Col. C.S. LINTON, D.S.O., M.C.
   2/Hampshire Regt.   Capt. K.A. JOHNSTON.
   1/Essex Regt.   Lt-Col. Sir G.E.R. STIRLING, Bart. D.S.O.
   Newfoundland Regt.   Lt-Col. A.L. HADOW, C.M.G.

2. **Disposition of Troops at Zero.**

   86th Inf. Bde.   In the area Q.23, Q.29.a. and b.

   87th Inf. Bde.   In the area Q.24, Q.30.a. and c.

   88th Inf. Bde.   In the area Q.29.c. and d., Q.35.a. and b.

   Field Coys. R.E. In the area Q.34.c. and d., Q.35.c. and d.

   The Assembly areas are shown on the attached Map.

3. **Objectives.**

   The task allotted to the Division was, to pass through the 20th and 6th Divisions as soon as these had captured the BROWN LINE and the 12th Division had captured the BONAVIS Plateau, force the crossings over the Canal at MASNIERES and MARCOING and, breaking through the enemy's last line of resistance the MASNIERES - BEAUREVOIR line, to enable the Cavalry to pass through the gap thus formed.

4. **Plan.**

   To carry out this task successfully, it was essential that both MASNIERES and MARCOING should not only be captured, but that strong bridgeheads should be established on the Eastern side of the Canal. Both these villages are of considerable size and are some two miles apart, and it was considered that in each case one Infantry Brigade would be required.

- 2 -

Moreover NINE WOOD at the Eastern edge of FLESQUIERES Ridge overlooks MARCOING from the North at a range of 1000 yards and is 100 feet above it. The capture of MARCOING was therefore dependent on the capture of this position, thus necessitating the use of my third Brigade.

No reserve of Infantry was kept in hand as I considered that being a pursuing force, extraordinary risks might be taken and the holding back of any portion of the fighting force might seriously hamper the success of the operation.

The 88th Brigade was therefore directed on MASNIERES, the 87th Brigade on MARCOING, and the 86th Brigade on NINE WOOD.

5. Concentration.

The Division entrained at BOISLEUX AU MONT on the night of 17th/18th November, resting for the day of the 18th at MOISLAINS.

On the following night it marched to FINS, EQUANCOURT and started at 2 a.m. on the morning of the 20th November for the Assembly position north of GOUZEAUCOURT a distance of 5 miles.

This assembly march was accomplished by 5.30 a.m. without any trouble. Routes had been previously reconnoitred and all road and track junctions piquetted to guard against loss of direction.

It will be noticed that the 3 nights prior to the attack the troops had been on the move.

6. The Approach March.

By the scheme the Division was not to advance until the BONAVIS Plateau and the BROWN LINE (HINDENBURG Support Line) had been gained by the 12th, 20th and 6th Divisions but as time was an important factor in a complete success, the leading Battalions of Brigades were moved at Zero into our front line which had been vacated by the above Divisions.

Further, each Brigade of this Division pushed out Advanced Guards up to the BLUE LINE as soon as this object

- 3 -

had been gained, with patrols following the troops as they attacked the BROWN LINE.

It was intended that Contact Planes should drop situation reports at this H.Q. to enable me to start this Division at the earliest possible moment. The fog however made the work of contact planes impossible, and the news of the capture of the BLUE LINE of which the scheduled time was 8 A.M. did not reach this H.Q. until 9.15 A.M., 1¼ hours later.

To have waited for news of the complete capture of the BROWN LINE would have so delayed the start of the 29th Division that at 10 A.M. on hearing that the troops of the 6th and 20th Divisions were well on their way to the BROWN LINE, I asked permission to take the risk and move my Brigades to their objective. At 10.15 A.M. the order was issued and was conveyed to all Units of each Brigade by Bugle Call.

The Division therefore moved off simultaneously with the 88th Brigade on the Right directed on MASNIERES, the 87th Brigade on MARCOING, from a point due South of it, and the 86th Brigade on NINE WOOD at the Eastern end of the FLESQUIERES Ridge.

Brigades adopted a Diamond formation, with one Battalion at each point, the long axis being 1800 yards, and the short axis, parallel to the direction, 1200 yards. Each Battalion placed their four Companies in a similar formation. This formation was adopted with a view to saving time, the flanking units being in position to envelope should opposition be met by the leading Battalion acting as Advanced Guard to each Brigade. Four tanks were allotted to each Brigade and moved in advance of the Infantry Advanced Guards.

7. **Narrative of the Action of the 86th (Right) Brigade.**

On approaching the BROWN LINE in K.5. and L.35. hostile fire was opened from rifles and Machine Guns and 3 of the Battalions were forced to attack it. This caused a delay

/ of

of ¾ hour and accounted for over 150 prisoners. On the left
the Newfoundland Battalion had some difficulty and sustained
many casualties, but with their accustomed dash they broke
down all opposition, using covering fire from rifles, Machine
Guns and a Stokes Gun. This delay however was unfortunate
as it gave time for the enemy to partially organise the
defences of LES RUES VERTES. The right Battalion
(4/Worcestershire Regt.) however, pushed on to its objective,
the lock in G.27.c, and got one Company across to form a
Bridgehead, sending another along the eastern Canal Bank
to outflank the defence. This manoeuvre was entirely
successful.

A tank now endeavoured to cross the Main Iron Bridge
at MASNIERES but the bridge, previously partially destroyed,
gave way. No assistance from tanks could then be expected
on the east side of the Canal.

Finding the leading Battalion held up at the Canal Bridge
at MASNIERES, the 2/Hampshires, skilfully led by Acting
Lieut-Colonel JOHNSTON, moved down to the Lock 1000 yards to the
S.E. crossed there and attacked the RED line with 2 Companies
and captured these prepared trenches as far North as G.21.c.8.8.
The other half Battalion was sent to attack MASNIERES from the
east and gained the outskirts of the town.

The death of Lieut-Colonel LINTON, D.S.O., M.C.,
4/Worcesters, left this Battalion without a leader and the
Companies somewhat disorganised, but Lieut-Colonel JOHNSTON
quickly took over the situation, organised the defences to the
North and East as far as MONT PLAISIR FARM, and continued to
press on his attack of MASNIERES until dawn of the 21st.

About 4 p.m. on the 20th a squadron of Canadian Dragoons
crossed the Canal at Lock in G.27.c. and rode up over the
RUMILLY Ridge.

On the left the N.F.L.D. crossed at the Lock in L.24.d.
and attacked to the East gaining the gun pits in L.19 & 20,

/ but

but were unable to cross the open ground between this cover and the town.

Heavy fighting was in progress during the night but at dawn we held the town as far North as L.20.d.7.9. with the exception of a pocket in the centre. Here a number of the enemy were sheltered in the Catacombs, to which there are 7 openings. These were not captured until midday of the 21st.

8. Narrative of the Action of the 87th (Centre) Brigade.

The Centre Brigade marched straight on MARCOING and MARCOING Copse. In the former place the enemy hurriedly evacuated the town. The Commander General VON KEPPEL had not even time to remove his personal belongings. At MARCOING Copse, some resistance was experienced and many enemy killed in the Wood. The leading Battalion of this Brigade, 1/Kings Own Scottish Borderers marched through the town and crossed by the Railway Bridge. Only 1 tank succeeded in crossing, the others for various causes being unable to get there. The right flank Battalion, 2/South Wales Borderers, crossed at the Lock L.24. These two Battalions, as ordered, immediately prepared Bridgeheads covering the crossings, where the other two Battalions, 1/Royal Inniskilling Fusiliers on right, and 1/Border Regiment on left, passed over and advanced again at the RED LINE.

After a long advance of about a mile the attack was brought to a standstill some 300 yards behind our present line L.14.c.3.0. to the Lock at L.17.d.8.7. The RED LINE was seen to have been reinforced just before the attack of our troops, and the Machine Gun fire from it made any further advance impossible without the aid of Artillery or tanks. On the left one Company of the 1/Border Regiment gained the RED LINE in 13.a. and took 19 prisoners there, but owing to the right of the line being held up, this Company was withdrawn, retiring firing by alternate platoons. The above line was consolidated the same night.

/ The

The following day with the assistance of 9 Tanks, the 87th Brigade made another attempt to take the whole of the RED LINE, but without success. The tanks suffered from armour piercing bullets, 50 per cent of the personnel becoming casualties, and the Infantry came under heavy Machine Gun fire both from the front and from PILOT FARM where a number of guns firing indirect prevented the troops gaining the top of the ridge in L.20.a. & b.

9. **Narrative of the 86th (Left) Brigade.**

The 86th Brigade advanced without opposition to the Quarry S.E. of BIER WOOD, but here the leading Regiment (16/Middlesex Regiment) was checked. The flank Regiments however, 2/Royal Fusiliers on the right and 1/Royal Guernsey L.I. on the left, continued to push on enveloping the Wood from the S.E. and N.W. and so gaining all objectives by 1 p.m.

A Company was then sent to occupy NOYELLE and form a bridgehead on the eastern bank of the Canal. Between the R. ESCAUT and the Canal opposition was met and the troops were unable to accomplish the crossing.

10. **Counter-attacks.**

On November 21st three counter-attacks were launched against the new line of defence.

(a) At 11 a.m. a heavy attack from the N.E. was launched against the 88th Brigade by 2 Battalions which advanced in dense waves. This was caught by Artillery and Machine Gun fire and could not approach closer than 500 yards.

(b) The second attack at 1 p.m. moved S.W. against the 87th Brigade but came under heavy fire as it crossed the Support line in G.14 and did not get beyond the German front line.

(c) The third attack advanced on NOYELLE from the Wood north of the village and drove back our outposts to the southern end of the village. Reinforcements were sent down from BIER WOOD until we had 3 Companies in the village opposed to 6 Companies of the enemy. Our troops gradually drove the enemy

/ back

back, and at dusk had cleared the village except for 28 Germans who later surrendered. A relieving Battalion of the 6th Division took over the village the same night without a shot being fired. The troops of the 66th Brigade fired 200 rounds per man and expended all bombs and Stokes bombs. In the end they were fighting entirely with German weapons and ammunition.

11. **General Remarks.**

(1) This being the first occasion that this Division has been engaged in open warfare, it was necessary to adapt the training to the probable requirements. Fortunately the area, South of ARRAS, allotted by the VI Corps for this purpose was ideal in every way. By means of Brigade and Divisional Schemes Battalions were enabled to gain very valuable instruction. The difficulty in training Company and Platoon leaders to act correctly according to the situation and ground is far greater than training them to lead in a trench to trench attack, and the time available was inadequate. Much however was done by lectures and Brigade Exercises prepared by my General Staff.

(2) The diamond formation was found most suitable, saving time, and being less liable to casualties under shell fire.

(3) One Stokes Gun with 64 rounds was attached to each Battalion and this was found invaluable.

(4) One section Machine Guns was attached to the leading Battalion of each Brigade and a flank detachment of 2 Machine Guns and ½ Company was maintained on the flank of each Brigade, a precaution which has always proved useful.

(5) The rapidity of the advance of the 3 Brigades enabled them to gain the crossings before resistance could be organised and had it been possible to get tanks across in time before German reinforcements arrived from CAMBRAI, the success would have been even more complete. The breaking of the MASNIERES Bridge was fatal to the co-operation of the tanks.

/ (6)

- 8 -

(6) A remarkable feature of these operations was the physical endurance of the troops. From 8 a.m. on the 20th November, the Division marched 10 miles to the Canal, carrying over 60 lbs. of equipment. They fought till dark on the 21st, and have since consolidated a position 5000 yards long and 1500 yards deep.

After 10 days in the line, they are certainly worn out but still capable of defence.

This remarkable performance is due to the careful attention of Regimental Officers to the comfort of the troops and to the excellent discipline in all Brigades.

I append a statement of casualties incurred by the Units engaged in this attack, prisoners and war material captured.

6 December 1917.

Major-General,
Commanding 29th Division.

29th DIVISION - CAPTURED MATERIAL.

Field Guns and Howitzers.

    105 mm.   4
    77 mm.   16

Trench Mortars.   3

Machine Guns.   42

Spare barrels.   50

Machine Gun Limbers.   6

Field Kitchens.   3

Fuel, wood.   350 tons.

Coal   300 tons.

In addition 15 head of cattle were released from MASNIERES, of which 2 were killed by shell fire during evacuation.

TOTAL NUMBER OF PRISONERS CAPTURED.

Officers.   9
Other Ranks   746

TOTAL.   755

29th Division No. 3 11/66.

General Staff.

I forward herewith statement shewing:-

    Material Captured
    Number of Casualties incurred, and
    Prisoners captured and
    Civilians evacuated.

during recent operations.

                                             Lieut. Colonel,
30.11.17.   A.A. & Q.M.G., 29th Division.

CIVILIANS EVACUATED DURING RECENT OPERATIONS.

                MANDOING   -   Nil.

                MESNIERES   -   414

                NOYELLE   -   102

CIVILIANS EVACUATED DURING RECENT OPERATIONS.

          MARCOING   -   311.

          MASNIERES   -   414

          NOYELLE   -   102

29th DIVISION - CAPTURED MATERIAL.

Field Guns and Howitzers.

    105 mm.   4
    77 mm.   16

Trench Mortars.   3

Machine Guns.   42

Spare barrels.   50

Machine Gun Limbers.   6

Field Kitchens.   3

Fuel, wood.   360 tons.

Coal   300 tons.

In addition 15 head of cattle were released from MASNIERES, of which 2 were killed by shell fire during evacuation.

TOTAL NUMBER OF PRISONERS CAPTURED.

    Officers.   9
    Other Ranks   746

    TOTAL.   755

29th DIVISION - CAPTURED MATERIAL.

Field Guns and Howitzers.

    105 mm.   4
    77 mm.   16

Trench Mortars.   3

Machine Guns.   42

Spare barrels.   50

Machine Gun Limbers.   6

Field Kitchens.   3

Fuel, wood.   360 tons.

Coal   300 tons.

In addition 15 head of cattle were released from MASNIERES, of which 2 were killed by shell fire during evacuation.

TOTAL NUMBER OF PRISONERS CAPTURED.

    Officers.   9
    Other Ranks   746
                   ———
    TOTAL.   755

ACTION S.W. OF CAMBRAI.

29th. DIVISION.

SUMMARY

STATEMENT OF CASUALTIES. INCURRED 20.11.17 to 23.11.17 INCLUSIVE.

	Killed		Wounded		Missing	
	O.	OR.	O.	OR.	O.	OR.
86th. Infantry Brigade.						
2/Royal Fusiliers.	3	12	3	36	-	19
1/Lancashire Fusiliers.	2	5	2	37	-	1
16/Middlesex Regt.	2	7	2	31	-	12
1/R.Guernsey Light Inf.	1	3	2	45	-	8
86/Machine Gun Co.	-	4	-	4	-	2
86/Trench Mortar Battery.	-	-	2	-	-	-
87th. Infantry Brigade.						
2/S. Wales Borderers.	-	20	10z	127	3	90c
1/King's Own Scott.Bords.	-	12	3	80	-	15
1/R.Inniskilling Fuslrs.	-	20	6	115	-	18
1/Border Regt.	-	33	2	103	-	17
87/Machine Gun Company.	-	-	-	8	-	-
87/Trench Mortar Battery.	-	-	-	-	-	-
88th. Infantry Brigade.						
4/Worcester Regt.	2	9	2	37	-	14
2/Hampshire Regiment.	-	13	4x	67	1	2
1/Essex Regiment.	3	21	2	114	2n	60
1/Newfoundland Regt.	2	36	7	164	-	48
88/Machine Gun Company.	-	3	-	4	-	3
88/Trench Mortar Battery.	-	-	-	4	-	-
227/Machine Gun Company.	-	-	-	-	-	-
1/2nd.Monmouth Regiment.	-	-	-	3	-	-
226 Employment Co.	-	-	-	1	-	-
Divisional Headquarters.						
Headquarters, R.A.						
15/Brigade R.H.A.	-	-	1	8	-	-
17/Brigade R.F.A.	-	1	-	-	-	-
29/Divl.Ammn.Col.						
Headquarters, R.E.						
510(London)Field Co.R.E.	-	-	1	2	-	-
455(W.Riding) Fld.Co.R.E.	-	-	-	2	-	-
497(Kent) Field Co. R.E.						
87/Field Ambulance.	-	-	-	4	-	-
88/Field Ambulance.						
89/Field Ambulance.	-	-	-	2	-	-
18/Mobile Veterinary Sec.						
29/Divl.Signal Co.R.E.	-	-	-	3	-	-
29/Divl.Train.						
29/Divl.Supply Column.						
R.A.M.C. attached 1st Border Regt.	-	-	1	-	-	-
Attached Artillery	-	-	-	1	-	-
TOTAL.	15	199	50	1002	6	309

x includes 1 at duty.
n includes 1 since rejoined.
z includes 2 since died of wounds.
c includes 30 since rejoined.

Total. 71 officers 1510 O.R.

Major-General,
Commanding, 29th. Division.

P.T.O.

GOUZEAUCOURT.

510th. (London) Field Coy. R.E.,

1. This Coy. was withdrawn from the MASNIERES Sector, 29th. November to work with 1 Coy. 1/2nd. Monmouthshire Pioneers on hutting in GOUZEAUCOURT.

At 8-45 a.m. 30th. Nov. on vacating QUENTIN MILL Quarry, G.O.C. directed me to turn out the Pioneers. I ran to find them, and met Lt. ROSEBAUM, who said that as they were working on hutting they were unarmed, and now they were unable to get hold of their rifles. They were slowly marched towards FINS and armed en route with abandoned rifles.

I found however the London Field Coy. R.E. forming up with their attached infantry in W.6.d. (IRVINE LANE), and they were directed to send off their transport, hold the ridge at that point, and rally all stragglers who were coming by in numbers, (chiefly riflemen).

On their right flank some infantry had been rallied under a Brigade Staff Officer of the 12th. Division.

Their lift flank was not in touch with any formed Troops.

2. The Staff Officer told me that he was short of ammunition (the R.E. also had only 50 rounds per man), and so I rode across the GOUZEAUCOURT-HEUDICOURT Road to get some, and to rally the fugitives.

On my way I passed through some battery lines, and finding that the men had arms and some ammunition, turned them out and directed them to form up on a ridge in the rear of the London R.E.

3. Later a Brigadier took command of the London R.E., and the Infantry on their right, and under his orders the line retreated slowly across the HEUDICOURT-GOUZEAUCOURT Road to a wired trench West of the Road facing East.

Int the trench some ammunition was found and distributed and connection made with the R.A. (mentioned above) on the left.

4. On arrival on the GOUZEAUCOURT-FINS Road, I met the 470th. Field Coy. marching up, which was ordered on to GOUZEAUCOURT by G.O.C.

On arriving there I found some men of the D.L.I., under a Major of that Regt. just in front of the village and at his request 1 section R.E. was sent forward as a reinforcement, and the remaining 3 sections directed to hold the fringe of the village facing East.

5. On leaving GOUZEAUCOURT I met a small party of infantrymen marching up and I gave the Oi/c. a sketch of the position and state of affairs.

They went forward and reinforced the London R.E.

A little later three or four men were sent back for ammunition, which was very short. I found a few boxes on the road-side which were opened, and the whole sent forward with some of the men on a small car, which I stopped on the road.

I rode to the 6th. Division "Q" Headquarters (W.3.c.) informed "Q" of the state of affairs, and begged him to use one of his cars there to fetch ammunition and to send it up. This he did.

I posted here an Officer of the A.V.C. and a traffic policeman to rally stragglers.

At this point also a mixed platoon of some 30 armed men were assembled under Lt. BRUNNER, R.A., I ordered a Lieut: of the Heavy Artillery (who was present and not in action) to assist Lt. BRUNNER. This party was led forward and came into action.

6. Runners now arrived with a message from Capt. COMINS R.E. London Field Coy R.E., asking for ammunition water and food. Ammunition had been sent up to GOUZEAUCOURT, so I sent one runner back with a message, giving information, and saying I would send up water and food.

I happened to find close by a water-cart of some Canadian non-combatant unit which was just moving off. This I took with its driver, and putting on boxes of food, sent it off with a guide. It reached the men in due course.

Through an Officer of the D.A.C., whom I met, I arranged for more ammunition to be sent up and provided a guide for it.

7. By now Cavalry were arriving. They came into action on either flank of the London R.E., several Tanks were advancing with them.

8. The counter-attack was begun by the Guards attacking GOUZEAUCOURT on the left. Then the whole line of details advanced by short rushes, reforming at the various stages of the advance.

Near IRVINE LANE the left was held up for a short time, as connection was imperfect; but Tanks protecting the left flank, and the dismounted Cavalry swinging round on the right, enabled the line to advance, and at dark IRVINE LANE and the Bank above it were held.

9. The London Field Coy. was now dispersed over a broad front, so at 7-30 p.m. Capt. COMINS began to collect and to reorganise it, which he successfully accomplished during the night.

It was concentrated and marched to SOREL on the morning of the 1st. December 1917.

On 2nd. December it joined 88th. Bde. in the line, on Welsh Ridge, taking part in the defeat of the heavy German attack on that Brigade on the 3rd. December, and was withdrawn that evening with the 88th. Bde. on relief.

II   MARCOING.

455th. (West Riding) Field Coy. R.E.,

1. This Coy. was under the orders of the G.O.C. 87th. Brigade from 30th. November 1917 until the Brigade was relieved on evening of the 2nd. December, and their work forms part of that of the 87th. Bde.

2. On afternoon of the 2nd. December 1917, I arranged personally with G.S.O. 1, 6th. Division, for the relief of this Field Coy., informing him of details, especially the arrangements for the destruction of the MARCOING Bridges; and added that my men would remain until relieved.

3. The demolition parties were never relieved by the 6th. Division, and remained in MARCOING under Major B.T. WILSON, and Lt. DISTURNAL R.E., until the very last, successfully destroying their five bridges, after the infantry of the 6th. Division had been withdrawn on the night 3/4th. December 1917.

III   MASNIERES.

497th. (Kent) Field Coy. R.E.,

1. On the night of the 29/30th. November 1917, this Coy. was working as usual, and had returned to its dug-outs before dawn, situated in the extreme S.W. edge of RUES VERTES.

2. Their dug-out was a long brick tunnel with main openings on the MARCOING-MASNIERES Road, where two sentries were always posted.

The rear entrance opened by a ramped incline into the interior of the Courtyard of the Brasserie, which contained the Field Ambulance, all the Officers of the Coy. lived at this end of the tunnel, and there was no partition in the tunnel anywhere, except blankets.

3. The first intimation received that anything was wrong, was Germans rushing in and bombing the tunnel from its back entrance, i.e. from the S.E., the Officers being trapped with their men at once.

4. Five Officers and 87 men are missing, but no certain information exists as to the fate of individuals; as the tunnel never came into our possession again.

8th. December 1917.

Lt-Col. R.E.,
C.R.E., 29th. Division.

GOUZEAUCOURT.
-o-o-o-o-o-o-

510th (London) Field Coy. R.E.

1. This Coy. was withdrawn from the MASNIERES Sector, 29th November to work with 1 Coy. 1/2nd Monmouthshire Pioneers on hutting in GOUZEAUCOURT.

    At 8-45 a.m. 30th Nov. on vacating QUENTIN MILL Quarry, G.Q.C. directed me to turn out the Pioneers. I ran to find them, and met Lt. ROSEBAUM, who said that as they were working on Hutting they were unarmed, and now they were unable to get hold of their rifles. They were slowly marched towards FINS and armed en route with abandoned rifles.

    I found however the London Field Coy. R.E. forming up with their attached infantry in W.6.d. (IRVINE LANE), and they were directed to send off their transport, hold the ridge at that point, and rally all stragglers who were coming by in numbers, (chiefly riflemen).

    On their right flank some infantry had been rallied under a Brigade Staff Officer of the 12th Division.

    Their left flank was not in touch with any formed Troops.

2. The Staff Officer told me that he was short of ammunition (the R.E. also had only 50 rounds per man), and so I rode across the GOUZEAUCOURT - HEUDICOURT Road to get some, and to rally the fugitives.

    On my way I passed through some battery lines, and finding that the men had arms and some ammunition, turned them out and directed them to form up on a ridge in the rear of the London R.E.

3. Later a Brigadier took command of the London R.E., and the infantry on their right, and under his orders the line retreated slowly across the HEUDICOURT - GOUZEAUCOURT Road to a wired trench West of the Road facing East.

    In the trench some ammunition was found and distributed and connection made with the R.A. (mentioned above) on the left.

4. On arrival on the GOUZEAUCOURT - FINS Road, I met the 470th Field Coy. marching up, which was ordered on to GOUZEAUCOURT by G.O.C.

    On arriving there I found some men of the D.L.I., under a Major of that Regt. just in front of the village and at his request 1 section R.E. was sent forward as a reinforcement, and the remaining 3 sections directed to hold the fringe of the village facing East.

5. On leaving GOUZEAUCOURT I met a small party of infantry marching up and I gave the O. i/c a sketch of the position and state of affairs.

    They went forward and reinforced the London R.E.

    A little later 3 or 4 men were sent back for ammunition, which was very short. I found a few boxes on the road-side which were opened, and the whole sent forward with some of the men on a small car, which I stopped on the road.

    I rode to 6th Division "Q" Headquarters (W.3.c.) informed "Q" of the state of affairs, and begged him to use one of his cars there to fetch ammunition and to send it up - This he did.

    I posted here an Officer of the A.V.C. and a traffic policeman to rally stragglers.

    At this point also a mixed platoon of some 30 armed men was assembled under Lt. BRUNNER R.A. I ordered a Lieut. of the Heavy Artillery (who was present and not in action) to assist Lt. BRUNNER. This party was led forward and came into action.

6. Runners now arrived with a message from Capt. COMINS R.E. London Field Coy. R.E., asking for ammunition, water and food. Ammunition had been sent up to GOUZEAUCOURT, so I sent one runner back with a message, giving information, and saying I would send up water and food.

    I happened to find close by a water-cart of some Canadian non-combatant unit which was just moving off. This I took with its driver, and putting on boxes of food, sent it off with a guide. It reached the men in due course.

    Through an Officer of the D.A.C., whom I met, I arranged for more ammunition to be sent up and provided a guide for it.

7. By now Cavalry were arriving. They came into action on either flank

- 2 -

of the London R.E., several Tanks were advancing with them.

8. The counter-attack was begun by the Guards attacking GOUZEAUCOURT ON THE left. The whole line of details then advanced by short rushes, reforming at the various stages of the advance.

Near IRVINE LANE the left was held up for a short time, as connection was imperfect; but Tanks protecting the left flank, and the dismounted Cavalry swinging round on the right, enabled the line to advance, and at dark IRVINE LANE and the bank above it were held.

9. The London Field Coy. was now dispersed over a broad front, so at 7-30 p.m., Capt. COMINS began to collect and to reorganise it, which he successfully accomplished during the night.

It was concentrated and marched to SOREL on the morning of the 1st December, 1917.

II.   MARCOING.

465th (West Riding) Field Coy. R.E.

1. This Coy. was under the orders of G.O.C. 87th Bde. from 30th November 1917 until the Brigade was relieved on evening of the 2nd December, and their work forms part of that of the 87th Bde.

2. On afternoon of the 2nd December 1917, I arranged personally with G.S.O. 1, 6th Division, for the relief of this Field Coy., informing him of details, especially the arrangements for the destruction of the MARCOING Bridges; and added that my men would remain until relieved.

3. The demolition parties were never relieved by the 6th Division and remained in MARCOING under Major B.T. WILSON, and Lt. DISTURNAL R.E., until the very last, successfully destroying their five bridges, after the infantry of the 6th Division had been withdrawn on the night 3/4th December, 1917.

III.   MASNIERES.

497th (Kent) Field Coy. R.E.

1. On the night of 29/30th November, 1917, this Coy. was working as usual, and had returned to its dug-outs before dawn, situated in the extreme S.W. edge of LES RUES VERTES.

2. Their dug-out was a long brick tunnel with main openings on the MARCOING - MASNIERES Road, where two Sentries were always posted.

The rear entrance opened by a ramped incline into the interior of the Courtyard of the Brasserie, which contained the Field Ambulance; all the Officers of the Coy. lived at this end of the tunnel, and there was no partition in the tunnel anywhere (except blankets).

3. The first intimation received that anything was wrong, was Germans rushing in and bombing the tunnel from its back entrance, i.e. from the S.E., the Officers being trapped with their men at once.

4. Five Officers and 87 men are missing, but no certain information exists as to the fate of individuals; as the tunnel never came into our possession again.

                                              (Sd) R. BIDDULPH,
                                                     Lt-Col. R.E.,

8th December, 1917.   C.R.E., 29th Division.

Narrative of the Events at MARCOING on December 3rd. 1917.

The 87th Brigade handed over on the night of the 2/3rd December, in the big dug-out at L.22.d.4.3. to the 16th Infantry Brigade, 6th Div.
I saw General WALKER with General LUCA, and took part in a slight discussion on the merits of the "Peninsula" position.

The morning of December 3rd opened quite quietly - Lt. DISTURNAL, R.E., and 50 O.R. (West Riding Fd.Coy. R.E.) were with me in the concrete artillery dug-outs, 100 yards N.E. of Brigade Headqrs., which were now empty, as the 16th Bde. had moved to L. 27.B.1.8. about 1000 yards S.W.

At 10-0. o'clock, the shelling of the town increased, and we went out to look at it.

At 11 o'clock it became severe, and direct hits were received on our rather fragile shelters.

At 12-30 p.m., we took advantage of a lull in the shelling of 87th Brigade Hdqrs., and moved across with them.

At 1-30 p.m. while we were at lunch, a wounded man reported that the Germans were in the town - we went out, and saw that the enemy barrage was on the W. edge of the MARCOING COPSE.

2-30 p.m. At General NELSON'S request, I walked across to the 16th Infantry Brigade to urge upon General WALKER, the very urgent need of reinforcing the "Peninsula", especially the S.E. end. This I did.

He said that 2 Coys had been sent and a Company to advance in the direction of MARCOING COPSE.

At 4-0 p.m. I returned to Brigade H.Q., the barrage was still being put down W. of MARCOING, but looked inconclusive - I ordered Lt. DISTURNAL to look at his charges once more, and withdrew the remaining men from in front of the sunken road as there appeared to be nothing more to anticipate for the enemy.

At 4-10 p.m. Lt. DISTURNAL reported that men of the Division were streaming over the Railway Bridge, and along the Railway S.W., and appeared to have been doing so for some time - in fact all the time I was with General WALKER.

At 4-30 p.m. Heavy barrage on all the bridges. Retreat of the British stopped. No signs of any Germans. Lt. DISTURNAL'S attendants, (2) were both hit on the Railway Bridge, while looking at the leads.

5-5p.m. Situation quieted down - Rifle fire audible S.E. of the Railway Station - Very lights being fired - No sign of the enemy.

6.45.p.m. I went out to reconnoitre the town, looking at, and crossing the Railway Bridge.
A.T. Bridge at L.23.B.1.8.
Canal at L.23.B.1.8.

I looked at our two sappers at the house near the Canal Bridge L.23.B.1.8., and went on through the main street leading to the Mairie - At the Bridge over the ESCAUT, there was a patrol of about 12 men of the Leicester Regt., who said they were looking for a Bosche patrol of 4 men. I urged them to hold the Lock Bridge at L.23.B.1.8.

I had been told on the 'phone that General WALKER himself was collecting men at CRUCIFIX CORNER, L.22.a.8.6 to reinforce the "Peninsula" so I walked round there to find him, but saw no-one.

7.15 p.m. I returned via the Church and 86th Bde H.Q. of the 20th Nov., to the 87th Bde H.Q. Dug-out, and found General LUCAS - He ordered me away to the C.R.E. at TRESCAULT.

7-45 p.m. I returned to rear H.Q. and TRESCAULT, returned to rear H.Q. afterwards in the HINDENBURG Line.

Lt. DISTURNAL remained in Brigade H.Q. until about 9-30 p.m., until he received a 'phone message from the B.M., 16th Bde. ordering him to be ready to blow up the bridges in about ½ hour time, as they were evacuating the Peninsula.

Sgt. THACKER, R.E., No.4 Section had been ordered up in the afternoon to do the demolitions and arrived about 7-15 p.m.

A patrol

A patrol was sent out from his section to reconnoitre the Decauville bridge at L.25.D.9½.2½. which was reported clear, with Germans about 200 yards away.

Lt. DISTURNAL, R.E., on order of the Bde. Major, took his section out and laid his charges - He found a patrol of the Leicester Regt. asleep in a farm near the Railway bridge, where our exploder was sited. The Officer was awake, he said they were looking for the - some - Regt. (Y.& L.?)

He had sent a patrol across the Railway Bridge, but had seen no sign of them, or the enemy - he refused to send another patrol for Lt. DISTURNAL. Our rifle fire at this time was still audible on the Peninsula. The sappers were only sufficient to carry on the demolition work.

Lt. DISTURNAL returned to Bde H.Q. about 10-30 p.m., to report that everything was ready, and that he had seen no signs of troops being evacuated. He spoke to General LUCAS on the 'phone, and his orders were to blow up all the bridges on the evacuation of all the troops, and in any case by 6.a.m. on Dec.4th.

Lt. DISTURNAL, R.E., then returned again to the Railway Bridge and was fortunate to find Colonel ROSHER supervising the evacuation of the D.L.I., Y.& L. and Bedfords - Colonel ROSHER stated that he was going to line the Canal - this appeared to be wrong, as the river was intended by the Brigade. - He sent his Adjt. to the 'phone in Bde. H.Q. the mistake was corrected. He gave 10.am. as the hour for the final blowing up of the last bridge - the Railway Bridge- which was the evacuation bridge.

At 1-10 a.m the Railway Bridge and the A.T. Bridge were sent up and the other bridges being demolished about 2 hours before. The men who evacuated disappeared along the W. bank of the river.

The sappers were sent back to rear H.Q. and Lt. DISTURNAL returned to report at RIBECOURT.

Shelling was intermittent on the bridge and canal throughout the night - up to 6.0.a.m. there was slight shelling of the village, after that, it was quiet.

M.G. fire on the South bank of the Canal in the neighbourhood of MARCOING COPSE continued most of the night.

Very Light appeared to go up from about the Bridge Head Line all night.

On the right the enemy seemed to be very close to the Lock at L.25.B.1.8., Rifle fire on the "Peninsula" was slight but continuous right up to the evacuation.

No Germans were seen at all anywhere, throughout the day, even, at 2-4pm the most critical period, although we had a look-out in a shell hole with glasses.

8/12/17.

Sd/ B.T. WILSON, R.E.
Major,
O.C. 455th (W.R.)Fd Coy. R.E.

SECRET. (Ref. No. SR.11/150.)

29th. DIVISION.

REPORT ON EVACUATION OF WOUNDED DURING OPERATIONS

20th November to 4th December, 1917.

by

A.D.M.S., 29th DIVISION.

Reference Maps:- France 57.C.)
                        57.B.) 1-40,000.
Trench Maps:- NIERGNIES.)
                     GOUZEAUCOURT.) 1-20,000.

20th NOVEMBER, 1917.

GENERAL SCHEME OF EVACUATION.

The Bearer Division of each Field Ambulance was attached to its respective Brigade in the Assembly Area on the evening of 19th instant. The duties of each Division were to keep in touch with the Regimental Medical Officers of their Brigades, and to carry the wounded back from the AID POSTS to RELAY POSTS at the following places:-

1st Relay. (G.25.c.9.2.
            (L.28.b.central.

2nd Relay. (L.36.a.5.0.
            (L.34.b.8.5.

As soon as the Division moved from our original Front Line, the extra Divisional Stretcher Bearers, consisting of 4 Officers and 200 Other Ranks, advanced along the LA VACQUERIE Road to get in touch with the Relays. At the same time the personnel and equipment of an ADVANCED DRESSING STATION was pushed up to R.5.b. The extra Stretcher Bearers were to carry back from the Relays to the ADVANCED DRESSING STATION, and from there to the Ambulance loading point on LA VACQUERIE Road.

It was hoped that Motor Ambulances could be pushed up close to the ADVANCED DRESSING STATION a few hours after Zero. Unfortunately this was not possible, owing to the bad state of the roads, and the ambulances were unable to get further than LA VACQUERIE.

A WALKING WOUNDED COLLECTING POST, and TEA KITCHEN was established at LA VACQUERIE shortly after the Division advanced.

METHOD OF EVACUATION.

Owing to the slight casualties sustained at the commencement, wounded were taken to the first RELAY POST only by the R.A.M.C. Bearers, the extra Divisional Stretcher Bearers carrying to the second RELAY and ADVANCED DRESSING STATION. There was thus a large number of R.A.M.C. Bearers in the Forward Area who were able to clear quickly from the AID POSTS. The difficulty was the long carry from the 1st RELAY POSTS to the ADVANCED DRESSING STATION, and LA VACQUERIE.

- 2 -

METHOD OF EVACUATION (Continued).

As there was no likelihood of the LA VACQUERIE Road being made fit for Motor Ambulances, and as AID POSTS were being made North of MARCOING and in MASNIERES, this route of evacuation was stopped during the afternoon, and Officers i/c Bearer Divisions were told to hold up their cases in buildings until the VILLERS PLOUICH Road could be used on the following day.

On the afternoon of 21st November, an ADVANCED DRESSING STATION and TEA KITCHEN were opened in the Square, MARCOING, and the Brewery, Les Rues Vertes, MASNIERES, and by 2 o'clock Motor Ambulances had arrived, and were clearing cases down the VILLERS PLOUICH Road direct from MARCOING to Casualty Clearing Stations at YTRES and TINCOURT.

The TEA KITCHENS both at LA VACQUERIE and MARCOING were used to feed a large number of French refugees as well as Walking Wounded.

TRANSPORT.

MOTOR AMBULANCES.

Ford Cars worked continuously between LA VACQUERIE, and the CAMBRAI Road, where cases were transferred to large cars, and evacuated in them either to 20th Division Advanced Dressing Station, GOUZEAUCOURT, or direct to Casualty Clearing Stations at YTRES and TINCOURT. The majority of the cases were evacuated direct to Casualty Clearing Station.

HORSE AMBULANCES.

These carried Walking Wounded from LA VACQUERIE to the Decauville Railhead, GOUZEAUCOURT, where they were placed in the Corps Ambulance Train, or Lorries, and taken to the Corps WALKING WOUNDED POST, FINS.

DECAUVILLE RAILWAY.

Owing to the length of broken line in No Man's Land, this method of transport was impracticable.

The VILLERS PLOUICH - MARCOING Road was reserved for Cavalry on 20th November, so motor ambulances were unable to get to MARCOING before the 21st November.

MEDICAL SITUATION FROM

21st to 29th November, 1917.

REGIMENTAL AID POSTS.

    4 in MASNIERES.
    4 on N. side of Canal between MASNIERES and MARCOING.
    4 in MARCOING.

ADVANCED DRESSING STATIONS.

    1. LES RUES VERTES ...... G.26.c.9.8.
    2. MARCOING .... L.22.b.7.6.

TRANSPORT.

A Motor Ambulance Stand was made on the VILLERS PLOUICH - MARCOING Road at L.33.c.9.0. One car was kept at each Advanced Dressing Station, and as it passed the stand on the outward journey, a fresh car was sent up.

EVACUATION.

R.A.M.C. Bearers were attached to each REGIMENTAL AID POST. Cases were carried to the ADVANCED DRESSING STATION, and evacuated direct from there to Casualty Clearing Station via VILLERS PLOUICH and GOUZEAUCOURT.

Each ADVANCED DRESSING STATION could accommodate at least 50 Stretcher Cases.

MEDICAL SITUATION FROM
30th November to 4th December, 1917.

30th NOVEMBER, 1917.

Owing to the enemy counter-attack in the early morning, the line of evacuation along the VILLERS PLOUICH Road was cut, and a new route had to be established. All communication with the ADVANCED DRESSING STATION, LES RUES VERTES, was cut off, that part of the town being in the enemy's hands for a time, and under direct enemy observation until the ADVANCED DRESSING STATION was evacuated on the following night.

A new line of evacuation was made by establishing a COLLECTING POST in RIBECOURT, and removing cases as quickly as possible from MARCOING to RIBECOURT, and evacuating from there at leisure by DECAUVILLE RAILWAY, HORSE and MOTOR AMBULANCES.

NIGHT OF 30th NOV./1st DEC.

The ADVANCED DRESSING STATION, LES RUES VERTES, was full of wounded, 95 cases were evacuated that night to MARCOING ADVANCED DRESSING STATION, leaving 10 stretcher cases in LES RUES VERTES. The Medical Officer in charge was informed that there would be no communication with him the following day until night when all his cases would be cleared, and he would evacuate his ADVANCED DRESSING STATION.

NIGHT OF 1st/2nd DEC.

The Bearers were again sent up, and evacuated 50 Stretcher and 90 walking cases. The ADVANCED DRESSING STATION was then closed down leaving only six Enemy stretcher cases in the building.

At the same time other stretcher bearers were sent up to clear the MASNIERES REGIMENTAL AID POSTS near the Lock, and in the CATACOMBS.

2nd DECEMBER.

The ADVANCED DRESSING STATION was removed to RIBECOURT, and MARCOING was used as a COLLECTING POST.
Motor Ambulances still evacuated cases from MARCOING.

3rd DECEMBER.

It was impossible to get Motor Ambulances into MARCOING SQUARE after 4 p.m. owing to the shelling. The COLLECTING POST there was evacuated in the evening, and a Post established on the RIBECOURT - MARCOING Road, the Ambulance Bearers keeping in touch the whole time with the REGIMENTAL AID POSTS during the gradual withdrawal.

WOUNDED.

The total number of wounded evacuated during the period under consideration was as follows :-

Officers.	Other Ranks.
105	2,590

R.A.M.C. CASUALTIES.

Killed.		Wounded.		Missing.	
Officers.	O.R.	Officers.	O.R.	Officers.	O.R.
-	4	5	48	2	1

TOTAL = 60 All ranks.

Attached hereto is a report on a hot air apparatus used in both ADVANCED DRESSING STATIONS.

                                    (Sd) H. E. M. DOUGLAS,
                                            Colonel,
8th December, 1917.   A.D.M.S., 29th Division.

Copies to :- D.M.S., Third Army.
             D.D.M.S., IV Corps.
             "A", 29th Division.
             G.S., "   "
             War Diary.
             File (3 copies)

REPORT ON THE USE OF HOT AIR APPARATUS AT AN ADVANCED
DRESSING STATION DURING RECENT OPERATIONS OF THE
29TH DIVISION.
-o-o-o-o-o-o-o-o-o-o-o-o-o-o-o-o-o-o-o-o-o-o-o-o-o-o-o-o-o-o-o-

A description of the apparatus employed (Blanket Heater and Hot air Generator) was forwarded on 12/11/17 under No. A.1519.

The object aimed at was to thoroughly warm up chilled and shocked patients before transferring them to the C.C.S. The procedure adopted in general was as follows :-

If the man's clothes were wet they were changed for dry pyjamas and Socks, and he was transferred to a stretcher covered by a double folded dry blanket. The cradle was then put on the stretcher and the whole covered with blankets and the hot air bath given. As far as the position of the wound permitted dressing was carried out during the administration of the air bath.

The blanket rack provided the necessary supply of dry and hot clothes and blankets.

The bath lasted about 15 minutes, the cradle was then removed and hot water bottles placed under the blankets, the temperature being thus sustained for the period of transport.

Hot drinks were given as usual. Clothes were not removed if they were dry.

The apparatus was employed at the Advanced Dressing Stations at MARCOING and MASNIERES, at both places most of the work was carried out underground. The transport and use of both blanket drier and heat generator was found to be simple. During heavy inflows of wounded it was not possible to use the hot air bath for any but the most seriously wounded, but a sufficient surplus of dry blankets was maintained for all cases.

From my own observations and from those of other Medical Officers working at the A.D.S. the condition of the patients treated as above was much improved both subjectively and objectively. In some cases the body temperature was raised two degrees F. (from sub-normal) and in all cases the pinched and shivering appearance of the patients totally disappeared or was much improved, this was particularly evident in cases which had been lying out for some time.

As all cars in use were fitted with the exhaust heater which maintained the temperature inside at from 60° to 70°, there was no chance of the patients becoming chilled while en route for the C.C.S.

The following practical points may be mentioned in relation to the use of the apparatus.

BLANKET AND CLOTHES DRIER.

Two "Beatrice" stoves, fitted as described should be used for this and kept going continuously; the air chamber should be practically closed at half hour intervals by placing a blanket on the top, this varies the temperature inside to from 90° to 100° F. more ventilation is then allowed in order to dry off the contents. It was found that a blanket could be dried in this way in about 20 minutes.
Additional wires should be added at a suitable level for hanging pyjamas, etc., on.

HOT AIR GENERATOR AND BATH.

A double or even triple fold of a blanket should be both above and below the patient. A single-wicked "Beatrice" stove in the box will raise the temperature in the air chamber to about 140° F. in 10 - 15 minutes and this I think is a sufficient dose for a man before transport.

In general it would appear that the hot air appliances referred to are of the highest value in the treatment of the wounded at a C.C.S. and some such apparatus should in Winter time be in the equipment of every Field Ambulance. The hot air generator would also be of value at the C.C.S. and Base Units not only in the treatment of shock but for Myalgia, nephritis, etc.

(Sd) C. M. PAGE, Capt.
88th Field Ambulance,
R.A.M.C. (T.F.)

4.12.17.

Report on Operations by 29th Division on 20th November 1917.

1. Order of Battle.

Divisional Commander. Major General Sir BEAUVOIR de LISLE, K.C.B. D.S.O.

86th Inf Bde Commander. Brig-Gen G.R.H. CHEAPE, M.C.
2/Roy Fusiliers.   Major J.S. HODDING.
1/Lan Fusiliers.   Major T. SLINGSBY, M.C.
16/Middlesex Regt.   Lt-Col. J. FORBES-ROBERTSON.
                       D.S.O. M.C. (Border Regt).
1/R. Guernsey L.I.   Lt-Col H.J. de la CONDAMINE.

87th Inf. Bde Commander. Brig-Gen C.H.T. LUCAS. D.S.O.
2/S. Wales Borderers. Lt-Col G.T. RAIKES. D.S.O.
1/K.O.S.B.   Lt-Col C.A.G.O. MURRAY.
1/R. Inniskilling Fus. Lt-Col J. SHERWOOD-KELLY. C.M.G. D.S.O.
                       (Norfolk Regt).
1/Border Regt.   Lt-Col A.J. ELLIS, D.S.O.

88th Inf Bde Commander. Brig-Gen H. NELSON, D.S.O.
4/Worcester R.   Lt-Col C.S. LINTON, D.S.O. M.C.
2/Hampshire R.   Capt K.A. JOHNSTON.
1/Essex R.   Lt Col Sir G.M.H. STIRLING, Bart, D.S.O.
Newfoundland R.   Lt Col A. L. HADOW, C.M.G.

2. Disposition of Troops at Zero.

86th Inf Bde in the area Q.23, Q.29.a. and b.

87th Inf Bde in the area Q.24, Q.30.a. and c.

88th Inf Bde in the area Q.29.c. and d. Q.35.a. and b.

Field Coys R.E. in the area Q.34.c. and d. Q.35.c. and d.

The assembly areas are shewn on the attached map.

3. Objectives.

The task allotted to the Division was, to pass through the 20 and 6th Divisions as soon as these had captured the BROWN LINE and the 12th Division had captured the BONAVIS Plateau, force the crossings over the canal at MASNIERES and MARCOING and, breaking through the enemy's last line of resistance the MASNIERES - BEAUREVOIR line, to enable the Cavalry to pass through the gap thus formed.

4. PLAN.

To carry out this task successfully, it was essential that both MASNIERES and MARCOING should not only be captured, but that strong bridgeheads should be established on the Eastern side of the Canal. Both these villages are of considerable size and are some two miles apart, and it was considered that in each case one infantry Brigade would be required.

Moreover NINE WOOD at the Eastern edge of FLESQUIERES Ridge overlooks MARCOING from the North at a range of 1000 yards and is 100 feet above it. The capture of MARCOING was therefore dependent on the capture of this position, thus necessitating the use of my third Brigade.

No reserve of infantry was kept in hand as I considered that being a pursuing force, extraordinary risks might be taken and the holding back of any portion of the fighting force might seriously hamper the success of the operation.

The 88th Brigade was therefore directed on MASNIERES, the 87th Brigade on MARCOING, and the 86th Brigade on NINE WOOD.

5. Concentration.

The Division entrained at BOISLEUX AU MONT on the night of 17th/18th November, resting for the day of the 18th at MOISLAINS.

On the following night it marched to FINS, EQUANCOURT, and started at 2 a.m. on the morning of the 20th November

/for

for the assembly position north of GOUZEAUCOURT a distance of 5 miles.

This assembly march was accomplished by 5.30 a.m. without any trouble. Routes had been previously reconnoitred and all road and track junctions piquetted to guard against loss of direction.

It will be noticed that the 3 nights prior to the attack the troops had been on the move.

6. **The Approach March.**

By the scheme the Division was not to advance until the BONAVIS Plateau and the Brown Line (Hindenburg Support Line) had been gained by the 12th, 20th and 6th Divisions, but as time was an important factor in a complete success, the leading Battalions of Brigades were moved at Zero into our front line which had been vacated by the above Divisions.

Further, each Brigade of this Division pushed out Advanced Guards up to the BLUE LINE as soon as this object had been gained, with patrols following the troops as they attacked the BROWN LINE.

It was intended that Contact Planes should drop situation reports at this H.Q. to enable me to start this Division at the earliest possible moment. The fog however made the work of contact planes impossible, and the news of the capture of the BLUE LINE of which the scheduled time was 8 a.m. did not reach this H.Q. until 9.15 a.m. 1¼ hours later.

To have waited for news of the complete capture of the BROWN LINE would have so delayed the start of the 29th Division that at 10 a.m. on hearing that the troops of the 6th and 20th Divisions were well on their way to the Brown Line, I asked permission to take the risk and move my Brigades to their objective. At 10.15 A.M. the order was issued and was conveyed to all Units of each Brigade by Bugle Call.

The Division therefore moved off simultaneously with the 88th Brigade on the right directed on MASNIERES, the 87th Brigade on MARCOING, from a point due South of it, and the 86th Brigade on NINE WOOD at the Eastern end of the FLESQUIERE ridge.

Brigades adopted a Diamond formation with one Battalion at each point, the long axis being 1800 yards, and the short axis, parallel to the direction 1200. Each Battalion placed their four Companies in a similar formation. This formation was adopted with a view to saving time, the flanking units being in position to envelope should opposition be met by the leading Battalion acting as advanced guard to each Brigade Four Tanks were allotted to each Brigade and moved in advance of the Infantry Advanced Guards.

7. **Narrative of the action of the 88th (Right) Brigade.**

On approaching the Brown Line in R.5 and L.35 hostile fire was opened from rifles and Machine Guns and 3 of the Battalions were forced to attack it. This caused a delay of ¾ hour and accounted for over 150 prisoners. On the left the Newfoundland Battalion had some difficulty and sustained many casualties, but with their accustomed dash they broke down all opposition, using covering fire from rifles, Machine Guns and a Stokes Gun. This delay however was unfortunate as it gave time for the enemy to partially organise the defences of LES RUES VERTES. The right Battalion (4/Worcestershire Regt) however, pushed on to its objective, the lock in G.27.c. and got one Company across to form a Bridgehead sending another along the eastern Canal Bank to outflank the defence. This manoeuvre was entirely successful.

A tank now endeavoured to cross the Main Iron Bridge at MASNIERES but the Bridge, previously partially destroyed gave way. No assistance from tanks could then be expected on the east side of the Canal. Finding the leading Battalion held up at the Canal Bridge at MASNIERES, the 2/Hampshire, skilfully led by Acting Lieut-Colonel JOHNSTON, moved down to the Lock 1000 yards to the S.E. crossed there and attacked the RED LINE with 2 Companies and captured these was sent to attack MASNIERES from the east and gained the outskirts of the town.

The death of Lieut-Colonel LINTON, D.S.O. M.C. 4/Worcesters left this Battalion without a leader and the Companies somewhat

/disorganised

- disorganised, but Lieut-Colonel JOHNSTON quickly took over the situation, organised the defences to the North and East as far as MONT PLAISIN FARM, and continued to press on his attack of MASNIERES until dawn of the 21st.

About 4 p.m. on the 20th a squadron of Canadian Dragoons crossed the Canal at Lock in G.27.c and rode up over the RUMILLY ridge.

On the left the N.F.L.D. crossed at the lock in L.24.d, and attacked to the East gaining the gun pits in L.19 and 20 but were unable to cross the open ground between this cover and the town.

Heavy fighting was in progress during the night but at dawn we held the town as far North as L.20.d.7.9 with the exception of a pocket in the centre. Here a number of the enemy were sheltered in the Catacombs, to which there are 7 openings. These were not captured until midday of the 21st.

8. <u>Narrative of the Action of the 87th (Centre) Brigade.</u>

The Centre Brigade marched straight on MARCOING and MARCOING Copse. In the former place the enemy hurriedly evacuated the town. The Commander General VON KEPPEL had not even time to remove his personnel belongings. At MARCOING Copse, some resistance was experienced and many enemy killed in the Wood. The leading Battalion of this Brigade, 1/Kings Own Scottish Borderers marched through the town and crossed by the Railway Bridge. Only one tank succeeded in crossing, the others for various causes being unable to get there. The right flank Battalion, 2/South Wales Borderers crossed at the Lock L.24. These two Battalions, as ordered, immediately prepared Bridgeheads covering the crossings, where the other two Battalions, 1/Royal Inniskilling Fusiliers on right and 1/Border Regt on left passed over and advanced again at the Red Line.

After a long advance of about a mile the attack was brought to a standstill some 300 yards behind our present line L.14.c.3.0 to the Lock at L.17.d.3.7. The RED LINE was seen to have been reinforced just before the attack of our troops, and the Machine Gun fire from it made any further advance impossible without the aid of Artillery or Tanks. On the left one Company of the 1/Border Regt gained the RED LINE in 13.a. and took 19 prisoners there, but owing to the right of the line being held up, this Company was withdrawn, retiring firing by alternate platoons. The above line was consolidated the same night.

The following day with the assistance of 9 Tanks, the 87th Inf Bde made another attempt to take the whole of the RED LINE, but without success. The tanks suffered from armour piercing bullets, 50 per cent of the personnel becoming casualties, and the Infantry came under heavy Machine Gun fire both from the front and from FLOT FARM where a number of guns firing indirect prevented the troops gaining the top of the ridge in L.20.a. & b.

9. <u>Narrative of the 86th (left) Brigade.</u>

The 86th Brigade advanced without opposition to the Quarry S.W. of NINE WOOD, but here the leading Regiment (16/Middlesex Regt) was checked. The flank Regiments however, 2/Royal Fusiliers on the right and 1/Royal Guernsey L.I on the left continued to push on enveloping the wood from the S.E and N.W, and so gaining all objectives by 1 p.m.

A Company was then sent to occupy NOYELLE and bridgehead on the eastern bank of the Canal. Betw ESCAUT and the Canal opposition was met and the t unable to accomplish the crossing.

10. <u>Counter-attacks.</u>

On November 21st the three counter-attacks against the new line of defence.
(a) At 11 a.m. a heavy attack from the N.E. wa against the 88th Brigade by 2 Battalions which a waves. This was caught by Artillery and Machine could not approach closer than 500 yards.

-4-

(b) The second attack at 1 p.m. moved S.W against the 87th Brigade but came under heavy fire as it crossed the support line in G.14 and did not get beyond the German front line.

(c) The Third attack advanced on NOYELLE from the Wood north of the village and drove back our outposts to the southern end of the village. Reinforcements were sent down from NINE WOOD until we had 3 Companies in the village opposed to 5 Companies of the enemy. Our troops gradually drove the enemy back, and at dusk had cleared the village except for 28 Germans who later surrendered. A relieving Battalion of the 6th Division took over the village the same night without a shot being fired. The Troops of the 86th Brigade fired 200 rounds per man expended all Bombs and Stokes bombs. In the end they were fighting entirely with German weapons and ammunition.

11. General remarks.

(1) This being the first occasion that this Division has been engaged in open warfare, it was necessary to adapt the training to the probable requirements. Fortunately the area, South of ARRAS, allotted by the VI Corps for this purpose was ideal in every way. By means of Brigade and Divisional Schemes Battalions were enabled to gain very valuable instruction. The difficulty in training Company and Platoon leaders to act correctly according to the situation and ground is far greater than training them to lead in a trench to trench attack, and the time available was inadequate. Much however was done by lectures and Brigade Exercises prepared by my General Staff.

(2) The diamond formation was found most suitable, saving time, and being less liable to casualties under shell fire.

(3) One Stokes Gun with 64 rounds was attached to each Battalion and this was found invaluable.

(4) One section Machine Guns was attached to the leading Battalion of each Brigade and a flank detachment of 2 Machine Guns and ½ Company was maintained on the flank of each Brigade, a precaution which has always proved useful.

(5) The rapidity of the advance of the 3 Brigades enabled them to gain the crossings before resistance could be organised, and had it been possible to get tanks across in time before German reinforcements arrived from CAMBRAI, the success would have been even more complete. The breaking of the MASNIERES Bridge was fatal to the co-operation of the Tanks.

(6) A remarkable feature of these operations was the physical endurance of the troops. From 2 a.m. on the 20th November, the Division marched 10 miles to the Canal, carrying over 60 lbs of equipment. They fought till dark on the 21st, and have since consolidated a position 5000 yards long and 1500 yards deep.

After 10 days in the line, they are certainly worn out but still capable of defence.

This remarkable performance is due to the careful attention of Regimental Officers to the comfort of the Troops and to the excellent discipline in all Brigades.

I append a statement of casualties incurred by the Units engaged in this attack, prisoners and war material captured.

6th December 1917.

Major General.
Commanding 29th Division.

29th December 1917.

Headquarters,
29th Division.

Herewith report on operations of 30th November and the following two days.

A. Johnson
Brigadier General,
Commanding 29th Divisional Artillery.

(no spares)

No.	Contents.	Date.
	G.S. 29th Div. December 1917	

Army Form C. 2118.

WAR DIARY
or
INTELLIGENCE SUMMARY.
(Erase heading not required.)

Instructions regarding War Diaries and Intelligence Summaries are contained in F. S. Regs., Part II. and the Staff Manual respectively. Title pages will be prepared in manuscript.

Place	Date	Hour	Summary of Events and Information	Remarks and references to Appendices
TRESCAULT SOREL.	DEC. 1st.		86th Inf.Bde. withdrew from MASNIERES salient to a position South of RIBECOURT - MARCOING Road. The withdrawal was carried out without interference by the enemy. The flank of the 87th Inf.Bde. was thrown back to join with the left flank of the 88th Inf.Bde. about the look in L.27.c. G.O.C. visited III Corps H.Q. 9 p.m.	App. 1.
	2nd.		G.O.C. visited H.Q. 87th and 88th Inf.Bdes. at MARCOING in very heavy barrage. 86th Inf.Bde. from Area N.E. of RIBECOURT to cellars in RIBECOURT. 87th Inf.Bde. relieved in line by 16th Bde., 6th Division, and withdrew to HINDENBURG LINE South of RIBECOURT.	
	3rd.		86th Inf.Bde. from RIBECOURT to HAURINCOURT WOOD.	
	4th.		86th Inf.Bde. from HAURINCOURT WOOD to FINS. 87th Inf.Bde. from HINDENBURG LINE South of RIBECOURT to SOREL. 88th Inf.Bde. in the line relieved by 108th Bde. arrived at Pack Transport Lines RIBECOURT 5.0 a.m., 4th/5th, and after hot meal continued journey to ETRICOURT Station.	
SOREL. LE GAUROY.	5th		Brigades entrained at ETRICOURT for new area. Divisional H.Q. moved from SOREL LE GRAND. SOREL and FINS shelled. G.S. 51/134	

Army Form C. 2118.

WAR DIARY
or
INTELLIGENCE SUMMARY.
(Erase heading not required.)

Instructions regarding War Diaries and Intelligence Summaries are contained in F. S. Regs., Part II. and the Staff Manual respectively. Title pages will be prepared in manuscript.

Place	Date	Hour	Summary of Events and Information	Remarks and references to Appendices
IV CORPS	DEC.			
LE CAUROY	6th		Arrival of Brigades in new area by rail complete. G.O.C. visited G.H.Q. 88th Inf.Bde. H.Q. AMBRINES& 87th Inf.Bde. H.Q. LIENCOURT. 88th Inf.Bde. H.Q. SUS-ST-LEGER.	C.G.S.58 30 A/h 2
	7th		G.O.C. visited Second Army H.Q. Representatives of TIMES and TELEGRAPH visited Divisional H.Q. and H.Q. 87th Inf.Bde. General NELSON, Commanding 88th Inf.Bde. broke down. Governor and Prime Minister N.F.L.D. lunched at Divisional H.Q. and visited 1/N.F.L.D. R.	
	8th		Conference of Brigadiers, Commanding Officers, Seconds in Command, held at Divisional H.Q. 11 a.m. General NELSON, Commanding 88th Inf.Bde. better. Capt. R. GEE, Staff Captain 86th Inf.Bde. returned to duty.	
	9th		G.O.C. attended Church Parade Divisional H.Q. Rain all day.	
	10th		Nothing of interest to report.	
	11th		G.O.C. to ENGLAND on leave. General LUCAS, Commanding 87th Inf.Bde. a/G.O.C. Division.	

Army Form C. 2118.

WAR DIARY
or
INTELLIGENCE SUMMARY.
(Erase heading not required.)

Instructions regarding War Diaries and Intelligence Summaries are contained in F.S. Regs., Part II. and the Staff Manual respectively. Title pages will be prepared in manuscript.

Place	Date	Hour	Summary of Events and Information	Remarks and references to Appendices
	DEC.			
LE CAUROY.	12th		Nothing of interest to report.	
	13th		Nothing of interest to report.	
	14th		G.O.C. inspected 1/K.O.S.B.	
	15th		G.O.C. inspected 1/R. GUERN. L.I.	O.O.142 cuf. 3
	16th		86th Inf.Bde. from AMBRINES to BOUBERS. Began to snow in the afternoon.	
	17th		Snowed all night. Roads very deep in snow. 86th Inf.Bde. from BOUBERS to HESDIN area. 87th Inf.Bde. LIENCOURT to BOUBERS area. Transport difficult owing to state of roads.	

Army Form C. 2118.

WAR DIARY
or
INTELLIGENCE SUMMARY.
(Erase heading not required.)

Instructions regarding War Diaries and Intelligence Summaries are contained in F. S. Regs., Part II. and the Staff Manual respectively. Title pages will be prepared in manuscript.

Place	Date	Hour	Summary of Events and Information	Remarks and references to Appendices
	DEC.			
HUCQUELIERS	18th		88th Inf.Bde. from HESDIN area to FRUGES area. 86th Inf.Bde. H.Q. VERCHOCQ. 87th Inf.Bde. BOUBERS area to HESDIN area. 88th Inf.Bde. SUS-ST.-LEGER to BOUBERS area. G.O.C. inspected Division on the road, and stayed the night at HESDIN. Divisional H.Q. moved from LE CAUROY to HUCQUELIERS. Side roads blocked with snow. G.O.C.'s car ran into deep snowdrift and had to be dug out. 88th Inf.Bde. transport lorries fail to arrive owing to the state of roads. Despatch Riders unable to get through and wires broken by snow. Hard frost. Division to X Corps, Fourth Army.	O.O.172 A.4.3.
	19th		87th Inf.Bde. HESDIN area to FRUGES area. 87th Inf.Bde. H.Q. CREQUY. 88th Inf.Bde. BOUBERS area to HESDIN area. G.O.C. arrives at Divisional H.Q. HUCQUELIERS.	O.O.172 A.4.3.
	20th		88th Inf.Bde. HESDIN area to TORCY area. 88th Inf.Bde. H.Q. G.O.C. visits Brigade H.Q. and new area. 88th Inf.Bde. H.Q. TORCY.	O.O.172 A.4.3
	21st		Nothing of interest to report.	
	22nd		Thawed during the day. Frost at night makes horse transport more difficult.	
	23rd		Nothing of interest to report.	

Army Form C. 2118.

WAR DIARY
or
INTELLIGENCE SUMMARY.
(Erase heading not required.)

Instructions regarding War Diaries and Intelligence Summaries are contained in F. S. Regs., Part II. and the Staff Manual respectively. Title pages will be prepared in manuscript.

Place	Date	Hour	Summary of Events and Information	Remarks and references to Appendices
	DEC.			C.G.S. 56/31.
HUCQUELIERS	24th		Conference of Brigadiers, Commanding Officers, held at Divisional H.Q. 11 a.m. Owing to break-down on the road 88th Inf.Bde. did not arrive at the Conference. G.O.C., X Corps lunched at Divisional H.Q. Divisional Artillery rejoined Division. D.A.H.Q. MARESQUEL.	
	25th		G.O.C. attended Church Parade at Divisional H.Q. Lieut.General Sir AYLMER G. HUNTER-WESTON, K.C.B., D.S.O., G.O.C. VIII Corps, lunched at Divisional H.Q., and accompanied G.O.C. on a tour of the Battalions to offer Christmas Greetings. Men's Christmas dinners visited by G.O.C. and G.O.C. VIII Corps. Snowed heavily in the evening.	
	26th		All roads blocked with snow. Traffic held up.	
	27th		G.O.C. visited 87th and 88th Inf.Bdes. and Divisional Artillery.	
	28th		Nothing of interest to report. ⎫ Training suspended owing to snow.	
	29th		Nothing of interest to report. ⎭	

(A7192). Wt. W12859/M1293. 75 v.o. 1/17. D.D. & L., Ltd. Forms/C.2118/14.

Army Form C. 2118.

WAR DIARY
or
INTELLIGENCE SUMMARY.
(Erase heading not required.)

Instructions regarding War Diaries and Intelligence Summaries are contained in F. S. Regs., Part II. and the Staff Manual respectively. Title pages will be prepared in manuscript.

Place	Date	Hour	Summary of Events and Information	Remarks and references to Appendices
	DEC.			
HUCQUELIERS	30th		87th Inf. Bde. commenced march to XIX Corps. See O.O. No. 176.	App. 7.
	31st		Nothing of interest to report.	
			A summary of messages period 30th Nov - 4th Dec. is attached.	App. 8.

W F L Oming
Lt Col
General Staff, 29th Division.

9/1/18.

SECRET

29th Div. No. C.G.S.87

29TH DIVISION WARNING ORDER.
-o-o-o-o-o-o-o-o-o-o-o-o-o-o-o-

29th November, 1917.

1. The 29th Division will probably be relieved by the 6th and 20th Divisions on the nights of 2nd/3rd and 3rd/4th December respectively, and will be withdrawn to the HAUT ALLAINES area.

2. In the event of its being possible to withdraw the 29th Division by broad guage railway from the forward area the dates of relief will be postponed 24 hours.

3. ACKNOWLEDGE.

BM.O 39.

Lieut-Colonel, G.S.,
29th Division.

Issued at 4 pm

Copies	1 - 4	G.S.	14	D.M.G.O.
	5	"Q".	15	227th M.G. Coy.
	6	C.R.A.	16	D.A.D.O.S.
	7	C.R.E.	17	D.A.D.V.S.
	8	86th Inf. Bde.	18	Div. Train.
	9	87th Inf. Bde.	19	S.S.O.
	10	88th Inf. Bde.	20	A.P.M.
	11	Off. i/c Sigs.	21	III Corps.
	12	1/2nd Monmouths.	22	6th Div.
	13	A.D.M.S.	23	20th Div.

M.

SPECIAL ORDER OF THE DAY No. 70.
By
Major General Sir Beauvoir de Lisle, K.C.B., D.S.O.
Commanding 29th Division.

I wish to express to the Troops of my Division my high appreciation of their gallant conduct and resolute determination during the operations from November 20th 1917 to the 4th December 1917, and to convey to all ranks the following messages which have been received by me:-

From Lieut. General Sir W.P. PULTENEY, K.C.B., K.C.M.G., D.S.O.
   Commanding III Corps.

"The Corps Commander would like to place on record his deep appreciation of the fighting spirit of the 29th Division.
   The magnificient defence of the MASNIERES-MARCOING Line at a most critical juncture, and the subsequent orderly withdrawal reflects the highest credit on all concerned.
   In the 15 days in which your Division has been in action on this front, all ranks have displayed an endurance which is beyond praise.
   He would be glad if this could be conveyed to your troops."

From General the Honble. Sir Julian BYNG, K.C.B., K.C.M.G., M.V.O.
   Commanding Third Army.

"I would like you to express to all ranks my sincere appreciation of the services which have been rendered to the Third Army by the 29th Division.
   Both in the attack on the 20th November 1917 and in their defence of their sector on the 30th November 1917 and subsequent days, the Division has more than maintained its splendid reputation.
   I ask you to accept my warmest congratulations."

From Field Marshal Sir Douglas HAIG, K.T., G.C.B., G.C.V.O., K.C.I.E.,
   Commander-in-Chief British Armies in France.

"Please convey to General de Lisle and men of the 29th Division my warm congratulations on the splendid fight successfully maintained by them against repeated attacks by numerically superior forces. Their gallant defence of MASNIERES throughout two days of almost continuous fighting has had most important results upon the course of the battle and is worthy of the best traditions of the British Army.

Beauvoir de Lisle

Major General,
Commanding 29th Division.

11th December 1917.

SECRET

29th DIVISION ORDER No. 172.   Copy No. 1

14th December 1917.

Reference Maps:— LENS.
CALAIS.
HAZEBROUCK 5A.   } 1/100000.
ABBEVILLE.

1. The 29th Division (less Artillery) is to be transferred from IVth Corps to Xth Corps (Second Army) commencing on the 16th instant, and is to be accommodated in the FRUGES area.

2. (a) The transfer will be carried out by march route in accordance with march table attached.

   (b) A map of the FRUGES area showing allotment of sub areas to Brigade Groups and accommodation tables for FRUGES and HESDIN areas are being issued to all concerned.

3. Lorries will be provided under arrangements to be made by the A.A. & Q.M.G. to carry:—
   (a) Blankets
   (b) Packs of Infantry and other dismounted personnel.

4. The Divisional Supply Column will move by road as required.

5. Distances of 200 yards will be maintained between Battalions on the line of march.

6. Divisional H.Q. will close at LE CAUROY at 12 noon on the 18th instant and will re-open at HUCQUELIERS at the same hour.

7. Acknowledge.

RMD 23

Issued at 11 p.m.

Lieut-Colonel, G.S.,
29th Division.

Copies			
1 - 4	Gen. Staff	22.	DADOS
5	Q	23.	DADVS
6	CRA	24.	SAA Sect. DAC
7	CRE	25.	C. Comdt.
8 - 9	86th Bde	26.	Div. Train.
10 - 11	87th Bde	27.	SSO
12 - 13	88th Bde	28.	29th Div. Supply Col.
14	Sigs	29.	Sub area Comdt. VERCHOCQ
15	Mons E.	30.	" " " CREQUY
16	ADMS	31.	" " " ROYON
17	APM	32.	" " " BOUBERS
18	DAGO		SUR CANCHE
19	227 Div. M.G. Coy.	33.	G.O.C. L of C areas.
20	IVth Corps	34.	Comdt. G.H.Q. Troops.
21	Xth Corps		

SECRET.

29th DIVISION OPERATION ORDER No. 175.

Copy No. 9

27th December 1917

Reference Maps :- CALAIS.)
ABBEVILLE.) 1/100,000
HAZEBROUCK.)
LENS.)

1. The 29th Divisional Artillery will move from the FRUGES Area (BEAURAINVILLE sub-area) to the THIEMBRONNE Area (Divisional Artillery sub-area) on the 4th January 1918, and will be held in G.H.Q. Reserve.

2. Detailed orders on the subject of troops which are held in G.H.Q. Reserve will be issued later.

3. The move will be completed in one day; all roads will be available. No restrictions as to time of march.

4. Map showing THIEMBRONNE Area (Divisional sub-area) is attached hereto. Billets will be obtained from area Commandant, THIEMBRONNE.

5. Completion of the move to be reported to this office.

6. Attention is drawn to Second Army No. 138/G copy of which is attached (C.R.A. only).

7. ACKNOWLEDGE.

Issued at 6.30 p.m.

Hugh. O. Holmes
Major R.F.A.
for Lieut-Colonel, GS.
29th Division.

Copies - 1 - 4   Gen. Staff.
            5   Q.
            6   CRA.
            7   CRE.
        8 - 9   86th Bde.
       10 - 11   87th Bde.
       12 - 13   88th Bde.
           14   Sigs.
           15   Mons.
           16   ADMS.
           17   APM.
           18   DADOS
           19   DADVS
           20   3aa Sec. DAC.
           21   Camp Commdt.
           22   Div. Train.
           23   SSO.
           24   29 Div. S.C.
           25   Area Commdt, THIEMBRONNE.

29th Div. No. C.G.S.67/10⁷⁄₃.

Copy No. 9

SECRET.

Ref. Maps   Addendum No. 1
CALAIS   to
ABBEVILLE   29th Division Order No. 175.
HAZEBROUCK
LENS 1/100000   -o-o-o-o-o-o-o-o-o-o-o-o-o-o-o-

1. Cancel para. 1 and substitute the following :-

"The 29th Divisional Artillery will move from the FRUGES area (BEAURAINVILLE sub-area) to the THIEMBRONNE area (Divisional Artillery sub-area) on the 3rd and 4th January, 1918, as shown below, and will be held in G.H.Q. reserve.

Date.	From.	To.
3rd January	BEAURAINVILLE sub-area	VERCHOCQ COUPELLEVIELLE CREQUY
4th January	VERCHOCQ COUPELLEVIELLE CREQUY	THIEMBRONNE area

"

2. In para. 3 erase the words

"The move will be completed in one day".

3. The 87th Field Ambulance will billet in RUMILLY on night of 3rd/4th January instead of at VERCHOCQ as previously ordered in 29th Division Order No. 177 of 31/12/17.

4. To be acknowledged by C.R.A., 86th Inf. Bde. and O.C. 87th Field Ambulance.

P. Fraser Major
for Lieut-Colonel, G.S.,
29th Division.

2nd January, 1917.

Copies 1 - 4   Gen. Staff.   16   APM
       5   Q   17   DMGO
       6   CRA   18   227th Div. M.G. Coy.
       7   CRE   19   C. Comdt.
   8 - 9   86th Inf. Bde.   20   Div. Train.
  10 - 11   87th Inf. Bde.   21   SSO
      12   87th Field Ambce.   22   29th D.S.Col.
      13   Sigs   23   Area Comdt. CREQUY
      14   Mcn. R.   24   Area Comdt. VERCHOCQ
      15   ADMS

"C" Form.
Army Form C. 2123.
(In books of 100).
MESSAGES AND SIGNALS. No. of Message_____

Prefix____ Code____ Words____	Received. From_____ By_____	Sent, or sent out. At_____ m. To_____ By_____	Office Stamp.
Charges to collect			
Service Instructions.			

Handed in at_____ Office_____ m. Received_____ m.

TO

Sender's Number	Day of Month	In reply to Number	A A A
	9th		
			29th

FROM
PLACE & TIME

"C" Form.
MESSAGES AND SIGNALS.

Army Form C. 2123.
(In books of 100).
No. of Message _____

Prefix ____ Code ____ Words ____	Received.	Sent, or sent out.	Office Stamp.
£ s. d.	From _____	At _____ m.	
Charges to collect	By _____	To _____	
Service Instructions.		By _____	

Handed in at _____ Office _____ m. Received _____ m.

TO _____ GOC Bde _____

*Sender's Number	Day of Month	In reply to Number	A A A
NC145	28th		

Reference ... Hellers ... 00176
Please ... ...
... ...
NOT to 10
... ...

Ack 18th D 23 ... 28/12/17

FROM
PLACE & TIME: 29 Div 10:30 am

* This line should be erased if not required.
(6334). Wt. W7496/M857. 500,000 Pads. 10/16. D. D. & L. (E 489). Forms C/2123/3

SECRET.

29TH DIVISION OPERATION ORDER NO. 176.

Copy No. 9

Reference Maps :- CALAIS)
ABBEVILLE)
HAZEBROUCK) 1/100,000
LENS)

December 27th 1917.

1. The 87th Infantry Brigade (less M.G. Company and T.M. Battery) and the 455th (West Riding) Field Company R.E., will proceed by road to XIX Corps area for work under the XIX Corps on December 30th 1917.

2. Movements will take place in accordance with the table overleaf.

3. XIX Corps will administer the 87th Brigade & 455th (West Riding) Field Company R.E. from 1st January 1918 inclusive.

4. Arrival in the RENESCURE area to be reported direct to XIX Corps.

5. 87th T.M. Battery will move to ROLLEZ on December 30th 1917, and occupy billets vacated by 1st R. Inniskilling Fusiliers.

6. 87th Machine Gun Company and T.M. Battery will be administered by 86th Brigade from December 30th inclusive.

7. ACKNOWLEDGE.

Issued at 7.10 p.m

Hugh. O. Holmes
Major HFA
for Lieut-Colonel, GS
29th Division.

```
Copies -   1 -  4    Gen. Staff.
                5    Q
                6    CRA
                7    CRE
           8 -  9    86th Bde.
          10 - 11    87th Bde.
          12 - 13    88th Bde.
               14    Sigs.
               15    Mons. R.
               16    ADMS
               17    APM.
               18    DADOS.
               19    DADVS
               20    SAA Sec. DAC
               21    C Commdt.
               22    Div. Train.
               23    SSO
               24    29 Div. S.C.
               25    Area Commdt. THIEMBRONNE.
               26    Area Commdt. RENESCURE.
```

MARCH TABLE ISSUED WITH 29th DIVISION ORDER No. 178.
==

Copy of MARCH TABLE issued with X Corps O.O. 154.

Serial No.	Date.	UNIT.	From.	To.	Route.	Billets from	Remarks.
1.	30 DEC. 1917.	87th Inf.Bde. (less M.G.Coy. & T.M.Bty.) 455th W.Riding Fd.Coy. R.E.	FRUGES Area. (CREQUY) Sub-area.	THIEMBRONNE Area. (ELNES Sub-Area).	All roads available.	Area Commandant. THIEBRONNE.	To be clear of billets by 10a.m.
2.	31 DEC. 1917.	ditto.	THIES-BRONNE Area. (ELNES Sub-Area).	RENESCURE Area.	WIZERNES ARQUES.	Area Commandant. RENESCURE.	To be clear of Billets by 10 a.m.
3.	1 JAN. 1918.	ditto.	RENESCURE Area.	XIN Corps Area.			Orders for this move will be issued by XIX Corps direct.

29th Division No. C.G.S. 67/105.

SECRET

ADDENDUM No.1 to 29th DIVISION
ORDER No.176.

---

1. The 87th Field Ambulance will N O T accompany the 87th Infantry Brigade to XIX Corps. They will remain at PREHEDRE and be administered by 83th Infantry Brigade.

2. ACKNOWLEDGE.

28th December 1917.

C Ambrose Capt.
for Lieut.Colonel, G.S.
29th Division.

To all recipients of Order No.176.

29th Div. No. C.G.S. 87/99

SECRET

29th DIVISION WARNING ORDER

12th December 1917.

1. (a) The 29th Division (less Artillery) will be prepared to move to the FRUGES area (XIth Corps) by march route commencing on the 16th instant.

   (b) The move will be completed on the 20th instant.

2. The move will be carried out in three marches by Brigade Groups, the 86th Bde. Group moving on the 16th, the 87th Bde. Group on the 17th, and the 88th Bde. Group on the 18th instant.

3. Each Brigade Groupe will billet for one night in the area about BOUBERS SUR CANCHE and for one night in an area south of HESDIN.

4. Lorries will be provided to carry

   (a) Blankets

   (b) Packs of Infantry and other dismounted personnel.

5. Headquarters of Brigades in the FRUGES area will be as under:-

   86th Infantry Brigade   VERCHOCQ
   87th Infantry Brigade   CREQUY
   88th Infantry Brigade   TORCY

6. Divisional Headquarters will move on the 17th instant with 87th Bde. Group and will be established HUCQUELIERS in the FRUGES area.

7. Acknowledge.

Ack. to......
20/0/12

Issued at 9.0 p.m.

J.H. Mone
Lieut-Colonel, G.S.
29th Division.

Copies 1 - 4 G.S.
      5   5 "Q"
           6 C.R.E
           7 86th Inf. Bde.
           8 87th Inf. Bde.
           9 88th Inf. Bde
          10 Off. i/c Sigs.
          18. S.S.O.
          20. IV Corps

11. 1/2 Monmouths
12. A.D.M.S.
13. C.M.G.O.
14. 227th M.G. Coy.
15. D.A.D.O.S.
16. D.A.D.V.S.
17. Div. Train.
19. A.P.M.

SECRET.

29th Division No. C.G.S. 67/106

29TH DIVISION WARNING ORDER.

1.   The 29th Division, less 87th Infantry Brigade and Divisional Artillery, will be prepared to move to the TILQUES Area on 3rd January, move to be completed by the 4th January.

2.   Detailed orders will follow.

3.   87th Infantry Brigade and Divisional Artillery will move as already ordered.

4.   ACKNOWLEDGE.

Ack BM 1D 29
of 29-12-17.

W E Shamus

December 29th 1917.

Lieut-Colonel, G.S.,
29th Division.

```
Copies to :-    1 - 4    Gen. Staff.
                  5      Q
                  6      CRA
                  7      CRE
                8 - 9    86th Bde.
               10 - 11   87th Bde.
               12 - 13   88th Bde.
                 14      Sigs.
                 15      Mons.
                 16      ADMS.
                 17      APM.
                 18      DMGO.
                 19      227th M.G. Co.
                 20      X Corps.
                 21      DADOS.
                 22      DADVS.
                 23      SAA Sec. DAC.
                 24      C. Commdt.
                 25      Div. Train.
                 26      SSO.
                 27      29th Div. S.C.
                 28      Area Commdt. FRUGES.
                 29      Area Commdt. TILQUES.
```

APPENDICES.

Appendix "A" comprises:-

l.	29th Div. No. C.G.S. 51/134	Move from SOREL LE GRAND.
ll.	29th Div. No. C.G.S. 56/30.	Conference at D.H.Q.
lll.	29th Div. Order No. 172.	Move from LE CAUROY area.
lV.	29th Div. No. C.G.S. 56/31	Conference at D.H.Q.
V.	29th Div. Order No. 174.	Move of D.A. to FRUGES area.
Vl.	29th Div. Order No. 175.	Move of D.A. to THIEMBRONNE area
Vll.	29th Div. Order No. 176.	Move of 87th Bde to RENESCURE area.

Vlll. Summary of Operations 30th November to 4th December.

Appendix "B" comprises:-

1.	29th Div No I.G. 93/181.	Locations for 8th December.
2.	29th Div No I.G. 93/189.	Amendment to locations.

APPENDIX A

Operation Orders
&
Moves.

Summary of Messages
for Operations 30th Nov - 4th Dec

SECRET.

29th DIVISION ADMINISTRATIVE ORDER No. 22.

1. The 29th Division, less Royal Artillery and 1/2nd Monmouth Regt, will move to LE CAUROY area, by road and rail on 5.12.17 in accordance with attached Table "A".

2. Transport less that portion moving by rail (see attached Table "B") will move by march route under O.C., Divisional Train.
   All Transport not moving by rail will assemble at a time and place to be selected by O.C., Divisional Train, and march under his orders as follows:-

   1st Stage............... BAPAUME.
   2nd Stage .... COUTURELLE (9 miles East of DOULLENS)

   From COUTURELLE Transport will march to Units Billets in new area. Instructions will be sent to O.C., Divisional Train at COUTURELLE on the 6th instant as to billets.
   S.A.A. Section will accompany this Transport.

3. Time table of Transport moving by rail is laid down in attached Table "A".

4. (a) Blankets, greatcoats and camp kettles are to be collected into dumps by Brigades as follows:-

   86th Brigade ..... FINS
   87th Brigade ..... SOREL
   88th Brigade...... as detailed in . (b)

   (b) Blankets of 88th Brigade, now on Transport, must be dumped at old 88th Brigade Store, SOREL, to be picked up there (with those now in the store) by lorries detailed below in para. (c).

   (c) Eleven lorries will report at Divisional Headquarters, SOREL, at 5 a.m. on the 5th instant to move these blankets etc. to entraining station for loading on to railway train. If necessary lorries must do a double journey. Brigades

   LOT
   87 Bde 4
   86 - 4
   88 - 3

   (d) will send guides to meet their Lorries at Divisional Headquarters at 5 a.m.
   (e) Six lorries will be provided at detraining station for each Brigade. These must do double journeys if necessary.

5. (a) Rations for consumption on the 5th are being delivered to Transport lines, A.13.b., for 86th and 87th Brigades and to ETRICOURT Station at 9.a.m. for 88th Bde.
   (b) Rations for consumption on the 6th are being delivered to ETRICOURT (entraining Station) by Divisional Train on the morning of the 5th instant. Units must arrange for a representative to take them over at 9 a.m. to report to R.T.O. Office.ETRICOURT.
   (c) Rations for consumption on the 7th instant will be delivered in new area by Divisional Supply Column.
   (d) Two days forage for horses and rations for personnel of transport moving by rail will be delivered at BAPAUME Station at 12.00 on the 5th instant. Brigade Transport Officers must arrange for a representative to ride on ahead and take it over.
   (e) Forage and rations of Transport moving by road will be delivered by Divisional Train en route.
   (f) All transport and horses not detailed to proceed by rail in Table B must proceed by road under O.C., Divisional Train.

P.T.O.

6. Headquarter Company Divisional Train will be located at 29th Divisional Ammunition Column Lines, V.3.c., (EPEHICOURT) and will proceed there under orders of O.C., Divisional Train on morning of the 5th instant. Supply Vehicles for Pioneers must be attached to this Company.

7. Instructions as to Units' Billets will be given at detraining station.

8. Divisional Headquarters will be at LE CAUROY.

R.B. Campbell.
Lieut. Colonel,
A.A. & Q.M.G., 29th Division.

4th November 1917.

86th Brigade	10	Signals	1
87th Brigade	10	227 M.G.Co.	1
88th Brigade	10	III Corps	1
C.R.E.	4	IV Corps	1
C.R.A.	1		
A.D.M.S.	4		
D.A.D.V.S.	1		
Supply Col.	1		
D.A.D.O.S.	1		
A.P.M.	1		
Div. Train	5		
S.S.O.	1		
1/2nd Mons.	1		
G.S.	2		
Camp Cmdt.	1		
Employt. Co.	1		
S.A.A. Section	1		

Tabl-A.

ENTRAINING TABLE.

Formation.	Billets from.	Entraining station on 5-12-17.	Time of entrainment to commence.	Detraining Station.	
86th Infy. Bde. Personnel.	FINS.	ETRICOURT	14-30	PETIT HOUVIN	
86th Bde. Transport.	W.13.b.	BAPAUME	15-00	do	
87th Infy. Bde. Personnel.	SOREL	ETRICOURT	11-30	MONDICOURT	
87th Bde. Transport.	W.13.b.	BAPAUME	13-00	do	
88th Bde. Personnel. *	ETRICOURT	ETRICOURT	17-30	do	* Personnel move by Decauville from TRESCAULT to vicinity of YTRES thence by road to Camp at ETRICOURT.
88th Bde. Transport.	W.13.b.	BAPAUME	17-00	do	

A.D.M.S. will arrange for personnel of Field Ambulances moving by rail to arrive at Entraining Station in time to entrain with respective groups. One train capable of holding Brigades will arrange for personnel of Field Companies to move with Brigades. 2000 men is allotted to each brigade Group. Divisional headquarters Personnel will proceed with 87th Brigade Train.

P.T.O.

Table B.

TRANSPORT TO PROCEED BY RAIL.

1. Each Brigade Group

1 Water Cart per Battalion.	4 axles.	
4 Kitchens " "	32 "	Note. This is
1 Mess Cart " "	4 "	to include T.M.
1 Maltese Cart " "	4 "	Coys, but ex-
2 Limbers (less 1 limber)		cludes Fd.
of 1 Battalion.)	14 "	Ambs. All
Bde. Headquarters		Horse Trans-
1 Limber	2 "	port of Fd.
M.G.Coy.		Ambs is to
1 Cook's Cart	1 "	proceed by
1 Water Cart	1 "	road
2 Limbers	4 "	
Field Co.		
1 Limber	2 "	

    68 axles only.

2. Divisional Headquarters will send 1 G.S. Limber with the 87th Brigade Group. This will necessitate only 1 G.S. Limber being sent by 1 Battalion of 87th Brigade.

3. In case of Units not having 4 cookers, 1 G.S. Limber can be substituted for 1 Kitchen.

4. A loading party of 50 from each Brigade has been sent to BAPAUME. This party will also unload Transport at detraining Station.

5. Times for entrainment to commence are notified in Table A.
    Brigades are to arrange for respective Groups of Transport to march to BAPAUME via EQUANCOURT - ROCQUIGNY LE TRANSLOY in time to reach BAPAUME to commence loading at the time ordered. The Senior Transport Officer of each Brigade to command the party.

6. The above allotment by rail may be altered by Brigades provided the number of 68 axles is not exceeded.

7. Riding Horses will be taken by rail as follows:-

Divnl. Headquarters.	30 on 87th Bde. Transport Train.
	30 on 88th Bde. Transport Train.
Each Bde. Headquarters	7
Each Field Co.	7
Each M.G.Coy.	7
227 M.G.Coy.	8
Each Battalion	11

8. The C.R.E. and Camp Commandant will ensure the Transport and Riding Horses detailed to move by rail to arrive at BAPAUME in time to entrain with respective Groups. Each party to march under an Officer.

9. The Remainder of the Riding Horses will move by road with respective Brigade Groups. C.R.E., A.D.M.S., and Camp Commandant will arrange direct with O.C. Divisional Train as to time and place of rendezvous for transport moving by road.

29th Div. No. C.G.S.56/30.

29th Divisional Conference held at LE CAUROY on December 8th, Brigadiers and Commanding Officers attending.
-.-

1. Leave allotment.

2. Period available for rest and training.

3. Training. 1st Phase - December 10th to 15th.
        (a) Rigid Ceremonial Drill.
        (b) Short hours.
        (c) Dismiss Platoons and Companies when efficient.
        (d) Dress and personal smartness and saluting.
        (e) Marching.
    2nd Phase - December 16th to 18th.
        Strict March discipline.
        Punctuality. Billeting.
        Outpost Schemes.
    3rd Phase - December 20th to 27th.
    Company Training. All Companies to be inspected
    in   (a) Simple Company Drill.
        (b) Attack under a Barrage.
        (c) Attack in open with covering fire.
        (d) Counter-attack.
    4th Phase - December 28th
    Battalion and Brigade Training. Battalions will be inspected by Brigadiers in similar exercises, and Brigades by G.O.C. Division.

4. Battalion Conferences daily.
Brigade Conferences twice a week. Lectures.

5. Daily Inspection of Billets. Fire orders.

6. Training of specialists. Musketry and bombing.
All officers to know how to use all Company weapons.
Practice with enemy weapons.

29th Div. No. C.G.S. 87/92

29th DIVISION WARNING ORDER

SECRET

12th December 1917.

1. (a) The 29th Division (less Artillery) will be prepared to move to the FRUGES area (Xth Corps) by march route commencing on the 16th instant.

   (b) The move will be completed on the 20th instant.

2. The move will be carried out in three marches by Brigade Groups, the 86th Bde. Group moving on the 16th, the 87th Bde. Group on the 17th, and the 88th Bde. Group on the 18th instant.

3. Each Brigade Groupe will billet for one night in the area about BOUBERS SUR CANCHE and for one night in an area south of HESDIN.

4. Lorries will be provided to carry

   (a) Blankets

   (b) Packs of Infantry and other dismounted personnel.

5. Headquarters of Brigades in the FRUGES area will be as under:-

   86th Infantry Brigade   VERCHOCQ
   87th Infantry Brigade   CREQUY
   88th Infantry Brigade   TORCY

6. Divisional Headquarters will move on the 17th instant with 87th Bde. Group and will be established HUCQUELIERS in the FRUGES area.

7. Acknowledge.

Issued at 9.0 p.m.

Lieut-Colonel, G.S.
29th Division.

Copies 1 - 4 G.S.
       5   5 "Q"
            6 C.R.E
            7 86th Inf. Bde.
            8 87th Inf. Bde.
            9 88th Inf. Bde.
           10 Off. i/c Sigs.
           18. S.S.O.
           20. 1V Corps

11. 1/2 Monmouths
12. A.D.M.S.
13. D.M.G.O.
14. 227th M.G. Coy.
15. D.A.D.O.S.
16. D.A.D.V.S.
17. Div. Train.
19. A.P.M.

Appx 3

29th DIVISION ORDER No. 172.   Copy No IV

14th December 1917.

Reference Maps:- LENS.
CALAIS.
HAZEBROUCK 5A.   } 1/100000.
ABBEVILLE.

SECRET

1. The 29th Division (less Artillery) is to be transferred from IVth Corps to Xth Corps (Second Army) commencing on the 16th instant, and is to be accommodated in the FRUGES area.

2. (a) The transfer will be carried out by march route in accordance with march table attached.

   (b) A map of the FRUGES area showing allotment of sub areas to Brigade Groups and accommodation tables for FRUGES and HESDIN areas are being issued to all concerned.

3. Lorries will be provided under arrangements to be made by the A.A. & Q.M.G. to carry:-
   (a) Blankets
   (b) Packs of Infantry and other dismounted personnel.

4. The Divisional Supply Column will move by road as required.

5. Distances of 200 yards will be maintained between Battalions on the line of march.

6. Divisional H.Q. will close at LE CAUROY at 12 noon on the 18th instant and will re-open at HUCQUELIERS at the same hour.

7. Acknowledge.

Issued at 11 hrs.

Lieut-Colonel, G.S.,
29th Division.

Copies 1 - 4   Gen. Staff   22. DADOS
            5   Q   23. DADVS
            6   CRA   24. SAA Sect. DAC
            7   CRE   25. C.Comdt.
        8 - 9   86th Bde   26. Div. Train.
       10 - 11 87th Bde   27. SSO
       12 - 13 88th Bde   28. 29th Div. Supply Col.
           14   Sigs   29. Sub area Comdt. VERCHOCQ
           15   Mons F.   30.   "   "   "   CREQUY
           16   ADMS   31.   "   "   "   ROYON
           17   APM   32.   "   "   "   BOUBERS
           18   DAGO   SUR CANCHE
           19   227 Div. M.G. Coy.   33. G.O.C. L of C area.
           20   IVth Corps   34. Comdt. G.H.Q. Troops.
           21   Xth Corps

29th Div. No. C.G.S. 56/31

appen 4

29th Divisional Conference held at HUCQUELIERS on December 24th at 11 a.m. Brigadiers and Commanding Officers attending.

TRAINING 24th – 31st.

(1) Ceremonial parade will be held by each brigade for presentation of decorations. The whole brigade group. March past. Brigade massed bands. Advance in review order. Form 3 sides of a square. Presentation of medals. Each band playing its Battalion past.

(2) Company Drill. Brigadiers will inspect at least one Company in each Battalion at an hour and place which will be notified to Divisional Headquarters.

(3) Reference 29th Division No. C.G.S. 56/30 Para. 3, 3rd Phase Demonstrations must be carried out in Battalions in all the following operations.

   (b) Attack under barrage.
Each battalion must have ground marked out and flagged for one company to carry out a trench to trench attack. Only one objective is necessary.
The same party of signallers under the battalion Intelligence Officer should represent the barrage and be at the disposal of any company using the area for this purpose. The advance must be practised from our trenches both through gaps in wire and across the open where no wire exists. The preliminary forming up must be practised as though the company had moved up in file along a C.T. to the "jumping off trench", and also forming up in open on Taped line. As company Training, this must be purely a drill. The line being held up by strong points will be held over until battalion training starts. The jumping off trench should be flagged out and should be at least 150 yards short of objective. There should be enough ground beyond objective to send out covering parties and patrols to cover consolidation.

   (c) Attack in the open with covering fire
A position should be selected as the objective of the attack of the company. The position should be manned by a dummy enemy consisting of four groups of three men each with flags, the flags of each group being of a different colour. A few single men should be put out in front to represent snipers each with a flag, and the flag waved to represent a shot. The company will move off in artillery formation, each platoon commander having an orderly with him carrying 4 flags (one of each colour used by the dummy enemy). A single flag shown by the enemy represents sniping, two shown by same group indicate desultory fire, all three flags shown by same group indicate heavy fire and necessitates covering fire to allow further advance. Each platoon as it opens covering fire will raise the flag of the same colour as the group it is firing on. As soon as two flags of the same colour are shown by the attacking infantry that group will lower its flags and the platoon or section immediately in front can advance, but immediately only one flag or none of that colour is visible in the attacking line the group will again commence to wave its flags.

   (d) Counter attack.
This exercise can best be carried out by a battalion. Arrange a dummy enemy in groups of three men, each group representing a half company, the men will carry flags. Place the company or battalion in position in a captured objective. Start an attack against one company with three flags. Every available weapon should at once be turned on to this attack. The support platoon will move forward at once up to the firing line to meet the attack. O.C. this platoon will send

back to Battalion Headquarters reporting its action, when it will be replaced in support by a portion of the battalion reserve. As soon as the line has been re-established the company must be reorganized and either the counter attacking platoon or the remnants of another one sent back into support again, relieving that portion of the battalion reserve which has been sent up. Later launch another attack with more than three flags, so that the whole of battalion reserves are employed.

(e) *Attack on strong point*
Mark out short length of trench or pillbox to represent the strong point. Place an intelligent N.C.O. in the strong point with a drummer or a man with a can full of stones to represent a machine gun. Place flags out in front to mark zone of fire of the machine gun, through which troops cannot pass. The company advances until it comes under fire from this point. Lewis guns and bombers then work round the flank while covering fire is kept up on strong point with rifle grenades, trench mortars and rifles.
All movements to be carried out by prearranged code of signals. When strong point is captured, company must at once be reorganized for further advance, and arrangements made to convert the position.

NOTES:

(1) Each Battalion must detail a company to give a demonstration to the battalion in each of (b), (c) & (e).

(2) In every case drums or tins containing stones must be used to represent hostile fire as well as flags.

ANTI - GAS MEASURES.

SYLLABUS OF TRAINING FOR ONE HOUR TWICE EACH WEEK.

1st quarter of an hour to be spent in a careful examination of Box Respirators and P.H. Helmets.

2nd quarter of an hour should comprise the practices A,B,C,D, E,F,G, as laid down in "DEFENSIVE MEASURES AGAINST GAS" (SS.334)

The remaining half hour to be employed in carrying out all Infantry Training if possible under the various Battalion Specialists.

Stretcher bearers should be frequently practiced in their work.

All Regimentally employed men, including Officers Servants, should attend at least one parade each week.

(sgd) L.Spere, Lt. R.E.,
29th Div. Gas Officer.

War Diary   CONFIDENTIAL

29th DIVISION ORDER No. 174.

Appx 5

Reference Maps:—   LENS   )
                        CALAIS   )   1/100,000
                        HAZEBROUCK)
                        ABBEVILLE   )

December 20th 1917.

1.   29th Divisional Artillery accompanied by the Ammunition sub-park will rejoin 29th Division in the FRUGES Area on the 23rd December.

2.   29th Divisional Artillery accompanied by the Ammunition sub-park will march from PREVENT Area via HESDIN into BEAURAINVILLE sub-area on 23-rd December.
No restriction as to time of march.
The following distances will be maintained :—
Between
          Batteries .... 100 yards.
          Sections of D.A.C......... 100 yards.
          Brigades .... 500 yards.

3.   A map of the FRUGES Area showing BEAURAINVILLE sub-area is being issued to all concerned.

4.   Railhead from 24th instant inclusive will be HESDIN.

5.   ACKNOWLEDGE.

                                       Hugh O. Holmes
                                       Major R.F.A
                            for Lieut-Colonel, G.S.,
                               29th Division.

Cop-ies to:—   CRA
                   Q
                   X Corps.e

SECRET.

29th DIVISION OPERATION ORDER No. 175.

Copy No. 4

27th December 191_

Reference Maps :- CALAIS.)
ABBEVILLE.) 1/100,000
HAZEBROUCK.)
LENS.)

1. The 29th Divisional Artillery will move from the FRUGES Area (BEAURAINVILLE sub-area) to the THIEMBRONNE Area (Divisional Artillery sub-area) on the 4th January 1918, and will be held in G.H.Q. Reserve.

2. Detailed orders on the subject of troops which are held in G.H.Q. Reserve will be issued later.

3. The move will be completed in one day; all roads will be available. No restrictions as to time of march.

4. Map showing THIEMBRONNE Area (Divisional sub-area) is attached hereto. Billets will be obtained from area Commandant, THIEMBRONNE.

5. Completion of the move to be reported to this office.

6. Attention is drawn to Second Army No. 138/G copy of which is attached (C.R.A. only).

7. ACKNOWLEDGE.

Hugh O. Holmes
Major R.F.A.
/r Lieut-Colonel, GS.
29th Division.

Issued at 6.30 p.m.

```
Copies -    1 -  4    Gen. Staff.
                 5    Q.
                 6    CRA.
                 7    CRE.
            8 -  9    86th Bde.
           10 - 11    87th Bde.
           12 - 13    88th Bde.
                14    Sigs.
                15    Mons.
                16    ADMS.
                17    APM.
                18    DADOS
                19    DADVS
                20    3rd Sec. D.A.C.
                21    Camp Commdt.
                22    Div. Train.
                23    SSO.
                24    29 Div. S.C.
                25    Area Commdt. THIEMBRONNE.
```

Appen 7

SECRET.

29TH DIVISION OPERATION ORDER NO. 176.

Copy No. 4

Reference Maps :- CALAIS)
ABBEVILLE)
HAZEBROUCK) 1/100,000
LENS)

December 27th 1917.

1. The 87th Infantry Brigade (less M.G. Company and T.M. Battery) and the 455th (West Riding) Field Company R.E., will proceed by road to XIX Corps area for work under the XIX Corps on December 30th 1917.

2. Movements will take place in accordance with the table overleaf.

3. XIX Corps will administer the 87th Brigade & 455th (West Riding) Field Company R.E. from 1st January 1918 inclusive.

4. Arrival in the RENESCURE area to be reported direct to XIX Corps.

5. 87th T. M. Battery will move to ROLLEZ on December 30th 1917, and occupy billets vacated by 1st R. Inniskilling Fusiliers.

6. 87th Machine Gun Company and T.M. Battery will be administered by 86th Brigade from December 30th inclusive.

7. ACKNOWLEDGE.

Issued at 7.10 p.m

Hugh. O. Holmes
Major HFA
for Lieut-Colonel, GS.
29th Division.

Copies - 1 - 4 Gen. Staff.
5 Q
6 CRA
7 CRE
8 - 9 86th Bde.
10 - 11 87th Bde.
12 - 13 88th Bde.
14 Sigs.
15 Mons, R.
16 ADMS
17 APM.
18 DADOS.
19 DADVS
20 SAA Sec. DAC
21 C Commdt.
22 Div. Train.
23 SSO.
24 29 Div. S.C.
25 Area Commdt. THIEMBRONNE.
26 Area Commdt, RENESCURE.

move postponed one hour

MARCH TABLE ISSUED WITH 29th DIVISION ORDER No. 176.
===

Copy of MARCH TABLE issued with X Corps O.O. 154.

Serial No.	Date.	UNIT.	From.	To.	Route.	Billets from	Remarks.
1.	30 DEC. 1917.	87th Inf.Bde. (less .G.Coy. & T.M.Bty.) 455th W.Riding Fd.Coy. R.E.	FRUGES Area. (CREQUY) Sub-area.	THIEMBRONNE Area. (ELNES Sub-Area).	All roads available.	Area Commandant. THIEBRONNE.	To be clear of billets by 10 a.m.
2.	31 DEC. 1917.	ditto.	THIEM-BRONNE Area. (ELNES Sub-Area).	RENESCURE Area.	WIZERNES ARQUES.	Area Commandant. RENESCURE.	To be clear of billets by 10 a.m. Not to start before 10 a.m.
3.	1 JAN. 1918.	ditto.	RENESCURE Area.	XIX Corps Area.			Orders for this move will be issued by XIX Corps direct.

29th Division No. C.G.S. 67/105.

SECRET

ADDENDUM No.1 to 29th DIVISION
ORDER No.176.

----

1. The 87th Field Ambulance will N O T accompany the 87th Infantry Brigade to XIX Corps. They will remain at PREHEDRE and be administered by 86th Infantry Brigade.

2. ACKNOWLEDGE.

28th December 1917.

Lieut.Colonel, G.S.
29th Division.

To all recipients of Order No.176.

Army Form C. 2118.

WAR DIARY
of
INTELLIGENCE SUMMARY.
(Erase heading not required)

Instructions regarding War Diaries and Intelligence Summaries are contained in F.S. Regs., Part II. and the Staff Manual respectively. Title pages will be prepared in manuscript.

NOVEMBER 30th, 1917.

Place	Date	Hour	Summary of Events and Information	Remarks and references to Appendices
S. end of GOUZEAUCOURT		5.12 am.	To III Corps. Situation generally quiet. Slight hostile shelling during the night.	
		9.10am.	To III Corps. Troops South of BONAVIS are retiring before German attack. Advanced German patrols have reached as far West as ST. QUENTIN MILL. which I have evacuated. All communications to front and rear cut. Have sent up to my Division my mounted Staff Officer to do all they can. Formed bodies of troops urgently needed as nothing bu working parties in vicinity.	
		9.40 am.	To III Corps. Enemy now hold Railway East of GOUZEAUCOURT and advancing up the village very cautiously. Am moving my Headquarters to high ground half a mile West of the village.	
		10.10am.	To III Corps. The enemy appear to be checked at GOUZEAUCOURT which is now being held by one Company of R.E. 59th Division which I stopped for the purpose. Enemy holding ridge East of GOUZEAUCOURT with advanced parties in QUENTIN MILL and working up towards the village. I have sent my A.D.C. to give 6th, 20th and 59th Divisions the situation and my G.S.O.I to MARCOING to do what he can to protect my right flank. A Division attacking from the North is recommended.	
		10.20am.	To III Corps. Enemy have cut road S.W. of GOUZEAUCOURT, moving my Headquarters towards RIBECOURT to see what can be done as I can do nothing here.	
		10.45am.	To III Corps. GOUZEAUCOURT captured by enemy from the South at 10.15 am. If troops can attack enemy from direction of RIBECOURT from indications they would succeed as enemy seems in small strength and much strung out. I am on my way to 6th Division H.Q. and have stopped at this Signal Station to send this message.	
6th Division H.Q. VILLERS PLOUICH		11.45am.	To III Corps. Have reached 6th Division H.Q. and find situation there is good. Wounded officer reports my right flank turned and enemy approaching MASNIERES. I am moving across country on foot to organise organise best defence possible under circumstances.	
			From 86th Brigade timed 12.25 p.m. Situation still in hand. We hold all our line and have defensive flank on outskirts of LES RUES VERTES. In touch with 87th Brigade and hold bridgeheads all along Canal.	

(A7092) Wt. W12359/M1933. 75,30 0. 11/17. D.D. & L., Ltd. Forms/C.2118/14.

Army Form C. 2118.

WAR DIARY
or
INTELLIGENCE SUMMARY
(Erase heading not required.)

Place	Date	Hour	Summary of Events and Information	Remarks and references to Appendices
			From III Corps Commander. Well done hang on at all costs - timed 11.55 a.m. - received 12.40pm.	
			From III Corps. Timed 11.25 a.m. Received 4 p.m. Giving situation. Guards Division ordered to capture ridge from GONNLIEU to GOUCHE WOOD. 2nd Cavalry Division are moving on REVELON Ridge and Cavalry Corps are moving two Divisions towards VAUCELLETTE Farm from direction of VILLERS FAUCON.	
			From III Corps. Timed 11.35 a.m. Received 4 p.m. If you are forced to withdraw your troops from MASNIERES do so via MARCOING. Hold WELSH Ridge (R.4 and R.9) in order to cover the withdrawal along the COUILLET Valley. You must hold on to WELSH Ridge at all costs and if forced back you must retire on HIGHLAND Ridge.	
			From 86th Brigade. Received 12.32 p.m. 88th Brigade driving enemy back. They are retiring through G.31 and 32. My line intact.	
			From 86th Brigade. Received 12.35 p.m. Holding out. Enemy in great strength attacking us from G.31 and G.32. They are in South end of LES RUES VERTES. Have stopped three attacks from along the CAMBRAI Road. Any orders ?	
			From 86th Brigade. Received 12.38 p.m. We are in touch with 87th at G.19.d.Central. Enemy appear to be running away from MARCOING towards G.32. Our line intact.	
			From 86th Brigade. Received 1 p.m. Still hold all bridgeheads and in touch with 87th. We hold all LES RUES VERTES. Patrol has been through copse in G.25.a. and reports no enemy within 200 yards of copse.	
			From 86th Brigade. Received 1.23 p.m. LES RUES VERTES clear of enemy. Our line intact. Enemy appears to be retiring on CREVECOURT.	
			From 86th Brigade. Received 1.30 p.m. Enemy massing about G.33.Central and again advancing.	
			From 86th Brigade. Received 1.14 p.m. Position intact. Large number of enemy behind camouflage about Cross Roads G.32.b.0.8.	

Army Form C. 2118.

WAR DIARY
or
INTELLIGENCE SUMMARY
(Erase heading not required.)

Instructions regarding War Diaries and Intelligence Summaries are contained in F. S. Regs., Part II. and the Staff Manual respectively. Title pages will be prepared in manuscript.

Place	Date	Hour	Summary of Events and Information	Remarks and references to Appendices
		From 86th Brigade.	Received 1.29 p.m. Enemy massed Cavalry in M.3 and M.9.	
		From 86th Brigade.	Received 1.57 p.m. Enemy in position close in front of artillery in R.11.a. Enemy running hard from West to East about R.12.	
		To III Corps.	Timed 2.15 p.m. G.O.C. just returned from MARCOING. Situation appears that enemy attacked LES RUES VERTES from South-East and gained footing in that place. Left Brigade line at 12.30 p.m. was intact and in touch with Right Brigade in MASNIERES who it is thought hold original line with exception of MONT PLAISIR FARM. Reserve Brigade now holding a line from LES RUES VERTES to VILLERS PLOUICH and has orders to clear LES RUES VERTES of the enemy.	
		To III Corps.	Timed 2.50 p.m. Have just returned from MARCOING and find everything satisfactory. Heavy attack from the North beaten off. Enemy entered LES RUES VERTES from the South-East and my Reserve Brigade is now counter-attacking and has reached the line G.31.c. - L.36.c. - R.5.b. My line East of Canal intact except for post at MONT PLAISIR FARM. Suggest one Brigade 6th Division be sent to R.4. to connect my right with 20th Division. Have ordered 29th Division to give no ground.	
		From 86th Brigade.	Received 2.31 p.m. Enemy infantry again advancing about R.12.	
		From 86th Brigade.	Received 2.44 p.m. Enemy guns and cavalry have retired over N.7. to East. All well here.	
		From 86th Brigade.	Received 2.50 p.m. Enemy artillery moving from LATTEAU WOOD from North and East. Enemy infantry entering LATTEAU WOOD from North and East.	
		From III Corps.	To 86th Brigade. Untimed. Withdraw Brigade through MARCOING on to Ridge at R.4. and R.9. This message was cancelled by telephone from III Corps at 2.40 p.m.	
		From III Corps.Commander.	Recd. Timed 4 p.m. Please congratulate Gen. CHEAPE and troops under him on their splendid defence of MASNIERES. Also convey to the 87th and 88th Brigades my appreciation of their fine work today.	

Army Form C. 2118.

WAR DIARY
or
INTELLIGENCE SUMMARY.
(Erase heading not required.)

Place	Date	Hour	Summary of Events and Information	Remarks and references to Appendices
			From G.S.O.I at 87th Brigade H.Q. Received 4.15 p.m. Situation 4 p.m. 87th Brigade hold original line. 86th Brigade hold original line and LES RUES VERTES also all Bridges over the Canal. 88th Brigade holding line approx. L.30.a. thence along Sunken Road through L.35.b. not yet known whether in touch with 20th Division on right. 88th Brigade have been ordered to advance and endeavour to consolidate the line of the Sunken Road through L.36. G.51.a. effecting a junction with the 86th Brigade at the Cross Roads G.26.c.1.3. Brigade Major 88th Brigade wounded slight. Send up S.A.A. reinforcements badly needed.	
			From Gen. LUCAS. Received 12 midnight. Situation MASNIERES and MARCOING unchanged.	
		To III Corps. Added to 3 Bdes. To 86th Bde. only.	Timed 6.10 p.m. I left GOUZEAUCOURT at 4.30 p.m. 1st Guards Brigade was holding Eastern fringe of the village and the enemy in apparent strength and well supplied with Machine Guns on QUENTIN Ridge. I saw enemy guns come into action 100 yards South of the GOUZEAUCOURT - VILLERS GUISLAIN Road where it cuts ridge. Attack by troops of 6th Division and three tanks still West of GOUZEAUCOURT when darkness fell. Squadron 5th Cavalry Division also West of village. My line intact at 4 p.m. and LES RUES VERTES in our hands. The attack will be continued tomorrow against GONNLIEU and VILLERS GUISLAIN. 29th Division to hold on. If 86th Brigade are forced out of MASNIERES they will fall back along Canal to MARCOING and will hold on to WELSH RIDGE at all costs but the operations tomorrow depend on your being able to hold your line.	
			From 86th Brigade. Received 6.20 p.m. Have beaten off another counter-attack on LES RUES VERTES. Situation otherwise unchanged. Heavy shelling from enemy guns at M.8.d.	
			From Gen. LUCAS. Timed 9.40 p.m. Situation remains the same. A fair defensive flank is being established from WELSH RIDGE to LES RUES VERTES by 88th Brigade with Kings Own Scottish Borderers attached. 2 Companies South Wales Borderers are filling in gap between 86th and 88th Brigades. CHEAPE says he doubts if he can hold on tomorrow without assistance but has been told to do so. NELSON's line is very much strung out. He has the 2/Hampshire Regiment in reserve but requires further help. I have now no reserve in hand. At least two battalions are required. One for CHEAPE and one for NELSON, to stand a fresh attack in force. CHEAPE cannot withdraw by day.	

Army Form C. 2118.

WAR DIARY
or
INTELLIGENCE SUMMARY.
(Erase heading not required.)

Instructions regarding War Diaries and Intelligence Summaries are contained in F. S. Regs., Part II. and the Staff Manual respectively. Title pages will be prepared in manuscript.

Place	Date	Hour	Summary of Events and Information	Remarks and references to Appendices
			From 86th Brigade. Received 10.50 p.m. Line intact. Heavy shelling from all sides. Have you any orders for me ?	
		10 p.m.	G.O.C. visited III Corps Headquarters.	
	DECEMBER 1st, 1917.			
			To III Corps. Timed 9.35 a.m. Very heavy enemy barrage on line GONNLIEU - LA VAQUERIE - WELSH RIDGE.	
			From G.S.O.I at H.Q. 87th Brigade. Timed 9.50 a.m. Situation 9.45 a.m. We hold same line as reported in my 9.40 p.m. despatch last night. Quiet night. 86th and ‡ 88th Brigades now in touch at LES RUES VERTES. 88th Brigade is in touch with 20th Division on their right. Between 7 a.m. and 7.45 a.m. enemy put down an intense barrage on MASNIERES and 86th Brigade has suffered heavy casualties from it. It is imperative that some reinforcements be sent as my last reserves have now been put in. If no reinforcements are forthcoming it may be necessary to evacuate MASNIERES. 9.45 a.m. Divisional Headquarters shelled out of VILLERS PLOUICH and moved to TRESCAULT.	
			To 87th Brigade. Timed 12.10 p.m. Corps Commander says well done and congratulates all troops on splendid defence. Definite orders will be sent you before dusk as to your future movements. Divisional Headquarters Town Major's Office TRESCAULT.	
			From 86th Brigade. Received 1.30 p.m. Attack on LES RUES VERTES at 7.45 a.m. was repulsed. Situation has quietened and our position seems more satisfactory.	
			From 86th Brigade. Timed 7.15 a.m. Received 1.30 p.m. Very heavy enemy barrage on whole village.	
			From 86th Brigade. Timed 10.20 a.m. Received 1.30 p.m. Enemy in numbers in quarry G.32.d.	

WAR DIARY
or
INTELLIGENCE SUMMARY.
(Erase heading not required.)

Army Form C. 2118.

Place	Date	Hour	Summary of Events and Information	Remarks and references to Appendices
			From 86th Brigade. Timed 11.15 a.m. Received 1.30 p.m. Our troops in LES RUES VERTES report being shelled by our own artillery.	
			From Gen. LUCAS. Timed 2.15 p.m. Received 2.15 p.m. 88th Brigade report Worcestershire Regiment has advanced about 200 yards and occupied enemy trenches in front of them.	
			From 86th Brigade. Timed 9.47 a.m. Received 2.30 p.m. Enemy guns in action at M.8.b.	
			From III Corps. Timed 9.55 a.m. Received 2.30 p.m. Reorganisation of Corps front. Extract :? 29th Division will continue to be responsible for their original sector and the portion of the line from LES RUES VERTES to R.5.a.Central.	
			From Gen. LUCAS. Timed 1 p.m. Received 2.45 p.m. Is there any hope of reinforcements being sent up tonight ? Otherwise 86th Brigade must evacuate MASNIERES. Reply urgent. (Repeated to III Corps 2.50 p.m.)	
			To Gen. LUCAS. Timed 3.25 p.m. I have seen the Army Commander who is most anxious to give up no ground. There is no hope of 86th Brigade being relieved tonight but will certainly be relieved tomorrow night. If you think and CHEAPE agrees that MASNIERES cannot be held you must withdraw 86th Brigade out of the line and throw back right flank of 87th to star cover Lock in 19.c. keeping the Eastern edge of gun pits in 20.a. and throw back the left of the 88th Brigade to connect with right flank of 87th Brigade. Report your action by wireless and inform artillery supporting you. In this case send 86th Brigade to RIBECOURT and hold on to above line at all costs with remainder of Division.	
			To 87th Brigade. Timed 3.30 p.m. Monmouth Pioneers will reach you tonight as a reserve.	
			From Gen. LUCAS. Timed 11.30 a.m. Received 3.30 p.m. 86th Brigade beat off another counter-attack at 7.30 this morning but had heavy casualties. Unless they are sent a fresh battalion tonight I doubt if they will maintain their position. I have used up the troops from the bridgehead line which is now empty. 88th Brigade plus Kings Own Scottish Borderers still have Hampshire Regiment in reserve. A second battalion is urgently required to hold bridgehead line with 2 companies and 2 companies in reserve. Cannot move Hampshire Regiment as they may / be	

Army Form C. 2118.

WAR DIARY

INTELLIGENCE SUMMARY.
(Erase heading not required.)

Instructions regarding War Diaries and Intelligence Summaries are contained in F. S. Regs., Part II. and the Staff Manual respectively. Title pages will be prepared in manuscript.

Place	Date	Hour	Summary of Events and Information	Remarks and references to Appendices
			be urgently required to protect our right rear.	
			To III Corps. Timed 4.35 p.m. Officer just returned from forward area reports :- 86th Brigade on right have beaten off eight attacks today.	
			From 86th Brigade. Received 4.51 p.m. Enemy in LES RUES VERTES but we hold all bridges as yet.	
			From 86th Brigade. Received 4.53 p.m. Situation critical.	
			From III Corps. Received 4.55 p.m. Instruct 86th Brigade under circumstances to withdraw to line West of MASNIERES in G.20.a. and c. and alter line of 88th Brigade accordingly. Convey Corps Commanders hearty congratulations to 86th Brigade on their fine performance.	
			To III Corps. With reference to above message timed 5 p.m. Instructions already issued but will only be carried out if absolutely necessary and both Brigadiers agreeing.	
			To 87th Brigade. In continuation of my message timed 3.25 p.m. this has Corps Commander's approval. Convey his heartiest congratulations to 36th Brigade on fine performance.	
			From Gen. LUCAS. Received 5.33 p.m. 88th Brigade report that we are being driven out of LES RUES VERTES.	
			To III Corps. Timed 7.15 p.m. Message just received from 87th Brigade. LES RUES VERTES retaken by 88th Brigade and 50 prisoners captured.	
	DECEMBER 2nd, 1917.			
			To III Corps. & Flank Divisions. Timed 7.50 a.m. After dark last night the 86th Brigade were withdrawn from the MASNIERES Salient into reserve. The line now runs 88th Brigade from about R.5.central along the Sunken Road in L.35.Central to L.30.Central - along the drain to Lock L.24.c. which is connecting point with 87th Brigade whose line runs along Canal to houses L.19.c. then North along Eastern	

(A7092. Wt. W12859/M1293. 75 y.o. 11/17. D. D. & L., Ltd. Forms/C.2118/14.

WAR DIARY
INTELLIGENCE SUMMARY.
(Erase heading not required.)

Army Form C. 2118.

Place	Date	Hour	Summary of Events and Information	Remarks and references to Appendices
			edge of gun pits in L.20.a. to our original front line. Enemy have persistently shelled MASNIERES all the morning and continue to do so unaware of our withdrawal.	
			To Gen. LUCAS. Timed 8.50 a.m. Following moves will take place after dark tonight December 2nd/3rd. 16th Brigade 6th Division will relieve 87th Brigade on that portion of the Divisional front North of the ST. QUENTIN Canal. The 36th Brigade will withdraw to area about TRESCAULT. 87th Brigade on relief will withdraw to Squares K.36., L.31, L.32. 88th Brigade will continue to hold their present line from the #5 ST. QUENTIN Canal to junction with Division on right about R.5.a. at present the 20th Division but tonight will be the 61st Division. G.O.C. 88th Brigade will remain in command of the Divisional front.	
			To III Corps. Timed 9.5 a.m. Enemy reported massing in MASNIERES. Please turn on all available heavies.	
			To III Corps. Timed 9.45 a.m. Enemy that was massing in MASNIERES attacked our line North of Canal about 8.30 a.m. He was successfully driven off. Please keep heavies on to MASNIERES.	
			From III Corps. Timed 10 a.m. All bridges over the ST. QUENTIN Canal will be prepared for demolition.	
			From III Corps. Timed 1.30 p.m. Giving details of reserve line to be consolidated. Extract :- 29th Division from R.7.b. to HINDENBURG SUPPORT in L.32.c.9.5.	
			From III Corps. Timed 4.15 p.m. Brigade of 29th Division holding the line from the Canal to the left of the 61st Division will be placed under the orders of the 6th Division on completion of the relief of the Brigades North of the ST. QUENTIN Canal by the 6th Division.	
			To 86th Brigade. Timed 3 p.m. You will be accommodated tonight in RIBECOURT.	
			From 6th Division. Instructions from Corps to take over the Battalion front South of the Canal were received too late to alter arrangements. This Battalion front will be taken over tomorrow night.	

Army Form C. 2118.

WAR DIARY
XX
INTELLIGENCE SUMMARY.
(Erase heading not required.)

Instructions regarding War Diaries and Intelligence Summaries are contained in F.S. Regs., Part II and the Staff Manual respectively. Title pages will be prepared in manuscript.

Place	Date	Hour	Summary of Events and Information	Remarks and references to Appendices
	DECEMBER 3rd, 1917.			
			To III Corps. Timed 3.30 a.m. Reference Order No. 228, para. 12, relief complete 1.30 a.m. of troops East of Canal. 87th Brigade still have two battalions in front line attached to 88th Brigade.	
		11 a.m.	86th Brigade obliged to vacate RIBECOURT owing to hostile shelling. Situation on front uncertain, but eventually Corps sanctioned the move of 88th Brigade to HAVRINCOURT WOOD.	
			From O.C. 17th Brigade R.F.A. Attack extends from MARCOING to South. Bombardment heavy. First wave of attacking enemy caught in our barrage in G.36 and G.25 and dispersed. Keeping up strong barrage.	
			From G.O.C. 88th Brigade. My left very hard pressed. South Wales Borderers and Newfoundland Regiment almost wiped out by shell fire. Am sending Hampshire Regiment to take their place. If enemy bombard again fear will be unable to stop infantry attack on left flank. Situation North of Canal remnants of Durham Light Infantry arrived here and Commanding Officer reported that he had been driven out of defences, also that left battalion was retiring. Enemy however did not appear to be in occupation so I ordered him back. Major WILSON is collecting men in MARCOING to send to hold defences. NO reinforcements have arrived. If MARCOING is to be held assistance is wanted at once or the enemy will be in before us. If MARCOING defences fall intend to hold line L.35.a. - L.29.d. - L.29.a. - L.28.b. but cannot remain there if enemy get MARCOING. Please advise me of any action contemplated. Fresh troops badly wanted, my men being shaken by today's bombardment and exertions of past four days.	
			From III Corps. Timed 6.30 p.m. Giving details of relief of 88th Brigade by 108th Brigade. Under instructions from Corps Gen. LUCAS proceeded to Headquarters of G.O.C. 88th Brigade to report on situation and if necessary to take over command from Gen. NELSON should the latter not be in a fit state to carry on.	

Army Form C. 2118.

WAR DIARY
INTELLIGENCE SUMMARY.
(Erase heading not required.)

Instructions regarding War Diaries and Intelligence Summaries are contained in F. S. Regs., Part II. and the Staff Manual respectively. Title pages will be prepared in manuscript.

Place	Date	Hour	Summary of Events and Information	Remarks and references to Appendices
			From Gen. LUCAS. Timed 6.10 p.m. Present situation. A few of the 16th Brigade in MARCOING defences, remainder driven back. G.O.C. 16th Brigade now on his way with one battalion to retake or rather restore line. Left two battalions very badly cut up by this morning's bombardment. My line at present runs a post of 20 men covering the Lock in L.24 and then a gap to the road in L.29.d. where there is a strong point. Then as before. Enemy very close to my posts on the road in L.29.d. Message received from 16th Brigade 6.25 p.m. enemy holding ridge North of Canal with outposts. Have brushed aside initial opposition and am endeavouring to re-establish reserve line and cover both bridges but I am weak.	
			From Gen. LUCAS. Timed 8.25 p.m. NELSON and Brigade H.Q. going strong. NELSON is throwing back his left flank to South-West corner of MARCOING Copse. 16th Brigade have promised to connect at this point. They were establishing line behind MARCOING only putting patrols out to the bridges. This must be stopped at all costs and a line established along West Bank of Canal in front of village to join up with us. Everything very satisfactory on this front. South Wales Borderers have been relieved by 16th Brigade and are moving back to RIBECOURT. Much regret Major GARNETT, South Wales Borderers, killed.	
DECEMBER 4th, 1917.			H.Q. 88th Brigade move to L.34.a.4.7.	
			To III Corps. Timed 3.50 a.m. Gen. LUCAS confirms Major WILSON's report that no German over crossed the bridges into MARCOING. At 8 p.m. last night enemy were still shelling bridges when Major WILSON examined demolition charges. 88th line runs L.29.a.2.4. to L.35.c.0.3. with Brigade H.Q. at L.34.a.4.7. WILSON confirms that parties of 70 men seen marching over bridges yesterday were our men.	
			To 86th Brigade. Timed 10 a.m. Orders for move to FINS.	
			To Brigades, Flank Divisions. Informing them of moves to take place 4th instant and night of 4/5th. Extracts :- 86th Brigade HAVRINCOURT WOOD to FINS. 87th Brigade to SOREL. 88th Brigade on relief by 108th Brigade to assemble at Brigade Transport Camp K.36.c.Central. 227th Machine Gun Coy. to FINS.	

WAR DIARY

INTELLIGENCE SUMMARY

Army Form C. 2118.

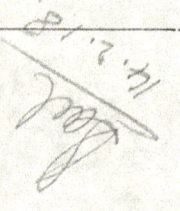

From 88th Brigade. ## Received 11.41 a.m. Situation quiet.

The relief of 88th Brigade by 108th Brigade was much delayed owing to a readjustment of the line ordered by the Corps having to be carried out by the 88th Brigade before relief could commence. The leading troops of the 88th Brigade did not arrive at the Brigade Transport Camp until 4 a.m. A hot meal was ready for the whole Brigade and after a short rest the march was continued to the entraining station at ETRICOURT a distance of 8½ miles, where the Brigade rested until entrainment that evening.

Advanced Divisional Headquarters closed at TRESCAULT at 3.30 a.m. and moved back to SOREL.

Army Form C. 2118.

WAR DIARY
XX INTELLIGENCE SUMMARY XX
(Erase heading not required.)

NOVEMBER 30th, 1917.

Remarks and references to Appendices: App. 8

Place	Date	Hour		Summary of Events and Information
		5.12 am.	To III Corps.	Situation generally quiet. Slight hostile shelling during the night.
S. end of GOUZEAUCOURT		9.10am.	To III Corps.	Troops South of BONAVIS are retiring before German attack. Advanced German patrols have reached as far West as ST. QUENTIN MILL which I have evacuated. All communications to front and rear cut. Have sent up to my Division my mounted Staff Officer to do all they can. Formed bodies of troops urgently needed as nothing bu working parties in vicinity.
		9.40 am.	To III Corps.	Enemy now hold Railway East of GOUZEAUCOURT and advancing up the village very cautiously. Am moving my Headquarters to high ground half a mile West of the village.
		10.10am.	To III Corps.	The enemy appear to be checked at GOUZEAUCOURT which is now being held by one Company of R.E. 59th Division which I stopped for the purpose. Enemy holding ridge East of GOUZEAUCOURT with advanced parties in QUENTIN MILL and working up towards the village. I have sent my A.D.C. to give 6th, 20th and 59th Divisions the situation and my G.S.O.I to MARCOING to do what he can to protect my right flank. A Division attacking from the North is recommended.
		10.20am.	To III Corps.	Enemy have cut road S.W. of GOUZEAUCOURT, moving my Headquarters towards RIBECOURT to see what can be done as I can do nothing here.
		10.45am.	To III Corps.	GOUZEAUCOURT captured by enemy from the South at 10.15 am. If troops can attack enemy from direction of RIBECOURT from indications they would succeed as enemy seems in small strength and much strung out. I am on my way to 6th Division H.Q. and have stopped at this Signal Station to send this message.
6th Division H.Q. VILLERS PLOUICH		11.45am.	To III Corps.	Have reached 6th Division H.Q. and find situation there is good. Wounded officer reports my right flank turned and enemy approaching MASNIERES. I am moving across country on foot to organise organise best defence possible under circumstances.
			From 86th Brigade timed 12.25 p.m.	Situation still in hand. We hold all our line and have defensive flank on outskirts of LES RUES VERTES. In touch with 87th Brigade and hold bridgeheads all along Canal.

Army Form C. 2118.

WAR DIARY
INTELLIGENCE SUMMARY
(Erase heading not required.)

Place	Date	Hour	Summary of Events and Information	Remarks and references to Appendices
				A/A. 5.
			From III Corps Commander. Well done hang on at all costs - timed 11.55 a.m. - received 12.40pm.	
			From III Corps. Timed 11.25 a.m. Received 4 p.m. Giving situation. Guards Division ordered to capture ridge from GONNLIEU to GOUCHE WOOD. 2nd Cavalry Division are moving on REVELON Ridge and Cavalry Corps are moving two Divisions towards VAUCELLETTE Farm from direction of VILLERS FAUCON.	
			From III Corps. Timed 11.55 a.m. Received 4 p.m. If you are forced to withdraw your troops from MASNIERES do so via MARCOING. Hold WELSH Ridge (R.4 and R.9) in order to cover the withdrawal along the COUILLET Valley. You must hold on to WELSH Ridge at all costs and if forced back you must retire on HIGHLAND Ridge.	
			From 86th Brigade. Received 12.32 p.m. 88th Brigade driving enemy back. They are retiring through G.31 and 32. My line intact.	
			From 86th Brigade. Received 12.35 p.m. Holding out. Enemy in great strength attacking us from G.31 and G.32. They are in South end of LES RUES VERTES. Have stopped three attacks from along the CAMBRAI Road. Any orders ?	
			From 86th Brigade. Received 12.38 p.m. We are in touch with 87th at G.19.d.Central. Enemy appear to be running away from MARCOING towards G.32. Our line intact.	
			From 86th Brigade. Received 1 p.m. Still hold all bridgeheads and in touch with 87th. We hold all LES RUES VERTES. Patrol has been through copse in G.25.a. and reports no enemy within 200 yards of copse.	
			From 86th Brigade. Received 1.23 p.m. LES RUES VERTES clear of enemy. Our line intact. Enemy appears to be retiring on CREVECOURT.	
			From 86th Brigade. Received 1.30 p.m. Enemy massing about G.33.Central and again advancing.	
			From 86th Brigade. Received 1.14 p.m. Position in G.32.b.O.8. Large number of enemy behind camouflage about Cross Roads G.32.b.O.8.	

Army Form C. 2118.

WAR DIARY
INTELLIGENCE SUMMARY
(Erase heading not required)

Place	Date	Hour	Summary of Events and Information	Remarks and references to Appendices
		From 86th Brigade.	Received 1.29 p.m. Enemy massed Cavalry in M.3 and M.9.	App. 8
		From 86th Brigade.	Received 1.57 p.m. Enemy in position close in front of artillery in R.11.a. Enemy running hard from West to East about R.12.	
		To III Corps.	Timed 2.15 p.m. G.O.C. just returned from MARCOING. Situation appears that enemy attacked LES RUES VERTES from South-East and gained footing in that place. Left Brigade line at 12.30 p.m. was intact and in touch with Right Brigade in MASNIERES who it is thought hold original line with exception of MONT PLAISIR FARM. Reserve Brigade now holding a line from LES RUES VERTES to VILLERS PLOUICH and has orders to clear LES RUES VERTES of the enemy.	
		To III Corps.	Timed 2.30 p.m. Have just returned from MARCOING and find everything satisfactory. Heavy attack from the North beaten off. Enemy entered LES RUES VERTES from the South-East and my Reserve Brigade is now counter-attacking and has reached the line G.31.c. - L.36.c. - R.5.b. My line East of Canal intact except for post at MONT PLAISIR FARM. Suggest one Brigade 6th Division be sent to R.4. to connect my right with 20th Division. Have ordered 29th Division to give no ground.	
		From 86th Brigade.	Received 2.31 p.m. Enemy infantry again advancing about R.12.	
		From 86th Brigade.	Received 2.44 p.m. Enemy guns and cavalry have retired over N.7. to East. All well here.	
		From 86th Brigade.	Received 2.50 p.m. Enemy artillery moving from LATTEAU WOOD from North and East. Enemy infantry entering LATTEAU WOOD from North and East.	
		From III Corps.	To 86th Brigade. Untimed. Withdraw Brigade through MARCOING on to Ridge at R.4 and R.9. This message was cancelled by telephone from III Corps at 2.40 p.m.	
		From III Corps.Commander.	~~Reccd~~ Timed 4 p.m. Please congratulate Gen. CHEAPE and troops under him on their splendid defence of MASNIERES. Also convey to the 87th and 88th Brigades my appreciation of their fine work today.	

Army Form C. 2118.

WAR DIARY

INTELLIGENCE SUMMARY

(Erase heading not required.)

Instructions regarding War Diaries and Intelligence Summaries are contained in F. S. Regs., Part II. and the Staff Manual respectively. Title pages will be prepared in manuscript.

Place	Date	Hour	Summary of Events and Information	Remarks and references to Appendices
			From G.S.O.I at 87th Brigade H.Q. Received 4.15 p.m. Situation 4 p.m. 87th Brigade hold original line. 86th Brigade hold original line and LES RUES VERTES also all Bridges over the Canal. 88th Brigade holding line approx. L.30.a. thence along Sunken Road through L.35.b. not yet known whether in touch with 20th Division on right. 88th Brigade have been ordered to advance and endeavour to consolidate the line of the Sunken Road through L.36. G.31.a. effecting a junction with the 86th Brigade at the Cross Roads G.26.c.1.3. Brigade Major 88th Brigade wounded slight. Send up S.A.A. reinforcements badly needed.	App. 8
			From Gen. LUCAS. Received 12 midnight. Situation MASNIERES and MARCOING unchanged.	
			To III Corps. Timed 8.10 p.m. I left GOUZEAUCOURT at 4.30 p.m. 1st Guards Brigade was holding Eastern fringe of the village and the enemy in apparent strength and well supplied with Machine Guns on QUENTIN Ridge. I saw enemy guns come into action 100 yards South of the GOUZEAUCOURT - VILLERS GUISLAIN Road where it cuts ridge. Attack by troops of 6th Division and three tanks still West of GOUZEAUCOURT when darkness fell. Squadron 5th Cavalry Division also West of village. My line intact at 4 p.m. and LES RUES VERTES in our hands. Added to 3 Bdes. The attack will be continued tomorrow against GONNLIEU and VILLERS GUISLAIN. 29th Division to hold on.	
			To 86th Bde. only. If 86th Brigade are forced out of MASNIERES they will fall back along Canal to MARCOING and will hold on to WELSH RIDGE at all costs but the operations tomorrow depend on your being able to hold your line.	
			From 86th Brigade. Received 6.20 p.m. Have beaten off another counter-attack on LES RUES VERTES. Situation otherwise unchanged. Heavy shelling from enemy guns at M.8.d.	
			From Gen. LUCAS. Timed 9.40 p.m. Situation remains the same. A fair defensive flank is being established from WELSH RIDGE to LES RUES VERTES by 88th Brigade with Kings Own Scottish Borderers attached. 2½ Companies South Wales Borderers are filling in gap between 86th and 88th Brigades. CHEAPE says he doubts if he can hold on tomorrow without assistance but has been told to do so. NELSON's line is very much strung out. He has the 2/Hampshire Regiment in reserve but requires further help. I have now no reserve in hand. At least two battalions are required. One for CHEAPE and one for NELSON to stand a fresh attack in force. CHEAPE cannot withdraw by day.	

Army Form C. 2118.

WAR DIARY
INTELLIGENCE SUMMARY
(Erase heading not required)

Appx. 8

Place	Date	Hour	Summary of Events and Information	Remarks and references to Appendices

From 86th Brigade. Received 10.30 p.m. Line intact. Heavy shelling from all sides.

10 p.m. G.O.C. visited III Corps Headquarters. Have you any orders for me ?

DECEMBER 1st, 1917.

To III Corps. Timed 9.35 a.m. Very heavy enemy barrage on line GONNLIEU - LA VACQUERIE - WELSH RIDGE.

From G.S.O.I at H.Q. 87th Brigade. Timed 9.50 a.m. Situation 9.45 a.m. We hold same line as reported in my 9.40 p.m. despatch last night. Quiet night. 86th and ¾ 88th Brigades now in touch at LES RUES VERTES. 88th Brigade is in touch with 20th Division on their right. Between 7 a.m. and 7.45 a.m. enemy put down an intense barrage on MASNIERES and 86th Brigade has suffered heavy casualties from it. It is imperative that some reinforcements be sent as my last reserves have now been put in. If no reinforcements are forthcoming it may be necessary to evacuate MASNIERES.
9.45 a.m. Divisional Headquarters shelled out of VILLERS PLOUICH and moved to TRESCAULT.

To 87th Brigade. Timed 12.10 p.m. Corps Commander says well done and congratulates all troops on splendid defence. Definite orders will be sent you before dusk as to your future movements. Divisional Headquarters Town Major's Office TRESCAULT.

From 86th Brigade. Received 1.30 p.m. Attack on LES RUES VERTES at 7.45 a.m. was repulsed. Situation has quietened and our position seems more satisfactory.

From 86th Brigade. Timed 7.15 a.m. Received 1.30 p.m. Very heavy enemy barrage on whole village.

From 86th Brigade. Timed 10.20 a.m. Received 1.30 p.m. Enemy in numbers in quarry G.32.d.

Army Form C. 2118.

WAR DIARY
INTELLIGENCE SUMMARY.
(Erase heading not required)

Place	Date	Hour	Summary of Events and Information	Remarks and references to Appendices
				App. 8
			From 86th Brigade. Timed 11.15 a.m. Received 1.30 p.m. Our troops in LES RUES VERTES report being shelled by our own artillery.	
			From Gen. LUCAS. Timed 2.15 p.m. 88th Brigade report Worcestershire Regiment has advanced about 200 yards and occupied enemy trenches in front of them.	
			From 86th Brigade. Timed 9.47 a.m. Received 2.30 p.m. Enemy guns in action at M.8.b.	
			From III Corps. Timed 9.55 a.m. Received 2.30 p.m. Reorganisation of Corps front. Extract :- 29th Division will continue to be responsible for their original sector and the portion of the line from LES RUES VERTES to R.5.a.Central.	
			From Gen. LUCAS. Timed 1 p.m. Received 2.45 p.m. Is there any hope of reinforcements being sent up tonight ? Otherwise 86th Brigade must evacuate MASNIERES. Reply urgent. (Repeated to III Corps 2.50 p.m.)	
			To Gen. LUCAS. Timed 3.25 p.m. I have seen the Army Commander who is most anxious to give up no ground. There is no hope of 86th Brigade being relieved tonight but will certainly be relieved tomorrow night. If you think and CHEAPE agrees that MASNIERES cannot be held you must withdraw 86th Brigade out of the line and throw back right flank of 87th to cover Lock in 19.c. keeping the Eastern edge of gun pits in 20.a. and throw back the left of the 88th Brigade to connect with right flank of 87th Brigade. Report your action by wireless and inform artillery supporting you. In this case send 86th Brigade to RIBECOURT and hold on to above line at all costs with remainder of Division.	
			To 87th Brigade. Timed 3.30 p.m. Monmouth Pioneers will reach you tonight as a reserve.	
			From Gen. LUCAS. Timed 11.30 a.m. Received 3.30 p.m. 86th Brigade beat off another counter-attack at 7.30 this morning but had heavy casualties. Unless they are sent a fresh battalion tonight I doubt if they will maintain their position. I have used up the troops from the bridgehead line which is now empty. 88th Brigade plus Kings Own Scottish Borderers still have Hampshire Regiment in reserve. A second battalion is urgently required to hold bridgehead line with 2 companies and 2 companies in reserve. Cannot move Hampshire Regiment as they may/ be	

Army Form C. 2118.

WAR DIARY
INTELLIGENCE SUMMARY
(Erase heading not required.)

Instructions regarding War Diaries and Intelligence Summaries are contained in F. S. Regs., Part II. and the Staff Manual respectively. Title pages will be prepared in manuscript.

Place	Date	Hour	Summary of Events and Information	Remarks and references to Appendices
				App. 8.
			be urgently required to protect our right rear.	
			To III Corps. Timed 4.35 p.m. Officer just returned from forward area reports :- 86th Brigade on right have beaten off eight attacks today.	
			From 86th Brigade. Received 4.51 p.m. Enemy in LES RUES VERTES but we hold all bridges as yet.	
			From 86th Brigade. Received 4.56 p.m. Situation critical.	
			From III Corps. Received 4.55 p.m. Instruct 86th Brigade under circumstances to withdraw to line West of MASNIERES in G.20.a. and c. and alter line of 88th Brigade accordingly. Convey Corps Commanders hearty congratulations to 86th Brigade on their fine performance.	
			To III Corps. With reference to above message timed 5 p.m. Instructions already issued but will only be carried out if absolutely necessary and both Brigadiers agreeing.	
			To 87th Brigade. In continuation of my message timed 3.25 p.m. this has Corps Commander's approval. Convey his heartiest congratulations to 86th Brigade on fine performance.	
			From Gen. LUCAS. Received 5.33 p.m. 88th Brigade report that we are being driven out of LES RUES VERTES.	
			To III Corps. Timed 7.15 p.m. Message just received from 87th Brigade. LES RUES VERTES retaken by 88th Brigade and 50 prisoners captured.	
	DECEMBER 2nd, 1917.		To III Corps. & Flank Divisions. Timed 7.50 a.m. After dark last night the 86th Brigade were withdrawn from the MASNIERES Salient into reserve. The line now runs 88th Brigade from about R.5.central along the Sunken Road in L.35.Central to L.30.Central - along the drain to Lock L.24.c. which is connecting point with 87th Brigade whose line runs along Canal to houses L.19.c. then North along Eastern	

Army Form C. 2118.

WAR DIARY
INTELLIGENCE SUMMARY.
(Erase heading not required)

Instructions regarding War Diaries and Intelligence Summaries are contained in F. S. Regs., Part II. and the Staff Manual respectively. Title pages will be prepared in manuscript.

Place	Date	Hour	Summary of Events and Information	Remarks and references to Appendices
				App. 8

edge of gun pits in L.20.a. to our original front line. Enemy have persistently shelled MASNIERES all the morning and continue to do so unaware of our withdrawal.

To Gen. LUCAS. Timed 8.50 a.m. Following moves will take place after dark tonight December 2nd/3rd. 16th Brigade 6th Division will relieve 87th Brigade on that portion of the Divisional front North of the ST. QUENTIN Canal. The 86th Brigade will withdraw to area about TRESCAULT. 87th Brigade on relief will withdraw to Squares K.36., L.31, L.32. 88th Brigade will continue to hold their present line from the 25 ST. QUENTIN Canal to junction with Division on right about R.5.a. at present the 20th Division but tonight will be the 61st Division. G.O.C. 88th Brigade will remain in command of the Divisional front.

To III Corps. Timed 9.5 a.m. Enemy reported massing in MASNIERES. Please turn on all available heavies.

To III Corps. Timed 9.45 a.m. Enemy that was massing in MASNIERES attacked our line North of Canal about 8.30 a.m. He was successfully driven off. Please keep heavies on to MASNIERES.

From III Corps. Timed 10 a.m. All bridges over the ST. QUENTIN Canal will be prepared for demolition.

From III Corps. Timed 1.30 p.m. Giving details of reserve line to be consolidated. Extract :- 29th Division from R.7.b. to HINDENBURG SUPPORT in L.32.c.9.3.

From III Corps. Timed 4.15 p.m. Brigade of 29th Division holding the line from the Canal to the left of the 61st Division will be placed under the orders of the 6th Division on completion of the relief of the Brigades North of the ST. QUENTIN Canal by the 6th Division.

To 86th Brigade. Timed 3 p.m. You will be accommodated tonight in RIBECOURT.

From 6th Division. Instructions from Corps to take over the Battalion front South of the Canal were received too late to alter arrangements. This Battalion front will be taken over tomorrow night.

Army Form C. 2118.

WAR DIARY
INTELLIGENCE SUMMARY
(Erase heading not required.)

Instructions regarding War Diaries and Intelligence Summaries are contained in F. S. Regs., Part II. and the Staff Manual respectively. Title pages will be prepared in manuscript.

Place	Date	Hour	Summary of Events and Information	Remarks and references to Appendices
	DECEMBER 3rd, 1917.			App. 8
		11 a.m.	To III Corps. Timed 3.30 a.m. Reference Order No. 228, para. 12, relief complete 1.30 a.m. of troops East of Canal. 87th Brigade still have two battalions in front line attached to 88th Brigade.	
			86th Brigade obliged to vacate RIBECOURT owing to hostile shelling. Situation on front uncertain, but eventually Corps sanctioned the move of 86th Brigade to HAVRINCOURT WOOD.	
			From O.C. 17th Brigade R.F.A. Attack extends from MARCOING to South. Bombardment heavy. First wave of attacking enemy caught in our barrage in G.36 and G.25 and dispersed. Keeping up strong barrage.	
			From G.O.C. 88th Brigade. My left very hard pressed. South Wales Borderers and Newfoundland Regiment almost wiped out by shell fire. Am sending Hampshire Regiment to take their place. If enemy bombard again fear will be unable to stop infantry attack on left flank. Situation North of Canal remnants of Durham Light Infantry arrived here and Commanding Officer reported that he had been driven out of defences, also that left battalion was retiring. Enemy however did not appear to be in occupation so I ordered him back. Major WILSON is collecting men in MARCOING to send to hold defences. No reinforcements have arrived. If MARCOING is to be held assistance is wanted at once or the enemy will be in before us. If MARCOING defences fall intend to hold line L.35.a. - L.29.d. - L.29.a. - L.28.b. but cannot remain there if enemy get MARCOING. Please advise me of any action contemplated. Fresh troops badly wanted, my men being shaken by today's bombardment and exertions of past four days.	
			From III Corps. Timed 6.30 p.m. Giving details of relief of 88th Brigade by 108th Brigade.	
			Under instructions from Corps Gen. LUCAS proceeded to Headquarters of G.O.C. 88th Brigade to report on Situation and if necessary to take over command from Gen. NELSON should the latter not be in a fit state to carry on.	

Army Form C. 2118.

WAR DIARY
~~INTELLIGENCE SUMMARY~~
(Erase heading not required.)

Instructions regarding War Diaries and Intelligence Summaries are contained in F. S. Regs., Part II. and the Staff Manual respectively. Title pages will be prepared in manuscript.

Place	Date	Hour	Summary of Events and Information	Remarks and references to Appendices
	DECEMBER 4th, 1917.		From Gen. LUCAS. Timed 6.10 p.m. Present situation. A few of the 16th Brigade in MARCOING defences, remainder driven back. G.O.C. 16th Brigade now on his way with one battalion to retake or rather restore line. Left two battalions very badly cut up by this morning's bombardment. My line at present runs a post of 20 men covering the Lock in L.24 and then a gap to the road in L.29.d. where there is a strong point. Then as before. Enemy very close to my posts ⊞ on the road in L.29.d. Message received from 16th Brigade 6.25 p.m. enemy holding ridge North of Canal with outposts. Have brushed aside initial opposition and am endeavouring to re-establish reserve line and cover both bridges but I am weak. From Gen. LUCAS. Timed 8.25 p.m. NELSON and Brigade H.Q. going strong. NELSON is throwing back his left flank to South-West corner of MARCOING Copse. 16th Brigade have promised to connect at this point. They were establishing line behind MARCOING only putting patrols out to the bridges. This must be stopped at all costs and a line established along West Bank of Canal in front of village to join up with us. Everything very satisfactory on this front. South Wales Borderers have been relieved by 16th Brigade and are moving back to RIBECOURT. Much regret Major GARNETT, South Wales Borderers, killed. H.Q. 88th Brigade move to L.34.a.4.7. To III Corps. Timed 3.50 a.m. Gen. LUCAS confirms Major WILSON's report that no German ever crossed the bridges into MARCOING. At 8 p.m. last night enemy were still shelling bridges when Major WILSON examined demolition charges. 88th line runs L.29.a.2.4. to L.35.c.0.3. with Brigade H.Q. at L.34.a.4.7. WILSON confirms that parties of 70 men seen marching over bridges yesterday were our men. To 86th Brigade. Timed 10 a.m. Orders for move to FINS. To Brigades, Flank Divisions. Informing them of moves to take place 4th instant and night of 4/5th. Extracts :- 86th Brigade HAVRINCOURT WOOD to FINS. 87th Brigade to SOREL. 88th Brigade on relief by 108th Brigade to assemble at Brigade Transport Camp K.36.c.Central. 227th Machine Gun Coy. to FINS.	App. 8

Army Form C. 2118.

WAR DIARY
INTELLIGENCE SUMMARY
(Erase heading not required.)

Instructions regarding War Diaries and Intelligence Summaries are contained in F. S. Regs., Part II. and the Staff Manual respectively. Title pages will be prepared in manuscript.

Place	Date	Hour	Summary of Events and Information	Remarks and references to Appendices
			From 88th Brigade. ## Received 11.41 a.m. Situation quiet.	A/4. 8
			The relief of 88th Brigade by 108th Brigade was much delayed owing to a readjustment of the line ordered by the Corps having to be carried out by the 88th Brigade before relief could commence. The leading troops of the 88th Brigade did not arrive at the Brigade Transport Camp until 4 a.m. A hot meal was ready for the whole Brigade and after a short rest the march was continued to the entraining station at ETRICOURT a distance of 6½ miles, where the Brigade rested until entrainment that evening.	
			Advanced Divisional Headquarters closed at TRESCAULT at 3.30 a.m. and moved back to SOREL.	

APPENDIX B

Locations

SECRET.   29th Div. No. I.G.93/181.

LOCATIONS - 29TH DIVISION
for 8th December, 1917.
-o-o-o-o-o-o-o-o-o-o-o-o-

Unit.	Place.	Remarks.

Div. H.Q. .... LE CAUROY
C.R.A. .... NURLU .... Sheet. 57c V.23.d.Cent.
C.R.E. .... LE CAUROY
Div. Train .... MANIN
A.D.M.S. .... LE CAUROY
D.A.D.V.S. .... LE CAUROY
227th M.G. Coy. .... DENIER

86th Bde. H.Q. .... AMBRINES
86th M.G. Coy. .... MAGNICOURT
86th T.M. Bty. .... AMBRINES
2/Roy. Fus. .... LIGNEREUIL
1/Lan. Fus. .... AMBRINES
16/Middx. R. .... MAIZIERES
1/R.G.L.I. .... HOUVIN-HOUVIGNEUL
497th (Kent) Field Coy. ...... BERLENCOURT
2 Coy. Div. Train. .... HOUVIN-HOUVIGNEUL
89th Field Ambulance .... GOUY-EN-TERNOIS

87th Bde. H.Q. .... LIENCOURT
87th M.G. Coy. .... GRAND RULLECOURT
87th T.M. Bty. .... LIENCOURT
2/S.W.B. .... LIENCOURT
1/K.O.S.B. .... BEAUDRICOURT
1/Bord. R. .... GRAND RULLECOURT
1/R. Innis. Fus. .... BEAUFORT
455th (West Riding) Field Coy.. BERLENCOURT
3 Coy. Div. Train. .... LIENCOURT
87th Field Ambulance .... DENIER

88th Bde. H.Q. .... SUS-ST-LEGER
88th M.G. Coy. .... WARLUZEL
88th T.M. Bty. .... SUS-ST-Leger
4/Worc. R. .... WARLUZEL
2/Hamps. R. .... SUS-ST-LEGER
1/Essex R. .... SUS-ST-LEGER
N.F.L.D. R. .... HUMBERCOURT
510th (London) Field Coy. .... BERLENCOURT
4 Coy. Div. Train .... COULLEMONT
88th Field Ambulance .... COULLEMONT

1/2nd Monmouth R. (Pnrs.) .... MANIN
226th Emplyt. Coy. .... LE CAUROY
S.A.A. Sec. .... HUMBERCOURT
Mob. Vet. Sec. .... LE CAUROY

                                                                 Simpson, Lieut.
                                              for Lieut-Colonel, G.S.,
                                                      29th Division.

8.12.17.

M.

War Diary

appen. 2.

SECRET. 29th Div. No. I.G. 93/189.

AMENDMENT to LOCATIONS 29th DIVISION
No. I.G. 93/186.

No.	Unit.	Place.	Remarks.
2.	C.R.A.	MARESQUEL.	
5.	No. 1 Co. Train.	CONTES.	
8.	15th Bde. R.H.A.	AUBIN ST VAAST.	
9.	17th Bde. R.F.A.	BEAURAIN CHATEAU.	
10.	D.A.C.	OFFIN.	
11.	D.T.M.O.& V/ 29) H.T.M.B.)	MARESQUEL.	
12.	X.Y. & Z.29 T.M.B.	MARESQUEL.	
13.	227th M.G.Coy.	CLENLEU.	
21.	497th (Kent) Fd. Co.	GOURNAY.	
46.	S.A.A. Section.	LOISON.	
47.	Mob. Vet. Sect.	PREURES.	

27th December 1917.

Hugh O. Holmes.
Major R.E.
for Lieut-Colonel, G.S.,
29th Division.

SECRET.   (Ref. No. SR.11/150.)

29th. DIVISION.

REPORT ON EVACUATION OF WOUNDED DURING OPERATIONS

20th November to 4th December, 1917.

by

A.D.M.S., 29th DIVISION.

Reference Maps:- France 57.C.)
                        57.B.) 1-40,000.
Trench Maps:- NIERGNIES.   )
              GOUZEAUCOURT.   ) 1-20,000.

==

20th NOVEMBER, 1917.

GENERAL SCHEME OF EVACUATION.

The Bearer Division of each Field Ambulance was attached to its respective Brigade in the Assembly Area on the evening of 19th instant. The duties of each Division were to keep in touch with the Regimental Medical Officers of their Brigades, and to carry the wounded back from the AID POSTS to RELAY POSTS at the following places:-

1st Relay. (G.25.c.9.2.
            (L.28.b.central.

2nd Relay. (L.36.a.5.0.
            (L.34.b.8.5.

As soon as the Division moved from our original Front Line, the extra Divisional Stretcher Bearers, consisting of 4 Officers and 200 Other Ranks, advanced along the LA VACQUERIE Road to get in touch with the Relays. At the same time the personnel and equipment of an ADVANCED DRESSING STATION was pushed up to R.5.b. The extra Stretcher Bearers were to carry back from the Relays to the ADVANCED DRESSING STATION, and from there to the Ambulance loading point on LA VACQUERIE Road.

It was hoped that Motor Ambulances could be pushed up close to the ADVANCED DRESSING STATION a few hours after Zero. Unfortunately this was not possible, owing to the bad state of the roads, and the ambulances were unable to get further than LA VACQUERIE.

A WALKING WOUNDED COLLECTING POST, and TEA KITCHEN was established at LA VACQUERIE shortly after the Division advanced.

METHOD OF EVACUATION.

Owing to the slight casualties sustained at the commencement, wounded were taken to the first RELAY POST only by the R.A.M.C. Bearers, the extra Divisional Stretcher Bearers carrying to the second RELAY and ADVANCED DRESSING STATION. There was thus a large number of R.A.M.C. Bearers in the Forward Area who were able to clear quickly from the AID POSTS. The difficulty was the long carry from the 1st RELAY POSTS to the ADVANCED DRESSING STATION, and LA VACQUERIE.

METHOD OF EVACUATION (Continued).

As there was no likelihood of the LA VACQUERIE Road being made fit for Motor Ambulances, and as AID POSTS were being made North of MARCOING and in MASNIERES, this route of evacuation was stopped during the afternoon, and Officers i/c Bearer Divisions were told to hold up their cases in buildings until the VILLERS PLOUICH Road could be used on the following day.

On the afternoon of 21st November, an ADVANCED DRESSING STATION and TEA KITCHEN were opened in the Square, MARCOING, and the Brewery, Les Rues Vertes, MASNIERES, and by 2 o'clock Motor Ambulances had arrived, and were clearing cases down the VILLERS PLOUICH Road direct from MARCOING to Casualty Clearing Stations at YTRES and TINCOURT.

The TEA KITCHENS both at LA VACQUERIE and MARCOING were used to feed a large number of French refugees as well as Walking Wounded.

TRANSPORT.

MOTOR AMBULANCES.

Ford Cars worked continuously between LA VACQUERIE, and the CAMBRAI Road, where cases were transferred to large cars, and evacuated in them either to 20th Division Advanced Dressing Station, GOUZEAUCOURT, or direct to Casualty Clearing Stations at YTRES and TINCOURT. The majority of the cases were evacuated direct to Casualty Clearing Station.

HORSE AMBULANCES.

These carried Walking Wounded from LA VACQUERIE to the Decauville Railhead, GOUZEAUCOURT, where they were placed in the Corps Ambulance Train, or Lorries, and taken to the Corps WALKING WOUNDED POST, FINS.

DECAUVILLE RAILWAY.

Owing to the length of broken line in No Man's land, this method of transport was impracticable.

The VILLERS PLOUICH - MARCOING Road was reserved for Cavalry on 20th November, so Motor ambulances were unable to get to MARCOING before the 21st November.

MEDICAL SITUATION FROM
21st to 29th November, 1917.

REGIMENTAL AID POSTS.

4 in MASNIERES.
4 on N. side of Canal between MASNIERES and MARCOING.
4 in MARCOING.

ADVANCED DRESSING STATIONS.

1. LES RUES VERTES .... G.26.c.9.8.
2. MARCOING .... L.22.b.7.6.

TRANSPORT.

A Motor Ambulance Stand was made on the VILLERS PLOUICH - MARCOING Road at L.33.c.9.0. One car was kept at each Advanced Dressing Station, and as it passed the stand on the outward journey, a fresh car was sent up.

EVACUATION.

R.A.M.C. Bearers were attached to each REGIMENTAL AID POST. Cases were carried to the ADVANCED DRESSING STATION, and evacuated direct from there to Casualty Clearing Station via VILLERS PLOUICH and GOUZEAUCOURT.

Each ADVANCED DRESSING STATION could accommodate at least 50 Stretcher Cases.

MEDICAL SITUATION FROM

30th November to 4th December, 1917.

30th NOVEMBER, 1917.

Owing to the enemy counter-attack in the early morning, the line of evacuation along the VILLERS PLOUICH Road was cut, and a new route had to be established. All communication with the ADVANCED DRESSING STATION, LES RUES VERTES, was cut off, that part of the town being in the enemy's hands for a time, and under direct enemy observation until the ADVANCED DRESSING STATION was evacuated on the following night.

A new line of evacuation was made by establishing a COLLECTING POST in RIBECOURT, and removing cases as quickly as possible from MARCOING to RIBECOURT, and evacuating from there at leisure by DECAUVILLE RAILWAY, HORSE and MOTOR AMBULANCES.

NIGHT OF 30th NOV./1st DEC.

The ADVANCED DRESSING STATION, LES RUES VERTES, was full of wounded, 95 cases were evacuated that night to MARCOING ADVANCED DRESSING STATION, leaving 10 stretcher cases in LES RUES VERTES. The Medical Officer in charge was informed that there would be no communication with him the following day until night when all his cases would be cleared, and he would evacuate his ADVANCED DRESSING STATION.

NIGHT OF 1st/2nd DEC.

The Bearers were again sent up, and evacuated 50 Stretcher and 90 walking cases. The ADVANCED DRESSING STATION was then closed down leaving only six Enemy stretcher cases in the building.

At the same time other stretcher bearers were sent up to clear the MASNIERES REGIMENTAL AID POSTS near the Lock, and in the CATACOMBS.

2nd DECEMBER.

The ADVANCED DRESSING STATION was removed to RIBECOURT, and MARCOING was used as a COLLECTING POST.
Motor Ambulances still evacuated cases from MARCOING.

3rd DECEMBER.

It was impossible to get Motor Ambulances into MARCOING SQUARE after 4 p.m. owing to the shelling. The COLLECTING POST there was evacuated in the evening, and a Post established on the RIBECOURT - MARCOING Road, the Ambulance Bearers keeping in touch the whole time with the REGIMENTAL AID POSTS during the gradual withdrawal.

WOUNDED.

The total number of wounded evacuated during the period under consideration was as follows :-

Officers.	Other Ranks.
105	2,590

R.A.M.C. CASUALTIES.

Killed.		Wounded.		Missing.	
Officers.	O.R.	Officers.	O.R.	Officers.	O.R.
-	4	5	48	2	1

TOTAL = 60 All ranks.

Attached hereto is a report on a hot air apparatus used in both ADVANCED DRESSING STATIONS.

                                (Sd) H. K. M. DOUGLAS,
                                      Colonel,
8th December, 1917.   A.D.M.S., 29th Division.

Copies to :- D.M.S., Third Army.
              D.D.M.S., IV Corps.
              "A", 29th Division.
              G.S., "   "
              War Diary.
              File (3 copies)

REPORT ON THE USE OF HOT AIR APPARATUS AT AN ADVANCED
DRESSING STATION DURING RECENT OPERATIONS OF THE
29TH DIVISION.

A description of the apparatus employed (Blanket Heater and Hot air Generator) was forwarded on 12/11/17 under No. A.1519.

The object aimed at was to thoroughly warm up chilled and shocked patients before transferring them to the C.C.S. The procedure adopted in general was as follows :-

If the man's clothes were wet they were changed for dry pyjamas and socks, and he was transferred to a stretcher covered by a double folded dry blanket. The cradle was then put on the stretcher and the whole covered with blankets and the hot air bath given. As far as the position of the wound permitted dressing was carried out during the administration of the air bath.

The blanket rack provided the necessary supply of dry and hot clothes and blankets.

The bath lasted about 15 minutes, the cradle was then removed and hot water bottles placed under the blankets, the temperature being thus sustained for the period of transport.

Hot drinks were given as usual. Clothes were not removed if they were dry.

The apparatus was employed at the Advanced Dressing Stations at MARCOING and MASNIERES, at both places most of the work was carried out underground. The transport and use of both blanket drier and heat generator was found to be simple. During heavy inflows of wounded it was not possible to use the hot air bath for any but the most seriously wounded, but a sufficient surplus of dry blankets was maintained for all cases.

From my own observations and from those of other Medical Officers working at the A.D.S. the condition of the patients treated as above was much improved both subjectively and objectively. In some cases the body temperature was raised two degrees F. (from sub-normal) and in all cases the pinched and shivering appearance of the patients totally disappeared or was much improved, this was particularly evident in cases which had been lying out for some time.

As all cars in use were fitted with the exhaust heater which maintained the temperature inside at from 60° to 70°, there was no chance of the patients becoming chilled while en route for the C.C.S.

The following practical points may be mentioned in relation to the use of the apparatus.

BLANKET AND CLOTHES DRIER.

Two "Beatrice" stoves, fitted as described should be used for this and kept going continuously; the air chamber should be practically closed at half hour intervals by placing a blanket on the top, this varies the temperature inside to from 90° to 100° F. more ventilation is then allowed in order to dry off the contents. It was found that a blanket could be dried in this way in about 20 minutes.

Additional wires should be added at a suitable level for hanging pyjamas, etc., on.

HOT AIR GENERATOR AND BATH.

A double or even triple fold of a blanket should be both above and below the patient. A single-wicked "Beatrice" stove in the box will raise the temperature in the air chamber to about 140° F. in 10 - 15 minutes and this I think is a sufficient dose for a man before transport.

In general it would appear that the hot air appliances referred to are of the highest value in the treatment of the wounded at a C.C.S. and some such apparatus should in Winter time be in the equipment of every Field Ambulance. The hot air generator would also be of value at the C.C.S. and Base Units not only in the treatment of shock but for Myalgia, nephritis, etc.

(Sd) C. M. PAGE, Capt.
88th Field Ambulance,
R.A.M.C. (T.F.)

4.12.17.

"A" Form.
MESSAGES AND SIGNALS.

TO **Chorus**

Sender's Number.	Day of Month.	In reply to Number.	AAA
102	24		

No sign of "upstart"

From **Church**
Time **8.35pm**

"A" Form.
MESSAGES AND SIGNALS.

Army Form C.2121 (in pads of 100).

TO	Chorus	

Sender's Number.	Day of Month.	In reply to Number.	AAA
102	24		

No sign of "expectant"

From: Church
Place:
Time: 8.35 pm

"A" Form.
MESSAGES AND SIGNALS.
Army Form C.2121
(in pads of 100).
No. of Message

Moon about half other quarter
in

www.ingramcontent.com/pod-product-compliance
Lightning Source LLC
Chambersburg PA
CBHW080824010526
44111CB00015B/2601